International Political Economy Series

General Editor: **Timothy M. Shaw**, Professor of Political Science and International Development Studies, and Director of the Centre for Foreign Policy Studies, Dalhousie University, Halifax, Nova Scotia

Titles include:

Pradeep Agrawal, Subir V. Gokarn, Veena Mishra, Kirit S. Parikh and Kunal Sen
POLICY REGIMES AND INDUSTRIAL COMPETITIVENESS
A Comparative Study of East Asia and India

Roderic Alley
THE UNITED NATIONS IN SOUTHEAST ASIA AND THE SOUTH PACIFIC

Dick Beason and Jason James
THE POLITICAL ECONOMY OF JAPANESE FINANCIAL MARKETS
Myths versus Reality

Mark Beeson
COMPETING CAPITALISMS
Australia, Japan and Economic Competition in Asia-Pacific

Deborah Bräutigam
CHINESE AID AND AFRICAN DEVELOPMENT
Exporting Green Revolution

Steve Chan, Cal Clark and Danny Lam (*editors*)
BEYOND THE DEVELOPMENTAL STATE
East Asia's Political Economies Reconsidered

Dong-Sook Shin Gills
RURAL WOMEN AND TRIPLE EXPLOITATION IN KOREAN DEVELOPMENT

Jeffrey Henderson (*editor*)
INDUSTRIAL TRANSFORMATION IN EASTERN EUROPE IN
THE LIGHT OF THE EAST ASIAN EXPERIENCE

Pierre P. Lizée
PEACE, POWER AND RESISTANCE IN CAMBODIA
Global Governance and the Failure of International Conflict Resolution

Cecilia Ng
POSITIONING WOMEN IN MALAYSIA
Class and Gender in an Industrializing State

Ian Scott (*editor*)
INSTITUTIONAL CHANGE AND THE POLITICAL TRANSITION IN HONG KONG

Mark Turner (*editor*)
CENTRAL–LOCAL RELATIONS IN ASIA–PACIFIC
Convergence or Divergence?

Fei-Ling Wang
INSTITUTIONS AND INSTITUTIONAL CHANGE IN CHINA
Premodernity and Modernization

International Political Economy Series
Series Standing Order ISBN 0–333–71708–2 hardcover
Series Standing Order ISBN 0–333–71110–6 paperback
(*outside North America only*)

You can receive future titles in this series as they are published by placing a standing order. Please contact your bookseller or, in case of difficulty, write to us at the address below with your name and address, the title of the series and one or both of the ISBNs quoted above.

Customer Services Department, Macmillan Distribution Ltd, Houndmills, Basingstoke, Hampshire RG21 6XS, England

Bangladesh, India and Pakistan

International Relations and Regional Tensions in South Asia

Kathryn Jacques
School of Classics, History and Religion
University of New England, Armidale
New South Wales
Australia

© Kathryn Jacques 2000

Published by PALGRAVE
Houndmills, Basingstoke, Hampshire RG21 6XS and
175 Fifth Avenue, New York, N.Y. 10010
Companies and representatives throughout the world

PALGRAVE is the new global academic imprint of
St. Martin's Press LLC Scholarly and Reference Division and
Palgrave Publishers Ltd (formerly Macmillan Press Ltd).

Outside North America
ISBN 0–333–74824–7

In North America
ISBN 0–312–22386–2

This book is printed on paper suitable for recycling and made from fully managed and sustained forest sources.

A catalogue record for this book is available from the British Library.

Library of Congress Cataloging-in-Publication Data
Jacques, Kathryn, 1957–
Bangladesh, India and Pakistan : international relations and regional tensions in South Asia / Kathryn Jacques.
p. cm. — (International political economy series)
Includes bibliographical references and index.
ISBN 0–312–22386–2 (cloth)
1. Bangladesh—Foreign relations—India. 2. India—Foreign relations—Bangladesh. 3. Bangladesh—Foreign relations—Pakistan. 4. Pakistan—Foreign relations—Bangladesh. 5. South Asia—Politics and government. I. Title. II. Series.
DS394.73.I4J33   1999
327.5491054—dc21   99–33849
                                                                CIP

10   9   8   7   6   5   4   3   2
08 07 06 05 04 03 02 01

Printed and bound in Great Britain by
Antony Rowe Ltd, Chippenham, Wiltshire

Contents

List of Maps, Figures and Tables

Chronology

1971

December   Creation of independent Bangladesh.

1975

August 15   Assassination of Sheikh Mujibur Rahman. Khondakar
                  Mushtaque Ahmad became President.

November   Short-lived insurrection led by Khalid Musharraf. Ziaur
                  Rahman (Zia) emerged as the key political figure in
                  Bangladesh.

1976

November   Zia became Chief Martial Law Administrator.

1977

April 21   Zia took over Presidency of Bangladesh from A.S.M. Sayem.
                  (Zia kept position of CMLA and Commander in Chief of the
                  Armed Forces.)

May 30   Zia held a Referendum on his continuance in office.

July 5   Zia ul-Haq took over leadership of Pakistan from Zulfikar Ali
                  Bhutto.

November 5   Five-year agreement signed between Bangladesh and India
                  over the Farakka Barrage.

1978

June 3   Abdus Sattar was elected as Vice-President.

1979

February 18   Parliamentary Election gave Zia's party 207 of 300 seats.

April 15–17   Indian Prime Minister, Morarji Desai, visited Bangladesh.

July   India's Desai Government collapsed.

Novermber 4   Armed conflict in dispute between India and Bangladesh
                  over the Muhuri Char border.

1980

May   Zia first proposed a South Asian forum (to become the South
                  Asian Association for Regional Cooperation (SAARC)).

August   India Foreign Minister, Narasimha Rao visited Dhaka for
                  talks.

1981
May 9   India landed troops on New Moore/South Talpatty Island.
May 30   Zia was assassinated in Chittagong.
November 15   Abdus Sattar was elected as President.

1982
March 24   Abdus Sattar was overthrown in a military coup led by Hussain Muhammad Ershad.
October 6–8   Talks between Ershad and Indian Prime Minister, Indira Gandhi in New Delhi.
December 6–10   14th Islamic Foreign Ministers' Conference held in Dhaka.

1983
December 11   Ershad assumed the Presidency of Bangladesh.

1984
April   Indo–Bangladesh clashes over border.
May 31   Indo–Bangladesh accord signed on sharing the Ganges.
October 31   Indian Prime Minister Indira Gandhi assassinated.

1985
March 21   Ershad called for a referendum to seek legitimacy.
December 7–8   First SAARC Summit held in Dhaka.

1986
May   50,000 Chakma refugees fled from the Chittagong Hill Tracts into India's northeast.
May 7   Parliamentary election gave Ershad's party, the Jatiyo Dal, a slight majority. The Awami League and allies won about one third of the seats.

1988
March 3   Ershad's party won 250 out of 300 seats in Parliamentary elections.
August   Severe flooding in Bangladesh.
August 17   Pakistan leader Zia ul-Haq died in a plane crash.

1990
December 12   Ershad and his wife arrested.

Preface and Acknowledgements

I would like to thank Dr Denis Wright for his invaluable assistance regarding the content and structure of the book and for his generous encouragement and support. I am also much indebted to Professor Peter Reeves, Associate Professor Jim Masselos and Dr Habib Zafarullah for their perceptive and encouraging scholarly advice.

I would also like to make special mention of Associate Professor Jack Hobbs for his inspiring and enthusiastic assistance with all aspects of the book, and for giving me the benefit of the different perspective of a geographer.

For his unstinting encouragement and proof-reading assistance, I offer warm thanks to Kris Jacques.

I would also like to express my gratitude to the History Department, University of New England, for providing me with the facilities to assist in undertaking my research.

Grateful acknowledgement is also made to the following for their valued advice and encouragement:

Associate Professor Howard Brasted; Dr I. Bruce Watson; Professor Sinnappah Arasaratnam; Professor Carl Bridge; Associate Professor Geoff Quaife; Dr Kim Lawes; Nafis Ahmed; Dr Emdadul Haque; Staff of the Dixson Library, University of New England; Sally McFarlane; Madeleine Hyson; Corinne Buckland; Gloria Obbens; Trish Cluley; Elizabeth Richards; Janice Lord; Associate Professor David Kent; Associate Professor Amarjit Kaur; Professor Alan Atkinson; Dr Jo Woolmington; Associate Professor Miriam Dixson; Gail Binnie; Kev Condon; Professor Robin Jeffrey; Melva and Alf Crawley; and Mike Roach.

KATHRYN JACQUES

List of Abbreviations

ADB	Asian Development Bank
BAKSAL	Bangladesh Krishak Sramik Awami League
BDR	Bangladesh Rifles
BJP	Bharatiya Janata Party
BSF	(Indian) Border Security Forces
CIA	Central Intelligence Agency
CHOGM	Commonwealth Heads of Government Meeting
CHT	Chittagong Hill Tracts
EEC	European Economic Community
ESCAP	Economic and Social Commission for Asia and the Pacific
GDP	gross domestic product
IJI	Islamic Democratic Alliance
JCE	Joint Committee of Experts
JRB	*Jatiyo Rakkhi Bahini*
JRC	(Indo–Bangladesh) Joint Rivers Commission
JSD	*Jatiyo Samajtantrik Dal*
MOU	Memorandum of Understanding
MQM	*Muhajir Qaumi Mahaz*
OIC	Organisation of Islamic Conference
OPEC	Organisation of Petroleum-Exporting Countries
PPP	Pakistan People's Party
PRC	People's Republic of China
RAW	(Indian) Research and Analysis Wing
SAARC	South Asian Association for Regional Cooperation
SARC	South Asian Regional Cooperation
TNV	Tripura National Volunteers

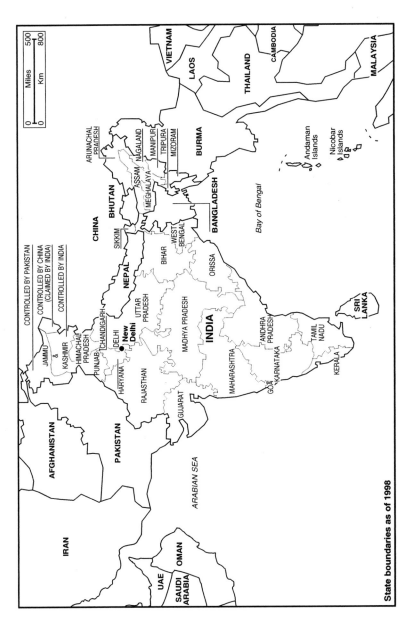

Map 1   South Asia, 1998

State boundaries as of 1998

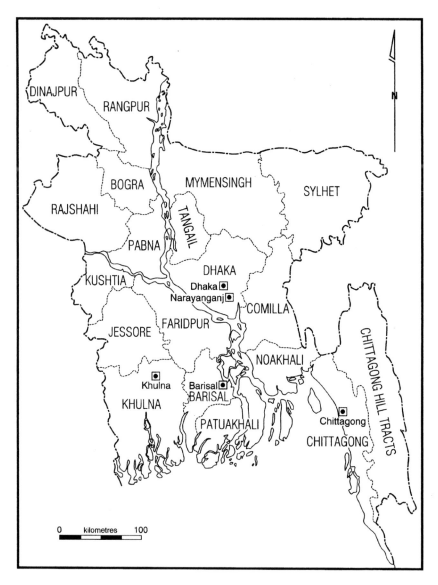

Map 2   Bangladesh, 1975
Source: Based on Johnson (1975), p. 2.

Part I
Overview

1
General Influences on Bangladesh's Foreign Policy

Domestic, regional and extra-regional pressures have combined to shape Bangladesh's foreign policy and its relations with the two most powerful and influential states in the South Asian region, India and Pakistan.[1] Studies of Bangladesh's foreign relations since 1975 have been minimal, tending to be descriptive, biased accounts. The most common themes of those studies are ones which point either to Bangladesh's turbulent political life and economic woes or to India's desire for regional dominance as being the principal influence on regional international relations. This study, by contrast, emphasises and illustrates the way in which both domestic and external pressures have impinged on Bangladesh's foreign relations. A range of perspectives is applied in order to give depth to the study and to minimise bias as much as possible. These perspectives take into account what is taking place within and outside the region generally; as well as what is happening within Bangladesh. A study of Bangladeshi foreign policy shows that the regional perspective requires greater emphasis than it has been given hitherto. For this reason, the regional viewpoint precedes the domestic in subsequent chapters dealing with Bangladesh's most critical relationship: that with India.

Maintaining security of national independence has been an important foreign policy consideration for each of the South Asian states. Similarly, cultural and economic pressures have also fuelled insecurities and moulded foreign policy direction in the region. Traditionally, India and Pakistan have loomed large in Bangladesh's foreign policy and relations between each of the three states have been shaped by their differing security perceptions and fears.

For a newly formed state, as Bangladesh was in 1971, the most pressing problems are often domestic. Bangladesh's position was no exception, but even a supposedly inward-looking perspective has repercussions for interstate relations. A new or brittle regime plagued with domestic strife may seek out external supporters in order to preserve its privileged position, with major repercussions for the character of the state's foreign policy and, in turn, for regional relations. From the time of Bangladesh's creation, it has been, either directly or indirectly, a vital constituent in the conduct of South Asian regional affairs.

At the same time, a small, militarily weak state, such as Bangladesh, is not impervious to pressures deriving from the South Asian region or, more broadly, from the activities of the superpowers or global trends, such as a growing emphasis on religious and cultural identities, extending beyond the artificial confines of national sovereignty.

Broad, underlying pressures and themes have become intrinsic to Bangladesh's foreign policy and to the conduct of Bangladesh's relations with India and Pakistan. Subsequent chapters illustrate these themes in terms of specific regional and domestic events associated with Bangladesh's relations with India and Pakistan. Bangladesh's foreign policy has been shaped by a number of factors: its colonial past; its political underdevelopment; the issue of sovereign independence; cultural and religious identity; fear of Indian dominance; Indian security concerns; and poverty and dependence on foreign aid.

Several ingredients are common to the foreign policies of the states of the South Asian region, but in Bangladesh's case one element can be singled out as meriting special consideration. The legacy of colonialism is borne by each of these states, but for the inhabitants of Bangladesh, the process of extrication from a colonial relationship not once, but twice, has had a pervasive impact on their state's political structure and foreign policy dealings. Bangladesh was subjected to colonial rule not only under the British Raj, but also from 1947 to 1971, as Pakistan's east wing, subordinate to the central government located in the west wing.[2]

The many problems associated with a colonial past, such as political underdevelopment and the ensuing susceptibility to military intervention in domestic affairs, indicate the diversity of influences. This complexity is reflected in Bangladesh's foreign policy. The focus on preservation of sovereignty and the development of national identity underlies much of foreign policy decision-making throughout Bangladesh's history.

The slow progress in South Asian regional cooperation is also traceable partly to colonial imposition, impinging in turn on Bangladesh's foreign relations. The hasty and artificial delineation of the Indo–Pakistan border in 1947 resulted in an inevitably lopsided bipolarity in the region, with India far surpassing each of the other states in size and military capability. This imbalance was conducive to ethnic disharmony and unfavourable for regional integration. As a result, there has been a propensity for the individual South Asian states to seek links outside the region, and for the smaller states to be distrustful and wary of a predominant India. Both of these tendencies apply strongly to Bangladesh, despite its intrinsic cultural bond with India.

The imbalance which gave India its pre-eminence in the region and the accompanying lack of rapport between the states can be linked directly to South Asia's colonial past. India saw itself as the natural 'successor' state to the British Raj in the subcontinent,[3] or at least that was the way in which the smaller states nervously interpreted India's self-perception, and continue to do so up to the present.

It is a widely held opinion amongst scholars studying Bangladesh and other post-colonial states that colonial misrule leads to post-independence problems such as political instability, factionalism and the concentration of power and wealth in the hands of minorities. The partial borrowing or inheritance of colonial institutions, many of which fostered patronage, frequent state intervention, repression and authoritarianism, also hampers political stability, making it difficult for the newly independent state to develop strong political parties and a sense of national identity.[4]

The region which became Bangladesh, as part of a former British colony, subsequently as a province under West Pakistani dominance, and finally as an independent state, endured all of these destabilising legacies over a much longer period than did any of the other South Asian states.[5] It was not until December 1971 that cultural and national concerns were convergent enough to create at least some degree of political stability in the region which became Bangladesh. Nevertheless, the very fact that Bangladesh finally managed to gain independence, despite such an oppressive and turbulent political past, points to the underlying strength and resilience of Bengali cultural unity.

The resultant disparity between Bangladesh's opportunity to develop a stable political structure and that of the other South Asian states must therefore be kept in mind throughout any examination of Bangladesh's relations with India and Pakistan. The quest for internal political stability and cohesion is an aim common to most states, and requires at least a minimum level of development in the political structure to have some chance of attainment. For a comparatively new state like Bangladesh, which also has had to bear an excessive colonial legacy, this quest has been an elusive one, despite the advantage of cultural homogeneity. Problems such as extreme poverty, civil disorder, a politicised military and the existence of elite groups determined to preserve a monopoly of power, have all interfered with the various attempts to implement a democratic political structure in Bangladesh.

Because Bangladesh's nation-building strategies have had less time to develop than those of India and Pakistan, the various attitudes and responses of the successive Bangladeshi governments to regional or global affairs have often been moulded by quite different concerns.[6] More often than not, these concerns have been dictated by sheer necessity rather than by ideological considerations, although the latter have played a part. The difficulty of finding the balance between a foreign policy determined by necessity and one which reinforced national identity and sovereignty has beset each of the Bangladeshi governments. Their dilemma of bridging the gap between policy and practice in international relations has been particularly acute.

A state needs political maturity in order to achieve internal stability and prevent external intervention, the assumption being that as a new state eventually matures, the governing elites should be more able to evaluate what is practicable as well as desirable in their foreign policies.[7] Ingredients considered to exemplify the ideal of political maturity in foreign policy dealings include the mutual recognition of and respect for other states as political equals, and the commitment not to interfere in each others' affairs.[8] Unfortunately, such an ideal is not easily put into practice, as has been pointed out by Henry Kissinger:

> When the domestic structures are based on fundamentally different conceptions of what is just, the conduct of international affairs grows more complex. Then it becomes difficult even to define the nature of disagreement because what seems most obvious to one side appears most problematic to the other... Incompatible domestic structures can passively generate a gulf, simply because of the difficulty of achieving a consensus about the nature of 'reasonable' aims and methods.[9]

Such impediments to harmonious foreign relations have permeated Bangladesh's relations with India and Pakistan.

The complexity of Bangladeshi foreign policy, engendered partly by the unique qualities of the state's colonial heritage, becomes apparent particularly when examining the theme of national security. The term 'security' has been defined as meaning the 'protection and preservation of the minimum core values of any nation: political independence and territorial integrity'.[10] If these values are considered to be minimum necessities, then for Bangladesh, a state weakened and unstable from the outset, the notion of security is of vital importance.

The difficulty of translating formal independence into political reality has not been unique to Bangladesh, but the degree of difficulty has been considerable. Even the initial process of obtaining world-wide recognition of sovereignty was protracted and involved, arousing considerable anger and disillusionment in Bangladesh.[11] Preserving Bangladesh's independence remained a politically emotive issue played upon continually by successive leaders. For example, in consolidating his new regime in 1976, Ziaur Rahman assured the populace that he would do all in his power to protect Bangladesh's hard-won sovereignty and independence:

> I would like to state that the name of this country is Bangladesh. This is an independent country, and it will for ever remain independent. If there is an aggression on us the seven and a half-crore [75 m] people of this country will rise to one man and resist it and defend the independence.[12]

Similar rhetoric pervaded Hussain Muhammad Ershad's inaugural speech following his coup in March 1982:

> The Armed Forces had to take over the administration of the country to safeguard [the] nation's sovereignty and independence and to save and rescue the country from administrative, social and economic disaster... We shall continue our efforts to improve our relations with the Big Powers. But I want to declare it categorically that we want friendship with any country of the world but no domination.[13]

Both leaders were tapping into popular sensitivities which were inevitable in a newly created and militarily weak state.

Like many other weak and politically unstable states, Bangladesh has been vulnerable to external pressures which impinge on its autonomy or greatly reduce its influence in the international arena. The consequent heightened sense of insecurity has helped to shape Bangladeshi foreign policy, an impediment which has been exacerbated by the tendency of the more powerful nations to be unsympathetic towards such fears or desires to exercise sovereign rights.[14]

Applying the principle of security to Bangladesh's foreign policy draws attention to the many political problems and weaknesses which have placed the state at a distinct disadvantage in the South Asian region. As already pointed out, these weaknesses are due partly to Bangladesh's colonial past, and they provide an important stimulus in the forging of Bangladesh's interstate relations. Political instability is not unique to Bangladesh, but particular elements have been isolated by analysts as being the cause of an instability which is inherent to the state, rather than a temporary or intermittent problem.

Another important ingredient in forming Bangladesh's foreign policy has been the high degree of factional rivalry, not only within Bangladesh's political parties, civil service and armed forces, but also between each of these groups. The problem of factionalism was particularly convoluted and destabilising during the first decade of Bangladesh's existence,[15] but throughout Bangladesh's history it has fostered state insecurity and restricted the governing elites' opportunities to pursue an assertive or autonomous foreign policy. These domestic weaknesses have played an important part in extending Bangladesh's foreign policy concerns beyond the regional context, causing Bangladesh governments to seek assistance and support where possible from the superpowers (United States, Soviet Union and the People's Republic of China) and the United Nations.

Bangladesh's comparative military weakness[16] (see Table 1.1) has also played a part in reducing the negotiating options available to the state's leaders and hence, by necessity, the tendency has been for them to use various methods of diplomacy in conducting foreign affairs. Diplomacy through negotiation

Table 1.1 Statistical comparison between Bangladesh, India and Pakistan, 1995

	Area (sq. km)	Per Capita GNP mid-1995 (US$)	Population (million) 1995	Population Density (per sq. km)	Military Personnel 1995
Bangladesh	143 998	240	120.0	833.3	156 000
India	3 287 263	350	929.4	282.8	1 311 000
Pakistan	796 100	460	129.7	162.9	844 000

Sources: *The Statesman's Year-Book 1996–1997*; *The Europa World Year Book 1996, Volume 1*, London, 1996, p. 503; *Statistical Outline of India 1994–95* (Tata Services Ltd); *World Bank Group* (cited 22 January 1997) <http://www.worldbank.org/html/extdr/offrep/sas/>.

has been the only practical option for a state with such internal weaknesses as Bangladesh, but diplomatic acumen on the part of Bangladesh's leaders has been used to greater effect in the extra-regional rather than the regional, arena. The study of Bangladesh's foreign policy is very much a study of diplomatic manoeuvring, focusing upon personalities and their coteries. The absence of a strong, well established and unified central government, and the prevalence of political instability and factionalism means that, certainly for Bangladesh, much of the diplomatic negotiation is conducted by the state leader, or at least closely adheres to the policies of that leader.

The notion of 'security' carries strong military and territorial connotations, but there is another aspect of security which has relevance to the study of Bangladeshi foreign policy. There is some controversy over whether or not strategic considerations should have precedence over those of a cultural, economic, ideological or religious nature when looking at the influences upon foreign policy formulation. Most scholars engaged in the debate appear to be agreed that the loss of sovereignty is the greatest fear a state is likely to hold, a fear which will be the most dominant compulsion behind foreign policy-making.[17] Others point out that the importance of socio–cultural influences has been underestimated.[18] In Bangladesh's case, both territorial and cultural concerns have been extremely, perhaps equally, influential in moulding Bangladeshi foreign policy.

The defence of cultural identity has special relevance to Bangladesh because even the state's very existence can be attributed, to a large extent, to the ramifications of cultural discrimination. The East Bengali language movement, which gathered momentum soon after Partition in 1947, was provoked by the Pakistan government's insensitivity to east-wing aspirations of political equality. The language dispute, in turn, transformed into a powerful, unifying movement demanding regional autonomy, with Bengali language and culture being the focus for regional identity in the east-wing. The notion of religious identity was inextricably linked with the language issue, with the estrangement between the two wings interpreted by the Pakistan government as a confrontation between secularism and Islam.

East Bengali political aspirations and cultural pride were therefore perceived to be a threat to the validity of the two-nation theory, the original premise on which Pakistan's creation was based. While Bangladesh's relative cultural homogeneity has reduced the potential for multicultural and multilinguistic problems to impinge on international relations, socio–cultural concerns are nevertheless a vital, underlying component of Bangladeshi foreign policy. The East Bengali language movement had extraordinary repercussions not only for east-wing inhabitants, but also for the course of South Asian politics as a whole.

This analysis does not attempt to resolve the long-standing debate over whether or not the cultural loyalties existing in Bangladesh are based on inherited, 'primordial' attachments or whether they have been created and strengthened largely because of the manipulations of self-seeking political elites.[19] Both positions have relevance to Bangladeshi polity, with both ensuring that cultural concerns have remained a vital, integral part of Bangladeshi political life. Particular elements can be highlighted as having contributed towards a 'cultural focus' in Bangladeshi politics, or having prompted feelings of cultural insecurity and discrimination: the relative uniformity of language and culture in the region; the tussle between Islamic and regional Bengali cultural loyalties which became prominent with the growth of Muslim separatist politics in the nineteenth century and again after Pakistan came into being;[20] the uniqueness and syncretism of Bengali Islam,[21] the existence of which ran counter to exhortations of pan-Islamic unity as being the justification for Pakistan's creation; the geographical constraint against Pakistani unity after Partition, whereby culturally homogeneous East Pakistan was separated by a vast distance from the west wing, the centre of government; and the ensuing political and economic exploitation of East Pakistan by the central government. Whatever emphasis may be applied in the 'primordialist/instrumentalist' debate, the cultural perspective cannot be ignored with regard to Bangladesh. According to Paul Brass, one of the most prominent scholars engaged in the debate, it is the strength of the cultural heritage which needs to be assessed:

> [O]ne possible route towards reconciling the perspectives of primordialists and instrumentalists may lie in simply recognizing that cultural groups differ in the strength and richness of their cultural traditions and even more importantly in the strength of traditional institutions and social structure.[22]

In Bangladesh's case, that strength is considerable, making the task of political manipulation of cultural loyalties a risky and unpredictable one, where huge political gains might be the reward, or perhaps the reverse: political annihilation. An examination of the influence of security – or, more appropriately, insecurity – considerations on Bangladesh's foreign policy therefore also requires an appreciation of the degree to which intense indigenous cultural loyalties and fears can direct the state's foreign policy, as pursued by the governing elite.

The interplay between strategic and cultural insecurities and their influence on foreign policy is especially evident when studying the relationship between Bangladesh and India. India's place as the largest and dominant power in South Asia is a geopolitical reality which concerns each of the other regional states, none more so than Bangladesh which is virtually encircled by India. Indian assistance may have helped to bring Bangladesh into existence, but even this indebtedness was not sufficient to offset the fear of Indian, or more subtly, Hindu, domination which had long been a fundamental aspect of East Bengali Muslim politics. In its efforts to foster a separate national identity, the Pakistan central government was able to play on and exacerbate these fears, leaving the east wing with a deep-seated distrust of India's intentions. Being indebted to India soon became regarded in Bangladesh as the equivalent of being subordinated by India's will, especially once the debt quickly acquired a more literal, financial tenor.[23] One of the greatest fears engendering insecurity in Bangladesh is that India might intervene directly in curtailing Bangladesh's sovereign rights.[24]

The fear of Indian dominance or interference is a concern shared by each of India's South Asian neighbours, and the extent to which it is justified has little bearing on the reality of this fear. If insecurity can be regarded as an important element in shaping foreign policy-making, then the insecurity invoked by India's comparative strength in the region would warrant pre-eminence. Such apprehension defines much of the character of Bangladeshi foreign relations, not just with India, but with the regional states generally. The reasons for the trepidation which India's might has instilled in the smaller states, such as Bangladesh, are intricate and subtle, with inherent cultural as well as territorial bases. The notion of pan-Islamism is one which currently receives much discussion and debate, but the idea of pan-Asianism is also one which has been very influential, even if superseded by movements such as Islamic revivalism in recent decades. The idea of an intrinsic Asian unity, where the 'spiritually and morally superior' east was bound by a common philosophical 'love for the ultimate and the universal', became popular in the nineteenth century, as part of the emerging Asian nationalist response to western imperialism.[25] In India the notion of Asianism was propounded by intellectuals such as Keshab Chandra Sen and Swami Vivekananda, gaining momentum in the early twentieth century, largely due to the writings of Rabindranath Tagore.[26] Tagore's belief in Asia's spiritual, as opposed to materialistic, ethos and his universalist desire for nations to transcend their territorial boundaries are typified by the following statements:

we do not slip into the habit of looking on man as a machine, or as a tool for the furtherance of some interest. There may be a bad as well as a good side to this; anyhow, it has been the way of our country; more it has been the way of the East.[27]

European civilization puts all emphasis on the progress of this cumulative acquisition, forgetting that the best which each individual can contribute to the progressive life of humanity is in the perfection of his own life. So their end comes in the middle of things; there is no game, but only the chase.[28]

How to be free from arrogant nationalism is today the chief lesson to be learnt. Tomorrow's history will begin with a chapter on internationalism, and we shall be unfit for tomorrow if we retain any manners, customs, or habits of thought that are contrary to universalism. There is, I know, such a thing as national pride, but I earnestly wish that it never makes me forget that the best efforts of our Indian sages were directed to the abolition of disunity.[29]

Tagore's philosophy nevertheless contains a powerful, rallying call for Indian cultural solidarity:

Since India has this genius for unification, we do not have to fear imaginary enemies. We may look forward to our own expansion as the final result of each new struggle. Hindu and Buddhist, Muslim and Christian shall not die fighting on Indian soil; here they will find harmony. That harmony will not be non-Hindu; on the contrary, it will be peculiarly Hinduistic. And however cosmopolitan the several limbs may be, the heart will still be the heart of India.[30]

Such sentiments held widespread appeal, particularly in Indian nationalist circles, during the struggle for independence from imperial Britain. With partition in 1947, the ideal of Asian unity received a jolt, but continued to be espoused by the Indian prime minister, Jawaharlal Nehru. Like Tagore, Nehru saw India as a cultural and religious focus of the entire South and Southeast Asian region.[31] The creation of Muslim Pakistan represented a direct challenge to the assumption of India's destiny to provide the mantle of political and cultural leadership in the South Asian region, a belief which had become embedded in the psyche of many in India and which proved difficult to dispel,[32] despite the implications associated with Pakistan's existence. The depth of this sentiment has been explained thus:

Having gained independence after nearly a thousand years of colonial bondage, India's sights are set on becoming a world class power commensurate with its size, population and past glory.[33]

The Indian scholar, Ravinder Kumar, has provided a contemporary voicing of ideas in keeping with the spirit of Nehru and Tagore, sentiments which affirm Indian cultural, as opposed to national, unity and strength as being the basis for Indian political identity:

> There is a consensus among historians, that if we look upon India as a 'nation', then we cannot make much sense of what happened to us prior to the 19th century. However, the moment we look upon ourselves as one of the autonomous world civilisations, then we can clearly relate our present condition, through a chain of cause and effect, to happenings in the past ... The political experience of the post-freedom decades, when the affairs of the Indian polity have been conducted upon the assumption that it is a nation – rather than a 'civilisational society' – has made it amply clear that our attempt to create a political society within our country on the pattern of a 'nation-state' is doomed to failure ... We would be much more at peace with ourselves, politically speaking, if we frankly accepted the fact that we are not a 'nation' but a 'civilisation'.[34]

American scholar, Ainslee Embree has, also assessed the political significance of India's rich cultural heritage, providing insights concerning the origins of the notion of the fundamental unity of an over-arching 'Indian' civilization.[35] Embree points out that the underlying unity provided by the extraordinary continuity and pervasiveness of the Brahmanical cultural tradition has been idealised and expanded, particularly by the Indian nationalists, to include the additional connotation of political unity.[36] He thoroughly explores the validity of such an assumption, concluding that the vision of historical Indian political unity was an ill-founded one, ironically based partly on the idea of 'India' as it existed in western historical imagination.[37] Embree explains that western images of India as a political and cultural unity, ranging from those of Herodotus to Kipling, were incorporated into the 'emotional and intellectual inheritance' of the Indian nationalist elites.[38] These images were all the more appealing because they resembled those expounded in the Sanskritic texts, which also contained universalist notions of political unity.[39] Adding to this complexity, according to Embree, was the influence of contradictory western imperial assumptions, which in India's case, denied the possibility of effective, unified self-government without British assistance.[40] In response, the Indian nationalists sought to prove that India, as unified by the British, corresponded with their image of the India of the past, thereby rendering western power and administration unnecessary.[41] Embree's observations have relevance when considering the reasons behind the Hindu–Muslim rivalry which culminated in the creation of Pakistan. The Indian nationalist emphasis on the intrinsic political unity of India provided little reassurance for the Muslim minority that their particular needs would be met, thereby contributing towards the Muslim League's insistence on the necessity for a separate Muslim nation.

The emergence of Bangladesh was therefore a cause for jubilation in India as the occurrence appeared to confirm the non-viability of Pakistan,[42] no doubt reviving for some the dream of a 'greater India', a hope seemingly thwarted by partition. Such enthusiasm carried the deeper connotation of Indian cultural and territorial designs and expectations which Bangladeshis feared might go so far as to consider that the reabsorption of the new state into India's fold was predestined. These anxieties were suppressed in the euphoria immediately following independence, but soon began to re-emerge,[43] despite, or perhaps because of, Bangladeshi leader Mujibur Rahman's close affiliation with the Indian government. Such fears were easily manipulated and brought to the fore upon Ziaur Rahman's ascendancy, becoming an on-going impediment to the resolution of Indo–Bangladesh conflict. In closely examining the interaction between these two states in later chapters, it will be shown that the legacy of pan-Asianist appeals and associated claims about Indian cultural pre-eminence has been a pervasive and lasting one, considerably exacerbating the labyrinthine and tense character of post-partition South Asian foreign relations.

There are many layers to the idea of Indian hegemonistic designs as a cause of insecurity in the region. The pan-Asianist ideal, as espoused by Indian intellectuals, and the associated notion of Indian cultural leadership, both imply that the territorial and cultural fears held by the smaller South Asian states have due cause to exist. It is not difficult to find examples of Indian preparedness to meddle directly with the internal politics of its neighbours in an almost contradictory attempt to preserve the so-called status quo.[44] It has been pointed out that India's superior military strength in South Asia virtually dictates that force rather than diplomacy will be the most likely option chosen by India to resolve regional disputes.[45] According to S.P. Cohen, India has gradually increased its influence in the region, particularly since 1971, to the extent that a type of civilian militarism has come to dominate.[46] India's strategic concerns are seen to encompass the entire South Asian region, consequently creating an image of India as a nation which has come to expect 'habitual obedience' from its smaller and less powerful neighbours.[47] Instead of fostering regional security, Indian strength has instilled the opposite, the smaller states' overriding fears being exacerbated, rather than appeased, by Indian protestations of regional beneficence. India's typical perspective is exemplified by the following comment made by Indira Gandhi during the November 1975 coups in Bangladesh. Her assurance of non-interference contains an opposite message:

[T]hings happening in 'our neighbourhood were not entirely good and cause us grave concern.' India was very careful not to interfere in the internal affairs of any country and had kept itself scrupulously aloof from them. But it could not help expressing its concern 'when stability of the region is disturbed' and could pose a threat to India itself.[48]

India's habitual stance has been to dismiss, rather than acknowledge such fears of Indian domination and interference, and this attitude is sometimes reflected in the writings of Indian scholars, such as P.S. Ghosh:

> The smaller nations of South Asia have no grounds for anxiety as far as India's relations with them are concerned. In fact because of a relative authoritarian power structure in our neighbourhood, an artificial fear psychosis has been created in the minds of their peoples by the ruling elites particularly in Islamabad and Dacca.[49]

The dismissive approach is also manifested in the constant attempts by India to minimise the international importance of intractable disputes with its neighbours, the aim being to discourage external interference in what India regards as virtually a domestic preserve.[50] It has been pointed out that this down-playing tendency by a regionally dominant state can be an important contributor towards conflictual interstate relations. International harmony is dependent upon the states generating 'a sensitivity to the impact of their own behaviour' on other regional states which is 'at least equal to their sensitivity to the impact of the behaviour of other actors on them'.[51] Each state therefore needs to be aware of and acknowledge the fears of other states, whether or not those fears are justified. The ever-present tension between a large state such as India and one much less militarily powerful such as Bangladesh can thus be explained partly by such a maxim. While the view that Bangladesh is of no real significance to Indian political considerations[52] is extreme, there has been little cause for Indian apprehensions to include a serious concern for Bangladeshi territorial designs, and hence there has been no great effort to empathise with or accommodate Bangladeshi insecurities. In matters of national self-interest, for the dominant power, the concerns of smaller states tend to be lost.

The desire for security has provided an important driving force in interstate relationships.[53] Just as the smaller South Asian states hold various fears and insecurities, so do India and Pakistan, despite their size and military strength. Like the smaller states, both India and Pakistan fear threats to their sovereignty and independence, as exemplified by Indira Gandhi's comment above. Bangladesh's foreign relations in South Asia are subject not only to domestic security concerns, but also to the security concerns of India and Pakistan. For example, by sharing a fear of Indian dominance, the foreign policies of Bangladesh and Pakistan were given a fundamental nudge in a common direction. The sharing of insecurity concerns between these two states has enabled them to suppress historical antagonisms and differences in national outlook.[54]

In a fundamental way, Indian security concerns have been at odds with those of Bangladesh. The grand Indian vision of cultural leadership and pan-Asian unity may have been dented somewhat over time, but as explained above, it has been an enduring one and has played an underlying part in fostering Indian expectations of regional pre-eminence. This outlook contrasts sharply with the aspirations generally existing in a state such as Bangladesh, in which, apart from a brief period of post-independence euphoria, there has been little historical cause to entertain such idealistic and expansive ambitions. Indian idealism partly owed its resilience to the reasonably stable and long-term liaison between India and the Soviet Union. This alliance offered a degree of stability which Bangladesh was denied, even during its existence as the colonial wing of Pakistan.[55]

The emergence of Bangladesh altered the Indo-centrism of the region, but at the same time, it did much to boost Indian influence and status. Its creation symbolically, and pragmatically, weakened India's rival, Pakistan. In defeating Pakistan and in helping in Bangladesh's creation, India attained an international reputation as being a powerful, skilfully managed state.[56] The prevailing regional political arrangement, to which each of the smaller states has had to adapt, is therefore one in which the successive Indian governments have perceived the state's minimum sphere of territorial and cultural influence to include the whole of the South Asian region. This perception contrasts markedly with that existing in Bangladesh, the newest South Asian state, where considerable effort has been expended simply in asserting sovereignty over the state's borders. The difficulty in determining their precise location, as mutually agreeable to India, has been a consistent source of antagonism, and at times enmity, between the two states. The essentially contrary nature of their security concerns therefore almost guarantees that comparatively minor dealings between the two will be accompanied by an exaggerated tension. In keeping with this assumption is the following observation made by Indian scholar, Surjit Mansingh:

> In New Delhi, Bangladeshi officials gained the reputation of being the toughest, most demanding, and most sensitive of all national groups with whom the Indian government has regular dealings.[57]

The Indian tendency to consider all South Asian activities to be of Indian concern has given rise to an intricate dilemma to be faced by successive Indian governments; a problem which has impinged directly on Bangladeshi foreign policy. The Indian predicament is characterised on one hand by the wish to ensure that the state continues to enjoy the post-1971 'unprecedented concentration of unchallenged power'.[58] On the other, there is a combination of pragmatism and idealism, whereby excessive interference in the region could prove too costly financially and politically. India has always prided itself on its non-aligned status in the international arena and, particularly during the Cold War era of superpower rivalry, on its support for the non-aligned movement. Expansionistic actions on India's part would undermine its self-perceived role as a bastion of non-alignment.

The term 'non-alignment' has been given a multiplicity of meanings, but according to former Indian Prime Minister, Narasimha Rao, the pursuit of a non-aligned foreign policy was synonymous with the assertion of sovereignty and independence. Rao believed that non-alignment was as relevant as ever, if not more so, for developing nations such as India in recent times.[59] Like his predecessors, Rao projected the Indian government as a staunch defender of the ideal of non-alignment, partly in response to the controversy associated with India's long-term liaison with the Soviet Union.

Because of India's self-proclaimed commitment to non-alignment, its security concerns over Bangladesh have fluctuated between fearing the ramifications of having a politically unstable neighbour in an already sensitive and at times turbulent area; and, as would be expected of an advocate of non-alignment, providing the conditions to ensure that Bangladesh is able to adopt an independent stance in the international arena. The quandary of Indian foreign policy-makers has been given a more pragmatic emphasis in the following statement:

> Any attempt to softpedal India's stakes in the South Asian power structure and security environment in a deliberately created maze of moral platitudes and demands of good neighbourliness may only result in serious weakening of the Indian position with no tangible corresponding gains in terms of sustained goodwill and cooperation from its neighbours. A more pronounced Indian profile, on the other hand, would meet increasing resistance from the neighbouring countries and become counterproductive.[60]

India's sensitivities regarding non-alignment were easily played upon by the other South Asian states, as occurred at the Fifth Non-Aligned Summit, held in Colombo in August 1976. The Summit provided an ideal forum for Ziaur Rahman to air his grievances against the Indian government and to secure sympathetic international attention. His strategy was to undermine the traditional image presented by India as being the state which epitomised the spirit of non-alignment, by appealing for support to withstand the 'foreign interference' instigated by India in the affairs of Bangladesh.[61] Without directly naming India, but with obvious intent, Zia made these comments on the eve of the summit:

> The strength of the non-aligned movement... was its flexibility and they had to look at the Movement in the context of the present complex problems when some bigger nations were trying to dominate the smaller ones, when one was trying to interfere with the political and economic

sovereignty and independence and interfering in the internal affairs of other states, when some were trying to extend their hegemony over the smaller ones.[62]

Zia was using what he considered to be the most effective diplomatic means to keep India in check.

Possessing regional strength has not meant that India has been exempt from having to engage in the intricacies of diplomatic manoeuvring in order to preserve its position. Indian foreign policy fears and concerns have been no less real than those of a weaker state such as Bangladesh, but much of the focus of Indian unease, at least during the period under study, has been aimed specifically towards Pakistan and its links outside the region, particularly with superpowers China and the United States. Just as Indian political aspirations have tended to encompass a wider sphere than those of the smaller South Asian states, so has Indian political insecurity. That is not to deny Bangladesh's and Pakistan's own attempts to seek alliances external to the region, but the focus of those efforts has been characterised by the aim to find a counterpoise to dominant India. Tension between India and Pakistan has been exacerbated by the clash between India's desire to maintain the regional status quo and Pakistan's cultivation of superpower military and financial assistance.

Former Indian prime minister, Mrs Gandhi, whose foreign policy goals dominated the Indian government for almost two decades, believed that there was a tangible link between instability within the region and external interference. Her fears were expressed when interviewed by Surjit Mansingh in 1981:

> It is not good for us economically, militarily or from any other point of view to have weak neighbours. Some of our present problems are because they are so instable. But we also think that there is a deliberate move to keep the subcontinent unstable.[63]

She reiterated her opinion in a *Times of India* interview in 1983, when asked about external threats to India's unity and integrity:

> We see all over the world how countries are being destabilised. Other governments look to their own interest rather than the interest of the country concerned (the country in whose affairs they intervene)... I don't think people can destabilise a government merely from outside. But there are plenty of people who wish to take advantage of the trouble, who like to encourage it in one way or another.[64]

The tension between Bangladesh and India therefore can be explained partly by the fundamental difference in the foci of their foreign policies.

Indian concerns are typified by the broader fear of Bangladesh's potential to produce destabilising conditions in the subcontinent which, in the long term, could invite external meddling and perhaps, ultimately, the disintegration of the Indian Union. Superpower interference in South Asia has tended to have been driven more by 'external' strategic considerations, rather than by 'the intrinsic value of the Subcontinent itself', but India has remained suspicious of any superpower activities in the subcontinental region.[65] By contrast, Bangladeshi foreign policy has been moulded by the fear of India's regional hegemonistic designs. While it is highly unlikely that India would resort to a take-over of Bangladesh in an attempt to restore regional stability in a crisis, the Indian government's obvious concern for regional security has fostered popular Bangladeshi fears of Indian domination. Indian fears regarding Bangladesh's instability are based not only on the latter's political fragility, but also on its deepseated and extreme poverty[66] and dependency on large amounts of foreign aid for survival.

Poverty is increasing in Bangladesh, despite the best efforts of the United Nations and various indigenous organisations like the Grameen Bank.[67] According to a study by Rehman Sobhan, one of Bangladesh's foremost economists, the number of the poor has been increasing each year since 1983, at about 1.5 per cent per year.[68] Approximately 60 per cent of all households are below the poverty line and over half of those are below the so-called hard-core poverty line.[69] Being one of the most densely populated countries in the world, Bangladesh has a serious overpopulation problem[70] which has contributed towards the worsening poverty. The rate of population growth has declined in recent years to less than 2 per cent per year,[71] but even conservative population estimates put Bangladesh's population at approximately 195 million by 2025.[72] Poverty, and the state's growing dependency on foreign aid, have become integral to Bangladesh's foreign relations and have ensured that Indian concerns over Bangladesh's viability have not diminished. The validity of those concerns is evaluated below.

Analysts have debated at length the impact of Bangladesh's increasing dependency on foreign aid, either pointing to the benefits of obtaining foreign capital and technology or to the burdens they have inflicted. The latter view has become increasingly accepted, where aid dependency is considered to have inhibited the nation's economic development, perpetuated poverty; and, ultimately, threatened the state's stability and sovereign independence.[73] Aid-donors have acknowledged some of the adverse consequences of aid, but have tended to blame mismanagement of aid within Bangladesh. Their criticism has been focused instead on the 'low rate of project implementation, slow rate of growth in the agricultural sector, and the fall in some of the social indicators'.[74]

Economic analyst Anisul Islam has provided evidence to show that Bangladesh has become increasingly subject to economic difficulties associated with foreign aid. According to Islam, Bangladesh's dependence on foreign capital has increased steadily since independence.[75] From 1971 to 1991, Bangladesh received a total of US$22.46 billion in foreign aid.[76] The amount of aid received per year increased from US$270 million in 1972 to US$1809 million in 1990, the latter amount constituting 8 per cent of the 1990 Gross Domestic Product (GDP).[77] By 1990, 96 per cent of Bangladesh's development budget was reliant on foreign aid (compared with 17 per cent in India's case), and approximately half of Bangladesh's total imports were financed by foreign aid.[78] At the same time, the international aid climate deteriorated after 1987, reducing the rate of 'real dollar' (inflation-adjusted) aid flows into Bangladesh.[79] As a result, much more of Bangladesh's aid is now received in the form of loans, rather than outright grants,[80] adding increasingly to the cost of debt servicing. Bangladesh's total outstanding debt has increased dramatically over the last two decades, growing from US$501 million in 1974 to US$ 13 879 million by the end of 1993.[81] Debt-service repayment figures also show that Bangladesh's debt burden will continue to increase. Loan conditions have tightened, becoming much more of a burden, particularly since 1985, resulting in higher interest rates and a corresponding decline in the repayments of principal.[82]

Sobhan has taken a vigorously anti-aid standpoint, declaring that the process of development and the acquiring of aid for Bangladesh has contributed towards 'the growth of external linkages, dependency and domination of the domestic policy'.[83] The external linkages have become 'critical to the emergence and development of an indigenous bourgeoisie, whose entire fortunes are intimately tied up with access to external resources in the name of development'.[84] Ownership of wealth has become concentrated and poverty for the majority has become entrenched as a result.[85] Sobhan scathingly considers that the 'immiserization of the masses' has grown correspondingly as the 'parasitic and unproductive . . . bourgeoisie has accentuated the need for external resource flows to both sustain subsistence consumption and to feed the growing appetites of the aspirant bourgeoisie'.[86] He warns that this process has marginalised the masses, threatening Bangladesh's domestic social order and, in turn, hampering Bangladesh's 'linkages with the world economic system'.[87] As well as reinforcing economic inequalities, foreign aid has produced dependency in large sections of the urban and rural population.[88] Employment, income and consumption have become increasingly dependent on aid availability, as has 'virtually every area of government activity'.[89]

Sobhan's views are supported by T. Maniruzzaman who argues that foreign aid has hampered Bangladesh's economic development by the creation of an affluent, opportunistic class of entrepreneurs.[90] According to Maniruzzaman, Bangladesh has come under the sway of a monied business and industrial class which emerged partly because of the massive foreign aid received since independence.[91] The Bangladesh bureaucracy has also flourished artificially with the continuous flow of aid, increasing the country's dependency on aid, as explained by Maniruzzaman:

> Indeed, a vicious circle developed where Bangladesh commission agents, Bangladesh bureaucracy, and officials in the donor countries or aid organizations kept the flow of foreign aid going to Bangladesh, such aid sustaining the rentier class which foreign aid itself helped to grow in the first place.[92]

Many of the *nouveau riche* class have further impaired the country's economic and political instability by indulging in conspicuous consumption, using corrupt trading practices, defaulting on loan repayments and seeking personal political gain.[93]

According to Sobhan, Bangladesh's increasing dependency on foreign aid has undermined the state's autonomy, giving donor countries an 'unusual measure of leverage' over domestic policy.[94] Many development decisions, such as those associated with investment priorities and choice of technology, have to be 'tailored to the ideological predilections of donors, the types of aid provided and the terms on which it is made available'.[95] Anisul Islam supports this argument, pointing out that the true cost of loans is much higher because of 'aid tying', where the 'recipient country is given very little flexibility or freedom to purchase inputs (or supplies) from cheapest sources or to select the most appropriate technology or projects'.[96]

B.N. Ghosh puts forward similar arguments, emphasising that 'aid is granted only when the ideologies and interests of the aid-givers and aid-receivers coincide'.[97] He argues further that supplying 'so-called' aid has become a highly profitable exercise on the part of donor countries whose business and political elites aim to prop up sagging domestic industries and to perpetuate the dependent status of the aid recipient.[98] In short, he considers foreign aid to be an instrument of 'foreign policy and even of blackmail'.[99] Sobhan believes that popular Bangladeshi fears regarding the impact of aid dependency on Bangladeshi sovereignty and independence have been particularly justified:

> The decision makers of the developed world hold the lifeline of any regime in Bangladesh in their hands and can create havoc in the life of a country...The sovereignty of the Bangladesh nation state, in its prevailing social configuration, is therefore, a polite fiction which is perpetuated by the courtesy of the donors as long as Bangladesh does not challenge their current strategic assumptions and ideological perceptions.[100]

Heavy reliance on foreign aid is not restricted to Bangladesh in the South Asian region,[101] but when combining this dependency with the problem of extreme population density and the widespread nature of frequent natural disasters,[102] Bangladesh is particularly vulnerable to any reduction in the supply of foreign aid. Considerable fluctuations have occurred in the supply of aid, forcing Bangladesh governments to seek new donors and forms of aid, particularly during the last decade, as explained below.

The largest provider of aid to Bangladesh has always been the World Bank, supplying 25.6 per cent of Bangladesh's aid in 1990.[103] The Asian Development Bank (ADB) has quadrupled its aid to Bangladesh since 1984, providing about 15 per cent of total aid by 1990.[104] Contrary to common perception, Saudi Arabia and the Organisation of Petroleum Exporting Countries (OPEC), have given comparatively little aid to Bangladesh in recent years, the Saudi portion declining from a peak of 10.8 per cent in 1977 to a mere 0.4 per cent in 1990 and the OPEC share dropping from a peak of 2.3 per cent in 1982 to about 0.5 per cent in 1990.[105] E. Ahamed's comment that the 'Muslim countries in general and the oil rich Arab countries in particular are important sources [of aid]'[106] may have had some foundation in the early 1980s, but Islamic aid has declined substantially. Instead, the Islamic Middle East Gulf States have assisted Bangladesh indirectly by providing employment to migrant Bangladeshis who remit valuable foreign exchange back to Bangladesh. Remittances from abroad, largely from the Gulf States, amounted to US$1300 million in 1994–5, an increase of 20 per cent compared with the previous financial year.[107] Bangladesh's dependency on the Gulf States is therefore considerable, as exemplified in late 1990 during the Gulf crisis caused by the Iraqi occupation of Kuwait, when Bangladesh's economy deteriorated rapidly because of the loss of remittances from Bangladeshi workers.[108]

Like the Islamic states, the United States has also greatly reduced its supply of direct aid to Bangladesh, dropping from the considerable portion of 36 per cent of total aid in 1976 to only 5.5 per cent in 1989. Similarly, aid from the Soviet Union and China also declined, dropping to just 0.5 per cent and 0.4 per cent respectively, in 1990. Indian aid has also become negligible, in contrast to the initial period between 1971 and 1975, when India had considerable political stakes in Bangladesh's survival and supplied Bangladesh with the extraordinary sum of US$304.3 million in aid when India itself was a major aid-recipient.[109] Japan has taken over the role as the largest individual supplier of aid to Bangladesh, increasing from 2.7 per cent of total aid in 1973 to a substantial 8.5 per cent in 1990.[110] The next largest individual supplier is Canada, surpassing even the United States by 1990.[111]

Whether or not aid has been of benefit to Bangladesh, it is integral to Bangladesh's economic structure and foreign policy. Successive Bangladesh governments have continually cultivated aid-donors wherever possible in the name of progress and development, despite the debatable benefits of aid. Ziaur Rahman, for example, 'embarked on an unprecedented quest to woo aid donors', undertaking many fund-raising visits to wealthy countries during his regime: the EEC, the Arab States, the United States, and Japan.[112]

Zia's foreign policy wholeheartedly embraced the notion that foreign aid was the key to domestic economic development, a naive and military-minded view, according to Marcus Franda.[113] As self-appointed champion of the 'third world cause', Zia urged developed countries to double their flow of aid to the least developed countries (LDCs) in the interests of easing the world's 'grim economic situation' and promoting cooperation.[114]

The corollary to Zia's search for aid was the emphasis he placed on Bangladesh's neutrality in the international arena and on espousing the necessity for global peace. Being vulnerable and dependent, Bangladesh's best option, in Zia's view, was to take a non-aligned stance whenever possible, preferably via an international body such as the United Nations, in the hope of generating a broader source of political and economic support.[115] His platform of neutrality included a commitment to establishing the Indian Ocean as a 'Zone of Peace'[116] and to creating a regional association of the South Asian states for the purpose of fostering 'regional friendship and bilateral interests'.[117] Zia's initiative regarding the latter was eventually fulfilled posthumously in 1985, with the first summit of the South Asian Association for Regional Cooperation (SAARC).[118] The themes of non-alignment and regional cooperation advanced by Zia were aimed ultimately as counters to India's regional dominance. They also flouted India's traditional preference for maintaining the regional status quo and for dealing bilaterally with the other South Asian states.

Like Zia, Ershad espoused a foreign policy ostensibly aimed at promoting global peace and non-alignment, but in reality partly aimed to curb Indian dominance over Bangladesh. The underlying message to India appears in Ershad's statement made during a visit to the United States in 1983:

> We have been governed by principles of sovereign equality of states, territorial integrity and non-use of force, non-interference and non-intervention in the internal affairs of other states and peaceful settlement of disputes.[119]

Ershad's foreign policy also resembled that of Zia regarding foreign aid for Bangladesh. Ershad believed in the necessity of aid for Bangladesh's development and principally appealed to the same states for assistance: the United States, China and the oil-producing Gulf States.[120]

Bangladesh's extreme poverty, economic instability and aid dependency have directly and indirectly fuelled and reinforced Indian fears of external interference in the region. These fears have been justified to the extent that severe and worsening economic problems exist in Bangladesh which is, in turn, indebted towards and dependent on assistance from states external to the region. Zia and Ershad also played on Indian fears by emphasising and exaggerating Bangladesh's strengthening links with the United States, China and the Arab states, long-standing allies of Pakistan, India's main adversary.[121] Whether or not the aid was forthcoming, Zia and Ershad were sending a clear message to India that their foreign policy leanings favoured Pakistan. Indian fears of external stratagems to destabilise its volatile north-east and northwest were widely known and easily provoked, as expressed by Nancy Jetly:

> India has reasons to be wary about Bangladesh's potentially disruptive role in the northeast, in the context of continuing uncertainty in the strategic region. India has also reasons to be uneasy about any major destabilization in Bangladesh which would lead to the involvement of an extra-regional Power in the area and have major repercussions in India. A hostile Bangladesh, in league with China and Pakistan, or both, will be able to exploit the turbulence in the northeast to India's patent disadvantage.[122]

A similar, more subtle argument has been put forward by Marcus Franda and Ataur Rahman:

> The inability of Bangladesh to become economically self-sufficient, together with its terribly restricted power position *vis-à-vis* India, significantly affect the security environment of Bangladesh. Possibilities for big power penetration are, therefore, considerable. Given the volatility of Bangladesh politics, the intensity and depth of Indo–Bangladesh differences, and Bangladesh's economic vulnerability, it is difficult to envisage an extensive period in the future when the big powers would not be tempted to at least probe Bangladesh's internal affairs.[123]

Zia and Ershad fostered, rather than allayed, Indian fears of external interference in their efforts to counter India's dominating presence in the region. As noted above, the level of aid to Bangladesh from the United States, China and the Arab states dropped markedly in the 1980s. Indian fears concerning the ramifications of Bangladesh's economic plight did not reduce correspondingly. If anything, they increased as India's domestic stability deteriorated in the 1980s.[124]

Bangladesh's poverty and aid dependency have been woven into the conduct of its foreign relations, but it is impossible to link economic ingredients precisely to outcomes in Bangladeshi foreign policy. On balance, economic factors appear to have been manipulated by, rather than instrumental in shaping political considerations and foreign policy. India will continue to see Bangladesh's economic strife in terms of a blend of political and ideological concerns, despite the reality that Bangladesh's economic dependency now principally involves either countries which are no threat to India, or organisations to which India is similarly indebted, such as the World Bank.

The above review has identified the most important influences on Bangla-deshi foreign policy; those considered to remain valid throughout the period under study, despite the variations in policy which may have been instigated or implemented by the successive Bangladeshi regimes. These influences range from those which have general applicability to interstate relations, to those which apply specifically to Bangladesh. Bangladesh's foreign policy has been moulded not only by monumental domestic difficulties and insec-urities: external pressures, insecurities and ideological concerns have also shaped Bangladesh's foreign relations. Subsequent chapters illustrate the interplay between these two realms, the domestic and the external, in the conduct of Bangladesh's relations with India and Pakistan.

India's regional supremacy has played a central role in the development of Bangladesh's foreign relations. For each of the smaller South Asian states, India's intentions are of great concern, but particularly to Bangladesh. Apart from being almost surrounded by India, Bangladesh is particularly vulner-able because it lacks the military strength and extra-regional alliances to withstand a serious challenge to its sovereign independence. Neither can Bangladesh take heart from the fact that it does not, like Pakistan, pose a military threat to India. Bangladesh's overpopulation and extreme political and economic fragility have become fixed in the Indian psyche as represent-ing one of the most ominous, unpredictable and worrisome threats to India's stability and integrity, compounded further if the Bangladeshi leader-ship is perceived to be anti-Indian.

Part II

Regional Influences on Bangladesh–India Relations, 1975–90

2
1975–81: Indo–Pakistani Rivalry and Indian Party Politics

The following extracts from three South Asian analysts provide typical examples of a perspective commonly adopted regarding Indo–Bangladesh relations during Ziaur Rahman's regime:

> Indo–Bangladesh relations in the post-Mujib era were more or less governed by the domestic compulsions of Bangladesh. At the domestic front, political instability and economic crisis dominated the scene. Trade between the two countries was on the path of decline. The political elites of Bangladesh tried to make political gains by raising the Muhuri char and New Moore island controversies. Their main purpose was to divert the attention of the people from domestic miseries. These irritants no doubt spoiled the relations of India and Bangladesh.[1]

> The unstable [Indo–Bangladesh] relationship is rooted in past memories of Hindu domination and partition of India. Later the attitude and postures of successive governments of Bangladesh have influenced shaping of the relations.[2]

> [T]he psychological need of the Bangladesh Government to distance itself from India and the requirement of external aid and foreign investments from Western and Islamic countries led to a perceptible loosening of Indo–Bangladesh bilateral ties.[3]

As broad, but typical, appraisals of Bangladesh's relations with India, the above statements do not portray a complete picture. Each of the extracts points to India's role in the relationship as passive, benign and unwitting, requiring forbearance on India's part to deal with the ramifications of Bangladesh's excessive and unjustified insecurities. This chapter will explain why the above opinions should be considered deficient as appraisals of India's role and of the regional forces which have impinged on the relationship between the two states. As will be shown, the domestic determinants of

Bangladesh's foreign policy were of importance, but pressures external to Bangladesh also played a very influential part in moulding Indo–Bangladesh relations during Zia's regime. The latter perspective merits greater attention than it has been given in the literature.

Influences external to Bangladesh are taken to include those of a South Asian, regional nature; in particular, the pressures which have been exerted on Bangladesh's foreign policy by India and Pakistan.[4] Regional influences in general have been down-played in the above assessments of Indo–Bangladesh relations where the emphasis has been placed on the effects of Bangladesh's domestic political machinations, poverty and soliciting of aid from states traditionally antagonistic to India. India has always stressed its policy of non-interference towards Bangladesh, but a study of individual issues marring relations between both states reveals that India has actively and effectively used indirect methods to manage those issues according to Indian requirements. The evidence shows that a much greater degree of reciprocation has occurred in relations between Bangladesh and India than has been acknowledged in the sample extracts above. The cooler relations between India and Bangladesh during Zia's regime were not due solely to domestic pressures operating within Bangladesh, such as Zia's choice of foreign policy direction.

As analyst Partha Ghosh has pointed out, the dividing line between foreign and domestic policies is very thin.[5] Nevertheless, if some attempt to create a broad, flexible division is made, using a regional perspective, then a less restricted understanding of Bangladesh's relations with India emerges. In assessing the external regional influences, the following two aspects have been chosen as particularly prominent, although again, no clear separation exists between them: the traditional character of post-1949 interstate relations in South Asia, imparted largely by India's political, military and cultural predominance in the region accompanied by perennial Indo–Pakistan rivalry; and India's specific foreign policy concerns, as interpreted by the prevailing Indian government. The latter aspect in particular tends to be under-emphasised in appraisals of Bangladesh's foreign policy during Zia's regime.

The relative importance of long-term political influences needs to be evaluated against the impact of events occurring during the period under study. In assessing the wider regional forces which impinge on Indo–Bangladesh relations, it becomes obvious that the foreign policy of a theoretically independent, sovereign state such as Bangladesh, is, to some extent, a manifestation of those political forces which have become characteristic of the South Asian arena. Perhaps the most dominant characteristic is that of India's regional pre-eminence, a position not necessarily guaranteeing India the right to use a free hand in South Asia, but one which nevertheless has enabled India to keep a firm rein on the activities of the other South Asian states. Fear of Indian military strength and regional intentions, and the way in which that fear has been provoked and manipulated, provides an undercurrent which permeates Bangladesh's foreign policy. The repercussions of this fear and mistrust also provide an enduring link between all of the components to be discussed below.

The other characteristic of South Asian politics widely believed to have significant implications for Indo–Bangladesh relations is that of regional bipolarity, whereby sustained Indo–Pakistan rivalry has created considerable tension in interstate relations. The emergence of Bangladesh in 1971 may have provided a new ingredient in this bipolarity, but during the first years of independence, at least, the state's existence represented largely an extension of India's regional pre-eminence. The pressure of political polarisation in South Asia meant that once Bangladesh succumbed to military rule in 1975, the state was considered, particularly by India, to have reversed its diplomatic orientation, favouring Pakistan instead.

Given the long-standing background of Indo–Pakistan rivalry, as far as Indira Gandhi and the Indian government were concerned, Ziaur Rahman's entry into Bangladeshi politics in November 1975 meant that a Pakistani-style military regime had emerged in Bangladesh. This event evoked almost obligatory Indian wariness and distrust, despite India's vastly superior military strength. The Bangladesh military had already been involved in the August coup against Mujib, but the officers concerned were of junior rank and they appeared to be acting with political, rather than military backing.[6] The way in which Zia's coup had accelerated the post-Mujib reconciliation between Bangladesh and Indian arch-rivals, Pakistan and China, compounded Indian fears.[7] Such concerns were described in the *New York Times* thus, after Bangladesh and Pakistan had agreed to an exchange of ambassadors within a few weeks of Zia's coup:

> Although Pakistan and Bangladesh had agreed in principle on the exchange of ambassadors before the coup d'etat in Dacca last Aug. 15, that change of government gave a major impetus to their reconciliation... The new warmth between the two countries is regarded as bad news in India, ... Pakistan's traditional enemy. After helping to militarily divide the country, the Indians had a close relationship with Sheik Mujib, and their relations with the Ziaur Rahman government are considerably cooler.[8]

An extra incentive for the Indian government to portray events in Bangladesh as a threat to regional stability was to use them as a means of justifying the Emergency proclamation which had been in force for nearly six months in India, the intention being to quell domestic criticisms and national disunity. According to a comment made by the Congress Party president, 'had Mrs. Gandhi not taken the firm stand she did on June 25 [the day on which emergency was proclaimed] India would have gone the Bangladesh way'.[9] In an oblique reference to Bangladeshi political events, Indira herself commented:

> The main task...was to maintain stability and unity of the country. The need for doing so had been further highlighted by what was happening in 'our neighbourhood'.[10]

Both statements by Mrs Gandhi and the Congress party president were completely unsupported by historical evidence, thus being merely justifications for Congress party actions.

Ziaur Rahman's assumption of leadership in Bangladesh was resented by Mrs Gandhi from the start and the antagonism and distrust was clearly mutual, as indicated in a statement by Zia, made shortly after his coup:

> Our patriotic people know well who are friends of the country and who are its enemies. Our people are also aware of those who are working in the interest of the country and who are acting against it.[11]

Zia urged the Bangladeshi public to watch carefully 'those who were engaged in violence and sabotage and those external forces trying to destroy us'.[12] The accusations and counter-accusations between Zia and Indira Gandhi therefore began to acquire a pattern reminiscent of the relationship which traditionally existed between India and Pakistan, one tainted by suspicion, insecurity and bitterness. Relations between India and Pakistan were far from amicable, even by February 1976, despite the latter state having been governed by a civilian regime for four years:

> India has no diplomatic relations with Pakistan and, in fact, very few links at all...Very informally, Pakistan and India have been discussing such problems as air connections. But some officials here say that the moves towards a better relationship were stalled by the Bangladesh coup and the fact that it brought the halves of what used to be Pakistan back toward each other.[13]

The 1971 Indo–Pakistan war and its repercussions contributed towards the lack of progress in cooperation between India and Pakistan, reinforcing the entrenched pattern of behaviour.[14] Ziaur Rahman's coup also contributed towards the tension between India and Pakistan, further indicating the strong historical links existing between the three states. The problem of separating the domestic from the external influences on Bangladesh's foreign policy becomes particularly pronounced when considering the historical ties between Bangladesh, India and Pakistan. These links have tended to be antagonistic in character, and at times bitter, particularly between India and Pakistan. The traditional tension between the three states has also underlain what often appears superficially as a lack of cooperation or communication between them. Despite the appearance of independence and isolation, the foreign policy concerns of the three states have always been inextricably interwoven.

It was because of these links that the Indian government saw the events of November 1975 in Bangladesh in terms of Indo–Pakistan relations. A comment made by Mrs Gandhi is indicative of the way in which the Indian government had given those events a 'Pakistani complexion', although the prime minister did not specify Pakistan by name. After stressing India's desire for stable and friendly relations with its neighbours, Mrs Gandhi said that 'some countries had not liked this', and 'had intervened in the Bangladesh affairs and brought about the present situation in that country'.[15]

For the Indian government to resort to the accusation of foreign intervention implied that Indian apprehension regarding Bangladesh's new military regime, and what it in turn implied for the balance of power in South Asia, was significant. Such insensitive allusions to Pakistani involvement in Bangladeshi affairs could have exacerbated Indo–Bangladesh relations, a step which the Indian government had little hesitation in taking. The opportunity to deliver a warning to Bangladesh that it should not become too friendly with Pakistan was clearly a greater priority than safeguarding Bangladeshi sensibilities. Implying that the establishment of a military regime in Bangladesh had been instigated by Pakistan no doubt also offered the Indian government an ideal opportunity to justify, regionally and internationally, its traditional stance of mistrust and animosity towards Pakistan.

The increase in tension between India and Bangladesh was obvious in the media, once Zia secured his dominant position in Bangladesh. The tension focused particularly upon the pro-Mujib Bangladesh guerrillas who commenced activities on the Indo–Bangladesh border after Mujib's assassination, bringing the issue of Bangladesh's border security to the fore. Zia quickly portrayed his attempts to curb the guerrillas as being a necessary part of asserting the sovereign rights of Bangladesh.

The rapid deterioration in Indo–Bangladesh relations was not surprising considering that such a fundamental change in the nature and outlook of the Bangladesh government had also occurred under Zia's direction. It was not difficult for Zia to play upon deep-seated fears of Indian dominance, as occurred during the border conflicts. These disputes were indicative not only of the fragility of Bangladesh's relations with India, but also of the extreme sensitivity in Bangladesh towards any encroachments on the new state's independence and national unity, both well within the Indian government's power to destabilise.

The pattern of deteriorating relations between the two states, at least while Indira Gandhi was in power, became established in the border disputes associated with Zia's assumption and consolidation of power. While

India attempted to minimise the issues at stake, to preserve an automatically advantageous bilateral arrangement, Bangladesh tended to overplay and broaden those issues in order to achieve what was to its government a more equitable, just resolution. The following statement by a spokesperson for the Indian External Affairs Ministry represented a typical example of the Indian response when confronted by Bangladeshi accusations during the first months of Zia's regime:

> The allegation that India is providing arms, training, funds or sanctuary to such miscreants 'is utterly false and baseless'... The attempt to revive anti-Indian feelings is particularly regrettable... [and] [t]he government of India is led to the inescapable conclusion that allegations of Indian involvement are being made out of domestic compulsions or some other reason.[16]

The Indian government spokesperson's reference to the revival of anti-Indian sentiments exemplified the polarised Indian vision of subcontinental relations up to that time. Any criticism of Indian activities was likely to be interpreted as of Pakistani origin. This assumption was no doubt cause for considerable annoyance and anger in Bangladesh, where political autonomy from the Pakistan government had been sought with such determination and achieved at such a high cost of human suffering. The Indian government's preoccupation with Pakistani interference meant that whatever attempts were made by India to understand and resolve Bangladeshi grievances were given an extra impediment.

The pervasive influence of Indo–Pakistan rivalry in the region becomes especially pronounced when viewed in relation to the Kashmir dispute, a bitter impasse which has dominated and soured Indo–Pakistan relations from the time of Partition up to the present day.[17] The way in which the feud has been conducted over the decades has resulted in characteristic, entrenched behaviour on the part of both states. In focusing upon India, perhaps the most obvious legacy of the Kashmir dispute has been India's preference for bilateral negotiations in the region, and a concomitant unwillingness to support extra-regional involvement and mediation in South Asia, as undertaken intermittently by the United Nations in particular. Successive Indian governments had little reason to support United Nations attempts to reconcile the dispute because India, already ensconced in Kashmir, had little to gain but much to lose. The overall failure of the United Nations to resolve the dispute, or to act independently of the great powers,[18] provided a dual message for India: it was possible to flout the wishes of the United Nations and ignore international opinion; but at the same time, such disdain appeared to foster great-power involvement in the region. Moreover, the latter outcome ensured that India's diplomatic path would be far removed from the oft-espoused Nehru ideal of non-alignment.[19] The

Kashmir issue has played an integral part of Cold War politics in the region, the dispute fuelling Indo–Pakistan animosity and hence stimulating the desire for great-power military assistance.[20] The Kashmir issue's entrenched characteristics also came to bear on Indo–Bangladesh relations, particularly once Ziaur Rahman assumed leadership of the government.

Whether or not a military regime had taken control of the Bangladesh government, it is unlikely that Bangladesh's relations with India would have run smoothly, given the backdrop of the on-going Kashmir dispute and the fact that many of the ever-present problems between Bangladesh and India can also be placed in the category of border issues. The unlikelihood of the two states resolving territorially-based issues amicably and fairly becomes obvious when considering the intractability of the Kashmir dispute. Ranged against Bangladesh, militarily weak and newly independent, was a state which was not only vastly superior in military strength, enjoying the patronage of one of the great powers and experienced in large-scale warfare, but also one seasoned in defying international opinion and generally unaccustomed to compromise and diplomacy in territorial matters. It is worth noting that the interminable and particularly volatile nature of the Kashmir dispute is inextricably linked to the two-nation theory and the rationale for Pakistan's continued existence. Indo–Bangladesh border altercations should not necessarily be perceived in terms of Hindu–Muslim antagonism and the two-nation theory. Nevertheless, any defiance of the Indian government by predominantly Muslim Bangladesh could easily be construed in religious and ideological terms as a challenge to Indian ideals of secularism and democracy, particularly once Bangladesh came under a military regime which favoured warmer relations with Pakistan.

In attempting to resolve disputes with Bangladesh, the necessity for the Indian government to accommodate subtle differences in aspirations between Bangladesh's home-grown military regime and the succeeding governments of Pakistan would have found little Indian sympathy or support in the polarised arena of post-Partition South Asian politics. The protracted and emotive Kashmir dispute has acted to reinforce the polarity, ensuring that ideological anxieties on the part of both India and Pakistan remain a dominant ingredient in their stance on respective territorial issues. There was little reason to believe that Bangladesh, especially under a military, Islamic regime, could expect its border concerns to be seen by the Indian government in a tolerant, impartial and understanding light. The ramifications of the Kashmir dispute for Indo–Bangladesh relations will become clearer when specific border issues between the two states are examined in more depth below.

In assessing the extent to which India's general, shifting foreign policy concerns have been able to mould the course of Bangladesh's relations with India, an informative event occurring within India indicates that the effect of those concerns has been significant. The influence of this event was not all-embracing, but rather more subtle, resulting in the underestimation of its impact on Indo–Bangladesh relations.

In March 1977, Indira Gandhi and the Congress Party, widely criticised for undemocratic, dynastic, and authoritarian policies,[21] were ousted in a general election by the Janata Party, led by Morarji Desai. For almost two and a half years, the Janata regime maintained a somewhat tenuous hold on power, until forced to resign in July 1979 from lack of unity and support.[22] In the ensuing elections held in January 1980, Indira Gandhi, heading a reformed Congress-I (Indira) Party, was reinstated as prime minister, more or less returning regional interstate relations to their traditional positions.

The direction in which Desai's government took India's foreign policy, characterised by an emphasis on 'genuine' non-alignment,[23] undoubtedly had beneficial results for Indo–Bangladesh relations, clearing the air to some extent and allowing greater room for political manoeuvring for both Zia and Desai. Both leaders were relatively 'unhindered by inherited sentiments',[24] and just as Zia was at pains to dissociate his regime from the unpopular policies of his predecessor, Mujib, so did Desai and the Janata Party attempt to chart a new political course, away from the more militant, high-handed style which had become identified with Mrs Gandhi's rule and which had contributed to her election defeat.

The Desai government's diplomatic overtures to the United States[25] and China,[26] and its intimations that the Soviet Union had 'no special corner on Indian friendship',[27] represented an unprecedented attempt to remould India's traditional stance in international relations. At a Foreign Ministers' Conference of the non-aligned countries, the first international conference attended by India after the formation of the Janata government, Desai declared that India would remain non-aligned in the 'real sense of the term'.[28] Once installed as leader of the new government, Desai also made prompt reassurances to India's South Asian neighbours, explaining that 'his government was specially determined to make every effort so that India's relations with its immediate neighbours improved on the basis of dignity and mutual interest'.[29] In further emphasising the reorientation in Indian foreign policy, he added:

> Our purpose is to see that at least this Sub-continent overcomes old suspicions and discovers that through co-operation and peaceful efforts we make our neighbourhood stable against outside malevolence and can devote a greater share of our limited resources towards respective constructive endeavours.[30]

There is ample evidence that the Desai government's efforts to ease the tension in relations between India and Bangladesh did go considerably beyond the rhetorical level, managing, to some extent, to counteract the traditional influence of political polarisation in South Asian relations. At the

Commonwealth Heads of Government meeting held in London in June 1977, Zia and Desai, meeting for the first time, espoused their commitment to resolving the various problems existing between the two states, with particular reference to the pro-Mujib dissidents who had been operating under Indian sanctuary.[31] Warmer relations between India and Bangladesh were given substance due to the Desai government's encouragement of many of the so-called 'miscreants' to return to Bangladesh, declining to continue readily giving them Indian financial and political patronage.[32] In November 1977, Desai and the Indian Foreign Minister, A. B. Vajpayee reaffirmed that the government would not give any support or encouragement to 'elements wanting to carry on political activities against India's neighbours'.[33] Such reassurance represented a stark contrast to the attitude of the previous Indian government which had continually denied that any assistance was being given to the dissidents at all, virtually refusing to acknowledge even the existence of such groups in India.

Perhaps the best example of how India's foreign policy stance has been able to alter, at least temporarily, the shape of Indo–Bangladesh relations, is the way in which the Desai government chose to deal with the arguably most divisive issue existing between the two states: the sharing of the Ganges water. The dispute over Ganges water usage had been an on-going source of friction between India and Pakistan virtually from the time of Partition, but once Bangladesh achieved independence, the controversy assumed particular significance.

Bangladesh, the lower riparian state and economically dependent on the Ganges, was automatically placed in a position vulnerable to any plans which a prevailing Indian government might have to divert Gangetic water. Bangladeshi fears were brought into focus in 1975, with India's eventual completion of the Farakka Barrage which had been constructed across the Ganges, in a strategically vital position, only 17 kilometres upstream from Bangladesh's western border with India (see Map 3). The most publicised purpose of the barrage was, and is, to divert sufficient water from the Ganges into the Bhagirathi–Hughli river, a distributary which provides India with a significant economic link between the Ganges and the Bay of Bengal (see Figure 1). The augmented flow was deemed necessary to reduce the siltation which was impairing the navigability of Calcutta port at the river mouth, particularly during the drier months of the year.[34] Although the issue was not ignored, Bangladeshi concerns about the implications of the Farakka barrage were held in relative abeyance during most of Mujib's pro-Indian regime,[35] but once the barrage actually commenced operation, the character of the dispute became increasingly bitter, for a number of reasons.

The most obvious was the reality of less water being available to approximately one third of Bangladesh during the drier time of the year. This was to set in motion a chain of adverse environmental, social and economic effects for Bangladesh, consequences which were continually down-played by the Indian government.[36] Also significant in heightening the dispute, after the barrage commenced operation, was the Indian government's provocative decision to continue diverting the Ganges flow after the expiration of a temporary agreement with Bangladesh lasting from 21 April to 31 May

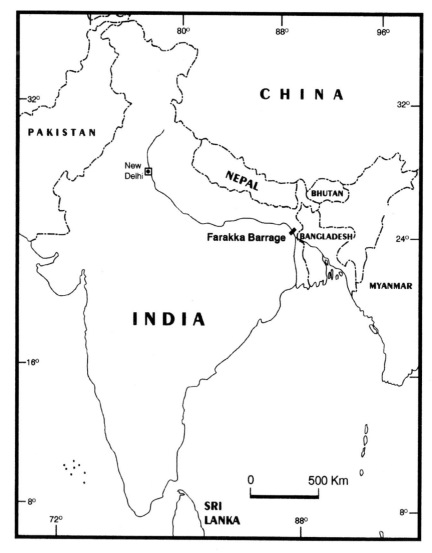

Map 3   Location of the Farakka Barrage
Source: Based on Crow *et al.* (1995), p.16.

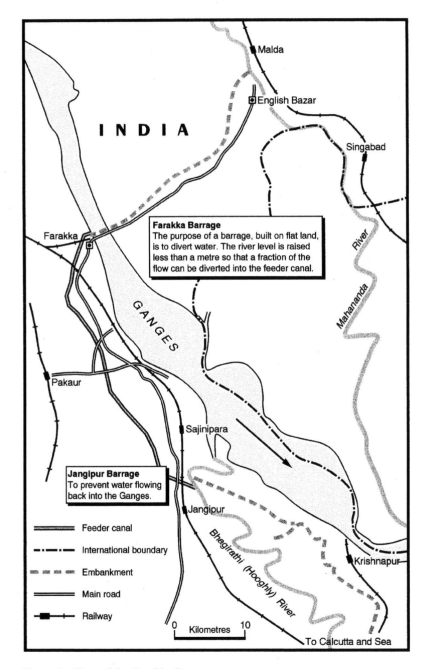

Figure 1 Plan of the Farakka Barrage
Source: Based on Crow *et al.* (1995), p. 52.

1975. Bangladesh had expected that further discussions would be held, but India's decision to keep the barrage in operation was undertaken without consultation or concurrence by Bangladesh.[37]

With the barrage already causing concern, it was not surprising that when General Ziaur Rahman came to power in November 1975 he should vindicate his anti-Indian stance and rally domestic unity and support by focusing on the emotive Farakka issue, thereby also contributing towards the escalation in tension between Bangladesh and India.[38] Until the Desai government came to power, the intermittent bilateral talks conducted to resolve the Farakka issue exhibited an obvious decline in cordiality. At talks held in Dhaka in June 1976, the Deputy Chief Martial Law Administrator of Bangladesh, Rear Admiral M.H. Khan, commented that views concerning Farakka were exchanged with India in a 'cordial atmosphere' and he was glad that the leader of the Indian team had appreciated the Bangladesh points of view.[39] By August 1976, M.H. Khan was taking a much stronger stand concerning Farakka, declaring that Bangladeshis would 'fight to the last and shed our last drop of blood to establish our right',[40] and adding that 'India wants to cripple us. Unless we stand united and fight out the issue, all our water resources and flood control measures will suffer'.[41]

Farakka talks held in New Delhi in September 1976 only reinforced the deadlock between the two states, with the Bangladesh government blaming India's unrelenting intransigence[42] for the failure of the talks and India accusing Bangladesh of taking an 'inflexible stand',[43] thereby preventing a solution being reached. Even involvement and encouragement from the United Nations, the stated intention of which was to negotiate and resolve the Farakka dispute by 'arriving at a fair and expeditious settlement',[44] did not make the subsequent bilateral talks more productive.[45] The following comment, which highlighted the lack of progress, appeared in an editorial in *The Statesman* (Delhi), after the conclusion of the January talks:

> The hopes generated by the 'consensus statement' on the Farakka issue in the U.N. Special Political Committee on November 24 have been frustrated. The two rounds of talks in Dacca, in December and earlier this month, did not yield an agreement, but it was said that much ground had been covered and some progress made. At the end of the third round in Delhi, neither side thought it worthwhile to pretend that anything had been, or was likely to be, achieved...In theory, the negotiations could be resumed; but, at the moment, neither side seems to think that this will serve any purpose.[46]

The lack of progress achieved in Farakka negotiations, up to the time of Mrs Gandhi's election defeat in March 1977, stood in marked contrast to the speedy developments occurring after the installation of the Janata government. Within three weeks of assuming power, the new Indian government

had taken decisive steps to comply with the UN's earlier consensus statement which insisted that India and Bangladesh should settle the dispute
bilaterally, a result which, until the Janata's investiture, had been far from
forthcoming.[47] On 18 April 1977, after three days of negotiations between
Ziaur Rahman and the Indian defence minister, Jagjivan Ram, an 'understanding' had been reached on the sharing of Ganges water, an agreement
which the Indian press claimed would go a 'long way in restoring and further strengthening the friendly relations between the two neighbouring
countries'.[48] Details of the understanding, revealed unofficially within days
of the negotiations, indicated a substantial concession on India's part,
enough to cause considerable concern in Calcutta and West Bengal generally.[49] The Indian government had agreed to halve the amount of water
drawn at Farakka during the driest period in April from 40 000 to 20 500
cubic feet of water per second, a reduction which the Calcutta newspaper,
Amrita Bazar Patrika dramatically declared would 'sound the death knell of
the vital Calcutta Port in [the] no distant future'.[50]

The formal signing of the Farakka accord did not take place until 5
November 1977,[51] and although the agreement was only a temporary one,
intended to last five years, it represented the most substantial step towards
resolving the 25-year-old dispute. Considering the lack of previous progress,
the signing of an accord, even if a short-term measure, was an achievement
easily underestimated.[52] It becomes an even more remarkable event when
also taking into account the domestic political turmoil in Bangladesh at the
time. In the intervening period between the initialling of the Farakka agreement, on 30 September 1977, and the formal signing of the agreement on 5
November, Zia was confronted with a particularly threatening and violent
military uprising. The mutiny was crushed mercilessly and, in order to rally
popular domestic support, Zia quickly resorted to claims of Indian interference, although the focus of his attack was directed at West Bengal rather
than the Desai government as a whole:

> [T]hose who take orders from other countries have to leave this country ...
> [T]he West Bengal Press have not accepted our rights on the Ganges and
> were also helping the miscreants. It is significant that the recent incid-
> ents took place after the miscreants were allowed to come back and settle
> down.[53]

In this way, Zia could use his traditional tactic of blaming India for Bangladesh's domestic political instability, without being too provocative towards
a relatively friendly regime. At the same time, the Desai regime, if it chose,
could easily have played upon Zia's accusations and his current political crisis to use them as excuses to delay signing of the Farakka accord or even to
renege on the terms of the agreement. The fact that neither leader had taken

a provocative stance at the time indicates that the Janata regime had succeeded in fostering a surprising degree of genuine political goodwill between Bangladesh and India.

The increase in warmth of Indo–Bangladesh relations was particularly pronounced during the post-accord euphoria, as exemplified by Ziaur Rahman's visit to India in December, where he was accorded a 'hearty welcome', in an 'atmosphere charged with friendship and enthusiasm'.[54] Retrospective criticisms of the accord usually centre on its failure to produce the expected study and recommendations for a long-term scheme to augment, from a source agreeable to both India and Bangladesh, the dry season flow of the Ganges. This failure should, more realistically, be regarded as an indication of the extraordinary difficulty of solving the problem of augmentation, rather than the ineffectiveness of the accord. Finding a mutually satisfactory means of augmenting the Gangetic flow has proved to be as formidable a task as sharing the Ganges itself.[55]

The fact that the Janata government collapsed in July 1979, years before the accord recommendations were due to be fulfilled, was also relevant in assessing the overall worth of the five-year accord. Even in the last months of the Janata regime, Desai and Zia were on amicable terms, asserting that a mutually acceptable solution for augmentation of the Ganges would be found 'as quickly as possible', and that 'great possibilities existed for increasing co-operation in economic trade, agriculture, shipping and technical fields'.[56] In April 1979, two weeks after the withdrawal of martial law by Zia, Desai paid a three-day visit to Bangladesh, the first visit in seven years of an Indian Prime Minister, providing Indo–Bangladesh relations with an additional warmth which was sufficiently noteworthy to attract comment in the *New York Times*.[57]

With the reinstallation in January 1980 of Mrs Gandhi and the Congress-I party as leaders of the Indian government, the Farakka accord (which they had opposed as being too generous to Bangladesh) quickly came under review, reviving some of the tensions which had dominated Indo–Bangladesh relations before the Janata party had come to power. The resurgence of the more habitual testiness traditionally associated with the Farakka issue could be predicted from the first comments made by the new Indian minister for Irrigation and Energy, Mr Gani Choudhury, in which he expressed his misgivings about the 'soundness of the agreement for sharing of Ganga waters', adding that the Congress-I 'was critical of the agreement when it was concluded by the Janata Government'.[58] In a similar vein, a contemporary Indian newspaper editorial declared:

> It is generally believed that Bangladesh asks for more water than it really needs and India is not unprepared to take less than the Calcutta Port needs...Bangladesh has been steadily pushing its ground and it is unlikely to give up any of the advantages which it has already secured.[59]

Nevertheless, the harder line followed by Mrs Gandhi's government with regard to Farakka, and the ensuing mutual recriminations between India and Bangladesh,[60] did not mean that the accord was scrapped. Mrs Gandhi's reassumption of power was met initially with at least some degree of optimism and cordiality in the Bangladesh press.[61] As a result, tension over Farakka did not escalate to the level it had attained before the Desai government came to power.[62] Although the various Farakka talks held in 1980–1 made little headway in resolving the problem of augmentation, the tone of the talks was somewhat milder than those held between 1975 and March 1977.[63] It would further confirm, therefore, that the Janata government's contribution towards the mellowing of Indo–Bangladesh relations was of more than temporary significance.

The Farakka stalemate and the way in which it came to dominate Indo–Bangladesh relations had shown no indication of breaking before 1977, under Ziaur Rahman and Indira Gandhi. The combination of the fact that the governments of both states were unequivocally convinced of the validity of their respective positions, along with the sheer logistical difficulty of sharing satisfactorily what was, during the drier months, barely an adequate amount of water just for Bangladesh, produced an intractable bone of contention reminiscent of the Kashmir issue. The essential reasons for the enduring stalemate of both issues had much in common, including ingredients such as India's military superiority, territorial possession and control and the other state's overwhelming sense of injustice, powerlessness and frustration. Although lacking the history of violence associated with the Kashmir dispute, the potential for violence erupting over Farakka and the sharing of Gangetic water cannot be ruled out. While Bangladesh may be far less capable than either India or Pakistan of waging a military campaign to settle an issue as vexing as the Farakka barrage, frustration and violence could be manifested in a number of other ways, such as mass demonstrations or support for rebel groups, either Indian or Bangladeshi. Like the effects of the Kashmir issue on Indo–Pakistan relations, disagreement over Farakka has continually marred Indo–Bangladesh relations up to the present day, being a focus of rhetoric, recrimination, political manoeuvring and, in Bangladesh's case, fear, defying long-term resolution and generally curbing any long-term warming of those relations.

Against such an unpromising background of irreconcilability, the efforts by Morarji Desai's government to settle the Farakka dispute stood out in contrast to the harder line followed by the preceding and succeeding Indian governments led by Mrs Gandhi. Adding to the unlikelihood of solving the dispute was the pressure deriving from Zia's regime to extract as much political advantage as possible, domestically and internationally, from a highly emotive and rallying issue. The approach taken by Desai's government regarding Farakka and the progress achieved were therefore all the more remarkable in view of these well entrenched problems which, as pointed out above, can be compared with those of the Kashmir dispute in their intractability. Considering the inability of India and Pakistan to find a long-term solution, (and the fact that 'long-term solutions' are all but absent in the history of major South Asian disputes), the short-term alleviation of the Farakka tension achieved by Desai's regime represented an important step forward, setting a precedent for the Indian government to compromise a little over Farakka and accommodate some of the Bangladeshi demands, thereby easing the considerable potential for a violent outcome.

The period of Janata rule was relatively short and unstable. The Janata government was also unable to fulfil, in the long term, its promises to institute a regime more attuned to the ideals of democracy and non-alignment. These shortcomings have resulted in a tendency for analysts to gloss over Janata achievements and to regard the regime as a welcome but ephemeral respite from the essentially dynastic character of the Indian government. The following comment about the Farakka issue typifies the commonly held opinion that the Janata regime's contribution provided little of lasting substance in resolving the dispute:

> The water treaty of 1977, an Agreement of the two countries to agree on the question of the best means of augmentation of the Ganga within a fixed period of 5 years ended without any consensus of the two parties. All the arrangements made at the cost of time and energy of the negotiators proved to be futile at the end of the 5-year duration of the treaty. In plain words, the two parties failed to make any significant progress towards the settlement of the dispute.[64]

This assumption may be valid on a superficial level, but it does not do justice to the fact that a Farakka agreement was actually reached in 1977, an achievement which had not been possible while Mrs Gandhi and Zia were both in power, despite the United Nation's attempts to encourage a settlement. Desai's government gave the first indication that India was prepared to make some concessions to Bangladesh. This move provided much-needed reassurance for the latter state, particularly as Mrs Gandhi and her government had, until ousted in the 1977 election, allowed the barrage to operate as they saw fit. Without the more amenable interlude, as represented by the Janata party's brief hold on power in India, the Farakka dispute, and Indo–Bangladesh relations generally, were likely to have deteriorated further.

The signing of a later interim Farakka accord in October 1982, an agreement which made marginal changes to the 1977 accord and gave only a slight advantage to India,[65] could also be regarded as the legacy of the warmer standing of Indo–Bangladesh relations developed during the Desai regime. Mrs Gandhi had disapproved of the 1977 agreement as being too generous to Bangladesh, but it would appear by the terms of the 1982 accord, that she did not have as free a hand as before March 1977. The Janata government had collapsed, but no doubt Mrs Gandhi was well aware that her hold on power was not as assured as it may have seemed during the Emergency.

The actions of the Janata regime would therefore confirm the sometimes overriding, influential role that domestic political events occurring within India, and subsequent shifts in Indian foreign policy orientation, have been able to play in the conduct of Indo–Bangladesh relations. Such events illustrate the extent to which a comparatively small, militarily weak state such as Bangladesh was and is at the mercy of the domestic, political machinations and fluctuations of a large, powerful neighbour.

An examination of the territorial disputes which flared up between Bangladesh and India after November 1979 reveals characteristics which clearly resemble those of the Farakka issue. The similarities between these issues emphasise the ways in which India and the broader regional pressures have moulded Indo–Bangladesh relations. On the other hand, studying the territorial disputes between Bangladesh and India also highlights the blurring of distinctions between the various internal and external influences on those relations. As with the Farakka issue, and for that matter, the Kashmir dispute, the rule of possession being virtually the equivalent of the law, applied to the tussles over border delineation between Bangladesh and India. At the same time, the influence of shifts in Indian foreign policy considerations can be observed in the course of those disputes. In other words, the nature of territorial disputes between the two states indicates the considerable influence of the traditional character of South Asian interstate relations, as exemplified by Indo–Pakistan rivalry and the fear of Indian domination. The course of the disputes also illustrates the way in which particular circumstances, such as the less antagonistic Janata regime's redirection in foreign policy, have impinged on that intrinsic character.

The most prominent Indo–Bangladesh border issues, the Tin Bigha Corridor, Muhuri Char and New Moore/South Talpatty/Purbasha island[66] have all tended to reinforce the traditional antagonisms, rivalries and fears existing in South Asia, the disputes being manipulated and protracted for political advantage by both Mrs Gandhi and Ziaur Rahman. A marked contrast can be observed between the relatively minor tension associated with the issues while the Janata party held power, and the bitterness which developed around them after the Janata collapse. Although little substantial progress was achieved in resolving the problems of border demarcation, the way in which the Desai government diplomatically addressed the issues differed particularly from the tactics used by the succeeding Indian government under Mrs Gandhi. By simply acknowledging that the problems, along with Bangladeshi concerns about Indian territorial designs, actually existed, and furthermore, required discussion and accommodation, the Janata regime was establishing a foundation for the possible, mutually satisfactory resolution of the border issues. In spirit at least, Desai's discussions with Zia in Dhaka in April 1979 were an attempt to do so.[67]

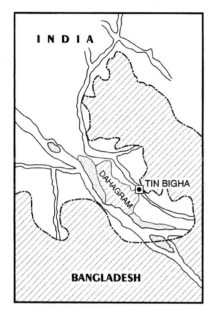
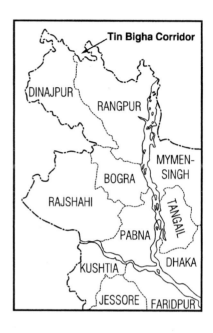

Map 4   **The Tin Bigha Corridor**
Source: Based on Gulati (1988), p. 175 (left) and Johnson (1975), p. 2 (right).

In dealing with a specific border issue, such as the Tin Bigha Corridor, the Desai government's approach was one of cordiality and compromise. The history of the Tin Bigha issue has been covered in depth elsewhere.[68] In essence the dispute stemmed from the difficulty of translating the theoretical border delineation, devised by Sir Cyril Radcliffe in 1947, into reality. As a result of Partition, various East Bengali/Bangladeshi enclaves of territory were located in India and vice versa. The arrangements regarding Bangladesh's access to two of its enclaves situated in Indian territory, close to the district of Rangpur in northern Bangladesh (see Map 4), also defied long-term resolution. According to the Border Agreement signed in May 1974, India was to lease, in perpetuity, an access corridor (Tin Bigha) between the two Bangladeshi enclaves and the mainsoil of Bangladesh.

The sticking point of the issue and the reason why the Indian government chose to procrastinate in fulfilling its part of the agreement was that by handing Tin Bigha over to Bangladesh, a portion of Indian territory would be placed in a similar predicament, no longer having a direct, mainland link to the rest of India. The Desai government made some attempt to break the Tin Bigha deadlock, which, although it ultimately did not succeed, nevertheless went far enough to evoke the following strong protest by the political representative of Cooch Behar, the Indian district affected by the Tin Bigha Corridor:

> It is learnt that the Government of India is going to introduce a Constitution Amendment Bill...in favour of its agreement with Bangladesh, for handing over the land of Tinbigha, an integral part of the Indian Union to Bangladesh...[A]ccording to the agreement, if the corridor (from Bangladesh mainland to Dahagram Angarpota enclave) is allowed *via* Tinbigha by perpetual lease, then, the Kuchlibari area will be cut off from the rest of the Indian territory and as such the people of this area will have to suffer untold miseries. They will be at the mercy of the Bangladesh Government. A new Indian enclave problem will arise. So, this type of gift of Tinbigha to Bangladesh must be stopped at all costs. Certainly, we want friendship with Bangladesh, but not at the cost of our motherland. No more appeasement. No more surrenders. No more cessation of our motherland.[69]

The Janata government's efforts may not have solved the Tin Bigha issue, but at the same time it did not appease such extreme sentiments or allow the dispute to reach such bitter heights as occurred in mid-1981 under the Congress-I government.[70] India had, in effect, reneged on the terms of the 1974 Border Agreement. The Tin Bigha Corridor itself was a very small area, being only 178 metres by 85 metres,[71] but by denying Bangladesh official access to the enclaves, India was effectively nullifying Bangladesh's ability to exercise sovereign rights over an area of 25 216 square kilometres. The conduct of the dispute, illustrating both the ease and the determination with which India could hold the reins, could hardly inspire the inhabitants of Bangladesh with confidence that the Indian government would deal with the more serious bones of contention between the two states with equanimity, impartiality and a willingness to compromise. The Tin Bigha issue did not attract significant attention outside the region, but as far as Indo–Bangladesh relations were concerned, it acted to reinforce popular, stereotypical images held of each other in both states and provided ample scope for both leaders to extract political mileage from the dispute,[72] impairing those relations as a result. The issue epitomised the way in which two antagonistic governments, as were those of Mrs Gandhi and Ziaur Rahman, could magnify a localised issue into one of considerable tension and emotive influence, in response to the pressures of political necessity and advantage. It also illustrated the ease with which the prevailing Indian government could regulate the climate of relations between the two.

Just as the Tin Bigha corridor issue did not become particularly divisive until after the collapse of the Janata government, neither did the other prominent territorial disputes between the two states: the rightful ownership of Muhurir Char[73] and New Moore Island.

In November–December 1979, both states clashed over which of the two should administer approximately twenty hectares of emergent charland in the Muhuri River (see map 5). As with Tin Bigha, the flare-up did not escalate to the point where it drew significant international concern. Nevertheless,

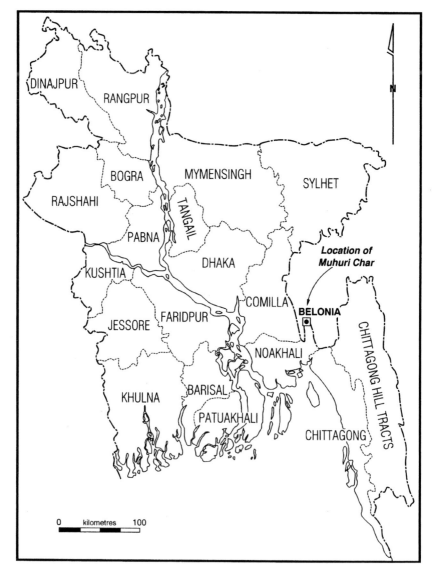

Map 5   Location of Muhuri Char
Source: Based on Johnson (1975), p. 2.

the Muhuri issue provided a clear indication that post-Janata Indo–Bangladesh relations would revert, to some extent, to their earlier abrasiveness.

Shifts in the course of the Muhuri River in the vicinity of the charland, and the Indian government's subsequent construction, without Bangladesh's approval, of nine spurs to control the effects of those shifts, made the area a focus of tension in October 1979. Earlier that year, in March, at a meeting of the Expert Committee of the Indo–Bangladesh Joint Rivers Commission, the Janata government had agreed, at the request of the Bangladesh government, to demolish the spurs by the 20 October.[74] According to Bangladesh, the construction of the spurs represented a violation of the terms of the 1974 Boundary Agreement, which had stipulated that the territorial status quo should be maintained on the Muhuri River, until the international frontier along the river had been demarcated officially.[75] When the succeeding Indian government did not demolish the spurs as agreed and, according to the Bangladeshi national press, instead began to strengthen and reinforce them, tension over the issue became particularly acute, leading to armed conflict within weeks.[76] The catalyst for the recourse to violence in the area, whereby the Indian Border Security Forces (BSF) and the Bangladesh Rifles (BDR) exchanged fire over a period of several weeks, derived from the attempts of Indian cultivators to harvest their crops on the Char in November. The Bangladesh government claimed that the Char was 'part and parcel of Bangladesh' and that the Indian cultivators had 'forcibly' harvested the crops under the cover of BSF assistance, thereby justifying the BDR's firing on the Char.[77] From the West Bengal press's point of view, Bangladesh was initiating 'war-like moves' in the area, and the BSF was acting merely in self-defence in order to protect the Indian cultivators and secure threatened Indian territory.[78]

A close study of the issue indicates that virtually no accurate account of the events can be presented confidently, particularly concerning which of the two states may have provoked or initiated the violence. Bias and contradiction in the contemporary sources, combined with vagueness, inaccuracies[79] and further contradictions in the secondary accounts provide a host of problems for any impartial assessment of the issue.[80] Even to ascertain fundamental details, such as the length of time the Char had been in existence, presents difficulties when opinions vary considerably. Accounts range from one which stated that the Char was 'newly surfaced land' in 1979[81] and its ownership therefore open to negotiation; to one which implied that the Char had existed for years, always having been under Indian suzerainty:

> But when this firing across Tripura border was taking place day after day, it was being alleged by Bangladesh authorities, according to the Press, that certain land, the charland which is in the middle of the river on which the Indian farmers were cultivating, they were cultivating that

land for quite a long time, that that land did not belong to India and that it rightfully belonged to Bangladesh.[82]

Another opinion goes so far as to declare that the disputed charland had always been part of the Indian mainland, being simply an extension of the Muhuri River bank:

> According to a BSF spokesman, the Indian side produced a map showing that about 4–5 acres[83] of cultivable land near Belonia on the bank of the Muhuri river were within the Indian territory and the Indian cultivators were cultivating the land from Tripura maharaja's time in 1952. The Bangladesh authorities, however, made a counter claim that it was their land.[84]

The *New York Times* appears to have accepted the Indian view, bypassing the points of contention raised by Bangladesh:

> Bangladesh has disputed an Indian claim to 44 acres of rice paddies on the banks of the Muhuri River, outside Belonia, 80 miles south of Agartala. The land has been customarily cultivated by Indian farmers, but this year Bangladesh objected to the harvesting.[85]

While an understanding of the issue may be impeded by conflicting sources and opinions, some broad conclusions may be drawn. By claiming ownership of the Muhuri Char and taking a strong stand against India, Zia was able to create a popular rallying point and enhance his domestic standing. Bangladeshi fears of Indian dominance were pervasive and easily provoked, providing a permanent source from which to extract political profit when appropriate. The strength of the Bangladesh government's claim to ownership, which appeared to contradict its own insistence that the status quo should be maintained until an official boundary could be agreed upon, also implied that there were genuine, deep-seated fears about India's intention to flout the 1974 Border Agreement and delay indefinitely the demarcation of disputed territory. Perhaps by insisting on more than could be expected, the Bangladesh government aimed at obtaining a reasonably fair settlement. A source of additional anxiety was, and is, the intrinsic problem of unpredictable shifts in the Indo–Bangladesh border, it being located in a deltaic region subject to heavy siltation and erosion arising from regular flooding and cyclones.

In contrast to these fears was the central Indian government's casual and protracted approach to the issue, while at the same time carefully (and literally) not giving ground – as exemplified in the following excerpt:

> The Government of India perceives the recent firing across the Tripura–Bangladesh border as a 'purely local issue' which can be solved through

discussions at the appropriate level. Thus, summing up the situation, the spokesman of the External Affairs Ministry today said that instructions had already been issued to the districts authorities and the BSF in Tripura to take up the matter with their counterparts.[86]

The *New York Times* again appeared to take the Indian view, emphasising the minor nature of the dispute and quoting the view of New Delhi officials who had dismissed the firing incidents as inconsequential.[87] Nevertheless, an additional comment contained in the article implied that matters were perhaps not as trivial as the Indian government portrayed:

> The Tripura Government has ordered the raising of the protective embankment along Belonia and has charged that the Government of Bangladesh was 'deliberately' trying to whip a minor dispute into an international incident.[88]

While India could afford to be complacent about Bangladesh's claims to a small portion of land which India already occupied, the Bangladesh government could not afford to ignore the issue or any provocations deemed to have been initiated by India. Zia's hold on power depended, to some extent, on cultivating popular appeal and, where possible, undermining the popularity of his rivals, particularly the Awami League. The issues of territorial integrity and Indian dominance and interference were perhaps the most emotive and receptive to manipulation in a newly independent South Asian state. Domestic compulsions of Bangladeshi politics were influential in moulding Indo–Bangladesh relations. Nevertheless, events occurring external to Bangladesh clearly played an important role. In March 1979, the Janata government had not only acknowledged, but attempted to accommodate Bangladeshi concerns over the Muhuri Char.[89] By November 1979, within a few months of the removal of Desai's government from office, those accommodations had shown little indication of being implemented and both sides had resorted to arms, in lieu of negotiation.

To an even greater degree, the dispute concerning which state had the right of sovereignty over an emergent island of silt in the Bay of Bengal provided a source of friction between Mrs Gandhi's re-elected government and that of Ziaur Rahman. Examination of the New Moore Island issue shows that the conduct of the dispute resembled those of Tin Bigha and Muhuri Char, but the stakes and tension were greater, particularly for Bangladesh and Zia's government. The ramifications for Indo–Bangladesh relations were therefore correspondingly greater.

Providing an accurate description of events surrounding the New Moore Island dispute is no less problematic than the border issues discussed above, given the excessive bias which permeates most of the contemporary and secondary sources. As with the Muhuri Char issue, simply to ascertain the geographical boundaries of the island under dispute is far from straightforward, the island being formed from eroded silt and gradually increasing in size.[90] A useful explanation has been provided by M. Habibur Rahman who views the New Moore island issue in terms of the wider problem of achieving a mutually satisfactory delimitation of the maritime boundaries for the two states.[91] The island, being formed in the estuary of the Haribhanga River on the border between India and Bangladesh, and probably having been created after the cyclone and tidal bore of 1970,[92] became the focus of a dispute which epitomised the difficulties which could be encountered in border delineation between the two states (see map 6).

The island's emergence was demonstrative of Bangladesh's unstable and erodable deltaic coastline. Having come into existence precisely on the Indo–Bangladesh border, the island's location posed problems not only for the border's delineation, but more significantly, for the demarcation of the surrounding sea bed and its resources. If New Moore island was taken to be the outermost tip of the Indian coast, then according to India's interpretation of

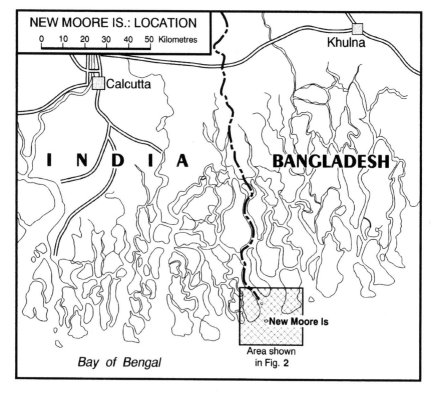

Map 6   Location of New Moore Island
Source: Based on Gulati (1988), p. 163.

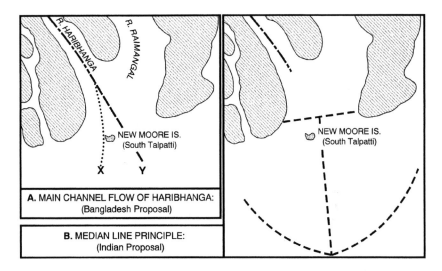

Figure 2   Bangladeshi and Indian proposals in the Haribhanga River dispute
Source: Based on Gulati (1988), p. 169

maritime boundary laws, the country stood to gain possession of a large area of sea bed which, hitherto, would have belonged to Bangladesh.[93] Rumours concerning the island's potential to form a land area of possibly 50 000 square kilometres[94] also played a part in amplifying what was considered to be at stake, consequently increasing the tension associated with the dispute.

Each of the two states claimed ownership of the island on a variety of legal and technical bases, and each presented the 'evidence' to its advantage. From Bangladesh's perspective, ownership depended upon which side of the island the midstream of the Haribhanga River flowed. If, as Bangladesh declared the satellite images revealed, the midstream flowed to the west of the island, then Bangladesh was the rightful owner.[95] The Indian government also used satellite images to prove its own right to claim the Island, emphasising instead the fact that the island lay closer to the Indian mainland than that of Bangladesh[96] (see Figure 2).

Further 'evidence' was produced by the Indian government, based on the results of the Indian survey of New Moore, conducted by the *INS Sandhayak:*

> The main sea channel dividing the Bay waters between India and Bangladesh was found clearly to be east of the New Moore Island ... Depth sounding of the main channel showed depths of over 20 metres and it was found to be easily navigable by ships. On the western and eastern sides of the main channel, depths decrease very rapidly over shallow banks lying on either side of it. This proved that the channel lay on the

eastern side of the New Moore Island and not on the western side as Bangladesh seemed to suggest.[97]

Obviously both governments could find suitable evidence to support their respective claims to New Moore Island. Of greater significance in attempting to shed light on the issue and the course of Indo–Bangladesh relations, was the way in which both states came to reinforce those claims with provocative and aggressive tactics, once Mrs Gandhi returned to power in January 1980. Under the Janata regime, the Bangladesh government had little cause to escalate the New Moore issue, owing to Morarji Desai's congenial, albeit vague, reassurances.[98] Furthermore, the Bangladesh government interpreted Desai's overtures regarding New Moore Island to include a pledge that a joint survey by a team of Indian and Bangladeshi experts would determine the island's ownership. Pressuring the Indian government to fulfil this 'pledge' became a recurring theme in the Bangladesh government's rhetoric over New Moore Island once the Desai government had been removed from office.[99] In early March 1980, less than two months after being installed, Mrs Gandhi's government reportedly instructed the West Bengal government to take possession of the island by formally hoisting the Indian flag, and renaming the island as Purbasha (Hopes of the East).[100] The decision to annex the island was made in defiance of Bangladesh's insistence that the island's sovereignty was still under question, a provocative move causing considerable alarm and anger in Bangladesh and prompting a large anti-Indian demonstration in Dhaka on 22 May 1980.[101]

Reassurances from India's external affairs minister, Mr P.V. Narasimha Rao, mollified Bangladeshi fears to some degree, during his three-day visit to Dhaka in August 1980. In a joint statement issued by Narasimha Rao and the Bangladesh foreign minister, Professor Shamsul Huq, it was agreed that India and Bangladesh 'would continue their efforts to maintain a climate of mutual trust and understanding and further consolidate and strengthen the friendly relations' between them.[102] The joint statement also commented that further discussions concerning 'Purbasha' island would be held after 'studying the additional information exchanged between the two governments on the issue'.[103] The Indian government's 'cooperative and friendly' stance on New Moore Island was noted in the Bangladeshi press,[104] and Indian gestures of appeasement – such as hinting that accepting Bangladesh's proposal for a joint survey for settling ownership of the island would 'not be ruled out' – were received favourably in Bangladesh.[105] Four months later, as agreed in the August talks, further boundary delimitation discussions were held, the seventh round since the 1974 Border Agreement was made. Again, these latest talks were regarded favourably in the Bangladesh press, being described as 'useful and constructive' and as being held in an atmosphere of 'cordiality and understanding'.[106] In what amounted to little more than a repeat of the August talks, it was agreed that ownership of New Moore Island would be determined 'following further talks'.[107]

Looking beyond the rhetoric expounded throughout the boundary discussions of August and December 1980, it would appear that these talks represented little more than an exercise in skilful procrastination on India's part. The larger state had already taken official possession of the island in March. Instead of addressing this action, those border discussions perpetuated a myth that the island's sovereignty was still undecided. Having already established a firm foothold on the island, the Indian government could afford to appear agreeable and accommodating during the subsequent talks, deriving such benefits as the placation of Bangladeshi fears and indignation and the allaying of potential international criticism.

The ineffectiveness of the 1980 talks on New Moore Island becomes obvious when considering the subsequent sabre-rattling over the issue in 1981. The hollowness of earlier reassurances given by the Indian government, such as the possibility of undertaking a joint survey of the island, or simply that the island's sovereignty was yet to be decided, was revealed in April 1981. On 2 April in the Lok Sabha, the Indian external affairs minister, Mr Narasimha Rao, revived the strong stand which India had taken on the issue in March 1980, again claiming India's unilateral title to the island.[108] This statement aroused protest and indignation in Bangladesh,[109] prompting the Bangladesh government to initiate a show of naval presence in the island's vicinity. The tension between the two states escalated as each state took retaliatory steps against perceived manoeuvres and naval threats deemed to be instigated by the other.

From India's perspective, three fully armed Bangladeshi gunboats had trespassed into Indian waters and threatened an Indian survey ship which was gathering information about New Moore Island.[110] According to the Bangladeshi press, India's accusations were 'totally unfounded and were used as a cover for her own unwarranted unilateral and illegal action', the landing of Indian troops on the island in May.[111] From the Bangladesh government's point of view, India had sent its survey ship, the *Sandhayak* into the area without any advance notification to Bangladesh and had taken the provocative step of using the ship to land naval personnel on the island to reinforce India's claim of ownership. The Bangladesh government condemned the latter action particularly, describing it as 'an aggression of Bangladesh territory and an attack on the sovereignty of Bangladesh'.[112] India's response was to strengthen its own naval presence near the island, at the same time playing down the issue, accusing Bangladesh of deliberately creating tension between the two states for political reasons:

Official sources here [India] also maintain that the sequence of developments since May 12 and the timing of giving them sensational publicity make it clear that the Bangladesh authorities deliberately intended to create an artificial crisis for internal political reasons though they were fully aware of the facts.[113]

The 'gunboat diplomacy' of the dispute roused an unprecedented degree of tension between the two states, pointing to Bangladesh's vulnerability to India's demands and superior military strength. The contrast was sufficient to evoke some sympathy for Bangladesh's position, even from a section of the Indian press:

[T]his confrontationist gesture towards neighbours is very much in Mrs. Gandhi's style, but is likely to prove counterproductive for several reasons. India can expect to receive little sympathy in the world for tangling with a small neighbour, and the Indian version of Bangladesh launching an attack on a small disputed island is simply not credible... [S]urely there are better methods of resolving a dispute with a small neighbour over a tiny island than through the Indian version of gunboat diplomacy.[114]

Regardless of whether or not the action was acceptable, or whether one of the two states could be held more responsible for escalating the tension, the reality was that both India and Bangladesh resorted to comparatively strong measures in the conduct of the dispute, only stopping short of direct armed conflict. The gravity of the issue, as perceived by Bangladesh, can be gauged by the increasing degree of political and popular attention which was paid to the dispute as it deteriorated into a military confrontation. Whatever motivations may have been behind Zia's decision to involve naval forces in the issue, the way in which the dispute developed caused considerable concern in Bangladesh, heightening fears of Indian dominance and providing a great deal of scope for the manipulation of those fears.[115]

The depth of concern in Bangladesh over the issue was also reflected in the drafting, by the Bangladesh Ministry of Foreign Affairs, of a White Paper on the history of the dispute,[116] the submission to be placed before the Bangladesh parliament for appraisal. In response to the White Paper, the parliament passed unanimously a resolution on 28 May which called upon the government of India to remove forthwith from New Moore Island 'all personnel, structures and materials including its flag and the remaining armed Indian naval landing craft and to desist from any use of force, threat of force or provocative acts of any form or kind'.[117] In support of the resolution, the Bangladesh foreign minister, Shamsul Huq, warned that 'if India refused to honour her agreements and remove her armed crafts, personnel, structures, materials and flag from South Talpatty Bangladesh would decide on adopting "appropriate measures as warranted by the situation"'.[118]

In the midst of the gathering tension associated with the dispute, president Ziaur Rahman was assassinated, as a result of domestic political causes.[119]

Not only was the New Moore Island issue overshadowed in Bangladesh as a result, but Zia's replacement with an (albeit temporary) civilian regime led to a redefining of Indo–Bangladesh relations: the traditional antagonism between Zia's military government and Mrs Gandhi's Congress-I government no longer applied. Predictably, therefore, the animosity, threats and tough rhetoric concerning the New Moore Island dispute lost their intensity, and, apart from some ineffective calls for international sympathy,[120] there was little indication that the subsequent Bangladesh government attempted to challenge India's occupation of the island with the same fervour.[121] After the confrontation of May 1981, New Moore Island, like Farakka and other border issues, became a drawn-out point of contention, with little prospect of achieving a resolution acceptable to both sides.[122]

The outcome of any of the tussles for territorial ownership between India and Bangladesh was unlikely to have been the result of compromise. The final lesson for Bangladesh was that neither bilateral negotiation nor a military stance would induce a determined Indian government to accommodate the countervailing wishes of a neighbouring state. With regard to New Moore, considerable maritime territory and access to potentially significant oil and natural gas resources were at stake in both governments' bids to claim the island. The yearning to enjoy the benefits of becoming an oil-producing country was particularly acute following the world oil boom of 1974, resulting in scrambling for sea-bed territory in the Indian Ocean region.[123] With India showing such a determined interest in claiming the island and surrounding territory, Zia was provided with an ideal opportunity for rousing fear and resentment against India, thereby uniting and consolidating his political support.

Being the considerably larger, longer-established and militarily more powerful state, India had comparatively much less to lose in any of the border issues, even with the prospect of an increase in oil reserves. Nevertheless, India's foreign policy was also subject to the wishes and demands of Mrs Gandhi's strong, personalised form of government, one which had inherited a political mandate to distrust military regimes and resist territorial encroachments. These bogeys had been reinforced by unrelenting hostility between India and Pakistan over Kashmir. The New Moore Island issue, in particular, delivered an unambiguous, sharp message to the inhabitants of Bangladesh: Mrs Gandhi and the Congress-I government would assume control of territory deemed to be Indian, no matter how small the area at stake, and no matter how much India's actions might damage relations with the other state or states involved.

From the perspective of regional influences, the course of Indo–Bangladesh relations during Ziaur Rahman's regime shows clearly that pressures emanating from outside Bangladesh were of great significance. Bangladesh's relations with India were not 'more or less governed by the domestic compulsions of Bangladesh'.[124] There was little reason or precedent set for

Mrs Gandhi's government to react to Zia's military regime in a way that differed much from the antagonism which typically had been shown towards Pakistan and its militarily-dominated governments. The Bangladesh government itself could not pose any real military threat to the Indian government, but a regime on close terms with Pakistan and China might have been able to create considerable havoc in India's politically sensitive and volatile northeast. Hence Mrs Gandhi's government tended to resort to displays of force and aggression against Bangladesh, when negotiation could no longer allow for procrastination, in the habitual manner of dealing with Pakistan. In refusing to cooperate with Zia in his efforts to bring the pro-Mujib guerrillas to heel, Mrs Gandhi had made it clear that she disapproved of Bangladesh's new military regime and would use the most appropriate indirect means to restore a pro-Indian, Mujibist-style of government to Bangladesh.

The influence of Zia's domestic political concerns cannot be ignored as an integral part of the conduct of Indo–Bangladesh relations. As will be shown, those concerns provided an important additional stimulus to the direction of relations between Bangladesh and India.[125] If Zia had not found it necessary to subdue pro-Indian forces and cultivate support from sources antagonistic towards India, then perhaps Mrs Gandhi might have used a softer approach. Nevertheless, as has been shown above, the role of the Indian government in moulding Indo–Bangladesh relations was greater than has been generally acknowledged.

Shifts in the Indian government's broad foreign policy concerns were reflected in the changes which occurred in the character of Indo–Bangladesh relations during Zia's regime. The Indian government's ability to modify the relationship between the two states is brought into sharp relief when contrasting Mrs Gandhi's direction of India's foreign policy with that of Desai and the Janata government. The Janata regime's foreign policy, which allowed room to accommodate some of the Bangladeshi fears over the Farakka Barrage and the various border issues, had genuine, and not all short-lived, results in improving the diplomatic relations between India and Bangladesh. An Indian government which was sufficiently inclined and strong enough to do so, could overcome to a considerable extent, the traditional obstacles to good relations between the two states, whatever form of government existed in Bangladesh. At the same time, the Indian government showed no hesitation in souring foreign relations in the interests of pursuing its political objectives. Given the way in which this message was driven home during Zia's regime, it was not surprising that his attempts to consolidate power in Bangladesh involved cultivating the support of countries and international organisations which might have been influential enough to modify India's foreign policy concerns and priorities.

3
1982–4: A New Beginning or the Darkest Hour?

This chapter concentrates on a brief period in the history of Indo–Bangladesh relations, but it is a period which reveals more than has been acknowledged regarding the conduct and character of those relations. Analyses of relations between Bangladesh and India during the regime of Ziaur Rahman rarely vary from the common theme that the difficulties which have dogged relations between the two states have usually been generated wittingly, or unwittingly, by Bangladesh. This chapter examines the period from 1982 to 1984, providing evidence to show that Indo–Bangladesh relations underwent both subtle and obvious changes due to pressures emanating not just from within Bangladesh but from the interaction between a variety of internal and external forces.

Bangladesh's relations with India during the regime of Hussain Muhammad Ershad were no less intricate or sensitive than those existing while Zia was in power. This view does not accord with most broad, generally mild appraisals of Indo–Bangladesh relations during Ershad's regime. It becomes evident, in studying the period from 1982 to 1984, that the relationship between Bangladesh and India was noteworthy for its extremes. At the time, the international media considered that Ershad's coup in March 1982 had ushered in a 'new beginning' for Indo–Bangladesh relations, one which indicated that prospects for warmer relations were substantial. On closer inspection, relations between 1982 and 1984 indicate that, despite an auspicious beginning, the three-year period as a whole represented perhaps the lowest ebb in Indo–Bangladesh relations experienced to date.

The first years of Ershad's regime, until Indira Gandhi's assassination on 31 October 1984, have also been treated as a distinct period in this chapter because Mrs Gandhi played a highly influential, personal role in directing India's government and foreign relations. Interpretations of Mrs Gandhi's foreign policy behaviour have been numerous and contradictory, ranging from those which have emphasised her selfless determination to ensure regional harmony,[1] to those which stress that her foreign policy simply reflected her dictatorial desire to maintain personal power.[2] According to South Asia analyst, Sashi Tharoor, Mrs Gandhi transformed both domestic and foreign affairs to 'ensure her personal survival and dominance', preferring to 'rule rather than reinstitutionalize, to control rather than reorient, to subvert rather than balance'.[3] In a similar vein, analyst James Manor has claimed that Mrs Gandhi 'developed a deep personal need to rule' and if impeded would take 'audacious, even draconian action'.[4] Whichever of the above opinions may be closest to the truth, Mrs Gandhi adopted a highly prominent and sustained presence in fashioning India's foreign policy for almost two decades. This warrants a specific study of her dealings with Bangladesh during the Ershad regime.

Given the deterioration in Indo–Bangladesh relations which accompanied Ziaur Rahman's military coup in 1975, the establishment of a second military order in Bangladesh in March 1982 might also be expected to have had an immediate and detrimental impact on those relations. Such an expectation would not be unreasonable if subscribing to the opinion that relations between the two states have been determined largely by the effects of political changes and instability occurring within Bangladesh; as exemplified by the following comment which places a clear emphasis on Bangladesh's primary role in directing the course of the relationship:

> [I]n the aftermath of the overthrow of Sheikh Mujib . . . internal changes in . . . Bangladesh polity were reflected dramatically in its external relations as well. There was a sudden warming up of Bangladesh's relations with the United States, China and the Islamic world, in particular Saudi Arabia and to a lesser extent with Pakistan. Relations with India correspondingly became somewhat patchy. In the past five years [1982–6] . . . Indo–Bangladesh relations have remained on an even keel. Bangladesh's response to India's efforts to nurture political, economic and cultural co-operation, while not negative, has been somewhat selective.[5]

The same sources which emphasise the role of Bangladesh's domestic politics in determining the status of the relationship have also tended to conclude that Ershad's military coup and Islamic-style regime heralded an overall upswing in the cordiality of relations. This view contradicts their assessment of Ziaur Rahman's own military/Islamic orientation, considered largely responsible for the cooling of Indo–Bangladesh relations.[6] The reasons given for the deemed improvement under Ershad are vague, although they imply that Ershad was judged as somewhat less inclined towards 'India-baiting' than Zia had been.[7]

Ershad's regime spanned a large portion of Bangladesh's history, also coinciding with an eventful and turbulent period of Indian domestic politics. His style of government did not replicate that of his predecessor, Ziaur Rahman, although there were some similarities. As a result, a study of Ershad's period of governance provides ample evidence to counter limited or stereotypical interpretations of Indo–Bangladesh relations, explanations which have tended to stress the adverse, overriding influence of Bangladeshi domestic strife; Bangladesh's military elite; and/or Bangladesh's shift to a non-secular form of government.[8] The unprecedented foreign policy shifts occurring under Ziaur Rahman's high-profile, charismatic style of leadership may have played an undue role in colouring broad assessments of Bangladesh's relations with India. Ershad, on the other hand, has been described as a bland personality, 'an administrator perhaps more than a combat officer',[9] qualities which nevertheless act to provide a balancing, tempering ingredient in drawing conclusions about South Asia's personality-dominated interstate relations.

Comparing the course of Indo–Bangladesh relations during the regimes of both Ershad and Ziaur Rahman provides an opportunity to gain a clearer understanding of the more influential determinants of those relations. Of particular relevance were the political conditions prevailing, not just domestically, but also regionally, at the time both leaders undertook their respective coups.

When Zia came to power in November 1975, the post-Mujib souring of relations which had begun between Bangladesh and India was given substantial momentum due to the combination of particular circumstances: the steps which Ziaur Rahman deemed necessary to strengthen his newly won hold on power, and the way in which Mrs Gandhi and the Congress government responded to Zia's establishment of a military regime in Bangladesh. The confrontational stance which Zia took towards the Indian government was vigorously reciprocated as Mrs Gandhi reacted to his regime in a cool, sharp manner appropriate to that which was used habitually in dealing with the Pakistan government.[10]

Several noteworthy differences emerge when comparing the circumstances surrounding the establishment of Zia's regime[11] with those concerning General Ershad's own successful bid for leadership. These differences were reflected in the way in which India reacted towards Ershad's coup. Indian reactions to Ershad's coup contrasted noticeably with those exhibited during Zia's assumption of power. The calm, even resigned, Indian reactions to Ershad's coup prompted general optimism that relations between India and Bangladesh would improve. In appraising Ershad's coup, a *Times of India* editorial adopted the following posture: 'It had to take place and it has taken place.'[12] Such a nonchalant reaction implied that broader pressures were playing a more important part in modifying India's attitude towards Bangladesh, as opposed to trepidation over Ershad's specific ambitions and strategies. The latter obviously had not aroused much concern because the same editorial described Ershad as an 'unknown and enigmatic figure'. Ershad was portrayed therefore as simply the instigator of a coup which more or less 'had to happen'; an image which contrasted markedly with that produced in India by Ziaur Rahman's bid for power. Indira Gandhi's reaction to

Ershad's coup was also mild, her comment being: 'India naturally preferred a democratically elected government, . . . [b]ut what has happened inside a country's borders was its own concern.'[13]

Of greater significance for Indo–Bangladesh relations at the time was the fact that Mrs Gandhi's response did not include raising the spectre of 'foreign' or Pakistani intervention. For example, in replying to a question concerning possible external involvement in Ershad's coup, Mrs Gandhi replied that the Indian government 'did not have any knowledge'.[14] India's External Affairs Minister, Mr Narasimha Rao also seemed little concerned by the military take-over in Bangladesh, concurring that it was an internal matter and that India 'attached fundamental importance to peace, harmony and cooperation with all its neighbours and stability in the subcontinent'.[15] Rao added: 'It is our hope that the continuing friendship and cooperation between India and Bangladesh will be maintained.'[16] Ershad's 'swift, smooth and bloodless' coup[17] fortuitously coincided with a period of tentative rapprochement between India and Pakistan, where both states had been taking hesitant steps towards signing a no-war pact. On the same day as Ershad's coup, Narasimha Rao commented that some encouraging signs were emerging with regard to Pakistan, indicating that state's desire to improve its relations with India and representing a 'rare opportunity' for India to come closer to Pakistan: a 'chance of peace' not to be missed.[18] It was not surprising that Ershad's rule was accepted with little fuss or criticism by India since India and Pakistan were also peddling a softer line towards each other.

This correlation again emphasises the influential nature of the historical ties between the three states, bonds which nevertheless were not marked by tolerance and equality. India's reactions to Ershad's coup underlined the reality of Bangladesh's peripheral status in India's foreign policy concerns and strategies, with Pakistan normally being the focus of far greater Indian attention.

As shown above, and in Chapter 5, the regional political circumstances which prevailed at the establishment of Zia's and Ershad's regimes were of considerable contrast. Differences in regional pressures and expectations coinciding with Zia's and Ershad's political ascendancy were equally compelling in shaping Bangladesh's relations with India. The Indian government had achieved a position of unquestionable regional dominance, partly due to its involvement in Bangladesh's independence war. Mujib's assassination and its aftermath had an undermining impact on that pre-eminence, delivering a sharp blow to euphoric notions of Indian regional patronage and, especially galling, providing psychological benefits to Pakistan. Because Zia emerged at a time when Bangladesh's relations with India were already politically charged, he presented a clear target for the venting of Indian anger and indignation.

Ershad, by contrast, came to power when Indo–Bangladesh relations had regained at least some degree of stability. Zia's regime had already established that a military take-over in Bangladesh did not necessarily equate with pure opportunism and oppression of the populace,[19] characteristics which could create additional problems for neighbouring India. Ershad's strategic, controlled coup[20] and his intended style of government augured that the uneasy but stabilised relations between the two states during Zia's regime would not be modified significantly or deteriorate further: a position which accorded with India's long-term regional strategy of maintaining where possible a status quo with its neighbours.

Adjustments occurring in India's regional and extra-regional relations were also working in Ershad's favour. Although restored to power in 1980, Mrs Gandhi and the Congress-I had been chastened to some extent by their 1977 election defeat, resulting in a less magisterial approach towards the other South Asian states. The Soviet Union's incursion into Afghanistan in 1979 had also brought new and wide-reaching pressures to bear on Indian foreign policy, modifying and improving, for a time, some of India's most preoccupying relationships: those with Pakistan, China and the United States. Any reconciliation between India and Pakistan inevitably had repercussions for Bangladesh. Whether by accident or design, Ershad's coup took place at a time of comparative regional rapprochement, a phase which eased the relationship between the Indian government and Bangladesh's new military order.

Once established in power in Bangladesh, Ershad had a reasonably free hand, initially at least, to direct Bangladesh's domestic politics and foreign relations. Opposition parties were disunified and muzzled, intra-military feuding was in abeyance, and the Indian government appeared to accept his occupancy of Bangladesh's leadership with equanimity. Ershad's relatively stable position on gaining power, compared with the more unpredictable one faced by Ziaur Rahman, had favourable repercussions for the way in which Ershad and the Indian government began their negotiations on some of the more prominent issues, long-standing and emerging, between their respective states. A stable and cordial relationship between Ershad and the Indian government seemed assured.

Nevertheless, as will be shown below, such promising pre-conditions for amicable relations were to be offset by more influential and wide-reaching regional pressures. Bangladesh's relationship with India during Ershad's regime was conducted under the shadow of India's increasing preoccupation with domestic and regional political traumas. Apart from the issue of mounting discontent amongst the Assamese in India's north-east, Bangladesh played only a peripheral role in the burgeoning crises facing the Indian government. Sinhalese–Tamil violence in Sri Lanka; Sikh agitation in the Punjab; Hindu–Muslim communalism; the Bhopal disaster; and Indira Gandhi's assassination in October 1984 all placed the Indian government under enormous pressure. The severity of India's domestic tension, particularly during 1983 and 1984, prompted South Asia analyst, Robert Hardgrave, to declare: 'Never in the thirty-seven years since Independence and the trauma of partition has India faced more difficult times than in 1984.'[21]

The political tumult occurring in India inevitably impinged on the course of Indo–Bangladesh relations during Ershad's regime, yet the link has tended to be down-played, particularly by pro-Indian analysts. The emphasis, as already pointed out, has too often been placed on Bangladesh's renowned domestic instability as determining the character of that state's relationship with India. Several examples of this type of interpretation have already been provided, but the following comment by Partha Ghosh encapsulates the sentiment which appears to underlie many of the stereotypical views of Indo–Bangladesh relations:

> This basic reality of Bangladesh politics, that except for the secularists, all [other political] forces ... are, for structural as well as historical reasons, hostile to India, needs to be borne in mind while discussing the nature of [the] Indo-Bangla relationship.[22]

Ghosh's conclusion implies that India is endowed with a fundamental benignity which has been subject to excessive and unjustified hostility from Bangladesh. Yet the evidence has pointed to a more intricate relationship, whereby neither one state nor the other can be held wholly responsible for directing its course. The nature of that relationship has been shaped more by the interplay of attitudes and beliefs which have evolved in both India and Bangladesh, a reciprocal association which this study illustrates.

1982 had the semblance of a 'honeymoon year' for Bangladesh's relations with India. Neither Ershad nor Mrs Gandhi had as yet become too enmeshed in the preoccupying demands of domestic political unrest of subsequent years. While Ershad was expressing assurances that his government's foreign policy would place special emphasis on fostering good relations with the neighbouring countries,[23] Mrs Gandhi had little reason to be concerned about any looming changes to the Indo–Bangladesh relationship. The existence of a cordial regime in Bangladesh, combined with an unconcerned Indian Government appeared to offer the best hope for smooth relations between the two states. Ershad's mild but amicable overtures to India merged well with Indira's conservative foreign policy approach which, in the opinion of one analyst, had been lacking initiative since her return to office in 1980.[24] According to the more caustic viewpoint of S. Tharoor, Mrs Gandhi's foreign policy had always lacked creativity due to her 'obsessive concern with independence'.[25] In over-zealously guarding Indian independence, Tharoor has considered that Mrs Gandhi limited India's foreign policy options, restricting the avenue of diplomacy and, ironically, distancing India still further from the Nehru ideal of non-alignment.[26] The prime minister's efforts to preserve India from external interference would have been more fruitful, according to Tharoor, if they had been spent instead on forging political, economic and strategic linkages in a world in which inter-dependence was the maxim.[27] Mrs Gandhi's personally conducted foreign policy, emphasising the traditional tendency to maintain the status quo, did little to promote regional harmony, yet fluctuations in cordiality did occur. The comparative warmth between India and Bangladesh during 1982 represents one example, but the reason for the improvement lies partly in the same weaknesses in India's foreign policy pointed out above. The following comment by Tharoor provides one explanation why the fluctuations have occurred, although his criticisms could also apply more broadly to describe typical aspects of post-Partition foreign policy formulation in the South Asian region:

> While some of the Nehruvian expectations of the international system may have been modified in the face of the new realities, ... Mrs Gandhi's 'pragmatism' was only of the short-sighted, reactive variety, a 'realism' that informed tactics and ignored strategy. She had, indeed, no foreign policy, only an inchoate collection of foreign policy decisions, emerging from a world-view that was an uneasy blend of predilection and principle.[28]

In keeping with Tharoor's comment, India's relations with Bangladesh have tended to be reactive and lacking in long-term strategy. Exceptions can be found, where both states appeared to be working towards a more stable and mutually beneficial relationship, but they become less convincing when examined further. The circumstances associated with Ershad's two-day visit to New Delhi in October 1982 for talks with Indira Gandhi represented an appropriate example. The October talks had eventuated after six months of promising shuttle diplomacy, begun in May with the successful goodwill visit to Dhaka by Indian External Affairs Minister, Mr Narasimha Rao.[29] The ensuing October summit was widely regarded at the time as a successful, mutually agreeable one in which both states had compromised a little to accommodate the other's wishes. The success of the talks suggested that a new phase in harmonious relations had begun for the two states. The Saudi Arabian news media was sufficiently impressed by the outcome of the talks to describe it as an historic achievement which spoke of the 'statesmenship of the two leaders', and which represented a 'good augury' for the subcontinent since it improved the quality of relations between India and Bangladesh.[30] The People's Republic of China also chimed in with a favourable view of the talks, expressing approval of the moves by both India and Bangladesh towards a 'permanent solution of the unresolved problems between them'.[31] The Indian press was particularly enthusiastic, lauding the summit as the first serious attempt to improve Indo–Bangladesh relations in eight years, the decline being portrayed as the consequence of political changes which had taken place in Bangladesh following the assassination of Sheikh Mujib.[32]

The October talks were especially important to Bangladesh because they tackled what most Bangladeshis considered to be the more worrisome bones of contention between the two states, issues in which the larger state consistently held the 'higher ground': the Farakka Barrage, the Tin Bigha Corridor, New Moore Island, the maritime boundary demarcation and the trade imbalance between the two states. Most of these issues had been slipping into a stalemated torpor, a condition which suited the Indian government's advantaged position in all those issues. The vulnerability of Bangladesh's position was especially significant at the time the talks took place because of the imminent expiry of the 1977 Farakka Agreement, due for reappraisal within a month, on 4 November. Anxiety on the part of Bangladesh was perhaps partly responsible for an over-enthusiastic response to the outcome of the talks, which when given closer inspection achieved less than it seemed. With the Agreement due to expire, however, just a continuation of the status quo would have been greeted with relief in Bangladesh.[33]

On the whole, the summit talks were cordial and, to some extent, fruitful, with the most obvious breakthrough being made regarding the Tin Bigha Corridor, the narrow strip of land linking two Bangladeshi enclaves with the mainsoil of Bangladesh. Under an official agreement signed at the talks, Bangladesh was provided with a 'lease in perpetuity' which granted 'undisturbed possession and use of' the Tin Bigha Corridor.[34] The Indian government still owned the Corridor, but the 10 000 inhabitants of the Dahagram and Angarpota enclaves were no longer obstructed in their access to the rest of Bangladesh. The Indian government had, according to an Indian editorial, 'done the right thing by its smaller neighbour'.[35] The Tin Bigha Corridor dispute did not, as it turned out, end there,[36] but the signing of the lease by India was a firm gesture of political goodwill.

Other, genuinely conciliatory, agreements were signed at the summit. The establishment of a Joint Economic Commission was agreed upon to address trade imbalance problems, as well as to improve scientific and technical cooperation 'on the basis of equality and mutual benefit'.[37] Less tangible results were forthcoming with regard to some of the more controversial issues, such as the demarcation of the maritime boundaries and the ownership of New Moore Island, but the Indian government had indicated that these matters were still open to negotiation and future talks were arranged.[38]

In resolving the issue of greatest concern to Bangladesh – the future of the Farakka Agreement – the talks were deemed by both states to have been successful, although the recommendations raised more problems than existed already. Ershad was certainly aware that if he could be seen as engineering a breakthrough in such a contentious dispute as the Farakka Barrage it would provide an exceptional boost in legitimising his assumption of Bangladesh's leadership. Perhaps this motive explains why he claimed, following his 'historic' visit to India, that Bangladesh and India had, for the first time, agreed to reach a 'permanent solution to the most pressing problem of the sharing

of the Ganges waters at Farakka'.[39] Despite the public expressions of optimism and Ershad's rhetoric, a study of the Memorandum of Understanding
(MOU) which was reached on Farakka at the talks, shows there was little of
substance to indicate that a permanent solution was within reach. According
to the MOU, the 1977 Farakka Agreement was to be terminated, although for
the following two dry seasons, sharing of the Ganges water was to continue
'exactly' as it had been implemented under the 1977 Agreement.[40] Within
that 18-month period, a pre-feasibility study on schemes to augment the
dry-season flow of the Ganges was to have been completed by the Indo–
Bangladesh Joint Rivers Commission (JRC). The summit euphoria obscured
the fact that some changes to the 1977 Agreement were made, alterations
which favoured India, especially during times of exceptionally low flow.[41]

More ominous was the MOU's endorsement that a permanent solution to
the Farakka issue would definitely be provided by augmentation of the
Gangetic flow. Both states had already mooted their preferred methods of
augmentation, Bangladesh opting for storage dams on the Ganges in the
Indo–Nepalese border region and India wishing to construct a canal across
Bangladesh, linking the Brahmaputra River with the Ganges[42] (see map 7).
Even during the cordial Janata years, both Zia's and Desai's regime had

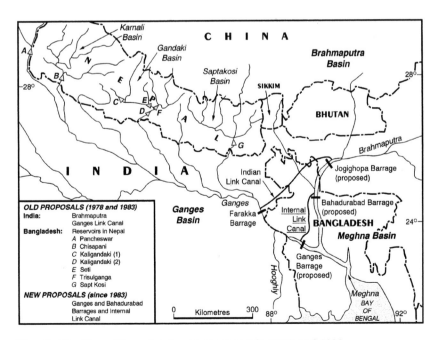

Map 7   The Three Rivers development proposals, 1978 and 1983
Source: Based on Crow *et al.* (1995), p. 187.

expressed their disapproval of the other's preferred option, each considering the alternative proposal to be unrealistic.[43] The strong stand taken by both states on each other's scheme, owing to the obvious pressure of political considerations, prompted the following comment by K. Begum in her rigorous study of the Farakka dispute:

> For an observer what is most striking is that the outright rejection of each other's proposal is not supported by any thorough investigation or study of the subjects. This indicates that the very ideas of the two proposals are unacceptable to the two parties; therefore, there is little scope to study the technical shortcomings or details.[44]

Even without a detailed study, it was not difficult to envisage that the social, economic, political and administrative implications of both proposals would have been substantial. Begum's study of the augmentation schemes has shown clearly that the impact of India's proposed link canal would have the more deleterious impact.[45] The sheer size alone of the so-called 'canal', estimated to be the largest in the world and the equivalent of seven Suez Canals,[46] pointed to likely technical and financial difficulties.[47] The adverse social, environmental and political consequences of the canal for Bangladesh have been pointed out by other analysts who, like Begum, concluded that the adverse effects of the canal would far outweigh the benefits.[48] Begum argued further that India's objection to Bangladesh's proposal of storage dams on the Ganges was not justified because India itself had constructed and planned to construct a number of storage dams, some of them involving Nepal.[49] Begum concluded that Mrs Gandhi's political penchant for bilateralism[50] was the principal reason why India rejected the Bangladesh proposal. Not only was Nepal involved in that proposal as a third party, but as an upper-riparian state to India, Nepal would have been in an ideal position to turn the tables on the Indian government. Nepal could then, if it had chosen, have exploited its advantageous location and exerted pressure on the India government over not only the Farakka issue, but perhaps also to more general political and economic advantage.[51]

Both India and Bangladesh had indicated unequivocally their rejection of the other's preferred option well before the MOU was signed at the summit talks in 1982. Whether either of the two augmentation proposals offered a realistic solution to sharing the Ganges water equitably was not the issue. The decision to pursue the avenue of Ganges augmentation in the expectation that the JRC would reach a compromise solution within 18 months seemed therefore to have been greeted with unjustified approbation and optimism. Predictably, the JRC was not able to fulfil its task of finding a mutually agreeable solution within the allotted time period.[52] It was very unlikely that an issue as vexatious and as politically charged as Farakka was would have been resolved by reworking schemes which had already aroused political hostility and veto. It was also possible that such schemes could have created more problems than they solved.[53] India's uncompromising decision to opt exclusively for a link canal across Bangladesh, a scheme with enormous social, environmental and political consequences for Bangladesh, evoked fears of the colonial tradition[54] and did nothing to dispel deep-seated Bangladeshi assumptions of Indian arrogance and dominance. Despite the debatable progress made by the MOU, which achieved less overall than the 1977 agreement, the summit talks were hailed as an outstanding success, or, as expressed by the Times of India, the summit 'could not have been friendlier or more fruitful'.[55]

In examining why the summit should have stimulated such an enthusiastic reaction, it would appear that the broad security concerns which had evolved in both states played an underlying role. The warmth associated with the 1982 summit and the promising signs for improved Indo–Bangladesh relations at that time has tended to be ascribed to Ershad's conscious decision to revive 'good neighbourliness in regard to India'.[56] While Ershad's attempts to restore warmth to the relationship in 1982 may have played a part, wider regional pressures were of greater influence. Ershad's debut as leader of Bangladesh was accompanied by signs of a more cordial relationship, but the dictates of India's traditional foreign policy concerns had a more substantial role in bringing about an improvement.

Indian foreign policy had been forged largely in response to Partition and the repercussions of the Cold War, producing a sense of weakness and vulnerability to great-power presence in the region. South Asia analyst, S.D. Muni, has concluded that while India's sense of vulnerability to greater global forces was eased by a growing confidence in the 1970s, the long-held fears and suspicions have lingered on in the form of a 'persecution psyche'.[57] Evidence of India's foreign policy having been permeated by an unjustified preoccupation with regional security can be found in the fluctuating course of disputes between India and Bangladesh.

The improvement in Indo–Bangladesh relations in 1982 can be linked clearly to India's traditional interest in the great powers and the security of the whole South Asian region. The more cordial relations between India and Bangladesh were largely a reflection of the simultaneous easing of some of India's most tension-ridden relationships with Pakistan, China and the United States. China had viewed the no-war pact being mooted between India and Pakistan with firm approval, also professing a desire to normalise relations with India.[58] In a similar fashion, Indo–United States relations were entering a new phase of cordiality and cooperation, exemplified by Mrs Gandhi's decision to pay a goodwill visit to Washington in July 1982, the first such visit in over 10 years.[59]

These auspicious developments in India's foreign relations in 1982 were further boosted by comparative domestic stability in India. Ominous signs of deep-seated political unrest[60] had not as yet become especially demanding of attention, allowing the Congress government to pursue the trivial but politically demanding pressures of increasing intra-party factionalism. The traditional insecurities and concerns which were habitually evident in Indian foreign and domestic policy were not prominent because of a more confident, flexible and conciliatory foreign policy stance being pursued.

The easing of tension between India and Bangladesh followed the relationship receiving what could be described as a shower of congeniality and brotherhood in the wake of the Indian government's pursuit of larger foreign policy stakes. This conclusion brings into question the relevance of regime compatibility to interstate relations in South Asia. Ideological affinity between states has often been pointed to as a prerequisite for warmer relations, as exemplified by the following comment by S.D. Muni, who has attempted to resolve the divergent pressures which have shaped Indian regional foreign policy:

> It may not be out of place here to mention that changes in the political structures of the neighbouring countries, if compatible with stated ideological preferences of the Indian state may result in lessening India's dilemma of choosing between security interests and ideological preferences while evolving policy responses to critical developments in the neighbouring countries. In general, the ideological character of the Indian state and its compatibility or otherwise with the characters of polities in its neighbourhood is a vital factor to be taken into account in understanding India's approach towards its neighbours.[61]

While the notion of ideological compatibility can provide one explanation for the establishment of warmer relations between the South Asian states, it is questionable whether that characteristic should be described as a vital factor in determining the conduct of relations between India and Bangladesh. The idea of ideological compatibility carries a connotation of political balance and equality, a position which had still not emerged between India and Bangladesh. There was little to distinguish ideologically the regimes of Ziaur Rahman and Ershad, yet both regimes had differing and fluctuating relationships with the Indian government.

More pragmatic considerations appear to have played a greater role in the relationship, such as political opportunism and the reality of Indian regional supremacy. The degree of warmth present in Indo–Bangladesh relations has tended to correspond with the extent to which the Bangladesh government has fitted in with the Indian government's particular foreign and domestic goals. The amount of free play which leaders of the Bangladesh government have had in moulding relations with India has generally been set according to the tolerances of the Indian government. The warmth of the 1982 summit talks between India and Bangladesh was in keeping with India's wider concerns at the time. Ershad's overtures to the Indian government were awarded gracious acceptance but the warmth was shallow. The outcome of the talks did not indicate that any substantial improvement in relations had occurred. On the contrary, the summit results, especially with regard to the Farakka Barrage, confirmed Bangladesh's subordinate and vulnerable position, one which could evince gratitude in the smaller state for India's decision not to press for an even more advantageous position.

The over-reaction to the summit exemplified the way in which the prevailing degree of political tension or goodwill between the Indian and Bangladesh governments had habitually outweighed more appropriate or logical foreign policy considerations. Fluctuations in tension associated with the Farakka issue, probably the most politically sensitive issue to impinge on the Indo–Bangladesh relationship, have shifted consistently according to the dictates of existing political warmth, a pattern least likely to produce a technologically feasible, mutually beneficial and long-term solution to the issue. As concluded previously,[62] the reaching of any form of mutually satisfactory agreement between India and Bangladesh was a noteworthy achievement not to be underestimated. The generally favourable reaction to the Farakka MOU may have gone beyond what was merited, but the agreement had stabilised the dispute temporarily. Yet if, as it happened, the 1982 summit talks and their outcome were regarded in the press as the zenith of warm relations between the two states, then the future of Bangladesh as an independent state receiving due regard for its sovereign wishes looked bleak indeed. Bangladesh's position in the relationship had remained a vulnerable one and even a high degree of widely acknowledged political goodwill between India and Bangladesh had not produced substantial benefits for Bangladesh.

Any attempt to appease the Indian government, as Ershad undertook in 1982, did not preordain a more favourable or equitable outcome, even if tension was reduced. The political stratagems, whims and fears of Mrs Gandhi and her Congress-I government easily outweighed whatever strategy was pursued by the Bangladesh government. The extent to which Ershad could initiate a significant change in Indo–Bangladesh relations appears therefore to have been limited. A more realistic view of Ershad's overtures towards the Indian government would be that he had embarked on a political gambit which fortuitously happened to accord with, or was prompted by, Mrs Gandhi's concurrent foreign policy designs; a manoeuvre which perhaps was aimed more at acquiring political approbation than to promote the interests of Bangladesh as a whole. Nevertheless, while the long-term benefits of the October summit may have been minimal for Bangladesh, Ershad had made some contribution towards the stability of Indo–Bangladesh relations, demonstrating in the process considerable political acumen. He had adopted a stance which did not exceed limits acceptable to the Indian government, but instead of damaging his public image, he had managed to reinforce his domestic and international popularity.

Tharoor's criticisms of Mrs Gandhi's foreign policy as being an uncoordinated series of reactive, idiosyncratic and uncompromising decisions has some justification when considering the history of the Farakka Barrage dispute. The overriding principle which seems to have governed Mrs Gandhi's perspective of the issue was that the dispute should not step beyond the bilateral level; whatever solution was to be implemented, it should not involve a third state, such as Nepal. India was not only the upper-riparian state to Bangladesh, but also by far the more powerful one, a relationship which meant that Mrs Gandhi could set the terms of the issue, controlling rather than accommodating the smaller state. Even during a time of comparative regional stability, as in 1982, Indian regional pre-eminence was manifested and maintained unequivocally. Concerning Farakka, Bangladesh received no more, perhaps less, by way of a mutually acceptable solution from the Indian government in 1982, despite the espousal by both governments of goodwill towards each other. Mrs Gandhi's regional policy could be described therefore as one which was consistent only in its determination to preserve Indian regional predominance; a policy which ran counter to the qualities of logic, fairness and vision.

Bangladesh has also been criticised for being unreasonably uncooperative towards India in finding an equitable solution to the Farakka dispute. S. Mansingh points to Bangladesh's failure to 'fully substantiate' complaints of environmental damage and to Bangladesh's refusal to carry out joint surveys with India on the environmental impact, both examples being evidence of a lack of vision on the part of Bangladesh.[63] Zia's government, in particular, was accused of protracting the issue for 'selfish motives' and 'political interests'.[64]

Neither the Indian nor Bangladesh governments could be praised for a conciliatory approach to the problem of sharing the Ganges, but if either state had been entitled to be intransigent over Farakka then Bangladesh appears to have had the greater reason to claim that right. The Farakka Barrage was constructed by India for India's benefit. Furthermore, while the advantages associated with harnessing the Ganges went largely to India, they were secured at the expense of Bangladesh which bore the brunt of the adverse side-effects. When the Gangetic flow was found wanting, both states turned to the remedy of augmentation, an avenue which emerged as a political and technological nightmare, ironically presenting the opportunity for India to extend its controlling influence over not only the Ganges, but Bangladesh's other major river, the Brahmaputra, as well.

The superficiality of the perceived improvement in Indo–Bangladesh relations under Ershad's new regime becomes obvious when examining the course of the relationship subsequent to 1982, when Mrs Gandhi's government slipped into a cauldron of domestic and regional crises and Indo–Pakistan relations regained some of their traditional tension. Ershad's government also faced mounting domestic strife. The character of relations between India and Bangladesh following the honeymoon year of 1982, up until Mrs Gandhi's demise, accorded even more closely with Tharoor's assessment of Mrs Gandhi's foreign policy, with little obscuring the fact that the relationship was reactive, ad hoc and lacking in initiative.

Peter Bertocci has stated that 'not all was darkness on the Indo–Bangladesh front' during 1983–4, citing as evidence the renewal of a trade agreement between the two.[65] While noteworthy, the trade agreement represented perhaps the only respite in a particularly uncooperative, indeed grim, period in Bangladesh's relations with India. Relations had also taken a plunge in 1975, after Mujib's death, but the parlous state of Indo–Bangladesh relations during 1983–4 represented an exceptionally inauspicious portent for the future of those relations.

Examination of the condition of relations between the two states during the last 18 months of Mrs Gandhi's regime has been relatively neglected in broad overviews of Ershad's regime, such as those noted above. Looking at Ershad's regime as a whole, relations between India and Bangladesh could be described as relatively stable when compared with Indo–Pakistan and Indo–Sri Lankan relations, for example. Nevertheless, the impression of stability between India and Bangladesh could have been generated partly by the effect of increasing domestic political instability impinging on the governments of both states. Even a very optimistic view of Indo–Bangladesh relations, emphasising their long-term stability, would be unlikely to conclude that Bangladesh had achieved a less subordinate position in the relationship.

From the more specific perspective of Indo–Bangladesh relations over 1983–4, the picture which emerges is much more serious than a superficial overview might reveal, with deep distrust, insecurity and mismanagement being exhibited by both states towards each other. Some of the least constructive characteristics of the Indo–Bangladesh relationship, such as India's imperiousness and disdain and Bangladesh's oversensitivity and unwillingness to negotiate bilaterally were epitomised. It was no coincidence that the plunging level of cordiality in relations between the two states in 1983 accompanied the sharpening of Indian domestic social conflict and the general heightening of tension in South Asia.

The eruption of ethnic and communal violence in Assam and the Sikh-majority Punjab in 1983 placed immense pressure on Mrs Gandhi and the Congress-I, which in turn responded with defensive measures lacking in 'political sense', exacerbating rather than defusing the conflicts.[66] According to W. Morris-Jones, Mrs Gandhi's Congress-I government bore a special responsibility for the extent of Sikh and Assamese unrest because of the way in which its ruling elite had continually sacrificed party institutions and constitutional integrity for the sake of personal political gain.[67] Morris-Jones has drawn a direct correlation between the Congress-I's corruption of the processes of responsible government on one hand and political mismanagement of the crises in Assam and the Punjab on the other. The corruption which was sapping Congress Party ideals therefore had direct and adverse consequences for Indo–Bangladesh relations which deteriorated sharply as a result of the violent unrest in Assam in 1983.

While stability of the Congress-I was not necessarily threatened by the conflicts in Assam and the Punjab (especially since the opposition parties remained in the grip of internecine struggle[68]), Mrs Gandhi's authoritarian and centralised form of government was proving to be incapable of responding adequately to the pressure of rising regional disaffection. Ironically, an amassing of power at the centre had reduced the government's ability to curb widespread social unrest. Centralisation had been achieved at the expense not only of Congress Party integrity, but also that of the institution which had traditionally played an important role in maintaining Indian social stability: the Indian civil service.[69] In Hardgrave's opinion, the Indian bureaucracy had steadily degenerated under Mrs Gandhi's regime to become 'a cheap alloy, corroded by low morale, corruption, and political interference'.[70] With India's governing elite having assumed a role beyond its capability, and with personal loyalties having been given precedence over the logic of sound political decision-making, it was to be expected that such politically eroding tendencies would also permeate India's dealings with Bangladesh. Adverse effects on the relationship were especially likely since Bangladesh played an integral part in the issue of Assamese discontent.

More often than not, the underlying cause of the unrest in Assam has been ascribed to the poverty-stricken, overpopulated conditions in East Bengal/Bangladesh which had caused many of the inhabitants to migrate illegally into India's northeast states in search of 'greener pastures'.[71] This argument was also the Indian government's long-standing official position on the matter, as exemplified during mid- to late 1980 when Assam and Tripura erupted in violence.[72] The inadequacy of an explanation based on Bangladeshi immigration as the sole foundation of Assamese political and economic grievances becomes clear when considering that migrations into Assam had been occurring in the millions since the 1820s, coming from a variety of locations apart from Bengal, such as Rajasthan, Punjab, Nepal and Bihar.[73] While the population of Assam has increased at a much faster rate than the rest of India, especially since 1961,[74] other ingredients apart from Bangladeshi immigration have exacerbated Assamese dissatisfaction. South Asia analyst Myron Weiner has illustrated the complexity and variety of reasons why Assam has become a region of political tension, pointing to the combined pressure of historical, social, demographic and cultural circumstances.[75] It is also evident that the increasing political corruption, mismanagement and inflexibility on the part of the Indian government played a part in fuelling the discontent, impairing relations with Bangladesh in the process. Not only did Bangladesh present the clearest target upon which to focus growing Assamese anger and frustration, but the methods by which the Indian government attempted to solve the perceived cause of the Assam problem also had adverse consequences for relations with Bangladesh.

Morris-Jones has concluded that Assamese unrest has grown due to 'real neglect and real deprivation'.[76] Assamese fears of being 'outnumbered, out-bought and . . . outvoted' in their own homeland have been fostered, accord-ing to Morris-Jones, by not only the influx of large numbers of Bengali Muslims but also by the policies of the central Indian government.[77] He has criticised Mrs Gandhi for having exploited the influx by placing the non-Assamese immigrants onto the electoral rolls in the expectation that mem-bers of this group would be 'docile', pro-Congress-I voters.[78] The validity of this criticism was reinforced by Mrs Gandhi's insistence that elections for the Assam state assembly and 12 vacant parliamentary seats should go ahead, despite the threat of a boycott by Assamese political parties.[79] The ensuing polls, held in February 1983, heightened political and cultural ten-sion in Assam to the extent of civil war, leaving thousands dead and requiring the presence of a virtual army of occupation to restrain further violence.[80]

From one perspective, therefore, Bangladeshi infiltration could be blamed for the increased unrest in Assam, but from another, the machinations of the Congress-I regime can be seen as a catalyst for fomenting political agita-tion in the region. Neither one perspective nor the other explains adequately the cause of Assamese unrest, yet both the Indian and Bangladesh govern-ments adopted a blinkered view of the problem, emphasising just one of the perspectives, the one most likely to absolve political responsibility.

In seeking absolution for the 1983 election carnage in Assam, described as the most serious violence in India since 1947,[81] the Congress-I gave 'top pri-ority' to the 'aliens' issue, announcing a package to appease Assamese demands.[82] The Government's solution focused on reinforcing the Indo–Bangladesh border, the porous state of which was considered ultimately responsible for the growing tension and violence in Assam. A programme to detect and deport 'foreigners' in Assam was 'vigorously taken up' by the central government which also increased the number of border outposts and stepped up police presence in Assam.[83] Perhaps interpreting the post-election calm which descended on Assam as 'an undetonated bomb that could go off at any moment',[84] the Indian government opted to supplement its offers of appeasement to the Assamese with a bizarre and questionable scheme: the sealing of the entire Indo–Bangladesh border with a 3300 kilo-metre barbed wire fence, estimated to cost half a billion US dollars.[85]

The fence plan was announced by the Indian government less than two weeks after the formal launching of an integrated programme for regional cooperation, a scheme mooted by Ziaur Rahman in 1980 for improving South Asian interstate relations. Known initially as the South Asian Regional Cooperation (SARC), the programme to enhance regional cooperation was described as an 'historic' and 'great beginning' which reflected the 'political will, sincerity and determination of the seven nations'.[86] Mrs Gandhi also praised the SARC initiative, expressing her hope that 'cooperation among the seven countries would increase their capacity to withstand pressures, enable them to move ahead to a future of freedom, peace and prosperity and give a strong impetus to closer friendship and greater stability in the region'.[87]

The SARC understanding offered economic benefits for relations between India and Bangladesh, prompting the Indo–Bangladesh Joint Economic Commission to take a wide range of measures to 'expand and accelerate' economic cooperation between the two states.[88] Political cooperation was another matter, the reality representing a stark contrast to Mrs Gandhi's rhetoric and her effusive support for attempts to foster regional cooperation. Those who had perceived the creation of SARC as a 'route to security'[89] – a potential means of diminishing the arms race and conflict in the region – would have had their optimism quickly curtailed. Even amidst the radiance of the new-found SARC spirit, India was delivering both defensive and provocative messages to Pakistan and Bangladesh.

Pakistan's increased military assistance from the United States in the wake of the Afghanistan crisis had been causing considerable unease within the Indian government. India's reaction to the perceived challenge to regional stability was sharp and direct, with little hint that a SARC-inspired approach would be implemented; as exemplified by the following comment by Indian external affairs minister, Narasimha Rao:

> We want peace. But it is not enough to have peaceful intentions if some quarters had different intention ... [I]f war comes, we are prepared for it.[90]

The ethics of the SARC proposal were not only ignored by India, they were also contravened with regard to diplomatic relations with Bangladesh. India's scheme to fence the Indo–Bangladesh border had been planned and announced without consultation with Bangladesh, a heavy-handed move described as 'not only unheard of in the present day world but also inconceivable even between two hostile neighbours.'[91] Narasimha Rao's assurances that the border fence would not sour relations were partly based on the far-fetched notion that taking direct action to prevent illegal migration would cause less friction than including the matter in bilateral talks which would 'only mean adding one more item to the long list of unresolved issues between the two countries'.[92] India could further justify taking matters into its own hands because Ershad had adopted the uncompromising position that no Bangladesh nationals were infiltrating illegally into India, using rhetoric rather than evidence to justify his stand:

> [W]e have achieved our independence after supreme sacrifices to belong to the country ... Our people are living in complete harmony and peace.

We have security of life and food to feed our people ... It is therefore out of the question for our people to leave for any other country illegally as has been alleged.[93]

Since, according to Ershad, the problem in Assam was not of Bangladesh's making, the issue was not a valid cause for negotiation, a stand of dubious logic and one virtually guaranteed to exacerbate tension over the matter. Whether open to negotiation or not, the fence plan itself represented an emotive and extreme course of action, inviting unpredictable and extreme responses.

The Indian government had hoped that the fence plan would soothe Assamese anger, but the announcement prompted the reverse, being greeted in Assam with cynical derision,[94] and rekindling anti-government activity which had been suspended in the region for four months.[95] In Bangladesh, national pride and the traditional fears of Indian dominance were easily manipulated regarding the fence proposal which offered a classic means of acquiring national and international support, the ultimate aim being to defuse the growing political opposition to Ershad's military regime.[96] Having denied Bangladesh's responsibility for Assamese grievances, Ershad wasted no time in pointing out to India the demeaning aspects of an iron curtain-style fence being constructed to encircle much of Bangladesh without Bangladesh's consent:

We were disturbed by your decision [to construct a fence] because it humiliates and belittles us before the world. We should live like good friends and as neighbours we expect to be consulted.[97]

It was doubtful whether Narasimha Rao genuinely believed that by presenting the fence proposal as a *fait accompli* he would minimise the risk of jeopardising the stability of Indo–Bangladesh relations. Bangladeshi indignation, if not outrage, were manifested immediately, yet the central Indian government remained unperturbed and determined to build the fence regardless of Bangladeshi opinion. Even Assamese and wider domestic criticism did not dent the government's resolution to implement the scheme, further exemplifying the Congress-I's political callousness and overcentralisation. Commencement of the fence's construction prompted sabotage activity by Bangladeshis, military mobilisation by both states, violent border skirmishes, mutual recriminations between the two governments, anti-Indian rallies in Bangladesh and heightened insecurity in Bangladesh concerning all the serious, unresolved disputes with India.[98] The Indian government remained unrelenting in insisting that the fence would go ahead,[99] making it clear that Bangladesh's 'aggressive action' would not be tolerated. Technically, the fence was being constructed within Indian territory[100] and, as with the Farakka Barrage, there was little that Bangladesh could do to vent frustration and anger without being accused of impinging on India's sovereign rights. Bangladeshi accusations, anger and indignation over the fence were little match for what the Indian government could do if it chose, as the Indian media sought to remind Bangladesh:

> Surely even Lt.-Gen. Ershad and his cohorts must know that . . . they are playing with fire, to put it no more strongly than that. The course on which Dhaka seems embarked at present is vastly more reckless than the despatch by it of gunboats to the disputed island of New Moore in 1982 [*sic*][101] . . . The patience India has shown despite the Bangladeshi provocations is a measure of its keenness to live in peace and harmony with Bangladesh. But the Ershad government must realise that there are limits to which this patience can be tried.[102]

Commentators on the fence issue pointed out the improbable and impractical aspects, problems such as its vast length and cost; the potential disruption for legitimate trade and immigration; and the virtual impossibility of making it impenetrable or actually finishing it without the wire being stolen as quickly as it was put in place.[103] Nevertheless, in any form, even as a draft plan, the decision to construct a patrolled fence around much of Bangladesh represented a stark symbol of contempt by the Indian government for Bangladeshi sensitivities. To emphasise the impracticalities of the fence plan simply side-stepped the fact that in any form it had considerable political and psychological implications for Indo–Bangladesh relations. India's decision to build the fence was intended to put Bangladesh in its place, in more ways than one. It also showed that despite India's domestic and regional problems, the Indian government had little fear from what Bangladesh might attempt by way of rousing international support.

With the stability of Indo–Bangladesh relations 'impaled on barbed wire',[104] the euphoria of the 1982 summit dissolved with little trace, followed unsurprisingly by the foundering of efforts to resolve long-standing disputes, such as the Farakka Barrage and the border demarcation. Even the leasing of the Tin Bigha Corridor, supposedly agreed upon at the summit talks, became embroiled in a legal challenge that was to last nearly eight years.[105] The glimmer of cooperation, essentially the SARC initiative, which came to Indo–Bangladesh relations between the 1982 summit and Mrs Gandhi's assassination, did little more at the time than rub salt into Bangladesh's wounds.

The condition of the relationship between Bangladesh and India during 1983 and 1984 was at least as tense as that which existed while Ziaur Rahman and Mrs Gandhi were in power, but 1983–4 presented a grimmer picture for relations in the long term. One of the main reasons for this appeared to be that India and the Congress government were in a far less comfortable position than in 1975–6 when Zia was establishing his position in Bangladesh. Despite the setback which the military take-over in Bangladesh meant to India, India still held a secure, commanding position of advantage in the region. The Indian government's reactions to Bangladesh's military take-over were strident but expected. In 1983–4, by contrast, the Indian govern-ment was proving to be increasingly corrupt and inept in the face of spiral-ling domestic turmoil and regional insecurity, the latter being heightened by the possibility of another war with Pakistan and by Tamil separatism in Sri Lanka.[106] The erratic and increasingly harsh way in which Mrs Gandhi's government attempted to restore domestic and regional security did not bode well for harmonious relations with Ershad's regime in Bangladesh, even if the latter had professed a desire for friendlier relations with India. Along with defensiveness and political mismanagement, the Indian government was becoming more prone to a reliance on the military to settle threats to internal security. Operation Blue Star, the Indian Army's forced entry into the Sikh Golden Temple in Amritsar in June 1984, was the government's answer to resolve a particularly volatile and critical domestic crisis.

There was little indication that India would act differently towards Ban-gladesh in a crisis that compared in severity with Assam. It seemed clear that while the Indian government felt vulnerable and while Mrs Gandhi remained in power, India would not hesitate to use whatever amount of force was necessary to counter action deemed to be threatening, irrespective of how friendly the prevailing Bangladesh government might be. At the very least, a pressured and insecure Indian government would give little quarter to Bangladesh's own sensitivities and insecurities, and would not necessarily act with pragmatism and discretion. The fence issue represented a classic example. With the momentum of communal tension rising in South Asia from 1983,[107] and the Congress-I's ad hoc remedies proving ineffective, there was little likelihood that relations between India and Bangladesh would not suffer as well.

The cordiality and stability of Indo–Bangladesh relations which accom-panied Ershad's inaugural year hinted that a more mature, perhaps egalitar-ian relationship would emerge. Yet despite the congeniality of regional conditions and the optimistic rhetoric of both Ershad and Mrs Gandhi, the brief period of cordiality had at best brought little more than a reinforcing of the status quo. By the end of 1983, the prospects for a 'new beginning' seemed less than non-existent.

The pressures of overpopulation and political instability in Bangladesh have always impinged on relations with India. General Ershad no doubt hampered the prospects for a genuine transformation in Indo–Bangladesh relations by preferring to manipulate domestic fears of India when political expediency demanded, rather than seeking practical solutions for the long-term benefit of Bangladesh. Nevertheless, the events of 1982–4 show that India's role in directly fashioning the shape of relations with Bangladesh has been a much greater one than has generally been acknowledged. At the same time, Indian foreign policy itself has been moulded, if not hindered, by the momentum not only of entrenched traditions harking back to Partition, but also protracted dominance by a powerful individual: Mrs Indira Gandhi. Combined, these two aspects represented a formidable foil during a large portion of the history of Indo–Bangladesh relations, driving home to Bangladesh that its viability and future were perennially circumscribed by India's agenda. Never was this message delivered more clearly than in 1983–4.

4
1985–90: The 'New Era' of Regional Amity and Cooperation

This chapter examines Bangladesh's relations with India from 1985 to 1990 and evaluates the impact of India's regional and domestic concerns on the relationship between the two states. The period covers both the remainder of Hussain Muhammad Ershad's regime and the post-Indira prime minister-ship of Rajiv Gandhi, a stage in Indo–Bangladesh relations on which very little research has been done. The second half of the 1980s was characterised by an unprecedented movement towards South Asian regional cooperation and this chapter will assess the extent to which the trend impinged on Indo–Bangladesh relations.

From 1985 to 1990, both Bangladesh and India were participants in the emerging, 'more truly world-wide', phenomenon of regional, transnational affiliation.[1] Regional coalitions were beginning to emerge in areas where the obstacles to cooperation had hitherto proved intractable, such as in South Asia, parts of Africa and parts of the Pacific.[2] Paradoxically, the period was also one in which the states of Bangladesh and India faced escalating domestic political, communal and ethnic instability. These tensions added new layers to the South Asian region's traditional political insecurities.

According to international relations analyst, Norman Palmer, a new, more realistic type of regionalism had been evolving globally during the 1980s. Unlike its earlier form, the regionalism of the 1980s was characterised by a non-European focus and by the replacement of ambitious notions of regional integration with those based on the principle of loose, flexible, mainly economic, cooperation between states.[3] Even South Asia, described as a 'region without regionalism',[4] was not immune to the 1980s trend towards regional associations. After five years of hesitant moves by various South Asian states towards fostering regional cooperation and self-reliance, these aims were given support in December 1985, in Dhaka, with the hold-ing of the first heads of state summit of the organisation for South Asian Regional Cooperation (subsequently called SAARC, the South Asian Associ-ation for Regional Cooperation).[5] The creation of SAARC indicated that a framework for multilateral, regional cooperation had emerged in South Asia, despite the civil strife which was occurring in several of the member states, and despite the fact that India, the largest and most politically powerful member, had a long-standing preference for bilateral political negotiations.

India's initial consent to the establishment of a regional forum was based on the proviso that the organisation's agenda should be restricted as much as possible to regionally non-contentious matters. Yet, even within the realm of trade (in India's view, an 'acceptable' area for SAARC involvement), the possibility of fostering genuine economic benefits in the region was minimal, apart from a strengthening of India's already dominant economic position. Since, in the opinion of the smaller states, Indian economic dominance was virtually synonymous with Indian political dominance, the potential for SAARC to offer an economic vehicle for regional reconciliation was limited at best. South Asia had always been 'conspicuous for the absence of even marginal intraregional trade',[6] a condition which substantially impeded the all-too-slim prospects for SAARC's long-term success.

Scepticism, as well as effusive rhetoric, accompanied the launching of SAARC. While the heads of state spoke glowingly about SAARC having ushered in a new era of amity,[7] many commentators were not as optimistic. For example, the editor of the *Times of India* stressed that it would be a miracle if SAARC did not founder under the 'strain of contradictions' which abounded in the region.[8] Despite the obstacles, SAARC was to acquire some standing over time,[9] defying extinction to date by broadening its agenda gradually to address some of the smaller states' political concerns,[10] but without provoking excessive Indian resistance.

Throughout the second half of the 1980s, South Asia was characterised by an incongruous blend of increasing political instability on one hand, and a cautious, yet resolute, fostering of regional consciousness on the other. The emergence of a regional awareness, exemplified by the creation of SAARC, had some beneficial consequences for Indo–Bangladesh relations. However, the emerging regional focus in South Asia did not result simply from the triumph of altruistic desires for regional harmony and cooperation. India's perennially sensitive and regionally-impinging security concerns were of much greater relevance than the promotion of regional awareness, the former having a direct impact on relations between India and its smaller neighbours. The Indian government's uncharacteristic support for a regional forum was driven by a transformation of Indian security perceptions. This shift was spurred to a considerable extent by the dual pressures of escalating regional strife, and the changing course of superpower interrelations.

The spread of increasingly uncontrollable civil unrest in India on many fronts, such as in the Punjab, Assam, Tamil Nadu and Kashmir forced a more regional outlook upon the central Indian government. From India's point of view, the underlying cause of the unrest in these trouble-spots was, without exception, linked to the policies and problems existing in particular neighbouring states. The more civil unrest increased in India, the more the

Indian government felt compelled, in the interests of political survival, to monitor, and modify where possible, the actions of neighbouring governments. Ironically, India's regional focus was stimulated by growing political fears and insecurity not, as the rhetoric suggested, because of a heartfelt realisation that by suppressing differences in the interests of regional unity, all the South Asian states would be much better off strategically and economically.[11]

The conduct of superpower interrelations had always had considerable ramifications for Indian foreign policy. Noteworthy changes in global politics emerged in the mid-1980s. These changes impinged upon India's relations with the Soviet Union and the United States, easing Indian security fears in some respects, but fostering them in others. On the whole, the changes contributed to a more regional preoccupation on India's part. Traditionally, India's self-appointed role of regional security manager was aimed largely at reducing opportunities for great power interference in the region. By the mid-1980s, this compulsion had moderated to some extent, due to an easing of superpower tensions and the accompanying development of a more diversified and less-aligned Indian foreign policy.[12] Global tensions, which had been heightened by Soviet intervention in Afghanistan in 1979, began to mellow by the mid-1980s. Soviet *glasnost* and *perestroika*[13] emerged, producing a mood of political reconciliation which embraced not only the Soviet Union and the United States, but also the People's Republic of China. The easing of global tensions, especially the new-found warmth between the USSR and China, produced foreign policy quandaries for India, highlighting the uneasy relationship which had existed between India and China since the Sino–Indian war in 1962.

In contrast to the moderation of superpower rivalry, Indo–Soviet rapprochement began to undergo a subtle distancing as both states began to broaden their foreign policies, even within the military sector.[14] The Indo–Soviet treaty of 1971 was still operative, but the peace and friendship alliance had been ratified in an era of global polarity, unlike the mid-1980s, where unequivocal Soviet support for Indian interests was less assured. Also contrary to established relations, the United States had begun to make expansive diplomatic overtures to India, offering the post-Indira government economic and military concessions and pandering to India's deep-seated desire to be considered a major world power.[15] The United States also appeared less inclined to meddle in South Asian politics, or to play upon Indo–Pakistani differences in the latter half of the 1980s.[16]

An improvement in relations between India and China was less forthcoming, although a mellowing did develop in response to the evolving mood of superpower reconciliation. In the wake of the 1962 war, China represented India's greatest military threat and was its chief rival for ascendancy in Asian and global affairs. Indian fears of Chinese influence and expansion in the subcontinent were well entrenched and not easily allayed. While of global benefit, warmer relations between the Soviet Union and China[17] presented a foreign policy dilemma to India. Any rapprochement between India's hitherto staunchest ally and one of India's most feared rivals meant a reappraisal of the deep stakes which India had in Soviet strength and support. India could no longer expect unequivocal Soviet support in resolving altercations and long running disputes with China. At the same time, Sino–Indian relations were no longer hindered by the weight of Soviet disapproval and were free to develop along new lines. Indian efforts to come to terms with the shifting nature of superpower interests were not noted for their strategic vision, tending to be hesitant and ad hoc. China, by contrast, acted promptly to exploit the foreign policy openings, extending overtures of warmth towards India in 1985. These initiatives were rebuffed warily by Indira's successor, Rajiv Gandhi,[18] pointing to India's deep-seated distrust of Chinese intentions. No substantial breakthrough was achieved with Sino–Indian border issues during the 1980s, although eventually some progress was made in the diplomatic sphere.[19] Between 1985 and 1990, China held an unequivocally commanding position over India's northern borders. India could no longer assume that Soviet assistance would be forthcoming and with large portions of India's border regions becoming increasingly volatile, scope for Chinese political advantage and interference was considerable.[20]

The new era of South Asian regionalism was therefore also a period in which Rajiv Gandhi and his government faced substantial foreign policy challenges. The reconfiguration in superpower relations and the unpredictable implications for Sino–Indian relations, together with India's increasing domestic instability, all combined to put pressure on the Indian government. These pressures meant that it faced a very difficult task in pursuing a foreign policy which was coherent and consistent with the developing mood of South Asian regional cooperation. The Indian government's foreign policy predicament impinged on the course of relations with Bangladesh, resulting in erratic fluctuations between antagonism and cooperation. These shifts reflected the interaction between the two prevalent and opposing forces of regional cooperation and regional conflict.

Although the movement towards regional cooperation did have an impact on Indo–Bangladesh relations, Rajiv Gandhi's personality and foreign policy predilections played a more dominant role. Initially lauded as 'Mr Clean' and praised for his affable nature,[21] Rajiv soon gained a reputation for impulsiveness, a managerial style of leadership, a contempt for politics and the bureaucracy and for restricting executive power to as few people as possible. These characteristics were noted in the Indian press. In assessing Rajiv's personality and style of regime, *The Times of India* commented: '[Rajiv] is not accessible to his ministers even of the cabinet rank, not to speak of MPs. All crucial decisions are taken by a small group.... The cult of personality has been in operation as never before ... [His] managerial approach is essentially a non-democratic one'.[22]

Like his predecessors, Indira and Nehru, Rajiv considered foreign policy formulation to be his personal preserve. He worked on establishing a high international profile, aiming to bolster his charismatic appeal and to counter the common accusation in the Indian press that he was inaccessible. His personal interest in foreign policy matters was evident in his penchant for undertaking international diplomatic visits himself, rather than delegating the task to a minister. During a four-year period of his Prime Ministership, Rajiv visited 48 countries, more than either his predecessors or successors.[23]

Rajiv's emphasis on diplomacy and conciliation towards India's South Asian neighbours was particularly pronounced during his first year of office. The western press appeared, at that time, to take a more approving view, compared with sections of the Indian media, of Rajiv's personality-dominated governance and foreign policy:

India is maintaining a brisk diplomatic pace to develop cordiality with its Sub-continental neighbours raising hopes of a breakthrough in relations with at least three countries: Pakistan, Bangladesh and Nepal. The important factor in the unfolding scenario is the personality of Indian Prime Minister Rajiv Gandhi, credited by many with a desire to break new ground.[24]

Rajiv's interest in foreign affairs was focused on South Asia, reflecting the wider trend towards regionalism. The initial period of his regime was marked by a particularly conciliatory demeanour towards India's neighbours. It was a period of comparative euphoria in which great hopes were held in the region that India's new leader would seek permanent resolution of regional disputes and would actively foster regional cooperation. Abundant enthusiasm and idealism permeated Rajiv's overtures towards the other States. In October 1985, at the eighth Commonwealth Heads of Government Meeting (CHOGM) at Nassau in the Bahamas, Rajiv espoused optimistic hopes for regional cooperation. This was in view of the imminent launching of SAARC, an organisation which Rajiv saw as a means of contributing towards 'creating understanding for fruitful cooperation in social, cultural and scientific fields and removing communication gaps and misunderstandings'.[25] SAARC would, according to Rajiv, provide 'a meaningful vehicle for forging a greater understanding among the member countries'.[26] He also hoped that SAARC would help promote 'fraternal feelings among the people, with the leaders of respective countries coming together for effective cooperation among themselves'.[27] He praised Bangladesh for its role in the creation of SAARC, describing Dhaka as the 'new strength of unity of the region'.[28]

The idealism and regional goodwill espoused by Rajiv at CHOGM were taken up eagerly by the Bangladesh press. Rajiv and Ershad formally agreed at the meeting to renew efforts to resolve the dispute over the Farakka barrage. *The Bangladesh Observer* declared boldly that the Farakka issue would be 'settled within one year'.[29] This was a very optimistic view of the agreement when considering that the 1982 memorandum of understanding (MOU) on Farakka had expired in June 1984, and no genuine progress had been made in finding a mutually agreeable solution to augmenting the dry-season Gangetic flow, despite attempts dating back to 1977.

The Nassau accord reached between Gandhi and Ershad did offer some hope for a resolution of the Farakka dispute. Despite the appearance of simply preserving the status quo, the accord did represent a positive step, eliciting the effusive media response in Bangladesh. The outcome of the accord was another three-year MOU, signed a month later at a meeting of the Ministers for Irrigation and Water Resources of both states. The agreement for sharing the dry-season flow was established on much the same basis as that of the 1982 MOU and took effect in 1986.[30] The Nassau accord also initiated the creation of a Joint Committee of Experts (JCE), a body which was to be assigned the task of completing, within 12 months, a study of alternatives for water-sharing and augmentation in the Ganges/Brahmaputra Basin.

The terms of reference of the JCE were much broader than those of the coexisting Joint Rivers Commission which had been formed in 1977 essentially to assess augmentation schemes for the Ganges. The JCE, by contrast, was expected to examine the river systems of the Ganges/Brahmaputra basin, the aim being to establish a formula for the equitable sharing of all major cross-border rivers between India and Bangladesh, not just the Ganges at Farakka.[31] The technical options to be considered by the JCE for flow augmentation were also correspondingly broad, such as the construction of additional barrages and canals within Bangladesh and dams on the Indian section of the Brahmaputra river.[32]

These developments in the Farakka issue indicated a promising degree of flexibility and initiative, both of which had been singularly lacking in the course of the dispute hitherto. Rajiv's agreement to allow Nepal to be included in the discussions on water augmentation with Bangladesh was a particular exception,[33] a concession which had not been entertained by the Indian government previously. The JCE was given permission by India to 'approach Nepal for the limited purpose of eliciting data on the feasibility of augmenting lean season flows at Farakka from storages in Nepal'.[34]

The SAARC ambience and Rajiv's fostering of regional cordiality contributed to further expressions of goodwill between India and Bangladesh in 1985–6. These included assurances between Rajiv and Ershad that the growing, mutual problems of tribal insurgency[35] and border infiltration in both India and Bangladesh would be addressed cooperatively.[36] Initially, at least, the launching of SAARC and the change of regimes in India had beneficial consequences for Indo–Bangladesh relations. The improvement was closely tied to the simultaneous warming of India's relations with Pakistan. The change of regime in India and the launching of SAARC prompted bilateral talks and agreements between Rajiv and the Pakistan President, Zia ul-Haq.

Following the SAARC summit, Zia made a diplomatic visit to New Delhi where he and Rajiv announced that various steps would be taken to normalise Indo-Pakistani relations.[37] The SAARC charter excluded the use, even the threat, of force by any of the South Asian states in settling mutual differences.[38] Building on the SAARC initiatives, India and Pakistan mutually agreed not to attack each other's nuclear facilities.[39] Other agreements were made or planned during Zia's December visit. They included: improved trade and communication links between India and Pakistan; a revision of the highly restrictive travel policy between the two states; a return visit by Rajiv to Islamabad;[40] and negotiation of differences over the Siachin glacier area in northern Kashmir.[41] Zia ul-Haq was especially delighted with the progress in relations with India, commenting: 'In such a short time we have achieved so much and in such a cordial atmosphere.'[42]

The improvement in India's relations with Pakistan and Bangladesh was welcomed by many, the 'smiles and salaams' receiving international media attention.[43] Nevertheless, the auspicious signs and rhetoric which pointed to a substantial breakthrough in South Asian international relations were of limited depth and duration; and were obviously dependent upon the Indian government's sense of political security. The initial waves of SAARC solidarity and Rajiv's foreign policy vigour did have a mellowing impact on Indo–Bangladesh relations for a period of about 12–18 months. Relations between the two states lost much of their SAARC-inspired warmth during the subsequent phase, from about mid-1986 to Ershad's removal from government in 1990. There were many reasons for the decline, and, as will be shown below, most were associated with the Indian government's attempts either to shore up a crumbling domestic power base or to ensure Indian stability and dominance in the region.

According to SAARC's charter, regional negotiations were supposed to be restricted to politically non-contentious matters. This restriction virtually guaranteed that, as a means of maintaining cordial South Asian relations, SAARC was very limited in scope. The 1985–6 warmth of South Asian relations was, to a large extent, a reflection of Rajiv Gandhi's bilateral foreign policy initiatives in the region. His initiatives were, in turn, dependent upon the prevailing degree of Indian domestic stability. As Indian political instability increased, Rajiv's initiatives began to falter, and so did the relative cordiality of international relations in the region.

An array of domestic and regional problems began to exert pressure on Rajiv's personalised regime in 1986. In circumventing the traditional and bureaucratic machinery, Rajiv and his coterie acquired considerable executive power. At the same time, with such a narrow power base, Rajiv became increasingly vulnerable to political challenges and the pressure of democratic processes. This became evident in 1987 when Rajiv's clean personal image tarnished rapidly with his perceived involvement in the Bofors scandal and his blatant attempts to bury the matter.[44] The subsequent loss of several by-elections by Rajiv's Congress-I party also undermined his domestic polit-ical strength,[45] prompting erratic and impulsive responses. These included arbitrary dismissals, such as that of the 'popular and articulate' Foreign Sec-retary, A.P. Venkateswaran.[46] Pressures increased further as Rajiv's domestic programmes, such as economic liberalisation, began to falter.[47]

A similar capriciousness infused Rajiv's foreign policy decisions, some of which were of questionable strategic benefit to India. In dealing with the People's Republic of China (PRC), Rajiv was particularly erratic. In 1985–6 he irritated the Chinese government considerably, ignoring Chinese over-tures for normalisation of relations, and adopting a 'forward policy' towards China which involved the deployment of troops and subsequent border clashes between the two states.[48] Rajiv then backed down in an attempt to mollify the Chinese, visiting China himself in 1988 and creating diplomatic embarrassment by his categorical endorsement of the Chinese claim to Tibet.[49] As explained by analyst S. Ganguly, '[p]ersonal whims rather than strategic imperatives seemed to have played a rather disproportionate role in the making of foreign and defence policy during the Rajiv Gandhi administration'.[50]

The ad hoc nature of Rajiv's personalised foreign policy was reflected in the fluctuating degree of cordiality present in the region. Signs of diplomatic tension between India and Pakistan appeared within a few months of SAARC's triumphant inauguration. In March 1986, Zia ul-Haq stated that India was 'cooling off' ties with Pakistan, applying the accusation, commonly used by both states, that troops had fired over the Kashmir border, killing civilians in the process.[51] The ease and speed with which tensions resurfaced between India and Pakistan drew attention to the superficiality of the 'new era of understanding, fraternity and cooperation'[52] deemed to have been stimulated by SAARC's creation. The broad issue of Kashmir, the major obstacle to a genuine improvement in Indo–Pakistan relations, was carefully skirted both at the SAARC summit and during Zia's December visit to New Delhi. The tendency for both states to avoid negotiations on the most intractable issues was illustrated in Zia's reply when asked about Pakistan's claim to Kashmir during his December visit. He commented: 'We have decided to start with areas of agreement and leave out disagreements for the time being. Kashmir will come at a proper time.'[53]

The incipient warmth of Indo–Bangladesh relations also faded as the euphoria of SAARC gave way to renewed regional antagonisms. As with Kashmir, several long-standing points of contention between India and Bangladesh received little attention because the SAARC charter excluded controversial bilateral matters. The atmosphere of SAARC cordiality did not generate noticeable progress in any of the disputes between the two coun-tries, apart from some attention to the Farakka Barrage and the sharing of the Ganges. Issues such as India's procrastination in handing over the Tin Bigha Corridor to Bangladesh; the disputed ownership of New Moore Island

and the Muhuri charland near Tripura; and the construction of the fence around Bangladesh continued to impair relations between the two states.

While these border disputes between India and Bangladesh remained unresolved, the issues settled into a desultory stalemate, with little indication that any serious efforts were being made by either government to improve matters. In mid-July 1985, Bangladesh repeated its claim to the entire area of the disputed Muhuri charland and a number of skirmishes along the Indo–Bangladesh border ensued over the next 12 months.[54] As in the past, no progress or compromise was achieved. The fence issue showed a similar lack of political interest on the part of both governments. The plan to construct a barbed wire fence around the entire Bangladesh border to restrict illegal immigration had been an emotive issue in 1983, incensing Bangladeshi popular opinion and souring Indo–Bangladesh relations considerably (see chapter 3). The fence construction had been suspended temporarily in 1984, but the announcement in October 1985 that work would be resumed, drew little response from Bangladesh.[55] The announcement was sandwiched between the cordiality of the Nassau CHOGM and the launching of SAARC, both events helping to defuse any tension generated.

The stalemated nature of the fence issue was exemplified by the following comment by a spokesperson for the Mission of Bangladesh to the UN in which he espoused the standard government line that there were no illegal Bangladeshi immigrants in India:

> The Government of Bangladesh has repeatedly made it clear that there are no Bangalees in Assam, and the question of their expulsion to Bangladesh has not arisen at all...There has not been a single case of communal disharmony in Bangladesh since independence. So does it stand to reason that Bangalees should have emigrated to Assam?[56]

At border talks held in New Delhi in April 1986, a similar stance prevailed, where the Bangladesh government delegation denied India's charge that continual large-scale illegal immigration of Bangladeshis into India was occurring. The delegation side-stepped the accusation by admitting that there may have been 'some cases of stranded Pakistani Biharis caught while crossing the Indo–Bangladesh border on their way to Pakistan'.[57] With regard to the fence itself, the Indian government still did not acknowledge the logistical impracticalities of the scheme, complaining instead of the disappearance of border pillars and fencing material, and demanding that Bangladesh be more cooperative in patrolling the border.[58] The mutual lack of political will to maintain stable relations was further exemplified by a border clash which occurred on the Muhuri River immediately following the April border talks.[59] Two members of the Bangladesh Rifles were killed in the clash. Neither India nor Bangladesh made a serious effort to negotiate a resolution of their outstanding border disputes.

For political reasons, the promising Farakka initiatives also lost their momentum in 1986. The Bangladesh, Indian and Nepalese governments each played a role in hampering implementation. By 1986, the discussed options for sharing and augmentation of Gangetic water had expanded well beyond the original limited proposals put forward by the Indian and Bangladesh governments. Methods to augment the Gangetic flow had been restricted to two options: India's proposal for a link canal from the Brahmaputra to the Ganges and Bangladesh's proposal for the construction of storage dams in Nepal. Alternative options were discussed in 1986–7 by the JCE. These included: the construction of barrages and a link canal within Bangladesh; Nepal's participation in discussions and plans to augment the Ganges; and a guaranteed minimum dry-season flow for Bangladesh on each of its major common rivers. As pointed out by Ben Crow, the mooting of these alternative options by the JCE was a worthy achievement in itself, regardless of whether or not the proposals were actually put into practice.[60] At the same time, the emphasis on finding an appropriate river-sharing formula, as opposed to Ganges augmentation, was driven to a large extent by Bangladesh's apprehension over India's construction of new barrages on other common rivers, such as the Teesta and the Gumti.[61] Bangladesh's vulnerability was increasing, so a package agreement for all shared rivers was particularly desirable from its point of view.

The new proposals foundered under a welter of political pressures and the weight of traditional antagonisms. The Bangladesh government was not blameless in preventing the proposals from coming to fruition,[62] and neither were the Indian and Nepalese governments. Frustrations, disagreements, and 'politicisation of technical differences' dogged the efforts of the JCE to establish the new line of river development proposals.[63] The JCE consisted of many of those who had been staunch proponents of the limited and divisive, but familiar old line, and who lacked the commitment or confidence to take the new proposals beyond the discussion table. As a result, the JCE easily fell victim to factionalism, indecision and political pressures, its meetings becoming less productive and increasingly intermittent into 1987.[64]

Despite the appearance of being a step forward, Nepal's involvement in the Indo–Bangladesh river sharing arrangements accentuated the hurdles facing the JCE. The inclusion of Nepal in negotiations, even tentatively, heightened entrenched and traditional antagonisms associated with Indo–Bangladesh border issues. Rajiv's magnanimous concession in allowing Nepal's participation in river-sharing negotiations did not sit well amongst conservative Indian government circles, causing discomfort, confusion and paralysis. The new tide of regionalism and the creation of SAARC did not dent India's traditional penchant for bilateral negotiations when dealing with important issues with its neighbours. Even the initial, tentative steps to bring Nepal into the water-sharing discussions between India and Bangladesh rapidly stalled.

Discussions were held in Nepal between three teams of experts from Bangladesh, India and Nepal in late October 1986 and in the following month between Rajiv, Ershad and King Birendra of Nepal at the second SAARC summit. Ershad described the talks as 'very positive',[65] but in fact little was achieved. The Nepalese government was particularly concerned that any plans for building storage reservoirs in Nepal would be of 'mutual benefit' and neither the Indian nor Bangladesh government was able to provide that assurance in a formal sense. Both 'accepted the principle of mutual benefit',[66] but both India and Bangladesh insisted that Nepal should first supply river-flow data before any formal, written commitment to Nepal could be made. The stalemated talks were described thus:

> The Nepal meeting was a complete waste of time and money. Even the request for data was a formality. Virtually all of the data requested had already been obtained through informal bilateral discussions between India and Nepal and Bangladesh and Nepal. The government of Nepal was, nevertheless, not willing to acquiesce in the formality of exchanging data because that would have set a precedent of involvement in river development without formal representation in the decision-making process.[67]

Essentially, what Nepal wanted was an official, trilateral arrangement with India and Bangladesh. The Indian government appeared to concede to this desire and promised to prepare a paper outlining Nepal's benefit and what was to be expected of Nepal in return. The paper never eventuated and Nepal's role in augmenting Bangladesh's Gangetic flow faded into oblivion.[68] The reasons why the Indian government failed to deliver the paper which would have resolved the deadlock with Nepal were the subject of controversy, although it appeared that the inertia of India's traditional adherence to bilateralism was the main ingredient, or perhaps 'masterly inaction', rather than deviousness or dishonesty. The Indian Secretary of the Ministry of Irrigation and Water Resources, July 1985–February 1987, later gave the following explanation:

> The Government of India was *not* convinced ... of the rightness of the multilateral or regional approach. It was not the Government of India which offered to produce a paper; Nepal and Bangladesh thrust on India the responsibility of producing a paper on a thesis which it was not enthusiastic about. There was genuine bewilderment in India on what kind of paper to prepare and how to prepare it. Even the bureaucracy could not produce a draft ... Quite possibly, there was equal bewilderment at the political level; in any case, directions never came.[69]

The bewilderment and confusion were a consequence of the way in which Rajiv Gandhi had taken a personal interest in Indian foreign relations and had come to dominate India's foreign policy. Gandhi's decision to include Nepal in the negotiations was clearly a personal whim, and did not reflect a fundamental, deep-seated change in India's traditionally bilateral foreign policy, as shown in the following extract based on an interview between Ben Crow and an unidentified, but senior Indian Water Ministry official:

> He [one of India's senior irrigation officials] recalls being called in with others to see Rajiv in July 1985, and asked to find new initiatives. According to this senior official: 'Rajiv came in with good intentions, even if they weren't always very well thought out. He wanted new initiatives.' Prime Minister Rajiv asked them, 'why can't we break this logjam in water relations with Bangladesh?' He also asked, 'why are we resisting the trilateral approach' of including Nepal in the water negotiations, as Bangladesh had long been pushing for? 'We have had long talks with Nepal, making very little progress. Wouldn't it help if Bangladesh came along?'[70]

According to Crow, the official's response to Rajiv's questions was to reiterate 'India's long-standing adherence to bilateral negotiations' and to warn of the danger 'that trilateral negotiations might establish a precedent for Bangladesh to demand, as a right, a share of water stored in Nepal'.[71] Crow's source added that 'Rajiv eventually accepted many of these arguments'.[72]

The Nepalese government's recalcitrance and the Indian government's subsequent indecisiveness had a moderating impact on Bangladeshi plans for Gangetic augmentation.[73] Less ambitious plans which did not involve Nepal were put forward in Bangladesh, but the controversial, political and factionalised nature of the issue promptly interfered with their implementation.

The JCE report, submitted at the SAARC summit in November 1986, reflected the failure of the experts to achieve anything of worth in determining appropriate sharing and management arrangements for the Gangetic basin rivers. The committee lapsed into old- and new-line factionalism. Even basic questions could not be resolved, such as the number of rivers which should be classed as common to both India and Bangladesh. Bangladesh considered 54 rivers to be common to both and requiring individual assessment, while India considered those to be parts of larger river systems and, hence, confined the figure to nine.[74] Not only did the teams disagree on how the water flow should be apportioned, they also disagreed on which rivers should come under a long-term sharing arrangement.

In turn, the JCE's fragility succumbed to the pressures of entrenched, old-line views on augmentation which focused on storage dams in Nepal as being the only viable option. Nepal's perceived recalcitrance in participating in Gangetic augmentation contributed to divisiveness and uncertainty amongst the Bangladesh members of the JCE. Implementing the old-line augmentation proposal also promised to be an extraordinarily difficult task. As pointed out by Crow, the Bangladesh proposal meant the submergence of a large area of Nepalese land (over 600 square kilometres); the dams were to have been amongst the largest in the world and opposition to such dams, for social and environmental reasons, was already widespread in South Asia; and the proposal would have required cooperation from Nepal and India for the foreseeable future.[75] Despite these expected difficulties, old-line proponents, such as the Bangladesh foreign minister, Humayun Rashid Chowdhury, continued to bring their political predilections to bear on the conduct of the Farakka issue.[76] The debate in Bangladesh over whether to concentrate on water-sharing arrangements or to augment the Ganges remained on-going for the rest of Ershad's regime, with little being achieved.

India, for its part, again began to push for its preferred option: augmentation rather than river-sharing schemes and, in particular, the construction of the Brahmaputra–Ganges link canal. India insisted that priority should be given to augmentation rather than water-sharing, once it became obvious that the JCE would not be able to present a unanimous report by the looming November 1986 deadline and would need an extension of tenure.[77] The JCE eventually expired in November 1987 and, more worrisome for Bangladesh, the three-year 1985 MOU was not extended in 1988.[78]

Because of the resurgence of old-line positions in both India and Bangladesh, negotiations on water-sharing had effectively ground to a halt by mid-1987. The particularly severe floods of 1987 and 1988 revitalised discussions on river development between the two governments, but the emphasis was placed on flood control, rather than water-sharing, and did little to foster cooperation between the two states.

Those of the old persuasion in Bangladesh used the floods to justify and strengthen their stance on Ganges augmentation, blaming India's poor management of the Farakka Barrage for the severity of the floods and insisting that the construction of headwater reservoirs outside Bangladesh was intrinsic to effective flood management. Despite the dubious scientific evidence for this view,[79] Ershad endorsed the traditional stance.[80]

Those advocating new initiatives, such as water-sharing in Bangladesh, focused on measures which did not require Indian cooperation and could be implemented wholly within Bangladesh. Large amounts of international aid were garnered to fund purely domestic flood-management projects,[81] but the inertia of the old line was considerable, with the result that Indo–Bangladesh relations deteriorated further. The uneasiness of relations was exemplified by the way in which Bangladesh reacted to India's attempt to provide flood relief. An Indian Air Force helicopter rescue and relief mission, sent within 8 hours of Ershad's international appeal for flood relief operations, was suddenly asked, less than a week later, to return to India on the pretext that it was no longer needed.[82] India retaliated with indignation, criticising Bangladesh for internationalising its domestic flooding problem in the hope of capitalising on international sympathy in its bilateral dealings with India over river management. India also rejected accusations in the Bangladeshi media which placed excessive blame upon the larger state for causing the severity of the flooding. Colourful accounts in the Bangladeshi press interpreted the severity of the floods as being caused by a variety of factors originating within India, such as Indian glacier-melting experiments in the Himalayas; excessive discharge from upstream dams in India; the Farakka Barrage; and recent earthquakes which were of India's making.[83]

Despite the political recriminations, some cooperative efforts were made by India and Bangladesh to address the issue of flood mitigation, but these were superficial and ineffective. In the wake of the 1988 floods, an Indo–Bangladesh Task Force was constituted at a summit meeting between the two heads of government in New Delhi in September. The aim of the Task Force was to study the Ganges and Brahmaputra waters jointly for flood management and water flow and to produce a report within six months. The *Far Eastern Economic Review* took a cynical view of the Task Force, drawing attention to the poor performance of similar bodies in the past:

> the decision to set up a high-powered task force of experts to study the two rivers jointly for flood management and water flow . . . merely places a new body on top of the moribund Bilateral Rivers Commission, created 10 years ago.[84]

While the Task Force was able to report some progress with short-term measures, such as improved flood forecasting and warning systems, larger-scale ventures which involved both countries did not come to fruition. According to Verghese, India hampered progress because of its reluctance to supply Bangladesh with detailed water-flow data concerning the Ganges and the Brahmaputra.[85] Bangladesh needed the data in order to develop more sophisticated flood-control schemes, based on dynamic river flood-routeing models which could have been implemented with World Bank assistance.[86] India was reluctant to provide the data on the grounds that such readily available information might invite third party interference or be used to advantage by states such as Nepal or China.[87] India's apprehension and excessive cautiousness were symptomatic of its bilaterally inclined foreign policy and its acceptance of the status quo.

The river-sharing and development negotiations between Bangladesh and India effectively entered a period of stagnation from 1987. This condition resulted from the increasing preoccupation by the respective governments with more politically threatening concerns. The domestic problems facing Ershad were mounting, as were those confronting Rajiv Gandhi, but the latter faced increasing difficulties on the regional as well as domestic front. The following developments were particularly troublesome and demanding for Rajiv: his decline in popular support from 1987 and eventual election defeat in November 1989; mounting domestic economic difficulties; the crisis in Sri-Lanka's Tamil–Sinhala ethnic conflict in mid-1987 and the ensuing controversy over direct Indian intervention;[88] the mobilisation of Indian and Chinese troops on India's northeast frontier; the increasing tension in Indo–Nepalese relations owing to the activities of the growing Gurkha National Liberation Front;[89] the increasing militant, secessionist demands from tribal groups in India's northeast; and the heightened Indo–Pakistani tension and brinkmanship in 1986–7 over Kashmir and Pakistan's alleged assistance to Sikh extremists in the Punjab.[90] Clearly, the increasing stress to which Rajiv Gandhi's regime was subjected, domestically and regionally, was reflected in the government's waning efforts to respond to Bangladeshi insecurities and concerns.

Contrary to 'international trends towards cooperation and reconciliation', and a brief improvement in 1985, Indo–Pakistani relations deepened in hostility during the 1980s.[91] Traditionally, the state of Indo–Pakistani relations was an indicator of the level of prevailing tension in the region. The growing tension in Indo–Pakistani relations from 1986 contributed towards the general sense of unease and suspicion in relations between India and its neighbours. Even issues which India perceived as minor irritants, such as Bangladesh's water-sharing fears and demands, were encumbered with excessive political constraints and rivalries. These increasing pressures easily outpaced the tentative moves towards regional cooperation.

The cordiality of Indo–Bangladesh relations in 1985–6 was partly associated with the launching of SAARC but, more significantly, the improvement coincided with the early phase of Rajiv Gandhi's regime. Rajiv's naively enthusiastic, but individualistic and erratic attempts to remould Indian foreign policy had beneficial consequences for Indo–Bangladesh relations, but the effects were temporary. Both regionalism and personality did have some bearing on the relationship between the two states, but the pressure of Indian domestic and regional security concerns was ultimately of much greater influence. The movement towards regional cooperation coincided with increasing regional instability. Indian insecurity and bellicosity grew correspondingly.

Just as Rajiv attempted to foster warmer regional relations during the first flush of his rise to power, similar efforts were made in 1990 by the newly elected Indian coalition government headed by V.P. Singh. The regime's dynamic External Affairs minister, Inder Kumar Gujral, showed particular initiative in trying to resuscitate India's relations with its neighbours, Bangladesh, Pakistan, Nepal and Sri Lanka.[92] In February 1990, Gujral visited Bangladesh[93] for wide-ranging and amicable discussions on the main outstanding issues: water-sharing, tribal insurgency, the Tin Bigha Corridor, ownership of New Moore Island, and the large trade imbalance between the two countries. The *Far Eastern Economic Review* praised Gujral's efforts in Dhaka as setting 'the right tone for future substantive talks'.[94] The talks were cooperative, but Gujral gave few firm assurances, even concerning the expired interim agreement on sharing the Ganges.[95] Bangladesh's Foreign

Minister, Anisul Islam Mahmud, took a more reserved line, commenting: 'The complex issues that remained as irritants in Indo–Bangladesh relations could not be resolved to our satisfaction.'[96] As with preceding Indian regimes, such as those of Desai and Rajiv Gandhi, the Singh government began with fresh and sincere intentions to tackle issues marring relations with the other South Asian states. For each of the Indian regimes, those intentions quickly succumbed to more dominant pressures, such as political expediency, domestic instability or traditional interstate rivalries and expectations.

The speedy demise of the Singh government, combined with India's growing political and communal instability,[97] ensured that negligible progress was made in resolving the issues between India and Bangladesh. By the end of 1990, optimistic hopes that a new era of cordiality had begun in the region were conspicuously absent. Bangladesh's relationship with India had not altered essentially, remaining subservient and stalemated. The following comment by former High Commissioner of Bangladesh in India, Abul Ehsan, indicated that hope for better relations with India had not disappeared entirely by 1990 but, given the history of relations to that time, his sentiments appeared rhetorical, idealistic and forlorn:

> India and Bangladesh are neighbours and it is imperative that both the countries remain good neighbours. If India means well for the people of Bangladesh, it should endeavour to give back to Bangladesh a share of water nearest to the historical flow of the Ganges at Farrakah which entered into Bangladesh through [the] centuries. This can be done through [a] realistic approach and good neighbourly relations. Once this is done, Nepal, West Bengal (India) and Bangladesh will be rejuvenated with economic growth of enormous dimensions, and the lower riparian Bangladesh will at least be saved from desertification, salinity and near ecological disaster in [the] course of a few years.[98]

A study of Indo–Bangladesh relations during the latter half of the 1980s shows that those relations did not improve in the long-term. The launching of SAARC had raised hopes for genuine and lasting regional cooperation in South Asia, but this did not eventuate. The subsequent period was, contrary to optimistic aspirations, one of heightened regional tension. The Indian government resorted increasingly to undemocratic and populist procedures and became more inclined to intervene directly in neighbouring affairs deemed threatening to Indian security. According to South Asia analyst, Ramesh Thakur:

> India has cut a sorry figure in recent times. It is ailing internally, wracked by political turmoil, social ferment and economic stagnation. By the end of 1989, after five years in power, the Rajiv Gandhi government had achieved the dubious distinction of being on bad terms with all its neighbors.[99]

India's more regional preoccupation and increasing tendency to intervene in regional affairs was not just a response to intensifying domestic and regional instability. It was also a reflection of a long-standing and growing determination to be unequivocally the most dominant power in South Asia.[100] Fundamental changes had occurred in superpower aspirations and rivalries, with the result that both the United States and the Soviet Union were taking a somewhat less partisan stance over South Asian politics and appeared less inclined to interfere. At the same time, the United States was establishing a broader interest in the region: continuing to supply arms to Pakistan,[101] but also working to improve traditionally strained US–Indian relations. As a result, two contradictory pressures were at work on South Asian international relations: on one hand, India was facing increasing domestic instability, but on the other, it was finding greater freedom to manoeuvre in South Asia. India was less answerable to a more detached Soviet Union, while a more agreeable United States offered India better leverage against Pakistan. The entrenched and universal fear of Indian domination in the region in turn ensured that traditional antagonisms were fostered, rather than resolved, at a time of regional awareness and reduced superpower meddling. By 1990, even an optimistic view of Bangladesh's relationship with India was unlikely to extend beyond the hope that the status quo would be preserved.

Part III

Domestic Influences on Bangladesh–India Relations, 1975–90

5
1975–81: Military Ascendancy in Bangladesh

Between 1975 and 1981 Bangladesh's foreign policy was given a new identity. This was partly the contribution of the leader at that time, Ziaur Rahman, who came to power on 7 November 1975. As noted in Chapter 1, both internal and external influences on a state's foreign policy need to be taken into consideration, so the identification and evaluation of the significance of both the domestic and external forces at work is required. The purpose of this chapter is to illustrate the ways in which long-term domestic political, cultural and economic pressures in Bangladesh, themselves inextricably interwoven, have combined with specific domestic political events, such as Ziaur Rahman's rise to power, and have influenced the relationship between Bangladesh and India.

External events beyond Zia's control, such as Indira Gandhi's ousting in the 1977 Indian election, played an important part in shaping Bangladesh's foreign policy, but due to the personalised nature of Bangladeshi politics and to Zia's leadership skills he was, at times, able to mould the state's foreign policy according to his own concerns, fears and predilections. At the same time, as will be shown below, the nature of those concerns correlated with prevailing political conditions in Bangladesh.

The notion of security, as discussed in Chapter 1, is an integral part of a state's foreign policy formulation, but a closer examination of Bangladeshi foreign policy reveals that the concept of security should also encompass the personal quest for power and political dominance which may be sought by those vying for supremacy in a politically volatile state. In concentrating on the domestic influences on Bangladesh's relations with India, it would appear that Zia's overriding ambition to retain power in Bangladesh, tempered by a genuine desire to put the economically fragile state on to the path of progress and prosperity, provided an important stimulus for the state's reorientation in relations with India after 1975. The many obstacles which Zia faced in holding on to power, as well as his methods used to deal with those obstacles, all played an important role in shaping relations between Bangladesh and India.

This premise does not imply that the long-term political, cultural, and economic domestic influences on foreign policy should be relegated to an inferior position. Rather, the way in which such influences are interwoven with Zia's ambitions and decision-making means that pervasive domestic influences assume considerable importance. Intrinsic differences in territorial and cultural concerns and perceptions between Bangladesh and India came to impinge upon Indo–Bangladesh relations after 1975, giving some basis to the rhetorical exchanges between the two state leaders. These differences, outlined in Chapter 1, detracted from any substantial, overall development in cooperative understanding between the two states.

Zia's actions in the realm of foreign policy should be examined against this background of underlying tension. The fate of Mujibur Rahman, who had been hindered by a strong sense of obligation towards India after the Independence War and who had also sacrificed his popularity by pursuing political gain at the expense of political ethics,[1] served as a reminder to Zia of the limitations that existed on the exercise of power in Bangladesh. Zia's subsequent efforts to accommodate popular sentiment[2] therefore had a pervasive impact on the shaping of Bangladesh's foreign policy. This was exemplified by his early disassociation with Mujib's political affinities, opting instead for a government which espoused Islamic sentiments and sought closer ties with the international Islamic community. The change in tack was an obvious course for Zia, despite the anti-Pakistani, anti-Islamic sentiments which flourished during the Independence War. The widespread disapproval of Mujib's government had become directly tied to his pro-Indian policies and his attempts to instigate the principles of secularism and socialism, goals which were modelled on those of the Indian government.[3] In rejecting those goals in order to gain popular support, Zia had little option but to turn away from India as well.

The relationship between Bangladesh and India during Zia's regime therefore became characterised by the way in which that relationship shifted, in many respects, to the reverse of the one which existed previously under Mujib. Nevertheless, while a notable reworking of Bangladesh's foreign policy did occur, those changes were not clear-cut and did not necessarily mean that a fundamental change in Bangladeshi sentiments towards India had also arisen. The relative warmth existing between the two states during Mujib's regime could be described more accurately as a cooperative understanding reached between Indira Gandhi and Mujib, representing an affirmation of the essentially personal character of not only Bangladeshi, but also of South Asian politics generally.

Between 1971 and 1976, the Indian government had come to identify itself with Mujib and the Awami League, at the same time becoming accustomed to the benefits of having a grateful, agreeable leadership in neighbouring Bangladesh. The suspicions and misconceptions which existed between India and Pakistan before 1971 were scarcely kept in abeyance during

Mujib's regime. A significant reason why resentment against India had not been removed in Bangladesh, despite Indian assistance during the war, was that India had confiscated all the heavy military equipment after Pakistan's defeat in 1971, leaving Bangladesh in an extremely inferior military position.[4] This had been widely publicised in Bangladesh and had considerable psychological repercussions at the popular level. Not only were India's actions interpreted as emphasising the inferior status of the newly independent state, but also that India simply did not think much about Bangladesh's concerns. The Indian government certainly would have taken into consideration that a Bangladesh equipped with an arsenal of Pakistani weapons might become a genuine threat to Indian security .

Another important reason for residual Bangladeshi fears about Indian intentions was the legacy of the Indo–Bangladesh Friendship Treaty signed in March 1972, an agreement which was interpreted by many as giving India the right to interfere in Bangladesh's affairs simply if any group hostile to India should take over the Bangladesh government.[5] According to Lawrence Lifschultz:

> Anti-Indian sentiment had been growing in Bangladesh for more than three years. The Mujib government was under heavy attack for permitting and having itself been involved in widespread rackets, including border smuggling of rice and jute to India which many Bengalis believed had brought the economy to the edge of ruin. India's training and backing of the now defunct Rakkhi Bahini, Mujib's repressive paramilitary force, aroused resentment within the army, as did the failure of India to return fully four divisions of Pakistani weapons captured in the 1971 war.[6]

Zia, on his accession to power, therefore had ample scope for the exploitation of popular fears and sentiments concerning India, and had no hesitation in doing so.

The change in the character of Bangladesh's foreign policy after 1975 was not just a consequence of the change to a militarily-backed regime. Mujib's liaison with the Indian government, combined with his efforts to consolidate personal power via one-party rule,[7] were viewed by many Bangladeshis as a fundamental threat to the fledgling state's precarious territorial and cultural sovereignty. A military regime, even if a factionalised one, might therefore offer greater administrative discipline and stability for a state labouring under political and economic chaos.[8] It was perhaps closer to the truth to say that when Zia came to power, his attempts to exploit such concerns were driven as much by necessity as ambition, a predicament which in turn added to the complex nature of Bangladesh's foreign policy during his regime. In order to strengthen his own position of authority, Zia had little option but to initiate policies which would counteract Mujib's unpopular pro-Indian stance. A contradiction thus came to permeate Bangladesh's foreign policy. On the one hand was the effort to 'look outward'; to remove India from the centre of that policy; on the other was the continual, often testy interaction which was unavoidable with such a large, powerful neighbour whose sphere of interests encompassed the entire South Asian region, and more importantly, whose approval of the new Bangladesh government was lacking. The difficulty which this contradiction presents for historical analysis is reflected in the writings on Bangladesh's relations with India during this period. Opinions fluctuate between one which stresses the complete reversal in Bangladesh's foreign policy and the other which considers that Zia made every effort to maintain harmonious relations with India. These differing approaches are represented by the following opinions.

> After the initial travails, Ziaur Rahman demonstrated a strong desire to keep the extremists at bay and to have good relations with India... In foreign policy, Ziaur Rahman charted a new course... [b]ut he refused to adopt an anti-Indian posture.[9]

> One remarkable feature of Bangladeshi foreign policy in the 1970s has been the shift of India from the centre to a negligent place within the foreign policy framework of Bangladesh... Once viewed as the greatest friend and ally of Bangladesh, India seemed to have become something like a hostile entity entertaining expansionist designs and hegemonic ambitions.[10]

> Zia's regime gave its closest attention to the problems of the subcontinent, and especially to those with India.[11]

Regardless of Zia's intentions towards India, the deep-seated distrust of India existing in Bangladesh meant that the removal of either Mujib or Mrs Gandhi from power would almost certainly upset the precarious harmony which had been established. In other words, the post-1975 shift in relations was not just a consequence of Zia's plans for augmenting personal power. The souring of relations had already begun with Mujib's assassination, but the deterioration was much more conspicuous once Zia sought control of the Bangladesh government, particularly as his triumph involved crushing a short-lived coup on 3 November by what were regarded as pro-Mujib, pro-Awami League forces.[12] The reasons for the failure of these forces, led by Khalid Musharraf, to win sufficient support would not have been lost on Zia. Within 48 hours of making his bid for power, Khalid Musharraf had been labelled as 'India's man' and what was even more damning, rumours had begun to circulate that India was about to invoke the Friendship Treaty to intervene on Khalid Musharraf's behalf.[13] Whatever course Zia took, it could not be one which would appear in Bangladesh as pro-Indian.

It is difficult to assess the potential for violence in Indo–Bangladesh relations after the November coups, but the escalation in tension was considerable. Political links had quickly moved away from the degree of measured cooperation which existed during Mujib's regime, a pragmatic cordiality which has been described thus:

> the period of Mujib's rule was one of careful negotiation... with the Indian government doing its best to avoid any serious confrontation but not prepared to budge on fundamental issues, and with the Bangladesh government determined to defend its interests very strongly.[14]

This explanation points to a level of maturity and stability having been attained in Bangladesh's relations with India, but it also indicates that those relations were finely balanced. Even Sheikh Mujib had to make some effort to appear independent of India, but for both Mujib and Zia, some degree of dependency on Bangladesh's larger and more powerful neighbour was unavoidable.

A multitude of domestic and external reasons, some more influential than others, played a part in the reversal of Indo–Bangladesh relations after 1975. From a focus on domestic influences in the policy shifts, it would appear that Zia's attempts to fulfil his ambitions did play an important role. The particular combination of Zia's attempt to consolidate his position and Mrs Gandhi's antagonism towards his regime meant that until Indira lost the March 1977 election, diplomatic relations between Bangladesh and India were cold and blunt. Rhetoric, word-sparring and, at times, open border hostilities all reflected the concerns of both leaders to be seen by their respective home audiences as acting consistently with espoused political goals. Just as Zia could not afford to be seen as following in Mujib's footsteps or adopting a conciliatory stance towards India, neither could Indira Gandhi be seen to be conciliatory towards a military regime which was opposed to Mujib's goals. Mujib's political aspirations interlocked neatly with those of the Indian government.

From an international as well as a domestic perspective, Zia's concerns were tied to his determination to acquire public support and legitimise his position by instituting what would appear to be a democratic rather than a military style of government. Seeking political legitimacy would bolster attempts to secure support from the powerful and wealthy United States, and building a democratic facade over a military foundation also offered a means of circumventing or dissipating the demands of the highly politicised and faction-ridden Bangladesh military.[15] The situation was complicated by the public disillusionment with Mujib who, in banning all political parties but his own, was widely considered to have compromised his espoused democratic ideals. In distancing himself from the memory of Mujib's failings, Zia was at pains to reassure Bangladeshis that his democracy would be genuine, informing them that although 'in the past their rights were taken away in the name of democracy', his political programme was for 'economic development of the country' and he would 'not allow anybody to use it for personal benefit'.[16] Zia's determination and efforts to establish the framework of a democratic political structure were considerable, being manifested in the holding of a presidential referendum in May 1977, a presidential election in June 1978, the formation of his own political party in September 1978, and the holding of parliamentary elections in February 1979. Nevertheless, Zia's grand pledge that he would 'take the democracy to every nook and corner of the country and...lay its root deep into the heart of the people so that it...[could] make a permanent place on the soil of Bangladesh'[17] contrasted sharply with the reality of his emasculation of democratic procedure in the government.

The essentially authoritarian, military nature of Zia's rule was best exemplified by the content of the 1979 Fifth Amendment to the Bangladesh Constitution, which effectively subordinated Parliament to the will of the President.[18] By protracting and manipulating democratic processes, Zia followed a path similar to that of many other military leaders who had sought legitimacy without relinquishing power. Former leaders of Pakistan, Ayub Khan and Yahya Khan, were typical examples.[19] In keeping with the methods used by both these military leaders to secure their positions was the necessity, ironically, for Zia to subdue potentially substantial political opposition before he could venture into the realm of democratic polity. His need to crush the most powerful sources of opposition had direct and significant repercussions on Bangladesh's relations with India.

The major obstacles to Zia's plans for political control and consolidation were the Awami League, faction-ridden and reduced in prestige because of its former tie with Mujib, but nevertheless the largest and most powerful opposition party, and the leftist party, the *Jatiyo Samajtantrik Dal* (JSD), the latter conditionally providing Zia with the opportunity to take control of the government in the November 7 sepoy rebellion and coup.[20] Both of these parties had powerful military fronts with enormous potential to undermine Zia's position in the government and in the armed forces. Zia therefore had to ensure that both the Awami League and the JSD were brought into line. This involved manipulation or imprisonment of their leaders, and even execution in the case of Abu Taher, the mastermind of the 7 November coup and Zia's most powerful rival.[21] Subjugation of the pro-Mujib elements in the military, as well as the suppression of former members of Mujib's private, loyal and ruthless paramilitary force, the *Jatiyo Rakkhi Bahini*, (JRB) proved more of a challenge for Zia as these pro-Mujib individuals had fled into India after Mujib's assassination. The former JRB members had forged a close relationship with the Indian military,[22] and hence turned to India rather than serve those who had been responsible for or failed to prevent Mujib's assassination. By fleeing to India, forces loyal to Mujib were able to receive sanctuary and military training from the Indian government and, in turn, launch a potentially powerful guerrilla campaign against Zia's regime.

In attempting to undermine remaining public support for these groups in Bangladesh, Zia drew upon an assortment of stereotypical and highly emotive images. These were given additional weight when combined with allusions to Indian hegemonistic designs, as exemplified by the following statement by Zia:

> Our aim is to re-establish democracy in the country through...free and fair elections...We will not tolerate any interference from any quarter that can create obstacles in the way of fulfilment of this aim...Certain circles forgetting their past misdeeds, are engaged in trying to join hands with the forces opposed to [the] country's sovereignty. These elements have clearly indicated that they are active with the help of external forces...Foreign agents engaged in conspiracy against our independence are warned that the heroic people of Bangladesh would frustrate all their evil designs. There is no place for Mirzafars[23] on our soil. Find out the Mirzafars and foreign agents and cooperate in inflicting adequate punishment on them. Allah is with us.[24]

The forcefulness of this rhetoric illustrates not only that Zia was determined to retain his new-found hold on power in Bangladesh, even to the point of antagonising the Indian government, but also that his dominant position was, in reality, a very tenuous one. The combination of Zia's efforts to expunge the threat to his authority, and the Indian government's continued assistance to the pro-Mujib guerrillas, therefore ensured that the politically tense state which arose between Bangladesh and India after Mujib's demise would, at best, continue.

Because of Zia's efforts to assert his authority and subdue the border raids of the Mujibist guerrillas, the possibility of violent conflict occurring, if only at a low level, between Bangladesh and India remained high throughout the first year of Zia's regime. Zia's particular determination to round up the 'miscreants', as they were called, and India's refusal to hand them over, quickly established a pattern of relations between the two states whereby the ready resort to an orchestrated show of force rather than diplomacy was the preferred option. Zia's diplomatic skills were to be used to great advantage in the international realm, but in bilateral relations with India, his greatest concern was to be regarded at home as a vigorous protector of Bangladesh's independence, avoiding any conciliatory actions reminiscent of Mujib's pro-Indian stance.

The reality of India's military superiority did not mean that Zia would refrain from making at least some provocative or aggressive military moves against the larger state. During the first year of Zia's rule, savage skirmishes occurred on the Indo–Bangladesh border.[25] The degree of violence involved appeared to act as a precedent for the border delineation disputes which became prominent after late 1979. The proven readiness of both sides to resort to military action ensured that those later challenges to what was regarded by the inhabitants of Bangladesh as the state's territorial integrity and sovereign rights would be potentially explosive. The political sparring and manoeuvres carried out by the Bangladesh and Indian governments during the first year of Zia's regime exhibited variations in the character of interaction between the two states. On a superficial level, the leaders of both states brought forth the rhetoric and military posturing which would tally with popular expectations and therefore provide domestic political profit. On another level, some attempt was made by both sides to be seen to be making an effort to resolve disputes, giving a limited degree of stability to Indo–Bangladesh relations.[26]

The pattern of action of both governments concerning the border skirmishes showed little variation while Mrs Gandhi remained in power. Even after 12 months of intermittent border conflicts involving largely the Bangladeshi 'miscreants' and the Bangladesh Rifles, the governments of both states were making declarations virtually identical to those made when Zia first came to power and had sought to round up those pro-Mujib activists who had sheltered under the Indian umbrella.[27] Zia's persistent attempts to quell the border activities of the pro-Indian, pro-Mujib guerrillas made a significant contribution towards establishing the redirection in Indo–Bangladesh diplomatic relations. Compromise and cordiality were replaced by political rhetoric and limited military engagements, both of which reflected the domestic concerns of the two state leaders. Militarily, neither side appeared willing to take matters too far, resulting in a political stalemate which had little chance of resolution, at least while Mrs Gandhi and Ziaur Rahman both remained leaders of their respective states.

The post-1975 tension in Indo–Bangladesh political rapport was nevertheless significant. It was closely associated with Zia's determination to strengthen his tenuous political position and, at the same time, to implement his chosen political programme. This shift in the relationship can be better understood against the domestic political background existing in Bangladesh. The deterioration in Indo–Bangladesh relations after 1975 may be interpreted as a reflection of the traditionally unstable character of East Bengali/Bangladeshi politics, the deep-seated factionalism within the Bangladesh military and the legacy of Mujib's treatment of the armed forces and the civil service.

If Zia was to survive politically, then it was imperative that he make every effort to assuage the resentment and disaffection which Mujib had created during his four-year rule. The factionalism which pervaded the military was an additional, but fundamental problem for Zia, one which had been exacerbated, rather than spawned by Mujib's policies. Rivalry within the Bangladesh armed forces was particularly pronounced after the Independence War, because those personnel who had been detained in Pakistan for the duration of the war had to be reabsorbed afterwards, into an army which differed greatly from the one they had known before the war. The victorious Bangladesh liberation army, the *Mukti Bahini*, had emerged with a distinctly leftist orientation, because many of those who had volunteered to join were politically motivated students and labourers who were steeped in the secular, socialist notions of Mujib's Awami League and the more leftist political parties.[28] After the war, the Bangladesh army therefore contained two distinct and mutually antagonistic groups: the 'returnees', who were generally higher-ranking, formally trained and ideologically conservative military personnel who naturally presumed they would reoccupy their positions of authority within the army, regardless of whether or not they had actually fought in the war. The other faction consisted of the more radical *Mukti Bahini*, the 'freedom fighters', who had played such an important role in the emergence of Bangladesh and therefore expected to be recompensed with positions of authority and responsibility within the post-independence military. Zia himself had an affinity with both groups, being a skilled and disciplined army officer who had participated in the war, commanding and training large numbers of freedom fighters, and in the process being exposed to leftist ideology.[29]

Maintaining control of the government of Bangladesh was very much a case of first controlling the politicised armed forces, hence Mujib's strengthening of his own trusted paramilitary force. In patronising this elite force, Mujib added significantly to the dissatisfaction and low morale of the remaining armed forces. Being an army officer, Zia's power base was much more of a military one than that of a civilian politician like Mujib, but one which, if not kept on a tight rein, would be very unstable. The armed forces were riddled with factionalism, and they were divided fundamentally into two irreconcilable camps. Although Zia was himself a freedom fighter, it was virtually unacceptable, because of prevailing anti-Mujib and associated anti-Indian sentiments, that Zia's military support base after the 7 November coup should be comprised of forces which had once fought a war in Mujib's name. Even Abu Taher, who fought in the war but came to condemn Mujib for his dictatorial actions, acknowledged the way in which Mujib had received universal Bangladeshi civil and military support during the Independence War:

> It was really tragic and painful to see Sheikh Mujibur Rahman, the leading personality among the founders of this state, emerge as a dictator. Mujib in his chequered political career had never compromised with autocracy or dictatorship. He was once the symbol of democracy and the national independence movement. With all his shortcomings, he was the only leader who had links with the masses and who had a broad base among the masses ... It is the people who glorified Mujib and magnified his image as a hero ... The very name of Mujib was a war cry in our Independence War. Sheikh Mujib was the leader of the masses. To deny this is to deny a fact.[30]

The aftermath of the 7 November coup, in which Zia found it necessary to subdue the extremist JSD,[31] would have provided Zia with ample confirmation that any attempt to wield power or administer largely via those who had been part of the *Mukti Bahini* would be difficult and dangerous at best.

The character of Indo–Bangladesh relations in the first months of Zia's regime was therefore shaped, to some extent, by the turmoil of domestic politics in Bangladesh and Zia's determination to strengthen his tenuous hold on power. With strong opposition coming from the secular, socialist groups, the JSD and the Awami League, Zia's choice of political direction was narrowed to one which inclined towards the remaining groups, more specifically towards those which were based on an Islamic platform. This direction was to allow the Muslim League and Islamic groups to prosper, the very groups which had been earlier discredited, pilloried or banned for their failure to support the struggle for Bangladesh's independence or their outright support of the Pakistan army. Even Maulana Bhashani, the socialist peasant leader of the pro-Chinese National Awami Party, whose popularity and influence had declined since independence, found Zia's Islamic umbrella to be a congenial one; one which perhaps offered him a better chance of implementing his own recipe for revolution in Bangladesh: 'Islamic Socialism'.[32] The same choice of Islamic direction also applied in Zia's attempts to establish military backing, whereby the essentially conservative and Islamic returnees were considered to be more supportive and controllable than the less militarily disciplined, leftist *Mukti Bahini*, despite Zia's historical affiliation with the latter group.

To gain further support, Zia worked to resurrect the ineffectual and faction-ridden civil service which, like the Islamic parties, carried the stigma of collaboration with the Pakistan government before and during the war.[33] The bureaucracy had been further undermined after independence by Mujib and his associates who purposefully acted to restrict its power and autonomy,[34] creating in the process a large disgruntled group from which Zia was later able to cultivate much-needed support. Again, in seeking that support, Zia was prepared to rely upon those who were either lacking in political influence or exceedingly unpopular in Bangladesh. The efforts required to make them acceptable to the Bangladeshi populace resulted in a fundamental redirection of domestic politics and, in turn, of foreign policy.

The civil and military backing which Zia acquired therefore represented an assortment of groups which seemed to have had little in common apart from their lack of mass appeal. In also sharing an antagonism towards Mujib and the Awami League, Zia's supporters could hope to counteract popular disapproval. That antagonism had become very widespread in Bangladesh, due to Mujib's failure to fulfil promises of social, economic and political reform and because of the increasingly undemocratic, dynastic character of his regime. Nevertheless, such disillusionment alone was not considered sufficient by Zia to guarantee public acceptance of those to whom he had offered patronage. An additional problem for Zia was the possibility that the extreme right-wing religious and military groups might prove to be even more difficult to control than those of the left. In order to win popular approval for himself and for those who were encouraged to participate in the new regime, Zia promoted the Islamic nature of his administration. This was done in a moderate fashion,[35] appealing to the Islamic traditions of Bangladesh's vast, poverty-stricken rural population, but, at the same time, aiming to keep the more extreme Islamic parties in check.[36] A simple appeal to Islamic sentiments to promote unity and support would also resemble too closely the Pakistan government's attempts to do likewise before the war. Zia's answer was to combine his Islamic exhortations with images of 'Bangladeshi' nationalism, an emphasis tailored to replace the emotive, unifying force which Mujib's appeals to Bengali consciousness had provided in the creation of Bangladesh but which had subsequently lost their relevance once independence was achieved. Zia began to promote his formula for national unity within a few months of his rise to power:

> Let us all [be] Bangladeshi first and Bangladeshi last...[L]ast year's development had clearly brought out our national identity and direction that the people of the country want...Our heritage and cultural traditions which are distinct by its character must find full play in all our activities. Our goal is to make our nation strong. It must be achieved through unity, discipline, patriotism, dedication and hard work and consolidation of nationalistic spirit.[37]

Zia was also drawing a clear distinction between the Bengali culture of India and that of Bangladesh through his emphasis on the uniqueness of Bangladeshi culture. His intention was to promote national unity, but his move also represented a rejection of traditional Indian cultural links, adding to the increasing tension between the two states. On the same day as he delivered the above statement, Zia also made a moral appeal to Bangladeshis to follow the teachings of the Prophet Muhammad in the 'true spirit',[38] an entreaty vague enough to allow Zia ample scope for manipulation of public sentiments. The dual combination of appeals to Bangladeshi cultural distinctiveness and to pan-Islamic sentiments provided Zia with a potent rallying point, taking advantage of underlying anti–Hindu sentiments. It also imparted a communal tone to Indo–Bangladesh relations, contributing towards long-term adverse repercussions for Hindu–Muslim unity within Bangladesh. Zia's Islamic emphasis also ensured that a secular pro-Indian political party such as the Awami League would have a guaranteed source of support from minority groups within Bangladesh. Nevertheless, Zia's political vulnerability and restricted manoeuvrability on gaining control of the government meant that such a traditionally effective political tactic as appealing to religious sentiments would seem an attractive one to pursue.

By May 1976, the direction of Bangladesh's foreign policy and Zia's public stand towards the Indian government were firmly in place:

Dear brothers and sisters, our people seek justice which emanates from Allah, and they must get their justice otherwise the people will fight for it... We want to practise our respective religion and to live under the umbrella of religion. This government of yours is determined to satisfy this requirement of the people... A handful of miscreants in our country are carrying on loot and plunder in the villages... So I want to tell you that the entire nation has to be determined to root out and destroy these miscreants [who]... claim to bring independence with foreign help... We do not want to interfere in the internal affairs of others. Likewise we want that no other country will interfere in the internal affairs of Bangladesh... We have religious, historical and cultural relations with all the Muslim countries of the world and we want to further our relations with them... If there is aggression on us the seven and a half-crore people of this country will rise to one man and resist it and defend the independence.[39]

Zia made an effective scapegoat of the Indian government by combining accusations of territorial aggression with the cry of 'Islam in danger'. This strategy not only deflected domestic criticism of his actions, but it also reinforced the notion of Bangladeshi nationalism which he was attempting to foster. Zia's ultimate aim was to accrue political prestige within Bangladesh and political leverage in the international arena. Zia risked long-term consequences, such as communal conflict and Indian retaliation, by cultivating such images of India, but his primary concerns on gaining power were immediate and domestic, requiring considerable political astuteness to maintain that power. Zia also had the advantage of being in a position to learn by Mujib's mistakes. Mujib and the Awami League had failed partly because they did not offer firm direction in the consolidation of a national identity for the people of Bangladesh. Mujib's emphasis on Bengali nationalism was easily construed as pro-Indian. At the same time, he could not renounce his secular position to exploit the potential force of Islam without suggesting that the 'division of 'Islamic' Bangladesh from 'Islamic' Pakistan' had been a mistake.[40] The difficulty in finding an appropriate focus for national identity 'pointed to a Bangladesh unlikely to look for Indian guidance'.[41] In resolving the dilemma and, in turn, rallying sufficient political and popular support, Zia's most advantageous strategy was to replace Mujib's unsuccessful form of secular government with one styled along Islamic lines. It was largely because of the necessity for Zia to find a more appealing and unifying formula for national identity that the orientation of Bangladesh's foreign policy shifted away from India towards the Islamic states.

In his efforts to forge a new national identity for the inhabitants of Bangladesh, Zia was attempting to grapple with a problem which had been in place since the growth of Muslim separatist politics in Bengal in the nineteenth century. A simple appeal to extra-territorial notions of Islamic ideology and unity would, as demonstrated clearly by the rise of the East Bengali language movement after 1947, have been unlikely to have succeeded unless such an appeal had also sought to accommodate the opposite pull of allegiance to an indigenous Bengali culture which transcended religious affiliations. According to Asim Roy, 'the history of Bengal Muslims is, in a very real sense, a history of a perennial crisis of identity'.[42] Such a description may be apt as a long-term view of Bengali Muslim political history, but at the same time, it should not obscure the significance and influence of particular circumstances, such as Mujib's experimentation with a secular form of government, which has been summed up thus:

[In 1975], [t]he period of aberration in Bangladeshi polity under Sheikh Mujibur Rahman was over, but there was a price which had to be paid. Part of that price was the yielding of illusions. Some were cast away lightly enough, for they were already based on ideals which had already taken a battering under Awami League rule. Secularism no longer meant anything in Bangladesh. Socialism had not worked, and there was no popular enthusiasm (and certainly no official encouragement) to rekindle the experiment... When Ziaur Rahman came to power, Bangladeshis were, if not baffled about what was expected of them in terms of political identity, then certainly disillusioned by the meagre results of the search. With the destruction of ideals by the activities of men on whom great faith had been bestowed, did the only hope of salvation lie in faith in God?[43]

Given the difficulty in resolving the problems associated with the issue of national identity in Bangladesh, it was therefore not surprising that it should have come to impinge on Indo–Bangladesh relations. The close cultural ties between the two states meant that the 'uniqueness' of Bangladesh had the least opportunity for expression and the very *raison d'être* of Bangladesh could have been open to question. Zia's efforts to cater to perennial Bangladeshi concerns regarding national identity represented a typical example of the way in which long-term domestic influences as well as immediate, personal domestic compulsions combined to provide foreign policy direction.

Perhaps the most significant step taken by Zia to establish that direction, one which diverged markedly from Mujib's pro-Indian path, was to dispose of the secular orientation of the Bangladesh constitution and substitute an Islamic one instead. Secularism was deleted as one of the fundamental principles of state policy in favour of an Islamic emphasis in a constitutional amendment announced in April 1977:

> The principles of absolute trust and faith in the Almighty Allah, nationalism, democracy and socialism meaning economic and social justice, together with the principles derived from them as set out in this Part, shall constitute the fundamental principles of state policy... Absolute trust and faith in the Almighty Allah shall be the basis of all actions.[44]

In addition, the phrase: 'Bismillah-ar-Rahman-ar-Rahim (in the name of Allah, the Beneficent, the Merciful)' was to be inserted at the beginning of the constitution. In keeping with Zia's plans to foster a more readily acceptable and more easily recognisable notion of national identity, the constitution was also modified so that the inhabitants of Bangladesh should henceforth officially be called 'Bangladeshis' rather than 'Bengalees'.[45] The latter description carried an Indian connotation which had, perhaps within months of Bangladesh's independence, become inappropriate. Even more specifically relevant to Indo–Bangladesh relations was the addition of the following clause to the constitution: '[t]he State shall endeavour to consolidate, preserve and strengthen fraternal relations among Muslim countries based on Islamic solidarity.'[46] Zia's political position was a precarious one, but in little over a year of gaining control of the Bangladesh government, he was able to strengthen that position somewhat by giving an official, legal and constitutional face to the state's Islamic orientation and redirected foreign policy.

In doing so, the benefits for Zia in consolidating his regime were considerable. First and foremost, he was able to demonstrate clearly to all that he would not be following in the disgraced Awami League's secularist footsteps. Zia could not only tap into the unifying strength of a religious and moral foundation by instituting his reforms via the constitution, but he could also be seen to be acting in some accordance with democratic procedure. The opportunity to couch his criticisms of political adversaries in anti-Islamic, pro-Indian terms was also useful, as typified by his following statement:

> [T]he real Muslim should have to be [a] patriot and should have love for the people and soil. One who is engaged in subversive activities against the state and the people with the assistances from a foreign power cannot be a real Muslim.[47]

In essence, Zia was creating a political environment which would be least conducive to the reestablishment and nurturing of Awami League and JSD strength. In the process, he restricted any redevelopment of close diplomatic ties with the Indian government, extending a diplomatic hand of friendship to the Islamic states instead. Those Islamic states represented an appropriate, alternative source of political, moral and economic support from that which had been provided beforehand, largely by the Indian government. Throughout his regime, Zia worked via diplomacy and the cultivating of Islamic values within Bangladesh to reinforce links with all the Islamic states,[48] the initiative for such an orientation being clearly linked to his need to establish political strength in Bangladesh. The brief, but revealing quote above also illustrates the tenor of Zia's Islamic message: one which tempered and modified a direct religious appeal with sentiments associated with Bangladeshi territorial and cultural pride.

The shift away from an Indian focus during Zia's regime can also be interpreted through a domestic, economic perspective. In evaluating the importance of economic pressures upon Zia's choice of foreign policy direction, it is worthwhile to examine the extent to which Zia's strong stand against India might be driven by economic considerations as well. As explained above, Zia's Islamic emphasis was an essential ingredient of his political platform, providing him with much-needed political strength and legitimacy in Bangladesh. Nevertheless, the lure of economic advantage, to be gained by taking an Islamic stance and reaping the benefits of a hitherto largely untapped source of international financial aid would have played some part in Zia's choice of foreign policy direction. There is no doubt that, initially, an enormous increase in financial support from Islamic states was provided to Bangladesh after Zia took control of the government. Aid from Muslim countries jumped from US$78.9 million between 1971 and 1975 to US$232 million between 1976 and 1979. For the shorter period between 1980 and 1981, the amount received increased to US$242.4 million.[49]

The domestic economic problems faced by Bangladesh throughout its history have been vast. To some degree these must be considered as a perennial influence upon the state's foreign policy dealings. The particular severity of the problem of poverty in Bangladesh[50] can be explained in terms which were noted in Chapter 1. These included Bangladesh's comparatively underdeveloped and weak political structure, and in particular, the state having to undergo the process of extrication from colonial domination and exploitation not once, but twice, as expressed in the following comment: 'For a people to have to build a new state from scratch is unfortunate. To have to do so twice in 25 years seems almost extravagant.'[51] Not only have political processes in Bangladesh been doubly disadvantaged compared with other ex-colonial states, but so too has economic development, resulting in extreme economic dependency in the international arena.[52] The unceasing quest for foreign aid, the corollary of such dire domestic poverty, has been described, in Bangladesh's case, as a vital component in foreign policy formulation: '[t]he simple fact is that time could be wasted arguing the merits and demerits of accepting foreign aid, whilst the reality that it has become one cornerstone of the Bangladesh economy and, by extension, of Bangladesh's foreign policy, is ignored.'[53] According to E. Ahamed's

interpretation, foreign aid, foreign policy and domestic policy are insepar-
able in Bangladesh:

> 'Foreign and domestic policy must be mutually supporting if national
> policy aspirations are to be achieved in an atmosphere of political
> stability.' But perhaps nowhere this dictum seems more true than in Ban-
> gladesh where almost 60 per cent of the annual budget and nearly 80 per
> cent of the development budget is financed by external assistance. In
> Bangladesh, foreign policy really begins at home. Each year the domestic
> policy makers appraise the foreign policy makers of the amount of for-
> eign aid which would be needed for that year.[54]

The existence of such extreme economic difficulties in Bangladesh has
dictated that an equally harsh pragmatism must permeate decision-making
in economic development; extremes which correlate with those of the political arena. In both economic and political spheres, therefore, either group or
individual self-interest has tended to prevail, a characteristic which could
also be regarded as the common ground between the political and economic
realms. This intrinsic link between political and economic concerns becomes
particularly obvious when considering the social and political elite class in
Bangladesh, as has been explained thus:

> In a state constantly gripped by economic uncertainty, burgeoning popu-
> lation growth and the omnipresent threat of massive natural or human
> induced disaster, the accumulation of money is an overwhelming pre-
> occupation, from top to bottom of the society. Those who have wealth
> have access to political influence and power if they want either or both.
> Those who desire both wealth and political power and do not have either
> see the political process as the quickest and easiest means of gaining
> them both. Those who fail to acquire wealth generally have neither polit-
> ical power nor access to it.[55]

Considering the nexus between wealth and political power in Bangladesh, it
is not surprising that economic pragmatism and expediency should coexist
with, and at times outweigh, equally pragmatic current political rhetoric.

Zia's search for foreign aid had deleterious consequences for Indo–Bangladesh relations, resulting in a coincidental reinforcement of the political
pressures already souring relations between the two states. Once Mujib was
removed from power, along with his strong sense of obligation towards
Indira Gandhi's government, there existed a far greater degree of flexibility
for the Bangladesh government, not only in forging diplomatic relations,
but also in obtaining foreign aid.[56] Zia's eclectic and pragmatic approach to
seeking foreign aid is typified by his statement made to the United Nations
in 1980:

Somebody has got to say this first, . . . [s]o we say it. Where lie the surpluses? They lie with OPEC, the socialist countries and the West. All these three groups should share the effort of developing the least developed.[57]

The most lucrative sources of aid for Bangladesh, the United States and the prospering, oil-producing Middle East states,[58] were also countries with which Mrs Gandhi's government and its pro-Soviet Union orientation had little rapport.[59] In addition, Zia's overtures to the West were readily reciprocated. The stamp of approval is obvious in the following comment made in *The Times*, which lauded the 'inspired general fighting a nation's apathy':

Bangladesh is beginning to haul itself up by its bootstraps, and no one is tugging harder than Zia ur-Rahman, who was at the heart of the liberation struggle, emerged as leader after the coups of 1975 and has been President for almost four years . . . He is an expert communicator, has done more than anyone to improve the lot of women and tries to educate his people politically. There has also been a grain surplus this year . . . In a country where corruption is embedded he is Mr Clean. There is no whiff of corruption about him and he has a horror of nepotism.[60]

The broadening and expansion of diplomatic and economic ties instigated by Zia and his regime provided an additional ingredient in the deterioration of Indo–Bangladesh relations after 1975. This was especially so when such ties also came to include those of a more disquieting nature for the Indian government: improved Bangladeshi diplomatic relations with Indian arch rivals, Pakistan[61] and China.[62]

Another economic development occurring within Bangladesh, after Zia came to power, contributed towards the distancing between Bangladesh and India: his campaign to reduce the flourishing smuggling trade between the two states. The economically disastrous post-independence years during Mujib's regime had encouraged the smuggling trade, an activity which drained the state financially,[63] and which was regarded in Bangladesh as being fostered by India since the latter was seen as the primary beneficiary.[64] By clamping down on smuggling activities, identifying them as a symptom of Indian interference, Zia appeased in the short term, but also reinforced, deep-seated Bangladeshi fears of Hindu economic exploitation. His declarations that 'the people of Bangladesh had achieved liberation through armed struggle for their economic emancipation and progress',[65] and that 'the corrupt elements, smugglers and miscreants were the enemies of the nation' were aimed at much more than simply attempting to remedy Bangladesh's economic plight, representing, rather, a skilful political manipulation of the Bangladeshi populace. By placing the smuggling trade in the same categories as the pro-Indian 'miscreant' forces and Indian domination, he could appear to be salving economic problems, but at the same time strengthening his power base by associating his opponents with corrupt practices. Zia's personal reputation for material austerity and financial incorruptibility no doubt further heightened the contrast he wished to cultivate between himself and his foes. He also made at least some impression on reducing the pervasive smuggling activities,[66] but the political overtones of his campaign added to the deterioration in Indo–Bangladesh relations.

It can be shown that the economic orientation of Zia's regime contributed towards the distancing between Bangladesh and India, but economic interests also ensured that at least some bounds would keep the antagonism between the two in check. Examination of Indo–Bangladesh economic relations during Zia's regime reveals that economic links operated in a sphere which, in some ways, can be regarded as independent of that in which Zia's political predicament required an anti-Indian stand. A statistical account of trade between Bangladesh and India does show that an overall decline occurred during Zia's regime, as illustrated in Table 5.1 concerning Indo–Bangladesh trade between 1973 and 1981:

Table 5.1   **Bangladesh's imports from and exports to India, 1973–81 (million US dollars)**

	1973	1974	1975	1976	1977	1978	1979	1980	1981
Import	114.8	82.0	83.3	62.7	48.9	43.0	40.0	55.6	64.0
Export	23.3	0.4	5.3	7.1	0.6	2.3	12.1	8.0	20.2

Source: United Nations. Economic and Social Commission for Asia and the Pacific, *Statistical Yearbook for Asia and the Pacific: 1982*, Bangkok, n.d., p. 94.

These statistics show that a reduction in trade with India began after 1973, prompting questions as to why it occurred. C.J. Gulati interprets the above statistics as being proof that the fluctuations in economic relations between India and Bangladesh were largely politically driven, concluding that the 'political turmoil in Bangladesh and friction-ridden Indo–Bangladesh relations have obstructed worthwhile [economic] cooperation'.[67] While the statistical evidence seems to imply that economic relations between India and Bangladesh have been moulded by Bangladesh's domestic political strife, the link becomes less clear when other possible causes are considered. A reduction in trade between the two states could be explained in a variety of ways, apart from being perceived as largely a reflection of political necessity and diplomatic reorientation deriving mostly from Bangladesh. The dictates of economic pragmatism in poverty-stricken Bangladesh also played an integral part, or, as expressed by Rehman Sobhan, 'the compulsion of needs and politics did not always fully coincide'.[68] As noted above, Ziaur Rahman sought more lucrative and assured economic ties for Bangladesh, particularly by approaching the United States and the OPEC states.[69] The difficulties in establishing stable and mutually beneficial economic relations between Bangladesh and India had already become apparent during Mujib's regime,[70] so it was not surprising that Zia sought additional options for the economic development of Bangladesh. India's substantial post-war aid to Bangladesh[71] and Indian efforts to bolster Bangladesh's economy during Mujib's regime could not be sustained indefinitely, especially as both states had competing major exports, such as jute and tea.[72] The political motive for India to ensure the fledgling state's viability by providing economic support also played a considerable part in creating an early impression of firm economic relations between the two.[73] In addition to the inevitable decline in Indian economic assistance, Bangladesh's post-liberation expectations of substantial economic assistance from the USSR were unfulfilled, thereby further encouraging a return to pre-Independence economic links which were traditionally based outside the Indo–Soviet sphere.[74]

The deterioration in economic links between India and Bangladesh had already begun before Ziaur Rahman came to power, the fluctuations and decline resulting from a wide variety of causes. Once Zia came to power, efforts to develop economic cooperation between Bangladesh and India were not abandoned, and in contrast to the political friction occurring between the two states after Zia's coup, a substantial trade agreement was signed between the two countries in January 1976. Under this agreement, the three-year decline in trade between the two states was to be reversed and the trade imbalance reduced, with India agreeing to supply coal at a cheaper price than before, and to increase its imports of jute, fish and newsprint from Bangladesh.[75] The signing of such an accommodating agreement,[76] at a time when political events occurring in Bangladesh were prompting an angry and indignant response from the Indian government, meant that the tension between the two states was not as deep-seated as it appeared, being manifested to a greater extent in the form of political rhetoric.

Under the Janata regime,[77] which portrayed itself as more accommodating towards the neighbouring states than Mrs Gandhi had been, further trade concessions were made by India to Bangladesh in 1978, following the 1976 Bangkok Agreement on trade expansion and economic cooperation among the developing countries of the Economic and Social Commission for Asia and the Pacific (ESCAP). At talks held in Dhaka in June 1978, India accepted almost all the import and export modifications proposed by the Bangladesh government.[78] Even after Mrs Gandhi returned to power in 1980, trading links between the two states did not appear to suffer a marked deterioration. Another three-year trade agreement between India and Bangladesh was signed on 4 October 1980, one which was considered to fulfil 'the need for exploring all possibilities for expansion and promotion of mutually advantageous trade between the two countries'.[79] This agreement indicated that prevailing political tensions existing between Bangladesh and India, sufficient to receive international attention,[80] did not automatically put a stop to trading links between the two states.

Whether or not the trade agreements actually managed to solve, in the long term, some of the trading imbalance problems between the two states has little bearing on the fact that these developments could take place in the midst of politically antagonistic periods in Indo–Bangladesh relations. The difficulty in finding an obvious correlation between economic policy and domestic political pressures can be illustrated further by arguing that Mujib's pro-Indian Awami League regime, eventually synonymous to many in Bangladesh with corruption, smuggling and Indian economic exploitation, impaired Indo–Bangladesh relations.[81] By contrast, Ziaur Rahman's anti-Indian foreign policy stance acted to reduce the economically debilitating effects of smuggling, and did not prevent the fostering of some improvement in economic relations between Bangladesh and India. The interplay between political and economic interests and the repercussions for Indo–Bangladesh relations are therefore not easily clarified by a reliance upon statistical evidence.

While trade did continue to decline between Bangladesh and India after Zia came to power, it appears that economic relations were less a source of friction between the two states. The signing of the various trade agreements with India between 1976 and 1980 indicates that Zia's efforts to obtain financial aid from the United States[82] and the Middle East were driven more by economic necessity than by a determination to achieve a broad severance of ties with India. Zia's public sentiments were aimed at portraying an independent Bangladesh which was leaving India's fold, but at the same time, economic pressures also ensured that trading links between the two states continued to function despite foreign policy orientation and political rhetoric.

The push and pull of economic demands existing alongside political considerations in Indo–Bangladesh relations demonstrates that both political and economic aspirations and activities need to be taken into account in the broader assessment of those relations. The post-1975 trading agreements between Bangladesh and India indicate that while the antagonism which characterised relations after Zia's rise to power was considerable, the antipathy did not have the same dimensions as that which had evolved between India and Pakistan, despite Mrs Gandhi's tendency to interpret the 1975 military coups in Bangladesh as of Pakistani origin.[83] Whereas the history of tension between India and Pakistan dictated that both diplomatic and economic links between the two should be minimal, Bangladesh's economic plight, particularly after the 1974 famine, meant that economic needs would have been more likely to counter the political ambitions and strategies of the ruling elite. At the same time, attempting to find the economic determinants of Bangladesh's relations with India shows that political and economic considerations are impossible to separate clearly. The following comment by Henry Kissinger illustrates some of the possible reasons why the links between political and economic pressures in Bangladesh have been contradictory, blurred and difficult to define:

> But to the charismatic heads of many of the new nations, economic progress, while not unwelcome, offers too limited a scope for their ambitions. It can be achieved only by slow, painful, highly technical measures which contrast with the heroic exertions of the struggle for independence. Results are long delayed; credit for them cannot be clearly established... Economic advance disrupts the traditional political structure. It thus places constant pressures on the incumbent leaders to re-establish the legitimacy of their rule. For this purpose a dramatic foreign policy is particularly apt. Many leaders of the new countries seem convinced that an adventurous foreign policy will not harm prospects for economic development and may even foster it.[84]

An evaluation of the significance of domestic economic pressures upon Bangladesh's foreign policy re-emphasises the inadequacy of isolating a single aspect, such as Bangladesh's domestic turmoil, as having the greatest influence. Even applying a very broad definition of 'foreign policy', such as that which focuses on the drive for state self-preservation being of overriding concern, seems idealistic and inappropriate when considering the course of Indo–Bangladesh relations. According to E. Ahamed, Bangladesh's foreign policy can be defined thus:

> As it is true for all other states, self-preservation is the most vital interest of Bangladesh... [T]he question of self-preservation takes precedence to all other considerations in Bangladesh.[85]

Choosing to give precedence to this aspect, that of national self-interest, is a standard approach of many foreign policy studies. For a relatively new state such as Bangladesh, any challenge to its sovereignty, no matter how slight, has exaggerated importance to the inhabitants. Nevertheless, the precise meaning of the expression, 'state self-preservation', is unclear. The implication is that the state, as an entity, has a unity of purpose and a well developed political structure, a generalisation which cannot be sustained in the case of Bangladesh. In studying the preconditions which led to Ziaur Rahman's stand against the Indian government, the notion of self-preservation does appear to have played an important part, but more in a personal, individual sense. Zia's accession to power and the consolidation of his political position were achieved against very difficult odds. His early political options were restricted considerably as he attempted to manoeuvre between and eventually triumph over the various political and military factions, particularly those headed by the Awami League, Khalid Musharraf and Abu Taher.

Combined with Zia's struggle to achieve and maintain supremacy was also his sincere belief that his policies would help to solve Bangladesh's political and economic strife.

Individual political machinations and aspirations, such as those of Ziaur Rahman, have tended to reflect the inherent structure of Bangladeshi polity, where sudden changes of leadership, intense rivalry, factionalism, personality cults and the threat of assassination were, and still are, ever present. This invites the question of how much influence individual self-interest has over these entrenched characteristics. The following viewpoint provides one possible answer:

> [W]here the cult of personality predominates, the political parties themselves, even that of the leader, may be peripheral to the entire decision-making process. It may well be too, that the conceptions behind the ideas of the leader may not be very relevant, for real power-broking may circumvent ideas. Indeed, there is some argument for saying that leadership is somewhat irrelevant to Bangladeshi politics, except where leadership simply operates according to crudely pragmatic motives, such as is now occurring in Bangladesh. Given the strength of inherent features, there is a case to be made for this opinion.[86]

Given the notable shift in foreign policy direction once Zia came to power, it would be very difficult to discount the strength of his individual concerns and actions. At the same time, nevertheless, he was virtually compelled to follow a course dictated by the inherently unstable character of Bangladeshi polity. It is impossible to isolate any single political, economic or cultural determinant which is applicable to all aspects of Bangladesh's interstate relations. The aim of this chapter has been to illustrate the interacting pressures upon Indo–Bangladesh relations, and in so doing, to draw out the unique as well as the general characteristics of that relationship.

If the 'norm' in South Asian interstate relations can be described as linkages infused by enmity and rivalry, rather than amity,[87] then domestic political events succeeding Mujibur Rahman's assassination resulted emphatically in a reassertion of that norm. For a brief period, the Bangladesh and Indian governments had exhibited a semblance of compatibility in national outlook, a characteristic which quickly succumbed to a variety of divisive influences. Mujib himself played a part in refuelling Bengali Muslim fears of Indian interference by instituting an autocratic, corrupt and inefficient regime which was identified partly by its sense of indebtedness towards Indira Gandhi's government. Zia, on becoming leader of the Bangladesh government, was able to strengthen his precarious political position by exploiting Bangladeshi disillusionment with Mujib's regime and fostering long-standing fears and insecurities with regard to Indian dominance in South Asia. India provided Zia with the perfect scapegoat to absorb domestic discontent and turn it into an asset. Combining this political tactic with one which offered a firm direction in national identity, Zia was able to boost his popular appeal and offset some of the inherent weaknesses of his hold on power. He was also able, to a limited extent, to reduce the undermining effects of prevalent military and political factionalism in Bangladesh, and deflect criticism of misdemeanours perpetrated in the past by his political support groups.

The need for Zia to cultivate popular appeal was especially important in Bangladesh for a variety of reasons, quite apart from the ineffectual attempts to institute a genuinely democratic system of government. Perhaps the most significant reason was the widely politicised character of the population, particularly within the peasantry, student groups, the middle classes, the urban elite and the military. These groups had responded to the rallying efforts of Mujib and Maulana Bhashani in particular, over the previous two decades, and had played an important role in resisting the Pakistan forces in the Independence War. The messianic, hallowed status awarded to the most influential leaders of East Bengali politics, at least while at their peak of popularity, virtually dictated that Zia would also be placed in this mould and be bound by the expectations which accompanied it.

In a similar fashion, Indira Gandhi was limited by popular expectations and the strength of political tradition, which, in India, centred on ideological images of civilian rule, democracy, secularism and regional dominance. These images were reinforced when contrasted with Bangladesh's militaristic, authoritarian and communalist regime, which Mrs Gandhi perceived Zia's rule to be. Regardless of the necessity for both leaders to accommodate domestic political demands, Mrs Gandhi's position, backed by a well established political structure, was relatively secure compared with that of Zia. Despite this advantage, not to mention that of overwhelming military supremacy, the Indian government's public reactions of bellicosity and suspicion towards Zia's regime apparently limited the sphere of diplomacy. These responses could be described as typical of post-Partition South Asian interstate relations where characteristics such as insecurity, instinctiveness, overreaction, brinkmanship and aggression had been predominant. Tempering these reactions, in the case of Indo–Bangladesh relations, were the tangential economic links between the two states, ties which suggested that the political and the economic dimensions were not wholly dependent upon each other.

While the Indian government's foreign policy concerns therefore reflected a preoccupation with regional influence, those of Zia and his regime represented largely the struggle for domestic political survival and acceptance. The methods by which Zia achieved his pre-eminent political position in Bangladesh ensured that the heightened souring of Indo–Bangladesh political relations after Mujib's assassination would have been unlikely to diminish. Moreover, many of the political problems which beset Zia on his accession, and which had played such an influential role in impairing Indo–Bangladesh relations, continued to apply throughout his regime.[88] Zia's attempts to manipulate and counteract the limitations on his domestic political options resulted in far more freedom to manoeuvre, but in the realm of foreign, rather than domestic, policy. Unlike Mujib, Zia was able to pursue a foreign policy which was not encumbered by gratitude towards the Indian government, developing into a policy which might extend beyond the boundaries of Indian approval. Nevertheless, political necessity and pragmatism modified his dealings with the Indian government to some extent. Continued economic links with India indicated that the deterioration in relations between the two states was not all-encompassing, relations being guided by pressures apart from those deriving from Bangladesh's domestic political turmoil. Further tempering relations between the two states was the possibility that an excessively defiant stance taken by the Bangladesh government towards its powerful neighbour could have provoked an Indian military response which, at the very least, might have ousted the troublesome regime from power.

6
1982–90: Political Manoeuvres and Ethnic Violence

This chapter examines the impact of selected domestic events on Indo–Bangladesh relations during Hussain Muhammad Ershad's regime, as part of the overall evaluation of the domestic and external determinants of Bangladesh's foreign relations. Aspects of three issues have been selected as appropriate examples for analysis: Ershad's assumption of power; the Farakka Barrage dispute; and the hill-people insurgency occurring in the Chittagong Hill Tracts of southeast Bangladesh. The chapter does not aim to explore these issues comprehensively. The intention is to use specific examples to illustrate the way in which each issue has been shaped, in part, by Bangladesh's domestic arena.

As with Ziaur Rahman, Hussain Muhammad Ershad's successful bid for leadership of Bangladesh influenced the course of Indo–Bangladesh relations, although to a more limited extent. Both leaders commenced their regimes via a military coup, but with differing reactions from India, further countering the common argument that relations were soured because of the shift to military rule in Bangladesh.

For those attempting to achieve supremacy in the wake of Zia's assassination in May 1981, political life remained volatile and precarious, although certain conditions offered advantages for an ambitious and shrewd individual such as Ershad. Ziaur Rahman's instinctive and vulnerable bid for leadership was made in highly dangerous circumstances, and in the face of Indian disapproval and indignation. Ershad, by contrast, had ample time to choose an opportune moment to take over the reins of government, an advantage which also minimised the risk of provoking Indian antagonism and interference. Ershad's initial decision to support the establishment of a civilian government following Zia's assassination aroused speculation in the Indian media that his 'mysterious' failure to seize power at that time was intended to 'cover up something'.[1]

Ershad was clearly regarded with some degree of suspicion in India, but his choice, or opportunity, to 'postpone' the expected coup proved to be an astute move which offered much greater scope for political gain, and in turn, smoothed Bangladesh's relations with India. There was a variety of domestic reasons why Ershad's eventual ousting of Bangladesh's civilian regime in 1982 occurred with little domestic opposition and hence ameliorated India's response.

Historical precedent had shown that the most dangerous threat facing a leader of Bangladesh usually came from within the military. Zia's unceasing efforts to eradicate powerful military opposition, exemplified by the thwarting of at least 20 attempts to overthrow his regime,[2] did not prevent his assassination from within the military.[3] Nevertheless, by means of execution and imprisonment, Zia had thinned and weakened the ranks of the most troublesome military factions, leaving the group which he had come to favour the most, the repatriates, in by far the most powerful position.[4] Being a member of the repatriate group, Ershad was able to reap the benefit of Zia's efforts to curb military opposition, bringing to heel with little difficulty those who had played a role in Zia's demise. Consequently, Ershad was under little pressure to stage a coup and enforce martial law at that particular time.

Ershad also had to take into account the prevalent, heightened public fear of the military and its violent and politically obtrusive factionalism which had culminated in Zia's assassination.[5] In being able to delay a bid for direct leadership, Ershad was able to concentrate on the task of consolidating his position as leader of the armed forces and, at the same time, minimise civilian apprehension. Ershad's attempt to deal with both of those problems was encapsulated in his open commitment to ensure that the military be given a decision-making, stabilising role in Bangladeshi political life,[6] governed by constitutional means and theoretically subject to popular approval.

In being able to choose the timing of his coup, Ershad had more scope to play upon political divisions which were bound to surface in the wake of a government which had been moulded around Zia's specific goals and ambitions. It was far more pragmatic for Ershad to allow Acting President Abdus Sattar's civilian government to bear the burden of trying to follow in Zia's idolised, martyred footsteps,[7] and to let Sattar run the risk of losing popularity if unsuccessful. Sattar's failure was a probability.[8] The ensuing necessity to restore political and economic stability would then have been used to justify a declaration of martial law, the earlier prospect of which had been viewed widely with alarm.

This type of strategy was used effectively by Ershad. In a style reminiscent of that pursued by former Pakistan President, Muhammad Ayub Khan in 1958, Ershad opted finally to impose martial law on the grounds that the civil administration was no longer able to function effectively and 'wanton corruption at all levels had become permissible as part of life, causing unbearable sufferings to the people'.[9] Sattar's regime and the opposition parties had both been plagued by intra-party squabbling and political disarray, and consequently had failed to galvanise popular confidence and support.[10] The picture of Bangladesh's general prospects was perhaps not as dire as Ershad's rhetoric portrayed,[11] depicting images of a nation having been gripped by an 'extreme crisis' since Zia's death.[12] Ershad's actions were also driven by the fact that after Sattar's sweeping election victory in November 1981, the President had felt secure enough to take a stronger stance against Ershad and the military, denying that the army was entitled to a share in governing the country.[13] At the same time, popular disillusionment with prevailing political conditions had been increasing,[14] prompting Ershad to initiate his bloodless coup while the civilian mood was comparatively favourable, and before Sattar could consolidate his own regime and become more obstructive.

Both the domestic and regional political circumstances which existed at the establishment of Zia's and Ershad's regimes were therefore of considerable contrast. The methods by which both military leaders sought to manipulate or adapt to those conditions also differed, of necessity. These differences were reflected in the fluctuating course of Indo–Bangladesh relations. Unlike Zia, Ershad did not have to deal with excessive opposition or resort to violent means to stage his coup. Ershad therefore had the opportunity to implement his political designs in a cautious, deliberative and methodical manner, synchronising his coup with the most politically advantageous domestic and regional conditions. Ershad's comparatively assured bid for leadership did not require a radical change in foreign policy direction, such as had accompanied Zia's more turbulent debut as leader of Bangladesh. While Zia was obliged to carry out sweeping foreign policy changes, Ershad was in a position to draw upon Zia's accomplishments and consolidate the more effective changes which had already been put in place by his military predecessor, rather than having to run the risk of trying an untested path.

As discussed in Chapter 3, a temporary upswing occurred in 1981–2 in the cordiality of Indo–Bangladesh relations.[15] Ershad's assumption of power was not the primary cause of the improvement, but neither did it impair relations, in sharp contrast to the downturn following Zia's coup in 1975. Ershad's effective manipulation of prevailing domestic political conditions in staging his coup reinforced rather than undermined the cordiality. In fact, the reaction by the Indian press to the non-violent coup could be described as favourable and optimistic.[16] Despite the auspicious beginning, relations between the two states did not strengthen to a significant extent during Ershad's regime. Some of the reasons have been examined elsewhere,[17] but domestically, it was partly due to Ershad's growing emphasis on cultivating the concept of Islamic identity in Bangladesh, and correspondingly, placing a greater emphasis on developing links with fellow Muslim countries.[18] His increasingly Islamic orientation in governance culminated in the official declaration of Islam as the state religion in June 1988.[19]

Even a brief analysis of India's differing responses to the two military coups underlines the extreme difficulty in isolating specific causes, whether domestic or external, which have moulded relations between Bangladesh and India. The argument that regime compatibility is a prerequisite for stable and cordial foreign relations is commonly applied to these two states, for example,[20] but as illustrated above, it is inadequate. Individual political aspirations have clearly played a very influential role during the course of Indo–Bangladesh relations.

* * *

The conduct of the Farakka Barrage dispute during Ershad's regime was also influenced by domestic pressures arising within Bangladesh. Analyst Ben Crow has brought to light little-known details concerning the politicised nature of the issue in a study which is balanced, thorough and based on a wide range of sources.[21] Crow's study includes what appears to be unique oral evidence concerning information and discussions on Farakka that were never put into writing. His research shows that the resolution of the Farakka dispute was hampered partly by features of Bangladeshi political life and partly by factionalism within the Bangladesh government, particularly during Ershad's regime.

Between 1983 and 1987, a conflict emerged in the Bangladesh government between hard-line conservatives and those who were attempting to implement initiatives to break the Farakka deadlock. Bangladesh Irrigation Ministers, Obaidullah Khan and Anisul Islam Mahmud, wanted to move away from the conservative, hard-fought line which insisted on Ganges augmentation via storage reservoirs in Nepal. The old-line option required Indian cooperation, but this was not forthcoming because the scheme clashed with India's bilaterally focused foreign policy. The new-liners therefore sought to devise water-management systems which were internal to Bangladesh and not dependent upon Indian acceptance. Both ministers pushed for a permanent sharing agreement for all rivers common to Bangladesh and India. Once a river-sharing arrangement was established, new methods to augment the Gangetic flow within Bangladesh could be put in place, thereby circumventing the need to involve India in the long term. Such methods included a scheme not unlike India's link canal-augmentation proposal.[22] In 1986, the new-liners began to put together a scheme to augment the Ganges with water from the Brahmaputra via a link canal constructed entirely within Bangladesh and completely under Bangladesh's control[23] (see map 7, p. 65). The new-liners' efforts to gain wider support for this scheme brought the highly politicised and sensitive nature of the Farakka issue into sharp relief.

According to Crow's study, the internal link-canal initiative represented a viable option for Bangladesh's water-resource development, but failed to make headway because of anticipated popular rejection of the proposal. It was believed, by both the old- and the new-line proponents, that the construction of any link canal, even one built entirely within Bangladesh, would be seen by the public as a pro-Indian, anti-Bangladeshi move, since it resembled the Indian augmentation scheme so closely.[24] Such sentiments were fuelled by the Indian government's own expression of support for the scheme because of the similarity to its own larger link-canal proposal.[25] In an interview between Ben Crow and Obaidullah Khan, the latter commented that the Indian Irrigation Minister Mirdha was 'very responsive' concerning the internal canal, but the plan was regarded warily by Ershad and his military coterie because they believed that the plan would be 'more in India's interest than Bangladesh's'.[26]

The new-liners struggled with the difficult task of trying to gain support for a fresh and promising scheme within a highly controversial, politicised and factionalised arena. The extreme political sensitivity of the internal link-canal proposal, combined with the inherent fragility of the Bangladesh government itself, meant that those attempting to implement the initiative had to act with discretion and garner as much political support from within government circles as possible. This was necessary in order to counter old-line arguments and, in turn, to gain the confidence of the ruling clique and the public. To push too vigorously for the proposal would have been political suicide, regardless of the scheme's practical advantages.[27] Because of the perceived need for secrecy, the proposal was the subject of much discussion behind closed doors for several years.[28]

As a result, new-line proponents felt compelled to maintain a dual course which consisted of an official, publicly palatable position and an unofficial one, where controversial initiatives could be assessed and developed away from public scrutiny. Anisul Islam Mahmud cautiously admitted to the existence of this parallel structure in an interview with Ben Crow in 1987, but was unwilling to provide details, justifying his reticence thus: 'If you discuss it in public you start taking public positions which you then cannot change.'[29] In Crow's opinion, Mahmud was 'trying to ride two horses: to pave the way for the new line without appearing to reject the old'.[30] While deemed necessary, a dual tack created many difficulties for the new-line proponents, keeping their overall position weak and tenuous and providing ample scope for exploitation by their opponents.[31] The dual tactic also meant that none of the main initiatives of the new line could be put into writing. Inevitably, attempts to present those proposals verbally to the Indian government were vague and lacked credibility,[32] causing Indian interest in the initiatives to wane. Even Rajiv Gandhi's compromising overtures in 1985–6[33] were not sufficient to overcome the reservations held in conservative Indian and Bangladesh government circles towards the new-line initiatives. Rajiv's attempts to break the Farakka deadlock were stymied in a similar fashion to those of the new-liners in Bangladesh, as pointed out by a senior Indian water official to Ben Crow: 'To some extent, the Prime Minister [Rajiv Gandhi] was in the position of Anisul Islam – he had not carried the Cabinet with him'.[34]

By early 1987, old-line proponents had strengthened their positions within both governments. The Farakka stalemate hardened correspondingly. The entire issue of water-sharing was so politically loaded in Bangladesh that even viable and reasonable proposals put forward by Bangladeshis themselves foundered on the obstacle of entrenched domestic political behaviour. The ad hoc and personalised political structure which existed in Bangladesh, and the strength of easily provoked Bangladeshi fears and prejudices concerning India's intentions, reinforced the process of politicisation of the Farakka dispute and impeded its resolution.

Political impediments like these were not unique to Bangladesh. Analyst B.G. Verghese considered these sorts of political difficulties to be common to both Bangladesh and India, emphasising that such problems had to be addressed by both countries in order to break the Farakka stalemate:

An objective analysis would suggest that over the years both sides have taken certain inflexible positions and made extravagant proposals and inflated claims without adequate technical, socio–economic or ecological data or sufficient regard for the other's reasonable needs. They have got locked into their own past rhetoric or perceptions, viewing enormously complex and diverse sets of propositions and aspirations in simplistic terms. Limited vision has precluded any meaningful consideration of potential trade-offs. Mistrust has hardened and none has calculated the opportunity costs of delay. Basically and ultimately, the eastern waters question, which includes water sharing and augmenting the lean [flow] of the Ganga ... is not just an engineering problem but a political question enveloping the long-term relationship between the co-riparians ... The problem is by no means incapable of a solution that is just and fair to both sides.[35]

As has been argued in preceding chapters,[36] the Farakka stalemate has benefited India rather than Bangladesh, with the former having had a greater impact in perpetuating the stalemate. Nevertheless, as shown above, political pressures deriving from within Bangladesh have also played an influential part in protracting and aggravating the Farakka barrage dispute.

*   *   *

The Chittagong Hill Tracts (CHT) Montagnard insurgency represents another example of the way in which Bangladesh's domestic problems have affected diplomatic relations with India. CHT insurgency impinged increasingly on Indo–Bangladesh relations between 1976 and 1990. The Bangladesh government blamed India for exacerbating the ethnic conflict, which otherwise might have been resolved with less difficulty; while India saw the issue as yet another example of Indian vulnerability to neighbouring domestic strife.[37] The history of insurgency in the CHT region has been described in more detail elsewhere.[38] The aim here is to illustrate the long-standing nature of CHT Montagnard unrest and to assess the extent to which Indo–Bangladesh tension has been exacerbated by or has contributed towards the escalating violence in the CHT.

The CHT of southeast Bangladesh comprise 13 000 square kilometres (10 per cent of Bangladesh) which form a strategic border area next to India and Burma. The Hill Tracts are part of a rugged and rainforested mountain range extending 1800 kilometres from western Burma to the eastern Himalayas in China (see map 8). The CHT region is inhabited by approximately a dozen non-Bengali, ethnically diverse Montagnard groups,[39] as well as a growing population of Bengali settlers. Estimates of population in the CHT vary from 500 000 to 650 000, with the largest group, the Chakmas, accounting for between 250 000 and 400 000.[40] The Bengali settler population figures are equally inconsistent, ranging between 300 000 and 470 000, or between 50 and 60 per cent of the total CHT population.[41]

Many factors contributed to the emergence of militancy amongst the hill people of the CHT. Most could be categorised as gross exploitation and mis-management by successive central governments: British, Pakistani and Bang-ladeshi. The Indian government contributed towards CHT militancy, but its role was minor when compared with the impact of long-term domestic pressures which were exerted upon the Montagnard groups.

Anthropologist Willem Van Schendel has produced pioneering work on state formation and ethnicity in the CHT, a subject which he considers to have been previously ignored, especially within Bangladesh, by anthropologists and historians.[42] According to Van Schendel, this neglect by scholars has resulted both in a lack of available information on the CHT, and in a 'remarkably stagnant view of the hill people' being held by many, particularly the Bengalis of Bangladesh.[43] Van Schendel has blamed the colonial era for this stereotyping process. Before colonial domination, the hill people were generally perceived as 'free agents', feared for their 'independence and military prowess' and regarded as 'invincible on their own turf'.[44] With colonialism, this perception changed to the common view that they were inferior, subordinate and dependent.[45] Van Schendel explains that nineteenth century descriptions of the hill people as 'primitives', 'savages', or 'wild hill tribes' are often found in contemporary writings in Bangladesh which have been dominated by the assumption that the hill people are '"isolated remnants" of some hoary past that have preserved their culture unchanged from time immemorial'. The Chittagong hill people have also been commonly regarded in Bangladesh as 'backward and childlike,... needing to be protected, educated, and disciplined by those who are more advanced socially'.[46]

Van Schendel has countered this stereotypical view of a primitive and static tribal culture with clear and concise evidence, emphasising the following:

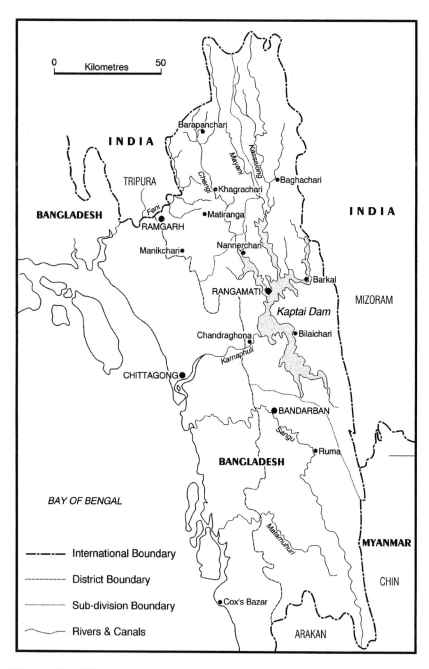

Map 8   The CHT
Source: Anti-Slavery Society (1984), p. 10.

the variety of cultures which exist within the Chittagong hill people; the many and different ways in which the hill groups have continually adapted and modified cultural practices in response to various stimuli; the complex patterns of wide-ranging migration which the hill people have developed over the centuries; and the long history of trade networks developed for the exchange of goods and ideas amongst not only themselves but also with the inhabitants of southeastern Bengal, Tripura, western Burma and perhaps further.[47]

Because the Chittagong hill people have been stereotyped as 'primitive tribals', as opposed to 'civilised Bengalis', it has meant that successive governments have been able to pursue authoritarian, militaristic and exploitative practices without fear of evoking widespread domestic condemnation. In fostering these stereotypical attitudes, colonial economic and political practices in the CHT created an increasingly antagonistic gulf between the Bengalis and the hill people. Such actions were carried out initially by the English East India Company in the eighteenth century. Monetisation and accompanying usurious money lending practices by plainlander Bengalis began to supplant the traditional subsistence and barter economy in the region;[48] indebtedness and economic dependency amongst the hill people were the result.

The British Raj officially absorbed the CHT into the Empire in 1860, but administered the strategically vital border region by military means, isolating the region from political reform occurring elsewhere, such as the establishment of an increasingly representative provincial legislature.[49] Shifting cultivation was further discouraged because of the problems associated with administering and controlling a moving population. By 1890, about 3000 hectares of scarce arable land were being cultivated, over half of which were being worked by the more experienced Bengali settlers.[50]

The CHT Regulation of 1900 restricted further Bengali migration into the area, essentially to isolate and consolidate the Empire's border regions.[51] Nevertheless, politicisation of the hill people was already well underway and the notion of a separate political identity gathered momentum. In isolating the CHT, the Regulation of 1900 appeared to provide a form of autonomy to the hill peoples, or to protect their rights. Van Schendel has argued that the opposite was true, that the Regulation marked 'the onset of a process of "enclavement" in which the hill people were denied access to power and were subordinated and exploited directly by their British overlords'.[52] The isolationist policy restricted major aspects of hill people life: administration and decision-making, migration and trade networks, and other economic activities intrinsic to hill culture.[53] The Regulation of 1900 therefore served to accelerate the politicisation of the CHT inhabitants.

After Partition, the rights of the hill people were further eroded as the Pakistan government continued the tradition of exploitation in the region. The isolationist policy towards the CHT was reversed but this was of little benefit for the hill people. Bengali plainlanders were again encouraged to move into the area, placing additional pressure on resources which were already suffering from the effects of inappropriate cultivation practices.[54] Although unreliable, population figures show that, when compared with the total number of indigenous inhabitants, the proportion of Bengali migrants living in the CHT increased greatly after Partition. At that time, the hill people were believed to have constituted between 89 and 98 per cent of the total CHT population.[55] By 1991, that figure had dropped to approximately 52 per cent, owing to the decades of government-sponsored Bengali migration.[56] Figures in Table 6.1 are approximations, but they do clearly indicate that the proportion of Bengali migrants living in the CHT has been increasing since Partition.

In reopening the area to migration, the Pakistan government's aim was mainly to ease growing overpopulation pressure in the east wing lowlands, ignoring the certainty that hill people's grievances and unrest would be exacerbated, especially as the latter were already facing overpopulation and economic decline. The government's move was characteristic of its broader nation-building strategy which involved the suppression of self-determination demands from disgruntled sections of the populace, such as the east Bengalis. The once-semi-independent Montagnard groups of the CHT felt increasingly threatened, culturally, politically and economically, under Pakistan, and subsequently, Bangladesh governments. This resulted in violent clashes for arable land and in their own growing demand for autonomy.

One of the most devastating acts of government exploitation in the CHT, from the Montagnard perspective, was the building of the Kaptai hydro-electricity project between 1959 and 1963. The Kaptai dam, the so-called 'Lake of Tears' (see map 8), flooded 20 000 hectares of the CHT (one-quarter of the best-quality arable land in the area), displacing 96 000 Montagnards, mostly of the Chakma group. Compensation fell far short of what was promised, and even by 1980, only US$2.6 million had been disbursed out of the original US$51 million supposedly set aside for this purpose.[57] The project had numerous other adverse consequences for the hill people, effects which have been highlighted by many, such as S. Mahmud Ali, who considered that for the majority of tribals displaced by the project, 'life had been an unmitigated disaster since 1959'.[58] Ali also drew attention to a letter which was delivered in his presence to Ziaur Rahman in 1976 by a Chakma elder who expressed his sorrow over the disastrous impact of the dam on the hill people:

> The vast expanse of water captured by the dam provides a scene that impresses every visitor with its beauty. But could anybody have thought that this immense body of water is to some extent filled with the tears of the local people? Through the cables of the electric lines not only current flows, but also the sighs of grief.[59]

Table 6.1 Population growth in the CHT, 1950–91 (Montagnards and Bengali migrants)

	1950			1981			1991		
	Montagnard pop.	*Bengali migrant pop.*	*Total pop.*	*Montagnard pop.*	*Bengali migrant pop.*	*Total pop.*	*Montagnard pop.*	*Bengali migrant pop.*	*Total pop.*
	240,000	28,000	268,000	439,458	268,998	708,456	498,595	468,825	967,420
Percentage of Total Pop.	89.6	10.4		62.1	37.9		51.6	48.4	

Sources: S.M. Ali (1993), p. 167, and *1991 Census*, Bangladesh Bureau of Statistics, cited in M. Rahman Shelley (1992), p. 50.

The Kaptai project and its aftermath typified the way in which the hill people were exploited, neglected and alienated by successive governments.

A strong military tradition was also reinforced in the CHT by the US Central Intelligence Agency (CIA) which undertook covert, anti-Communist operations in the area.[60] The late 1950s saw Dhaka as a 'centre of the CIA's struggle against Communism' and the CHT region became a command post for CIA operations against Chinese authority in Tibet.[61] Hill people militias were trained and armed by the CIA to help protect their operations. The CHT guerrillas were also covertly armed and trained by Pakistan's Inter Services Intelligence organisation in order to 'pursue a low-risk, low-intensity proxy war' against India.[62] The sensitivity of operations in the CHT was heightened further with China's later involvement.[63] According to Ali, the CHT tribal military wing which eventually formed, known as the *Shanti Bahini*, 'drew its roots from that old tradition' of clandestine militarisation.[64]

Bangladesh's independence war of 1971 exacerbated Montagnard grievances, despite the fact that the war was a secessionist struggle against similar problems: political, economic and cultural domination.[65] After the war, conflict over land ownership and regional autonomy demands became acute between the Montagnards and the new government which tended to favour the Bengali settlers. As leader of the fledgling state, Mujibur Rahman ignored hill people sensitivities, attempting to repress and absorb ethnic identities for the sake of 'greater "Bengali" nationalism'.[66] Mujib roused considerable anger in the CHT in 1973 when he declared that all hill people would be known as Bengali, and not by any other identity.[67] M.N. Larma, one of the most prominent Chakma leaders at that time, and later a Member of Parliament, led a constitutional struggle against Mujib's strategy of cultural assimilation. Larma's argument was:

> [Y]ou cannot impose your national identity on others. I am a Chakma, not a Bengali. I am a citizen of Bangladesh–Bangladeshi. You are also Bangladeshi but your national identity is Bengali...They [tribals] can never be Bengali.[68]

Following the 1975 coup which removed Mujib, Larma went underground, establishing the Montagnard armed wing, the *Shanti Bahini*. CHT unrest and militarisation evoked an often forceful and violent response from the government during both Zia's and Ershad's regimes. From 1976 onwards, the *Shanti Bahini* was involved in regular confrontations with government forces and armed CHT Bengali settlers, these clashes usually being followed by retribution massacres of Montagnard civilians by the military and the settlers.[69] The *Shanti Bahini* responded in kind, also killing many unarmed civilians.[70] According to a 1986 Amnesty International report, on no occasion did the Bangladesh government conduct an inquiry into the many complaints of 'unlawful and arbitrary killings of unarmed tribal people' in the CHT.[71]

Various patterns therefore emerged in the CHT, beginning over a century before Montagnard insurgency became associated with the declining warmth of Indo–Bangladesh relations from the mid-1970s. These patterns included: continual migration of Bengali plainlanders into the CHT, placing excessive pressure on arable land and other limited resources; political, economic and cultural exploitation of the indigenous inhabitants; a tradition of guerrilla warfare and military manoeuvres in the region; and increasing politicisation and militarisation of the Montagnards. Montagnard unrest intensified during Zia's and Ershad's regimes. The reasons for the unrest were so deep-seated that even well meaning attempts at domestic reform had little remedial impact. The bitterness and intractability surrounding the issue virtually dictated that the Bangladesh government would focus on India's involvement in order to divert domestic criticism.

In October 1983, for example, Ershad changed tack in dealing with the CHT issue, switching from excessive force to appeasement. Further plainlander migration into the CHT was halted,[72] and in hoping to pacify and disarm the *Shanti Bahini*, Ershad declared a general amnesty 'for the misguided persons in the Chittagong Hill Tracts to bring them back to normal life for a happy reunion with their parents and families'.[73] Ershad's overture was supported by a six-point programme which offered *Shanti Bahini* members food, land, low-interest loans, jobs and training.[74] By the end of 1985, 2500 out of an estimated 6000 had surrendered, but these belonged mostly to a less militant faction of the *Shanti Bahini*.[75]

Shanti Bahini guerrilla operations, led by M.N. Larma's brother, Shantu, increased in ferocity, reaching a peak in May 1986.[76] Killings and reprisals by both the *Shanti Bahini* and the Bengali settlers, the latter backed by government forces,[77] caused many thousands of Chakmas to flee into the neighbouring Indian state of Tripura, bringing the conflict under the international spotlight.[78] A subsequent offer of amnesty for the *Shanti Bahini* also had little success.

The refugee crisis in 1986 strained relations between Bangladesh and India, in part reflecting the general cooling of relations between the two states in 1986–7.[79] In an attempt to ease the refugee problem by encouraging the hill people to return to Bangladesh, the Bangladesh Parliament passed four laws in 1989, supposedly aimed to grant a form of autonomy to the CHT. The autonomy scheme, seen by the hill people as a 'sop to international opinion', was so obviously flawed that it did little to ease CHT unrest.[80] The most glaring fault of the autonomy plan was that it had no authority over the reserved and protected forests: the Kaptai hydroelectric project area and the industrialised parts of the CHT, which together made up 90 per cent of the region.[81] Hill people's distrust and suspicion of government intentions had been generated over decades and were simply too entrenched to be swept away by hasty legislation. As pointed out by an exiled Chakma newspaper editor living in Tripura: 'If properly implemented, the autonomy granted the three district councils in the CHT is not bad. But the problem is that it is on paper only'.[82]

The CHT insurgency and violence therefore remained a constant source of domestic pressure on Ershad's regime.[83] Simplistic and authoritarian solutions exacerbated the issue and the media emphasis on Bengali settler massacres fostered considerable domestic anger in Bangladesh.[84] The deterioration in the CHT region in the second half of the 1980s, and Ershad's inability to bring the *Shanti Bahini* into line through either force or appeasement, meant that the 'foreign-hand' ingredient was increasingly played upon. Ershad's regime was prepared to sour relations with India for the sake of countering adverse domestic opinion over the CHT dispute. The Bangladesh government's ineffective attempts to re-absorb and provide land for the thousands of Chakma refugees who had fled into India, not only in 1986, but at various times during the previous decade, prompted the following comment in the *Far Eastern Economic Review*:

[I]t is an open question whether Dhaka will ever permit real autonomy [for the CHT] – even as defined in its own 1989 laws. And even if it did, the problems of how to re-absorb the refugees who have lost their land, and how to deal with the intractable issue of the Bengali settlers will still remain . . . Nowhere in Bangladesh can so many landless people be accommodated without severe domestic political repercussions. Dhaka evidently prefers to have problems with a few hundred thousand ethnic minority peoples in the hills – and to have strained relations with India – than to face the possible wrath of 114 million Bengalis in the plains.[85]

The Bangladesh government and media essentially sought to blame the *Shanti Bahini* as the initiator of all unrest and violence in the CHT and, in turn, to blame India for providing the insurgents with the means to continue their guerrilla activities. Propaganda and stereotypical imagery were used constantly by the Bangladesh government. The advantages of this approach were considerable. Placing blame on the *Shanti Bahini* and the Indian government deflected domestic criticism of the Bangladesh government's inability to resolve the CHT conflict; it also justified the arbitrary use of extreme force to suppress *Shanti Bahini* activities; and it made the CHT problem appear more manageable and straightforward if it could be explained in the narrow terms of a small minority group of terrorists intent on waging a war based on their own limited political agenda. The following comments by President Ershad represented typical examples of government propaganda:

[I]f we review the whole situation in the hill districts, then we find that about 30 000 tribal population were forced into an exodus across the border through the creation of atrocities to serve [the] Shanti Bahini[86] ... who have been operating from their sanctuary in the other land [India] ... [T]hese Shanti Bahini men who have a Marxist mooring act at the instigation of 'others'. They are atheists and do not believe in the Allah, or the Buddha or the God or the Christ. They preach [a] godless cult which is contrary to the belief of [the] commonman belonging to the tribal and Bangalee ... population ... [F]rom the recovery of books and leaflets from the Shanti Bahini, it is explicit that they are Communists and promote the path of terrorism.[87]

[Shanti Bahini] atrocities were being let loose at times on innocent people which speaks of a conspiracy hatched outside against the people of the area ... [T]he rest of the refugees ... [want] to return to their homeland, but they are not being allowed to come back ... [because of] intimidation ... [by] vested quarters, including the Shanti Bahini, [who] are trying to prove that minorities are being subjected to harassment here.[88]

Similar rhetoric was used by Bangladesh's foreign minister, Humayun Rasheed Chowdhury, who stated that *Shanti Bahini* attacks 'were not isolated incidents but part of a conspiracy, ... the massacres ... being carried out under a blue print drawn and assisted by an alien country [India]'.[89]

The Bangladesh government attempted to add weight to its accusations by declaring that it had 'conclusive proof' that the *Shanti Bahini* were getting arms and sanctuary from India.[90] The accusations remained an integral aspect of the CHT issue, especially once it became clear that no substantial progress was being made in stemming violence in the region or in repatriating the thousands of Chakma refugees.[91] In June 1989, *The Bangladesh Observer* published a report appearing in the *New York Times* which stated that a senior Indian security officer had confirmed Indian assistance to the *Shanti Bahini*.[92] The officer was 'quoted as saying that his government was helping the "rebels" living in the camps of the para-military force of India along the border'.[93] The *New York Times* also stated that, according to Bimal Chakma, spokesperson for the *Shanti Bahini*, the Indian government had been giving 'arms and financial support' to his organisation since 1976, although he considered the degree of assistance to have been 'very low' compared with what was needed.[94] The *Far Eastern Economic Review* also concluded that some Indian assistance undoubtedly was provided to the *Shanti Bahini*:

The Bangladeshis frequently accuse India's intelligence agency, the Research and Analysis Wing (RAW), of providing sanctuary and training facilities to the Shanti Bahini. The charge is routinely denied by New Delhi, but it seems indisputable that the RAW maintains links with the rebels, though the extent is difficult to gauge.[95]

The Indian Government's official view of the CHT conflict was to consider it to be an 'internal problem for Bangladesh',[96] a domestic ethnic dispute for which India had no responsibility. On a three-day visit to Bangladesh in January 1987, Indian External Affairs Minister, Mr Narayan Tiwari, reiterated India's habitual response that no Indian assistance was being given to the *Shanti Bahini*. When asked whether or not the *Shanti Bahini* training camps in India would be dismantled, he jokingly replied: '[Y]ou are very clever to take a reply from me on camps which do not at all exist'.[97] In response to Bangladesh's accusations of Indian assistance to the *Shanti Bahini*, India not only denied involvement, but went so far as to accuse Bangladesh of the same type of activity: covertly aiding and harbouring Indian insurgents from Tripura, members of the Tripura National Volunteers (TNV).[98] Like India, the Bangladesh government vehemently denied providing insurgent assistance, pointing out that Bangladesh had 'neither the intention nor the means to train rebels from Tripura'.[99] The trading of accusations and the Chakma refugee problem placed additional stress on Indo–Bangladesh relations, further undermining the spirit of regional cooperation which accompanied the launching of the South Asian Association for Regional Cooperation (SAARC) in December 1985.

The CHT conflict has been heightened and manipulated by both the Bangladesh and Indian governments, according to political expediency. This has been carried out at the expense of the cultural, economic and political well-being of the Chittagong hill people themselves. The conflict has also reinforced the traditional fears and grievances between Bangladesh and India, such as Bangladeshi fears of Indian dominance, and disputes associated with the porous and ill-defined Indo–Bangladesh border.

At various times, according to political circumstances, the CHT issue has been down-played, overplayed, stereotyped, mismanaged or ignored. Many thousands have died in the CHT over the last two decades,[100] but the violence and acute ethnic divisions in the region have rarely received due international attention. This neglect was acknowledged in the *Far Eastern Economic Review*:

> While political concern has centred around the Indo–Pakistan friction and the security threat generated by the Soviet invasion of Afghanistan, the northeastern region of the Subcontinent, a potential powder keg, where South Asia meets Southeast Asia, has largely been ignored.[101]

It is noteworthy that the CHT conflict began to receive significant international attention after May 1986, when India's already unstable northeast was inundated with 50 000 Chakma refugees. Until then, the international media paid little attention to the dispute.

India, too, had taken a low-key official stance on the issue before the refugee crisis occurred. As long as the CHT ethnic conflict did not spiral out of control, the Indian government was able to reap certain benefits from Bangladesh's domestic strife. A Bangladeshi regime under domestic pressure was more easily manipulated than if it were in a secure, stable position. In the opinion of a Dhaka observer interviewed by the *Far Eastern Economic Review:*

> For India, the actual ethnic conflict in the CHT is of secondary importance,...but the Shanti Bahini provides India with an important bargaining chip for other, more crucial issues – such as the Farakka barrage and the sharing of the waters of the Ganga and the Brahmaputra river complex.[102]

India's own insurgency problem in Tripura had also provided opportunities to use the *Shanti Bahini* 'bargaining chip' in discouraging Bangladeshi assistance to the TNV.

If the Indian government had so chosen, it could have exerted effective pressure on the *Shanti Bahini* insurgents to cease cross-border operations, but until the refugee crisis in 1986, there was no political advantage in doing so. Instead, at the very least, India covertly condoned the *Shanti Bahini* operations. Once the cost became too great, India began to reconsider the strategy of giving the *Shanti Bahini* assistance. The 50 000–60 000 hill people in Tripura refugee camps placed considerable socio-economic pressure on India's northeast, costing the Indian government, according to a 1990 report, 80 million rupees (US$4.7 million) per year.[103] In order to ensure that the refugees returned to Bangladesh, and remained there, the Indian government was well aware that *Shanti Bahini* activities would have to be curbed to some degree. The considerable reduction in numbers of the *Shanti Bahini* and their increasing lack of mobility in the second half of the 1980s pointed to India's declining assistance to the insurgents.[104] In August 1988 the Indian government lifted its ban on the TNV, reducing the need to use the *Shanti Bahini* as leverage against Bangladesh. The breakthrough in resolving the nine-year-old dispute between the Indian government and the Tripura insurgents made Indian assistance to the *Shanti Bahini* much less politically profitable.[105] The cycle of mutual accusations of aiding and harbouring insurgents was therefore broken.

A change of central government in the 1989 Indian elections also eased tensions with Bangladesh over the *Shanti Bahini*. On a three-day goodwill visit to Dhaka, India's External Affairs Minister, Inder Kumar Gujral, emphasised his government's willingness to improve relations with Bangladesh.[106] Unlike his predecessor, Gujral adopted a more conciliatory approach in talks with Bangladesh regarding the *Shanti Bahini*. Instead of simply denying India's assistance to the insurgents, and therefore disclaiming any Indian responsibility, he stressed that 'no miscreants would be given sanctuary in the Indian side'.[107] He also assured the Bangladesh government of India's 'whole-hearted cooperation' in 'facilitating the return of refugees to the

Chittagong Hill Tracts'.[108] The conciliatory gestures were almost a repeat of those put forward by the previous non-Congress government, the Janata regime in 1977–9. Janata Prime Minister, Morarji Desai, also gave due acknowledgment to the insurgency issue, proffering assurances that India would not harbour tribal insurgents.[109] His pledge was reciprocated by the Bangladesh President, Ziaur Rahman.[110]

As has been pointed out by many analysts, regional tension is partly a reflection of the domestic conditions prevailing within each of the states of the region.[111] There is little doubt that the CHT conflict developed and intensified due to domestic causes and that the grievances of the hill people led, in turn, to increased tension between Bangladesh and India. The British Raj and the Pakistan government set the course for those grievances, and Mujib, Zia and Ershad compounded the depth of CHT unrest by forcefully implementing contradictory, insensitive and ill-conceived schemes, supposedly aimed to secure national integrity. As a fledgling state, Bangladesh's weak and underdeveloped political structure was characterised by inconsistencies in decision-making and by a preoccupation with promoting images of cultural homogeneity and national integration. Efforts to suppress expressions of CHT ethnicity, as undertaken by Mujib, were almost guaranteed to produce a violent backlash.

The relationship between the two seemingly contradictory objectives of national integration and ethnic fulfilment has been evaluated by anthropologist, Thomas Eriksen. His conclusion has been that if violent conflicts between the 'nation-state and ethnicity are to be avoided then the state must reduce its demands as regards the degree of cultural integration of its citizens'.[112] According to Eriksen, finding this equilibrium is an extremely difficult task since virtually any modern bureaucratic state will, almost by nature, 'promote cultural integration at any cost'.[113]

In a politically insecure state, such as Bangladesh, the difficulties associated with successful cultural integration are much more pronounced. Bangladesh's relative cultural homogeneity has often been contrasted with the ethnic diversity and tensions existing in Pakistan, India and Sri Lanka. Bangladesh's cultural unity has been emphasised and played upon by the state's successive leaders, almost in the hope that political unity and stability would automatically follow. As a result, for the small minority of non-Muslim inhabitants,[114] and the much smaller minority of non-Bengali inhabitants, there has been little scope to express and retain their cultural identity in an accepted and positive manner. Instead, violent conflict and cultural division have tended to accompany minority demands for cultural and political recognition, as has occurred in the CHT. A susceptibility to factionalism and a lack of coordination amongst the hill people have also prevented the effective articulation of their ethnic claims.

Bangladesh's relative cultural homogeneity has kept violent ethnic divisions to a much smaller scale than in the other large South Asian states, but the depth of bitterness and the degree of intractability associated with conflicts such as the CHT insurgency, are comparable. Until the validity and complexity of the hill people grievances are adequately accommodated by the Bangladesh government, the tension in the region will continue to simmer and, at times, spill over into Indian territory.

The CHT violence has a clear and deep-seated domestic origin, a causal link which has been emphasised by the Indian press and pro-India sources as evidence for the view that Bangladesh's domestic strife has been largely responsible for the difficulties which have marred Indo–Bangladesh relations.[115] In evaluating the evidence, there is much to counter this simple argument, indicating that India has had an intrinsic and active role in contributing towards the tension between the two states. The course of events associated with the Chittagong conflict shows that India played a subtle, but fundamental part in exacerbating the issue. The Indian government did not create the CHT unrest, nor did India prevent its resolution. India has, however, used the issue to its political advantage wherever possible, hindering rather than assisting the Bangladesh government in dealing with the problem. Tensions in the CHT were so easily exacerbated that it took very little effort, or risk, on India's part to exploit the issue.

The changes of Indian government in 1977 and in 1989 showed clearly that India had the power to turn the CHT violence into either a major or minor source of antagonism between the two states. Other Indian domestic political fluctuations, such as the extent of insurgent activity in Tripura, were also reflected in India's reactions to CHT unrest. To some extent, a degree of tension between India and Bangladesh over the CHT conflict was not undesirable from the point of view of both governments. As long as the conflict was manageable, it served the purpose of allowing each to use the other as a scapegoat to assuage domestic condemnation.

The events and issues above illustrate the way in which domestic pressures occurring within Bangladesh have affected the course of relations with India. Those stimuli have sometimes, almost coincidentally, helped to improve ties, but more often than not, they have had an adverse impact on cooperative relations. Problems arising from Bangladesh's colonial past and the state's subsequent political underdevelopment, insecurity and factionalism have been compounded by increasing socio–cultural pressures, such as severe and worsening poverty[116] and intensified expressions of ethnic identity. The manner in which the Bangladesh government has responded to these pressures has not helped to promote harmonious relations with India.

Isolating some of the domestic forces shaping Bangladesh's relations with India illustrates the intricacy of the relationship between the two states. Bangladesh's ever-present domestic turmoil provides an easy target for those wanting to understand why the problems between the two states have proved so difficult to resolve. The above analysis illustrates the inadequacy of such a narrow perspective. While some domestic pressures have clearly marred or improved Bangladesh's relations with India, others, such as the CHT insurgency, show that India's role has been far more pervasive than might appear initially. India's impassivity and subtle forms of hindrance have had a compelling, if not formidable, impact on the tenor of relations with Bangladesh, even concerning those issues over which the Bangladesh government has had considerable influence.

Part IV

Bangladesh–Pakistan Relations, 1975–90

7
1975–81: Catalysts and Convergences of Interest

As with Indo–Bangladesh relations, a wide range of pressures have impinged upon Bangladesh's relations with Pakistan, although comparatively little study has been made of the latter. The interaction between Bangladesh and Pakistan has been overshadowed by the political upheavals occurring within each of the two states, Pakistan in particular. Pakistan's long tradition of overwhelming concern for national identity and security, forged largely from decades of rivalry with India, has produced a domestic and foreign policy which strongly reflects that rivalry. The challenge therefore lies in defining characteristics which have been unique to Bangladesh–Pakistan relations and in assessing whether or not other influences, such as those deriving from Bangladesh, have also been able to play a significant role in shaping relations between the two states.

Diplomatic relations between Bangladesh and Pakistan following Mujib's demise contrasted sharply with much of the remaining political activity occurring in the region at the time. Domestically, each of the three largest South Asian states was experiencing considerable political turmoil, and apart from a new-found warmth emerging between Bangladesh and Pakistan, relations between the various South Asian states were showing little change for the better. In fact, Ziaur Rahman's rise to power in Bangladesh contributed towards a strong down-turn in Bangladesh–India relations, while Indo–Pakistan relations in 1976 were barely reaching the point where official diplomatic links could be restored, despite attempts to 'normalise' relations with the signing of the Simla Agreement in 1972. India's emergence as the first nuclear power in the region in 1974 played an influential part in ensuring that suspicion and distrust would continue to dog Indo–Pakistan relations. The stability being established between Bangladesh and Pakistan therefore represented a notable aberration in South Asian interstate relations, inviting questions as to why it occurred.

The standard approach of most works dealing with Bangladesh–Pakistan relations during this period has tended to be perfunctory, concentrating on domestic, as opposed to broader regional influences on those relations.[1]

Little attempt has been made to delve much beyond an acknowledgement that relations between the two states improved during Ziaur Rahman's regime. The period between November 1975 and July 1977, when Ziaur Rahman and Zulfikar Ali Bhutto held power in their respective states, has generally received brief attention,[2] while much of the emphasis is often placed upon succeeding events: from July 1977 onwards, particularly during the military regimes of Ziaur Rahman and that of Bhutto's successor, General Zia ul-Haq. This latter period, when both states came under military rule, is normally targeted as being the most indicative of strengthening relations between the two states, as exemplified by the following comments:

> Ziaur Rahman maintained cordial relations with [the] Bhutto government. However, the change of regime in Pakistan through a military coup (5 July 1977) opened a new chapter of relationship between Pakistan and Bangladesh ... During Mohammad Zia ul-Haq's military regime Pakistan's relations with Bangladesh considerably improved owing to identical objectives of military regimes in both the countries. Bangladesh President Ziaur Rahman provided fullfledged cooperation to Pakistan's military regime of General Zia ul-Haq.[3]

> [A] close and cordial relation manifesting itself in several spheres of interstate activity really started in 1977 when President General Ziaur Rahman visited Pakistan[,] ... [a]lthough ... the process towards normalization of relations between these two countries was initiated with the recognition of Bangladesh by Pakistan in July 1974.[4]

This chapter examines some of the assumptions encountered regarding Bangladesh–Pakistan relations, including those above.

Because of the lack of animosity and conflict manifested between the two states from 1975 to 1981, comparatively little has been written on Bangladesh–Pakistan relations during that period. Perhaps the view of 'no bad news' often being considered as 'no news at all' has played a subliminal part in discouraging closer study. There is little doubt that in contrast to the conduct of Indo–Bangladesh relations during Ziaur Rahman's regime, Bangladesh's relations with Pakistan can be described as harmonious and yet, as much may be revealed by harmony and cordiality as by conflict and instability. Far from being an unexceptional subject of study, the course of Bangladesh–Pakistan relations during this particular period provides much of relevance in gauging the strength of differing political pressures existing in the South Asian region.

Relations between Bangladesh and Pakistan improved remarkably after August 1975, but whether or not they can be described as entering a 'new chapter' after July 1977 is debatable. What would appear to be most in accordance with the available evidence is that the unprecedented calm which entered Bangladesh–Pakistan relations rested upon the critical event of Sheikh Mujibur Rahman's assassination, rather than upon Pakistan's formal recognition of Bangladesh in 1974, or upon Zia ul-Haq's rise to power in July 1977. While making such a distinction might seem unnecessary, this alternative perspective does have implications in the identification of the most influential reasons for the change in Bangladesh's relations with Pakistan. Defining when relations began to improve helps in understanding why the change occurred.

Relevant to this interpretation is the underemphasised point that the cordiality which came to Bangladesh–Pakistan relations was an extreme change in those relations. Furthermore, this change was not only an exceptional departure from the prevalent instability of South Asian foreign relations, but it was also counter to the historical lack of harmony in the region. According to Buzan's interpretation of South Asian politics, Indo–Pakistani rivalry has virtually defined relations between the states in the region.[5] He has also pointed out that the establishment of a high level of trust and friendship in the region has been very rare.[6] The improved relationship between Bangladesh and Pakistan appears to comply with that rarity, although the two aspects of Bangladesh–Pakistan cordiality and Indo–Pakistan rivalry are intertwined.

The shift in Indo–Bangladesh relations after August 1975 could not be described as one of sudden reversal, but the change in foreign relations between Bangladesh and Pakistan comes close to fitting such a description. Within four years of gaining independence in a brutal war instigated by the Pakistan government, Bangladesh readily accepted the establishment of diplomatic ties between the two states.[7] Both states were pioneering a link of unprecedented stability in the region, representing a diplomatic reversal which appeared to follow almost on the heels of savage conflict. The change confirmed that the pressures bearing upon both states' foreign policies were not only vast, but also that the source of those pressures had a much broader foundation than one specifically associated with Pakistan–Bangladesh interaction.

The extracts by Kaushik and Islam p. 146 interpret the cause of the extreme change in relations between Pakistan and Bangladesh generally in terms of the notion of regime compatibility. While this notion cannot be discounted as influential, examination of events from 1975 shows that a range of pressures, rather than one general, determining principle, has impinged on Bangladesh's relations with Pakistan. Catalytic events occurring in both Bangladesh and Pakistan had considerable influence on relations between the two states. The assassination of Sheikh Mujibur Rahman in August 1975 was critical for relations between Bangladesh and Pakistan. As mentioned in the extract by Islam, some steps towards improving Bangladesh–Pakistan relations had already been made, following the Pakistan prime minister Zulfikar Ali Bhutto's decision in February 1974 to give official recognition to Bangladesh. However, that decision had emerged from a compromise between domestic political pragmatism and Bhutto's desire to appease the expectations of the Muslim world.[8] It did not necessarily indicate that a substantial improvement in relations with Bangladesh would occur. Bhutto's public display of reluctance to condone recognition of Bangladesh[9] was symptomatic of the dictates of domestic Pakistani politics and of the long-standing, at times bitter, rivalry which coloured his dealings with Mujib. Bhutto's influential role in creating the political impasse after the 1970 elections, which in turn culminated in the Pakistan government's military assault on the east wing, provided a particularly potent source of friction between the two leaders.[10]

While relations between Bhutto and Mujib lacked empathy and solidarity, Bhutto's link with the Bangladeshi populace was different. His first official visit to post-independence Bangladesh in June 1974 was welcomed in a strong show of mass support,[11] but instead of taking advantage of these sentiments to increase his popularity, Bhutto was unforthcoming and evasive in resolving the divisive issues still marring relations with Bangladesh. These issues included the sharing of Pakistani assets deemed owing to Bangladesh and the transfer of hundreds of thousands of Bihari Muslims in Bangladesh who wished to retain their Pakistani nationality and begin a new life in Pakistan. Bhutto's visit was widely considered to have been a diplomatic failure,[12] having a withering effect on the beginnings of popular support which had been emerging in Bangladesh. Pakistan's official recognition of Bangladesh had not yet translated into firm, cordial relations between the two states.

Bhutto's unrestrained elation following Mujib's assassination, manifested in the immediate donation of 50 000 tons of rice and a large amount of clothing to Bangladesh,[13] emphasised the personal discord between the two men. The removal of Mujib and his pro-Indian regime offered Bhutto an ideal opportunity to capitalise politically on India's loss of influence in Bangladesh, but Bhutto's spontaneous offer of rice and clothing to Bangladesh carried a strong overtone of personal satisfaction with the August coup, particularly as beforehand he had been half-hearted in exploiting the growing anti-Indian sentiments in Bangladesh. Bhutto was clearly aware that Mujib's assassination meant the passing of an era and the undermining of the Awami League, developments which could precipitate a reversal of trends in Bangladeshi politics and foreign policy.

Bhutto's reaction to Mujib's assassination was not universal in Pakistan. Some took a more cautious, pragmatic line which they considered to be more appropriate in complying with the state's traditional, India-centric foreign policy stance. These feared that 'too sudden a shift in power [in Bangladesh] might prompt India's ambitious Prime Minister Indira Gandhi to take military action to prevent Bangladesh from slipping out of her grasp'.[14] The existence of these initial qualms had little effect in stemming Bhutto's enthusiastic overtures to Bangladesh, and his sentiments quickly became the official government line:

We knew that whoever had taken over there, it was likely to be better for us than it had been under Mujib... Moreover, the Pakistani people would not have understood any delay. After all, Mujib had been the architect of this country's dismemberment.[15]

Bhutto was the first state leader in the world to recognise the new regime, further underlining his approval of the change of government in Bangladesh.[16] This was a particularly pointed move in view of the fact that Bhutto was the last to accept the validity of Bangladesh's existence and Mujib's right to govern the new state. As indicated by the following extract from the *Pakistan Times*, Bhutto obviously felt some necessity to justify his speedy recognition of Bangladesh, and did so in terms that would mollify those in Pakistan who were apprehensive about India's reaction to Mujib's assassination. Bhutto's justification centred on what he regarded as the necessity to preempt the possibility that Indian intervention in Bangladesh would be undertaken on the plea that 'no Government existed in that country'.[17]

The political upheavals, coups and counter-coups in Bangladesh which followed Mujib's demise enhanced rather than dampened Bhutto's efforts to establish a close link between the two states. In broadly appraising the future of Bangladesh–Pakistan relations following Ziaur Rahman's ascendancy as leader of Bangladesh, Bhutto re-emphasised his satisfaction with the post-Mujib developments in Bangladesh, commenting:

[T]he situation has changed vastly... Our relationship is going to be a very decent, honorable and fair relationship... That is in itself a big achievement in terms of what we have gone through.[18]

Zia's assumption of power acted to reinforce the incipient warmth between Bangladesh and Pakistan. The political relationship between Bhutto and Zia was not burdened by a public history of estrangement. Ziaur Rahman had links with former Pakistani army officers and both leaders were relatively free to make diplomatic overtures to each other without arousing politically damaging accusations of hypocrisy and double-dealing.

It would appear that since the character of the relationship between Bhutto and Mujib was of substantial importance in prolonging the antagonism between Bangladesh and Pakistan after 1971, compatibility of individual leaders, rather than of 'regimes' or 'states', was and still is of greater influence, at least in the case of Bangladesh–Pakistan relations. The mutual antipathy which had become established between Bhutto and Mujib meant that any diplomatic initiatives to improve ties between the two countries would tend to lack commitment while they remained in power. Personal prejudice therefore had some bearing upon Bangladesh–Pakistan relations, at times even outweighing the dictates of political pragmatism. Furthermore, the considerable influence of powerful individuals, nepotism and personality cults in South Asian politics, as personified by Mujib and Bhutto, virtually dictated that the dispatch of Mujib in August 1975 would result in the eclipse of the Awami League and its policies, and in turn permit Bangladesh and Pakistan to break new ground in foreign relations.

From a more theoretical point of view, relations between Bangladesh and Pakistan were subject partly to the vagaries of highly personalised, unstable political systems which had existed in both states since their independence. The principle of regime compatibility, which is endorsed in the above extracts by Kaushik and Islam, carries an assumption of established political structure, and therefore would seem inappropriate as an explanation for the improved relations between Bangladesh and Pakistan. As a primary cause, the principle does not take into sufficient consideration the subtleties of both states' political traditions of individual influence. Mujib's regime of nationalism, socialism, secularism and democracy hardly could have been more compatible with the principles espoused by Mrs Gandhi's government, yet relations between the two states gradually deteriorated, the cause being popular dissatisfaction, rather than state-to-state disenchantment. Ziaur Rahman's and Bhutto's regimes were not obviously compatible, especially since the latter had a civilian, democratic beginning, yet considerable strengthening of Bangladesh–Pakistan relations took place once both were leaders of their states. The change in relations had already begun, well before Zia ul-Haq assumed control of Pakistan. It is not difficult to illustrate that the two Zias had characteristics in common: a military background and a strategy of loading their political policies with religious sentiments[19]; 'domesticating' pan-Islamic ideals for the purposes of political consolidation and advantage.[20] Consequently, it is also easy to presume that this appearance of political compatibility was largely responsible for bringing the two states together.

If a comparison is made of the character of Ziaur Rahman's and Zia ul-Haq's regimes, then the evidence for similarity becomes less clear-cut, undermining the notion of regime compatibility even further. Such a study has been made by Tushar Barua who has argued that although both Pakistan and Bangladesh succumbed to military rule, 'neither the structural and cultural affinity nor divergence' between the two states 'can explain the actual political systems in them'.[21] His main argument has focused on the personalised political structures in both states, where inter-elite relationships of cohesion and conflict aimed at sustaining power and privileges have been of greater influence in moulding both political systems.[22] Barua has also pointed out that although a military regime emerged in both states, the installation of military rule resulted from a variety of political, cultural, economic and administrative stimuli. Making an accurate comparison between the two regimes therefore becomes more difficult. Studying and comparing the particular goals of powerful individuals and factions in Pakistan and Bangladesh, as opposed to a general comparison between the types of regimes existing in each state, would perhaps provide a more useful method of interpretation. Even if the principle of regime compatibility could stand as an influential foreign policy determinant, it does not alter the fact that the sudden change to cordiality between Bangladesh and Pakistan occurred before Zia ul-Haq came to power in Pakistan.[23]

Barua's observations point towards a more comprehensive interpretation, one which can be extended further by questioning the extent to which private, individual political motives can be translated into public policies. In assessing Bangladesh's relations with Pakistan, it is pertinent to question the extent to which the recurring definition of foreign policy can be applied; that it is a manifestation of a government's desire to ensure state security and the 'protection and preservation of the minimum core values of any nation: political independence and territorial integrity'.[24] Examining the specific conduct of leaders such as Bhutto, Mujib and Ziaur Rahman indicates that such a definition is merely the ideal of what foreign policy should be and that personal self-interest plays a greater role in foreign policy decision-making than is usually indicated in the secondary sources. It may be more appropriate, for example, to explain the strong shift to cordial relations between Bangladesh and Pakistan in terms of the particular accordance between Ziaur Rahman's strategies to establish and hold on to power and Bhutto's ebullient overtures of friendship towards Bangladesh following Mujib's assassination. Considerable power has been held by individuals or small coteries in both states, a tendency which seems to indicate that the states' foreign policies have been determined by individual needs as much as anything else.

Scholars such as K.J. Holsti have evaluated this notion, Holsti concluding that in general, any explanation of a state's objectives in terms of the leader's 'images, values, ideological commitments, or private motives' is inadequate.[25] He has also stated that because 'policy, often undramatic, is the result of consultation, compromise, and bargaining among many individuals and advisers, the impact of subconscious psychological needs will be almost impossible to measure, identify, and may not help explain decisions in any case'.[26] Christopher Hill has added to the debate, declaring that a state's particular foreign policy is not simply a manifestation of the leadership's desire to stay in power,[27] because this impetus is common to most, if not all, ruling elites, and therefore becomes too general to be meaningful.[28]

While these arguments are applicable on a very broad scale, Barua's observations, which are based on particular circumstances occurring in Bangladesh and Pakistan, contain a slightly contrasting message, one which has given greater prominence to the actions of individuals and factions. Furthermore, both Holsti and Hill have qualified their arguments, taking them in a similar direction to that of Barua. Holsti has emphasised that the type of leadership existing in a state does have a considerable impact on the foreign policy decision-making which eventuates. He has pointed out that in an authoritarian political system, decision-making is sometimes limited to a few high-ranking individuals who are 'often cut off from objective analyses of internal and external conditions'.[29] These conditions, according to Holsti, mean that there are 'strong imperatives to undertake high-risk policies, or to command sudden switches in objectives, roles, orientations, or actions'.[30] Holsti has added that in regimes headed by charismatic leaders, (as Bhutto, Mujib and Ziaur Rahman are often described) those leaders can achieve 'considerable personal gratification from exercising power arbitrarily, seeking international prestige, or glorifying themselves through military displays and expeditions abroad'.[31] As shown above, and below, some of these stimuli and their ramifications (such as the sudden shift to warm relations between Pakistan and Bangladesh) are applicable to the conduct of Bangladesh–Pakistan relations.

Hill's added argument that 'all types of polity are prone to rule by dominant minorities'[32] may be valid, but it also suggests that foreign policy can be considerably dependent upon the fluctuating concerns of dominant individuals and groups. This perspective has also been supported by Christopher Clapham who has considered that foreign policy can be especially personalised in the absence of an 'effective range of domestic institutions' through which the leadership can work,[33] a condition which applied to both Pakistan and Bangladesh during the period under study.

In appraising the two states' foreign relations, the perspectives of Barua, as well as Holsti, Hill and Clapham, support to some degree the necessity to take into account the particular motives and circumstances associated with the leadership existing in Bangladesh and Pakistan between 1975 and 1990. An appraisal of the relationship between Bhutto and Mujib therefore should provide some insight into relations between the two states, as long as it also includes an examination of possible underlying reasons considered to have played a part in moulding the individual concerns and actions. Awareness of the type of regime occurring in both states can provide a very general basis for understanding their foreign relations, but this study attempts to take more into account, not only through examining the particular circumstances and motives involved, but also by looking at the underlying, long-term influences upon relations between the two states. A comparison of the evidence for warmer Bangladesh–Pakistan relations during Bhutto's regime and during that of Zia ul-Haq is warranted to try to ascertain the substance behind the rhetoric expounded. If the installation of a military regime in Pakistan was largely responsible for strengthening relations with Bangladesh, then an obvious increase in warmth and cordiality in those relations should have been evident upon Zia ul-Haq's rise to leadership of Pakistan.

The most significant step taken towards improved relations during the regimes of Bhutto and Ziaur Rahman was the establishment of diplomatic links in January 1976, as discussed above. It was this breakthrough which allowed further agreements, particularly economic, to be reached in the following months. For example, on 30 April 1976, both governments signed a general agreement which laid down the framework for the resumption of full-scale trade between the two countries.[34] A memorandum of understanding was signed to cover shipping arrangements to facilitate the trade, while a meeting to finalise banking arrangements to cover trade transactions was also organised.[35] The trade agreement was described by the leader of the Bangladesh trade delegation as providing 'an overall framework and official umbrella for the resumption of the trade ties' and representing 'the first official contact of its kind after Bangladesh was established'.[36] An achievement such as this tends to be overlooked by those scholars who link the cordiality of Bangladesh–Pakistan relations with the period of Zia ul-Haq's regime, as exemplified by the following incorrect comment by S.S. Islam who stated that '[i]n the early phase of independence of Bangladesh no trade agreement ... was signed between the two countries. They have been maintaining trade relations since President Zia's visit to Pakistan in 1977.'[37]

In the political arena, Bhutto offered firm support to Bangladesh, although there were considerable advantages for doing so, arising particularly from the latter's altercations with the Indian government. For example, in sympathising with Bangladesh in the Farakka debate conducted during the seventh Islamic conference of Foreign Ministers at Istanbul,[38] Bhutto's government could not only portray itself as acting clearly in the interests of Islamic unity, but it could also draw international attention towards Indian activities in the subcontinent. Bhutto was able to cultivate Pakistan's increasingly important Islamic ties, and at the same time, gain wider support in keeping Indian regional ambitions in check. Offering support to Bangladesh was an integral part of Bhutto's broader plans to win the support of wealthy and influential Muslim states (such as Iran, Saudi Arabia, the United Arab Emirates and Kuwait), a strategy which has been described as resulting from Bhutto's recognition that Pakistan had 'nowhere else to go given decreasing American interest'.[39] Bhutto's efforts to elevate his authoritarian and centralised regime by increasingly espousing Islamic sentiments[40] resembled Ziaur Rahman's own attempts to implement an Islamic style of government, providing an additional stimulus for rapprochement between the two states.

The evidence for a 'new chapter' emerging in Bangladesh–Pakistan relations once Zia ul-Haq had ousted Bhutto in July 1977 is far from conclusive. Zia ul-Haq's ascendancy in Pakistan was followed by effusive rhetorical reassurances from both states that their relations would continue to strengthen, due to the 'identity' of their views on international and regional issues, and thereby 'contribute to the stability of South Asia and to Islamic solidarity'.[41] Ziaur Rahman's visit to Pakistan in December 1977 was accompanied by similar assurances of cooperation and collaboration between the two states.[42] Nevertheless, despite such promising sentiments, the agreements reached between the two states did not go much beyond what had already been initiated, and those which went so far as to address unresolved legacies of the 1971 war achieved little of substance. As during Bhutto's regime, agreements concerning improved trading arrangements were made between the two states, in December 1977,[43] July 1979,[44] and July 1980.[45] Another shipping accord was signed in August 1978,[46] and an aviation accord was signed in January 1979 to facilitate the movement of people and the exchange of goods between Bangladesh and Pakistan.[47]

Agreements which would have represented a more substantial example of improved cordiality were those which might have addressed the two still unresolved problems associated with the Independence War, issues which had proved particularly intractable because they were logistically difficult to implement and would require the Pakistan government to incur a financial burden to the benefit of Bangladesh. Those problems were the repatriation of Biharis, numbering approximately 130 000 in 1977,[48] who as yet had not been able to fulfil their desire to relocate from Bangladesh to Pakistan; and the sharing of Pakistani assets which the Bangladesh government deemed should have taken place following Bangladesh's attainment of independence.[49]

The issues of Bihari repatriation and the division of assets had been virtually shelved once most of the other more pressing post-war differences had been resolved,[50] yet despite the obvious futility of extracting these concessions from the Pakistan government, successive Bangladesh governments continued to appeal to Pakistan to comply. For example, Ziaur Rahman had discussed the Bihari issue during his visit to Islamabad in December 1977, and although the Pakistan government had reportedly agreed to accept 25 000 more, little of substance actually came of the offer.[51] Optimistic reports concerning Bihari repatriation were still being presented in the Bangladesh press 12 months later. During a visit to Pakistan in December 1978, Bangladesh's foreign minister Professor Shamsul Haq commented confidently that 'both sides stressed the need for immediate start of the repatriation of stranded Pakistanis and agreed that the efforts should be made to remove the financial impediments affecting the process'.[52] By October 1980, at a meeting of foreign secretaries of Bangladesh and Pakistan, the earlier Pakistani offers of Bihari repatriation were shown to be meaningless, as indicated by the following reply by the Pakistan foreign secretary, Mr Reaz Piracha, to a question concerning repatriation:

> Since we have no dispute there was no question of agreement to be reached in this meeting . . . We have no divisive issues between the two countries.[53]

Later during the meeting Piracha acknowledged the 'human side of the problem of the three lakh stranded Pakistanis', clearly regarding the Biharis to be Pakistani citizens. Nevertheless, he justified Pakistan's back-pedalling on the issue by stating that 'this was not the only human problem and there were other such problems elsewhere and those also could not be solved'.[54]

A similar pattern of appeal and procrastination applied to the division of assets, although at the foreign secretaries' meeting in October 1980, a decision was reached to set up an 'expert level joint working group' to discuss the 'sharing of assets and liabilities between the two countries'.[55] Notwithstanding, no substantial progress was made by the joint body.[56]

The above study of some of the evidence for increasing cordiality in Bangladesh–Pakistan relations shows that while warmth had become characteristic of those relations, it did not appear to increase markedly beyond what was achieved during Bhutto's regime and certainly did not extend to the point of resolving the more politically contentious issues which had marred their relations since 1971. At the same time, this conclusion does not deny that a genuine, distinct shift in Bangladesh's relations with Pakistan did occur, but it confirms that the shift should be regarded as commencing after Mujib's assassination, rather than after the 1977 coup in Pakistan. Furthermore, while the solidarity achieved between the two states after 1975 appeared to be limited, the change to relative cordiality was nevertheless an extraordinary one, when taking into account the animosity and coolness which had been the most typical characteristics of official Bangladesh–Pakistan relations before that time. Even if little progress had been made in the assets-sharing issue, for example, the fact that representatives of both states had actually met to discuss the issue and could describe their talks as 'fruitful', being conducted in a 'spirit of frankness and understanding',[57] was an achievement easily underestimated in the light of traditional South Asian regional rivalry. The obvious procrastination by the Pakistan government over the Bihari problem also escaped noticeable criticism in the Bangladesh press. The improvement in relations between Bangladesh and Pakistan in 1975 was one of sharp contrast and appeared comparatively resilient.

A study of the timing of improved relations between the two states confirms that Mujib's assassination was an event of particular significance. The event needs to be taken into account when attempting to bring out the interconnections between individual political aspirations (deemed relevant in the discussion above) and some of the broader influences which may have contributed to the reshaping of Bangladesh–Pakistan relations. Mujib's assassination had fundamental ideological ramifications for both Bangladesh and Pakistan, and for relations between the two states. The effects were largely those which offered considerable political opportunities, openings which were capitalised upon in various ways and with varying degrees of success. In Bangladesh's case, Mujib's demise suggested to successors that a markedly different political approach should be adopted in order to distance themselves from the 'taint' of his style of administration. The civil and military dissatisfaction with Mujib's ineffective, autocratic and pro-Indian regime provided considerable political leverage for his opponents, particularly from within the regular armed forces which had been denied, until 1975, an influential role in the governance of Bangladesh. Mujib's unpopularity, particularly with the military, and his subsequent assassination therefore paved the way for the establishment of military rule in Bangladesh. The political path deemed by Ziaur Rahman as being the most politically expedient was one which was partly dictated by his perceptions of Mujib's failure. In order to cultivate support and legitimise his regime, Zia adopted a more independent stance towards the Indian government, espoused democratic sentiments, (which Mujib was perceived to have betrayed by instituting one-party rule) and promoted what he believed would be a more defined and acceptable formula for national identity and unity: a combination of Bangladeshi nationalism and Islamic consciousness. To a considerable extent, such goals were aimed at rejecting Indian political involvement in Bangladesh, and therefore were well suited to an acceptance of Bhutto's enthusiastic offers of rapprochement.

For Pakistan, the ideological implications of Mujib's assassination were also considerable and comparable, in some ways, with those occurring in Bangladesh. The creation of Bangladesh in 1971 had meant not only an overwhelming military defeat at the hands of arch-rival India. It also represented the greatest ideological challenge to the validity of Pakistan's existence yet encountered, an impact which has been described thus:

> The trauma associated with the 1971 dismemberment is not necessarily visible, but it permeates the attentive public's psyche. Jinnah's epochal creation has already been given a severe blow, and no politically conscious Pakistani can ignore or conceal the pain that secession has caused.[58]

It was likely, therefore, that any momentous event occurring within Bangladesh would be interpreted in Pakistan in terms which reflected the humiliation and insecurity which the 1971 defeat had generated, legacies for which both the Indian government and the Pakistan military were portrayed as most responsible.

The fortunes of Bhutto's political career at times hinged upon events occurring in Bangladesh. The convincing defeat of the Pakistan military in December 1971, and the subsequent ousting of Yahya Khan handed Bhutto the chance to fulfil his ambition to become leader of Pakistan. The opportunity easily could have been lost for a less seasoned politician, but Bhutto succeeded, until his eventual downfall in 1977, in turning possible pitfalls into advantages. In establishing his credentials, Bhutto especially had to play down his own part in the 1971 defeat, as pointed out by Tahir-Kheli:

> The first task for Zulfiqar Ali Bhutto as he came to power on December 20, 1971 in what was left of Pakistan was to gain some measure of

respectability for the country. He had not only to live down the image of a government committing atrocities against its own population but also to wipe out the lingering suspicion that he had played a critical role in the dismemberment.[59]

In attempting to remove that suspicion, Bhutto also aimed to turn the overwhelming defeat for Pakistan into something much less damning to the national psyche, and thereby accrue reflected political benefits. Since the military had already been discredited, Bhutto opted for the next most politically expedient course in legitimising his claim to the leadership: an approach which focused blame on the Indian government for the so-called 'dismemberment' of Pakistan. In early 1972, Bhutto terminated Pakistan's 24-year-old membership of the Commonwealth because the other members had agreed to recognise Bangladesh within a few weeks of Pakistan's defeat. Bhutto protested that the Commonwealth had sanctioned 'blatant aggression by one member against another and endorsed the use of force for the dismemberment of an independent, sovereign state'.[60]

Bhutto's visit to China in February 1972 was also aimed at bolstering his notion that India was responsible for a heinous violation of Pakistan's sovereignty; an accusation which received a sympathetic response from premier Chou En-lai who declared that China would assist the Pakistani people in their 'just struggle to preserve their State sovereignty and territorial integrity against outside aggression'.[61] The Chinese government had proved to be unreliable and unhelpful in the 1971 war, but Bhutto opted for the politically pragmatic course of ignoring, rather than criticising this slight. Accepting the rhetorical assurances of Pakistan's most powerful ally, rather than drawing attention to China's disloyalty, was much more likely to bear political fruit. While China had failed to provide tangible assistance to Pakistan during the war, Pakistan could at least glean some boost in morale from China's post-war rhetorical blandishments, in particular, China's interpretation of the phenomenon of Bangladesh's independence being put in terms of a state which had emerged due to Bengali elite interests, rather than because of a 'genuine grass roots peasant movement'.[62] In entertaining Chinese rhetoric, Bhutto was attempting to strengthen Sino–Pakistan relations and thereby restore at least some degree of credibility and prestige for Pakistan, and himself, in the post-1971 international arena.[63]

The 1971 war and its aftermath reinforced Bhutto's hand in Pakistan, while at the same time acting to undermine the normally powerful political influence of the military elite which otherwise would have posed the greatest challenge to his supremacy. The Indian government, the traditional scapegoat for Pakistani problems, fulfilled the role again perfectly. Despite the 'just and honorable peace' of the Simla Agreement',[64] the sensitivity of the links between Pakistan and India, associated particularly with the on-going

Kashmir dispute, ensured that leaders of both states would continue to capitalise on events in the region at the expense of each other.

Just as the emergence of Bangladesh offered Bhutto political advantages, Mujib's assassination also appeared to present fresh opportunities which Bhutto speedily adopted. Mujib's demise and the general lack of grief manifested in Bangladesh, as well as the ensuing decline in Indo–Bangladesh relations provided an ideological salve for Pakistan by representing a counter to the eroding effects of Bangladesh's emergence on the validity of the Two-Nation theory. These developments also appeared to confirm the propaganda used by Bhutto that Bangladesh had come into being as part of an Indian stratagem to reabsorb Pakistan and dominate the South Asian region. Bhutto was aware of the ideological leverage which Mujib's assassination offered, hence his alacrity in recognising Mujib's successor regime, led by Khondakar Mushtaque Ahmed. Since Bangladesh had so obviously declined to accept the Indian umbrella, and appeared willing to cultivate warmer relations with Pakistan, then such developments might be played upon to build national unity and identity in Pakistan. Amiable relations between the two states could be portrayed as evidence that Bangladesh's emergence did not necessarily bring Pakistan's *raison d'être* into question. A hint of these sentiments occurs in the following comment by Bhutto who, in criticising India's attempts to 'interfere and regulate the affairs of Bangladesh' and further justifying his recognition of the new regime in Bangladesh, declared:

> Pakistan wanted that the people of Bangladesh should not suffer any more. It respected them as the people of both the countries had lived together for 25 years and they share a common faith. We are interested in the welfare of the people of Bangladesh ... [T]he two peoples were once part of the same country. They had close relations. It was natural that even after separation we would not like to do anything which would add to the problems of Bangladesh.[65]

Unfortunately for Bhutto, the Pakistan military also reaped benefit from Mujib's removal. India's newly acquired nuclear capability had created fears in Pakistan,[66] acting to revitalise the Pakistan military to some extent, but the events occurring in Bangladesh in 1975 also offered a tangible opening for the restoration of military prestige in Pakistan. Mujib's assassination meant that the actions of the Pakistan military in 1971 could be reinterpreted in a less blameworthy light. The civil and military unrest which enveloped Pakistan in 1977 culminated in the reinstallation of military rule, but the renewal of military prestige and the acceptance of military power in Pakistan were also due partly to the face-saving ideological ramifications of Mujib's assassination and Bangladesh's subsequent spurning of Indian patronage.

The impact of events occurring within Bangladesh following Mujib's assassination also played a part in ensuring that the new course in Bangladesh's relations with Pakistan would become established. Ziaur Rahman's assumption of power and his attempts to consolidate his position as leader of Bangladesh required that he appeal to those groups which had been excluded from Mujib's generally pro-Indian cadre. Acquiring strong political support also led Zia to cultivate groups with an Islamic orientation, a political strategy which further alienated his regime from India's avowed secular government and in turn accorded more with Bhutto's increasing attention to his Islamic allies. To counteract possible Indian intervention in Bangladesh,[67] Zia's obvious option was to appeal to India's adversary, Pakistan, especially since Bhutto had expressed his approval of the changes occurring within Bangladesh.

Ziaur Rahman was also able to exploit Indo–Pakistani differences to strengthen his tenuous position. This strategy, in turn, played into the hands of the Pakistani government, thereby acting to strengthen the incipient warmth of Bangladesh–Pakistan relations. Such ploys drew attention to perceived Indian hegemonic designs. For example, in focusing on Zia's claim that 'foreign forces were out to destroy Bangladesh', the *Pakistan Times* had readily taken up Ziaur Rahman's appeal that 'certain elements inside the country... with the help of external forces [were] engaged in a conspiracy against the country's independence and sovereignty'.[68] The pressure of traditional Indo–Pakistani rivalry, combined with the ramifications of Mujib's assassination, was enough to set in motion the reversal in Bangladesh–Pakistan relations, quite apart from the convergence of political perspective between the two states in 1977.

The discussion above points to the intimate link between the political activities occurring within each of the three South Asian states and how events happening within the least powerful of the three, Bangladesh, have had influential, wider regional repercussions. It also indicates the underlying role which Indo–Pakistani rivalry has played in determining the direction of Bangladesh–Pakistan relations. It has been widely accepted, as illustrated in the extracts above, that once military regimes had emerged in Pakistan and Bangladesh, the diplomatic relations between the two states strengthened. Yet even without this convergence of political direction and outlook in 1977, the reversal in Bangladesh–Pakistan relations after August 1975 had already been initiated – speedily and with seemingly little grounds for doing so. The removal of Mujib and the subsequent shift in Bangladesh's foreign policy were sufficient to have considerable influence, not only on Bangladesh–Pakistan relations, but on Indo–Pakistan relations as well.

The Pakistan government interpreted regional events in terms of its preoccupation with India, as illustrated by the comment made by Bhutto, following Ziaur Rahman's coup in November 1975, that 'once diplomatic relations between Pakistan and Bangladesh were established he saw no difficulty in the restoration of diplomatic relations with India under the present conditions'.[69] His comment revealed how the changes happening in Bangladesh were viewed in Pakistan as representing a favourable shift in the balance of power in South Asia, one which enabled Bhutto to appear magnanimous and conciliatory by offering a return to diplomatic relations with India. Those relations were restored within eight months, in July 1976.[70]

The pressure of Indo–Pakistani rivalry, often regarded as the primary determinant of regional relations, has been shown above to have played an influential role in the conduct of Bangladesh's relations with Pakistan, but relying on this notion alone is not adequate to explain the change which occurred in relations between the two states. The change can also be explained partly in terms of the convergence between unique, chance events and individual political ambitions and acumen. Bhutto and Ziaur Rahman in particular were able to consolidate their uncertain hold on power partly by skilfully playing upon fears of Indian domination, a traditional rallying point in Pakistan and a legacy which could be revived in Bangladesh. In aiming to undermine their rivals and, in turn, cultivate popular appeal, both leaders used similar strategies which they also both realised could be enhanced by the cultivation of a diplomatic rapprochement between the two states. In establishing a new direction for Bangladesh–Pakistan relations, Ziaur Rahman and Bhutto were able to circumvent the traumatic heritage of the 1971 war, although both leaders were assisted by the fact that the most divisive matters which emerged from the war[71] had been settled already.

While the depth of cordiality reached between Bangladesh and Pakistan during this period could not be described as great, the two states did achieve stability in their relations. Acknowledgment of this stability has been limited in studies of South Asian regional relations which tend to centre on the rivalry between the various states. Relations between Bangladesh and Pakistan after 1975 represented a divergence from the general characteristic normally attributed to regional relations: that they 'have been characterized by mutual suspicion, unfriendly relations and, at times, open conflict'.[72] The divergence also counters S.P. Cohen's view of the interrelationship between the major South Asian states which he described as one of coexisting extremes; an 'ambiguous embrace of love and hate, expectation and dread'.[73]

Even though Indo–Pakistani rivalry played an influential part in moulding the relationship between Bangladesh and Pakistan, the two states had reached, quickly and unexpectedly, a degree of stability and maturity which was not typical of regional relations up to that time. The lessons of the 1971 war had forced Bhutto to reappraise Pakistan's foreign relations, resulting in a more diversified foreign policy which professed 'friendship with all', but aimed especially to establish closer links with influential Islamic states. Indian military supremacy had been confirmed in the 1971 war, while Pakistan had suffered international criticism and domestic instability. Caution, pragmatism, realism and consolidation were therefore especially appropriate for Pakistan's foreign policy which Bhutto redirected accordingly. The need to recognise and act upon opportunities for establishing new and beneficial international ties was intrinsic to that redirection. Events such as Mujib's assassination were seen by Bhutto as particularly opportune. Ziaur Rahman also took Bangladesh's foreign policy in a different, less aligned direction, one which echoed and converged with Bhutto's foreign policy aims, and hence reinforced the change from antagonism to cordiality and stability in Bangladesh's relations with Pakistan.

Despite the variety of pressures which have been isolated as impinging on the conduct of those relations, India's role has always been an integral one, extending beyond the notion of Indo–Pakistani rivalry. The methods by which Bhutto and Zia succeeded in establishing friendlier relations between Pakistan and Bangladesh indicated that popular fears of Indian domination existing in both states were easily played upon, outweighing whatever animosity and resentment lingered between their inhabitants.

8
1982–90: A Maturing
of Relations?

Little study has been made of the course of Bangladesh–Pakistan relations during Ershad's regime; even less than has been undertaken on relations during the Ziaur Rahman period.[1] This chapter approaches the subject by providing a broad interpretation of how Bangladesh's relations with Pakistan evolved during Ershad's regime, and by analysing the way in which both domestic and external events influenced the relationship. Again, the evidence contradicts the commonly held notion that Bangladesh's domestic turmoil has been largely responsible for moulding the character of its diplomatic relations in South Asia.

Bangladesh's relations with Pakistan during the regime of Hussain Muhammad Ershad were no less dominated by Indo–Pakistani rivalry, individual political aspirations and factional political turmoil than they were while Ziaur Rahman was leader. Additional, and at times contradictory, pressures came to impinge on Bangladesh–Pakistan relations in the 1980s. These developments were due to a wide range of causes: extra-regional, regional and domestic. South Asia was experiencing an emerging sense of fellowship and cooperation with the launching of SAARC in 1985. At the same time, regional tensions were increasing, particularly because of escalating ethnic conflict[2] and deepening Indo–Pakistani friction, the latter fuelled by the Soviet occupation of Afghanistan and the subsequent military strengthening of Pakistan by the United States. The threat of nuclear warfare also began to exacerbate regional tension in the 1980s, as both Pakistan and India were widely believed to have attained nuclear weapons capability.[3] Mutual fear and distrust of India remained characteristic of Bangladesh–Pakistan relations, guaranteeing them a degree of stability and harmony. At the same time, the negative bond of fear was not particularly conducive to innovative advancements in those relations. Domestic political, social and economic strife plagued both Bangladesh and Pakistan with increasing intensity during the second half of the decade, also tending to impede a maturing of relations.

The long-standing tension and rivalry between Pakistan and India has had an intrinsic role in shaping South Asian interstate relations, as evident in the relationship between Pakistan and Bangladesh. The conduct of Bangladesh–Pakistan relations in the 1980s was circumscribed to a considerable extent by the tension between India and Pakistan, as was the case during Ziaur Rahman's regime. Pakistan's foreign policy tended to react according to the dictates of habitual antagonism towards India, as illustrated in Chapter 7.

The strength of Pakistan's foreign policy fixation on India was great enough to outweigh the dangers posed to Pakistani sovereignty by the Soviet occupation of Afghanistan in December 1979. According to T.P. Thornton, even after the Soviet occupation, the 'Pakistanis remained aggravatingly preoccupied with the historic threat from the east, to the detriment of common efforts *vis-à-vis* the more real Soviet danger'.[4] H.W. Wriggins succinctly summarised the mutual preoccupation between Pakistan and India thus:

> Indeed, it is as if the principals on both sides simply cannot refrain from touching each other's raw nerves – rather like siblings who have lived too long in cramped quarters. Whether the difficulties derive from the bitterness of years of inter-communal suspicion, from thirty-five years of conflict-ridden interstate relations, or from the imperative need of hard-pressed leaders to evoke public support by calling up reliable xenophobic emotions, it is hard to say.[5]

Pakistan's Indo-centric foreign policy did not mean that Soviet activities in Afghanistan were not of considerable concern. The repercussions for Pakistan and the South Asian region were substantial. As expressed by Wriggins, the 'shadow of Soviet power hung over the entire subcontinent, as never before'.[6] For much of the 1980s, Pakistan's foreign policy was driven by the Soviet presence in Afghanistan and its corresponding augmentation of Indian regional strength. Pakistan's response to the Soviet occupation was of a dual nature. On one hand, Pakistan's India-focus was magnified greatly under the circumstances whereby it was sandwiched between India and the Soviet Union, India's most powerful and staunchest ally. On the other, Pakistan became preoccupied with expanding and strengthening its links outside the South Asian region, in order to offset the Soviet–Indian threat. For increased support, Pakistan turned to the Islamic Middle East states, the People's Republic of China (PRC) and the United States, the task made much easier because Pakistan was able to play on its vulnerability to Soviet expansionism.[7] Pakistan's initiatives bore considerable fruit, particularly in the form of a massive military aid package from the United States, worth US\$3.2 billion and including, what was, compared with India's arsenal, state-of-the-art military hardware.[8]

The Soviet occupation of Afghanistan therefore served to alter the balance of power in South Asia, heightening tensions between Pakistan and India and boosting the subcontinental arms race. Because of the historical link between India, Pakistan and Bangladesh, Soviet activity in Afghanistan inevitably had consequences for relations between Pakistan and Bangladesh. Those relations were strengthened, on the whole, particularly during the initial years, because both states held a mutual fear of India and the Soviet Union. At the same time, Pakistan's boosted extra-regional quest for military and financial assistance, neither of which Bangladesh could supply, tended to impede the incipient maturity of the relationship, as explained below.

During the early 1980s, interaction between Pakistan and Bangladesh exhibited a gradual improvement in the warmth and stability which had been developing since 1974. As well as the Afghanistan crisis, events occurring within Pakistan and Bangladesh reinforced friendly relations between the two states, at least during the first half of the decade. Relations improved despite Bangladesh's political upheavals following Ziaur Rahman's assassination in 1981, and the subsequent fluctuations between civilian and military rule. Ziaur Rahman's successors, Abdus Sattar and later Ershad, were essentially pro-Pakistani, their foreign policy positions and diplomatic overtures countering the impact on relations of domestic political uncertainty.

Following Zia's demise, mutual expressions of solidarity and support were offered between Bangladesh and Pakistan, with both states beginning to place great emphasis on their Islamic fraternity.[9] The Sattar government in Bangladesh began to take such a strongly-Islamic and pro-Pakistani stance that it aroused criticism from the Opposition. In vigorously defending his government's position, Sattar's Prime Minister, Shah Aziz Rahman, commented that the ties between Bangladesh and Pakistan could be strengthened even 'further within the framework of Islamic solidarity, and not merely bilaterally'.[10] He added that the 'promotion of Islamic solidarity' was one of the 'constitutional obligations' of the Bangladesh government.[11]

Within days of his coup in March 1982, Ershad acted to bring Bangladesh's foreign policy more into line with Pakistan's, adopting an assertively anti-Soviet, pro-United States stance. This was exemplified by the arrest of two Soviet attachés under suspicion of conducting espionage against Bangladesh,[12] followed up by Ershad's entreaties to the United States for greater support following the arrests, playing on US concern over the Soviet occupation of Afghanistan. Ershad commented in an interview after the Soviet incident that he considered the Soviet Union to be 'very dangerous', declaring: 'We cannot trust them so much. They are very crude. They have such a mighty military machine . . . We are really scared about what they may do next'.[13] He then drew attention to what he saw as the 'inadequate American responses to past Soviet moves'.[14] At the same time, Ershad tempered his criticism with placatory expressions of goodwill, declaring that 'Bangladesh felt nothing but friendship toward the United States' and that he thought President Reagan to be 'a strong leader'.[15] Ershad no doubt hoped that the United States would be more forthcoming with an anti-Soviet regime in Bangladesh. If Pakistan could obtain such vast amounts of financial and military aid while negotiating from a position of weakness and vulnerability, then perhaps Bangladesh, too, might be able to share in some of the largesse.

Ershad's concordant foreign policy was welcomed by Pakistan President, Zia ul-Haq, who responded along Islamic lines. In an effusive review of relations in August 1982, Zia lauded what he saw as the close Islamic bond which existed, and would always exist, between Pakistan and Bangladesh:

> Pakistan has got special regards for Bangladesh. We have lived for 24 years together. Then we were separated. But, whatever love, sympathy and affection we have for each other will never exhaust. None can snatch away our love. If Pakistan can maintain cordial relations with the countries like Sri Lanka and Nepal, why can she not have brotherly relations with Bangladesh. The love of a Muslim country for another Muslim country cannot be snatched away.[16]

The warm rhetoric was supported by a little substance in the following month, with Pakistan's recommencement of the scheme to repatriate the many thousands of Biharis stranded in Bangladesh after the Independence War.[17] The task of resettling the Biharis, supporters of Pakistan during the war, had been hampered by government apathy and political expediency on Pakistan's part. While it represented progress, the repatriation move in October 1982 was little more than a symbolic gesture, made possible by the financial contributions of the Kuwait and Qatar governments.[18] Approximately 4600 Biharis were moved on this occasion, while a further 250 000 awaited repatriation, languishing in 66 refugee camps scattered throughout Bangladesh.[19] More substantial indications of strengthening diplomatic relations did begin to emerge at this time, however. In the same month, both governments decided to expand bilateral trade further and to reduce existing trade constraints.[20] Trade turnover between the two countries had increased almost fivefold from US$30 million in 1976–7 to US$145 million in 1981–2, but both governments appeared determined to improve economic ties in the longer term, implementing strategies to create an equitable balance of trade.[21]

Diplomatic relations between Bangladesh and Pakistan continued to improve in the following year, the highlights being the Dhaka visit by Pakistan Foreign Minister Sahibzada Yakub Khan on 11–12 August 1983,[22] and Bangladesh's hosting of the Fourteenth Islamic Conference of Foreign Ministers on 6–10 December, as discussed below.[23] The August visit by Sahibzada Yakub Khan was significant in that it represented the first official visit by a Pakistani Foreign Minister since Bangladesh's creation in 1971. The visit followed upon the inaugural meeting of South Asian Foreign Ministers at New Delhi, held on 1–2 August to launch South Asian Regional Cooperation (SARC). Sahibzada Yakub and his Bangladesh counterpart, A.R. Shams-ud Doha, both espoused sentiments aimed to improve relations.

The 'free and frank' discussions between the two foreign ministers, and their foreign policy pronouncements, reflected the growing emphasis on Islamic consciousness emerging throughout the Islamic world. Doha declared that both Bangladesh and Pakistan were 'heirs to a rich civilisation and culture with ties rooted deep in... their shared faith, traditions and values', adding that the bonds between the two countries had been 'reinforced by many common aims and similarity of approach to problems'.[24] He also stated that 'Bangladesh as a member of the OIC [Organisation of Islamic Conference] was concerting its efforts with like-minded countries, including Pakistan, to uphold the causes and interests of the world of Islam', standing 'firmly for the unity and solidarity of the Islamic community'.[25] Doha assured the Pakistan foreign minister of Bangladesh's concordant stand on major international issues, such as those concerning Afghanistan and Israel.[26] Sahibzada Yakub responded in kind, declaring that 'both Pakistan and Bangladesh were linked by spiritual affinities of a glorious faith, a shared history and cultural heritage'.[27] He also commented that 'both countries experienced alike the gravitational pull of the Islamic world and the two countries had cooperated closely in efforts to promote fraternal solidarity of the OIC'.[28]

The mutual exchanges of goodwill were accompanied by firm initiatives to strengthen relations, such as the signing of an Agreement on visas. Under the Agreement, travel facilities for citizens of both countries were extended and streamlined, replacing the existing ad hoc arrangement. Slight, but tangible progress was made concerning at least one of the two long-term irritants in Bangladesh–Pakistan relations: the repatriation of the Bihari refugees and the sharing of assets and liabilities.[29] When asked by the Bangladesh media about these two issues, the Pakistan foreign minister gave assurances regarding the former, categorising those who would be repatriated.[30] While there was little evidence that his visit had much of an impact on Pakistani commitment to the Bihari issue, it did at least show that Pakistan was willing to continue discussing the matter. Shahibzada Yakub was much less forthcoming on the subject of assets-sharing,[31] as had been the standard approach of the Pakistan government since the 1971 war.

The Fourteenth Islamic Conference of Foreign Ministers in December 1983, held in Dhaka for the first time, capped a year in which Bangladesh–Pakistan relations strengthened markedly, compared with the remainder of the decade. Ershad embraced his role as head of the host state for the conference, emphasising Bangladesh's flourishing Islamic heritage and his country's wholehearted determination to 'step up efforts' to promote 'greater unity and solidarity' among the Islamic ummah.[32] The conference marked a maturing of Bangladesh's foreign relations. In being bestowed with the honour of hosting the conference, Bangladesh had won the acceptance and confidence of the other OIC members, despite the earlier controversy surrounding Bangladesh's creation and the break with Islamic Pakistan. The

OIC Secretary-General, Habib Chatty, praised Bangladesh's role in making the conference a success, commenting that Bangladesh was now 'capable of hosting an OIC summit'.[33] Bangladesh was clearly becoming integrated with the growing international pan-Islamic consciousness, drawing Bangladesh's foreign policy more closely into line with Pakistan and many of the middle east Islamic states.

The extent to which both Pakistan and Bangladesh were becoming ensconced within the international Islamic community was perhaps best exemplified by the generous Saudi offers of assistance to both states for the purpose of resolving the Bihari repatriation issue. An agreement was eventually reached, after several years of negotiations between a Saudi humanitarian organisation and the Pakistan and Bangladesh governments, to assist in the resettlement of Biharis who wished to move from Bangladesh to Pakistan.[34] Under the agreement, a trust fund was to be set up to raise US$284 million to repatriate and rehabilitate the Biharis, then estimated to number 259 100.[35] The plan was not fulfilled, for reasons to be discussed below, but even as a mooted plan it indicated the considerable potential for Bangladesh and Pakistan to resolve outstanding differences via the medium of Islamic fraternity.

Improved diplomatic ties between Bangladesh and Pakistan were also exemplified by Zia ul-Haq's unscheduled visit to Bangladesh in June 1985 to inspect the impact of a recent severe cyclone and storm surge, and to 'share the sorrows' of those affected.[36] Zia's visit, described by a somewhat biased source as 'demonstratively pretentious', was essentially a diplomatic exercise. The gesture was, nevertheless, symbolic of the gradual 'normalising' and strengthening of the once-bitter relations between the two states. The spontaneous initiative by Pakistan's President may have lacked substance, but it appeared no less sincere than the similar, brief inspection visits by the Indian Prime Minister, Rajiv Gandhi, and the Sri Lankan President, Jayawardene, carried out three days earlier. Ershad hailed all three leaders for their concern, despite the fact that little practical aid was forthcoming.[37] The high-level visits were partly prompted by the imminent launching of the South Asian Association for Regional Cooperation (SAARC), scheduled to take place in December 1985. The link between increasing regional awareness and Ershad's enthusiastic response to Zia's brief visit was exemplified in the following press extract:

> H.M. Ershad welcomed … Zia ul-Haq of Pakistan, saying that … [Bangladesh and Pakistan] were bound by 'innumerable ties of friendship' … President Ershad observed that friendly cooperation between Dhaka and Pindi was developing to the mutual benefit of the peoples of both the countries. He believed that such cooperation would get a new impetus with the gradual evolution of SARC. He hoped that President Zia ul-Haq's short visit would embolden 'our resolve to strengthen cooperation in this region'.[38]

During the early to mid-1980s, therefore, Bangladesh's relations with Pakistan were heavily influenced by extra-regional and regional pressures, more so than by those of a domestic nature. Stimuli such as the Islamic movement; direct superpower involvement in Afghanistan and South Asia; the associated unease and suspicion between India and Pakistan, and conversely, the movement towards South Asian regional cooperation; all contributed towards a strengthening of Bangladesh–Pakistan relations.

The extent to which relations between Bangladesh and Pakistan had improved was tested more rigorously in the second half of the decade. Revived tension between India and Pakistan in 1986–7[39] ensured that the stable relationship developing between Bangladesh and Pakistan would continue to be based on a mutual fear of Indian dominance, more so than on positive and constructive considerations. Domestic political events occurring particularly in Pakistan in the late 1980s showed that Bangladesh–Pakistan relations still required a more meaningful basis for long-term stability.

The majority of the South Asian states, India, Pakistan, Bangladesh and Sri Lanka, experienced increasing communal, ethnic and secessionist strife in the 1980s. Zia ul-Haq's democratically-elected successor, Benazir Bhutto, became prime minister of Pakistan in November 1988, but her regime was weak, becoming increasingly preoccupied with the basic task of holding on to power. Consequently, her dealings with Bangladesh came to be circumscribed largely by her domestic plight, as explained below.

Political secessionism and communal tension in Pakistan escalated particularly in the most ethnically diverse province, Sindh, and its capital, Karachi. The greatest rivalries existed between the four largest urban ethnic groups in the province: the Urdu-speaking Muhajireen (originally refugees who fled from India to Pakistan in 1947),[40] the native Sindhi-speakers, the Punjabis and the Pushtuns.[41] Further pressure was placed on native Sindh inhabitants by other ethnic immigrant groups, such as the Baluchis and the Biharis repatriated from Bangladesh. A virtual explosion of immigration in Sindh produced serious political and ethnic disharmony in the province, with most of the various groups finding it impossible to coexist without each fearing the loss of cultural identity and politico–economic power.[42] Extreme Sindhi nationalists demanded their own independent *Sindhodesh*, free of perceived Punjabi central-government dominance, while violent ethnic clashes erupted between the different ethnic groups vying for political dominance in Karachi.[43] The unrest was quelled by military force, but continuing tension in the province placed considerable pressure on the central government.[44]

Each of the ethnic groups established political wings to defend their rights, the *Muhajireen* forming the *Muhajir Qaumi Mahaz* (MQM)[45] in 1984. The MQM developed into a major, power-broking political party in Pakistan, dominating urban Sindh. The activities of the MQM were to have far-reaching consequences not only for the stability of the Pakistan central government, but also for the relationship between Pakistan and Bangladesh. For reasons of its own, the MQM began to push for the repatriation of the remaining Biharis in Bangladesh following the sudden death of Zia ul-Haq in August 1988.[46] In the ensuing struggle to lead the new government, Benazir Bhutto and her Sindhi-dominated Pakistan People's Party (PPP) emerged triumphant, but only after much intense political manoeuvring and bargaining. In order to secure an absolute majority in the National Assembly and to stabilise both urban and rural Sindh, Benazir was left with no option but to woo the PPP's rival, the MQM.[47] Benazir's political survival was also heavily dependent on appeasing the military and the bureaucracy, both of which remained powerful and politically influential, despite Zia's demise, as explained by S.V.R. Nasr:

> Democracy...emerged by default once the ruling regime voluntarily stepped aside after the sudden death of Zia and his top brass in a plane crash on August 17, 1988...The military made a grand exit before the time when the democratic movement could have matured and overwhelmed it. The military was thus able to continue to exercise political power, although indirectly; this clearly placed democratic forces at a disadvantage and instead emboldened political forces loyal to Zia's legacy.[48]

Benazir's hold on political power was thus exceedingly tenuous, being compounded by the weakening of the PPP's organisational structure with her nepotistic appointment of loyal, but inexperienced, advisors in place of the PPP 'old guard'.[49]

In trying to cultivate MQM support, Benazir inevitably alienated traditional PPP supporters: the Sindhi nationalists. In the struggle to maintain authority in Sindh, the ruling PPP was 'constricted and enfeebled' by the impossible task of fulfilling the opposing dictates of the two groups.[50] The repatriation of the Biharis, in particular, became a highly politicised issue in Karachi as the PPP tried, on the one hand, to be seen as complying with the MQM's stance on the issue, but on the other, procrastinating so as to avoid provoking the Sindhi nationalists.[51] The volatility associated with the Bihari problem in Sindh, and the PPP's vulnerability, forced Benazir to treat the issue with extreme caution, as was evident in her visit to Bangladesh in October 1989.

Benazir's visit to Bangladesh was touted as a 'new era of closer relations',[52] where Pakistan was prepared to cooperate with Bangladesh in 'all walks of life without any reservations or qualifications.'[53] In reality, the visit achieved very little of substance, Benazir's assurances clearly did not apply to the Biharis, with whom she refused to meet. In hoping to reduce both Pakistan's responsibility for the Biharis, and the extent of the violence in Sindh, Benazir was also 'believed to have requested that Dhaka resettle them [the Biharis] permanently in Bangladesh with financial assistance from Pakistan and other Islamic countries'.[54] Benazir's obvious evasiveness and back-tracking on the Bihari issue provoked not only criticism in Bangladesh but also precipitated a crisis in Sindh, prompting renewed and widespread political violence in the province.[55] Benazir's attempts to skirt the Bihari issue failed and the MQM withdrew its political support for the PPP, defecting to the opposition,[56] and contributing towards the downfall of the PPP government in the following year.

Benazir's vulnerable, unstable and erratic regime was in no position to initiate significant advances in Pakistan's relations with Bangladesh. Even domestically, the PPP government's performance was lack-lustre, with not a single new piece of legislation being passed or even introduced, apart from two annual budgets.[57] The larger state's increasing domestic instability overshadowed foreign-policy dealings, as had occurred with relations between Indian and Bangladesh. The chances for establishing very strong relations between Pakistan and Bangladesh were certainly there, particularly given the foreign policy characteristics common to both states. The Islamic link presented particular scope for manipulation, as had been undertaken by both Zia ul-Haq and Ershad, the latter declaring Islam to be the state religion in June 1988.[58] This step defined Bangladesh's increasingly Islamic outlook, presenting further opportunities to improve relations with Pakistan. Benazir Bhutto was unable to exploit either of these common bonds effectively; her policy on both India and Islam lacked clarity and consistency.

Concerning India, Benazir fluctuated between two extremes. In early 1990, she announced a policy of rapprochement with India with 'great fanfare'.[59] Indian analysts, such as P.S. Bhogal, were cautiously optimistic that Benazir's democratically elected regime and her cooperative overtures towards India heralded a break-through in relations, creating 'enhanced confidence and goodwill between the two countries'.[60] Benazir was forced to change her policy towards India during her ultimately unsuccessful struggle for political survival from mid-1989 to August 1990. The Kashmir dispute also re-erupted in early 1990, prompting Benazir to adopt a more antagonistic stance towards India in the hope of gaining domestic support.[61] In heightening fears of India, the Pakistan government was also using a standard technique to channel domestic criticism away from itself. Benazir's *volte-face* towards India was pronounced enough even to win the approval of Pakistan's extremist Islamic party, the *Jama'at-e Islami*.[62]

Benazir's regime was equally contradictory with regard to implementing a decisive policy on Islam. Increasing ethnic rivalry made it much more difficult for Benazir to promote Islam as a focus for national unity than it had been for her predecessor. Benazir had also inherited former PPP leader, Zulfikar Ali Bhutto's, comparatively secular political platform which she advocated wholeheartedly before being elected, denouncing Zia ul-Haq's Islamisation measures in 'the strongest terms'.[63] Once in power, Benazir realised, somewhat belatedly, that it was politically necessary to pursue a more moderate line or be condemned as anti-Muslim.[64] In attempting to find an appropriate Islamic stance, Benazir and the PPP were well behind their political rivals. While the PPP was being forced to reconsider its avowedly secular platform, parties such as the Islamic Democratic Alliance (IJI) were already thoroughly experienced in harnessing the emotive power of Islam.[65] The PPP's weak and vacillating approach to the notion of Islamic identity therefore meant that this avenue for strengthening relations with Bangladesh lacked the focus and momentum which existed under Zia ul-Haq.

Examining Bangladesh's relations with Pakistan in the 1980s shows that they fluctuated in warmth according to a wide range of pressures: extra-regional, regional and domestic. Some of these worked against an improvement in relations, some ensured that the relationship remained stable on the whole, while others, such as the Soviet occupation of Afghanistan, appeared to do both. There were many consequences of the Soviet activity in the region. One of the more fundamental results was that Pakistan gained an unprecedented amount of financial and military support and, just as importantly, a great deal of morale-boosting international sympathy. The latter had been in very short supply, particularly since Bangladesh's Independence War, where Pakistan had been humiliated in defeat and widely condemned for its actions. Certainly, before 1980, Pakistan had had a great deal of difficulty in developing and maintaining associations with other countries.[66] In gaining such vital support during the Afghanistan crisis, the stigma of Pakistan's earlier defeat and dismemberment was mitigated to some extent, perhaps reducing the psychological encumberment which had been integral to relations between Pakistan and Bangladesh. At the very least, the Afghanistan crisis assisted in keeping Bangladesh's relations with Pakistan on an even keel.

From one perspective, Bangladesh and Pakistan were drawn closer together by their mutual fear of Soviet–Indian intentions. From another, both became more interested in improving extra-regional links, opportunities for which were stimulated by Soviet activity in Afghanistan. Their extra-regional focus was developed at the expense of initiating improvements in relations with each other.

Pakistan was also beginning to realise that while it was advantageous to have friendly relations with Bangladesh, the smaller state was, nevertheless, starting to play a more influential role in South Asian political affairs. Bangladesh's regional and international stature and recognition had improved considerably, prompted by such factors as its election in 1978 for a two-year term on the United Nations Security Council and its instrumental role in the creation of SAARC. Bangladesh gained in confidence and independence as a result and, in turn, a cool cautiousness became more evident in Pakistan's attitude towards Bangladesh in the second half of the 1980s. In August 1989, for example, relations between Pakistan and Bangladesh became particularly strained because of Pakistan's humiliation over a pre-emptive

SAARC initiative made by Bangladesh.[67] A trade deal made by Bangladesh in the same year also incensed Pakistan. Bangladesh agreed to purchase 200 000 tonnes of rice from Bangkok at a higher rate than the concessional offer which had already been made by Pakistan.[68] In retaliation, Pakistan ceased buying tea from Bangladesh, cancelling a trade arrangement which was worth US$30 million per year to Bangladesh.[69] These disagreements showed that while relations between Bangladesh and Pakistan were maturing during Ershad's regime, the tradition of distrust in South Asian regional politics ensured that relations retained a degree of wariness. They also indicated that little rapport existed between Ershad and Benazir.

Pakistan's increasing domestic turmoil in the 1980s played a large part in hampering relations with Bangladesh, just as India's internal problems had marred relations with Bangladesh. Also common to both sets of relations was the manner in which they often varied according to the individual political aspirations of those in power. Benazir Bhutto, and Zia ul-Haq to a less blatant extent, reacted to the Bihari repatriation issue according to domestic political priorities, with little regard for the impact on the Biharis themselves or on relations with Bangladesh. The Bangladesh government also exploited, and continued to use such issues for political gain, and as a bargaining chip to extract possible concessions from the Pakistan government.[70] The Chittagong Hill Tract (CHT) problem (see chapter 6) exhibited a similar pattern, where a minority group became a pawn in the conduct of bilateral relations, politicising the group in the process, and ensuring that the issue would remain unresolved.

Relations between Bangladesh and Pakistan retained a degree of cordiality and stability during Ershad's regime, despite increasing domestic and regional strife. Nevertheless, the depth of the warmth did not mature to a notable extent, despite ample opportunities. In fact, as relations developed in the 1980s, they began to fall into some of the patterns associated with the ever-present rivalry between India and Pakistan. The Pakistan government did not effectively grasp the advantages which could have accrued from cultivating a staunch regional ally through skilful diplomacy. Instead, Pakistan tended to remain regionally aloof, preferring to court more powerful, external allies and the nuclear option,[71] rather than look to Bangladesh for moral support.

Conclusion

Bangladesh's relationship with India and Pakistan during the regimes of Ziaur Rahman and Ershad reflected the influence of a wide variety of stimuli, ranging from unique, catalytic events, such as Mujibur Rahman's assassination, to pervasive, long-term effects, such as those deriving from colonial domination. In resolving the multiplicity of pressures which have impinged on Bangladeshi foreign policy, three perspectives were applied: general, regional and domestic. This approach was used to counter the considerable bias in the contemporary and secondary sources and to appraise the common view that Bangladesh's foreign relations and the difficulties experienced in the course of pursuing those relationships were shaped largely by Bangladesh's inherent political and economic instability. The study of Bangladesh's most significant relationships – that is, with India and Pakistan – shows that they have a much broader and more intricate foundation than one which rests on stereotypical notions such as Bangladesh's 'inability to establish a stable regime'; its 'national chauvinism'; its ''anti-Indianism'; its 'disruptive role' in South Asia's northeast; or its heavy dependency on foreign aid.[1]

Many other pressures, apart from Bangladesh's domestic problems, have been identified as playing influential roles in Bangladesh's relations with India and Pakistan. While no single ingredient can be isolated as being the main determinant for the conduct of Bangladeshi foreign relations, the evidence presented suggests that it is possible to place the most prominent 'causal' pressures within a loose hierarchy. At the broadest level, Bangladesh's foreign policy is considered to be most influenced by pressures emanating from within the South Asian region. Such pressures have been consistently the most influential in shaping Bangladesh's foreign policy. Bangladesh's domestic realm has been placed second in the hierarchy; with the extra-regional arena considered to have had the least influence of the three. While the pressures exerted by the regional machinations of the superpowers and Bangladesh's aid-donors have played a part in determining the character of Bangladeshi foreign policy, this study shows that their roles have been of less influence than often suggested. The ending of the Cold War, for example, has not precipitated a reduction in South Asian tension nor an improvement in Bangladesh's relations with India and Pakistan.

The evidence suggests that, within the regional perspective, India's domestic and regional concerns have been most influential in the conduct of Indo–Bangladesh relations. Indo–Pakistani rivalry has been placed second in order of influence. Bangladesh's domestic political and economic instability appears to have been less influential than either of these.

The degree of political will exhibited by the Indian government has been the most consistently influential determinant shaping Indo–Bangladesh relations during the period. The ease with which those relations could be placed on either a cordial or a sour footing, depending on the prevailing Indian government's foreign policy, shows that India's influence over the course of the relationship has been considerable, and far greater than generally acknowledged. The concessions made by the Desai and Singh governments towards Bangladesh were minor as such, but when compared with the few initiatives shown during the regimes of Indira and Rajiv Gandhi, they were exceptional. The Desai and Singh overtures were not rebuffed by Ziaur Rahman and Ershad, both of whom responded positively. A longer term of office for either the Desai or Singh governments might have had a substantial impact on the course of Indo–Bangladesh relations.

For much of the period from 1975 to 1990, however, the theme which dominates is the Indian government's general unwillingness to compromise with or to offer concessions to Bangladesh. The rivalry between India and Pakistan is woven into India's reactions to Bangladesh, taking on a similar pattern, particularly with regard to matters of political geography. Disputes over the sharing of water and over ownership of small parcels of territory, such as the Tin Bigha Corridor, Muhuri Char and New Moore Island, were symptomatic of the essentially poor relationship between India and Bangladesh and fostered further ill-will between the two states. Both states added fuel to their mutual disputes, both overreacting with aggression and suspicion. Of the two states, India was in a far better position to compromise. Bangladesh did not represent a military threat and had much more to lose than India. The disputes should have been quickly resolvable through diplomatic channels. Instead, the conduct of the issues was characterised by belligerence and insensitivity on India's part, and oversensitivity and suspicion on Bangladesh's. The Indian government, particularly under Indira Gandhi, had great difficulty in differentiating between disputes with Bangladesh and those with rivals, Pakistan and China. A Bangladesh government which was not obviously pro-Indian, as it was under Mujibur Rahman, was automatically dubbed by India, Cold War-style, as being pro-Pakistan.

The possibility that India might soften its stance towards Bangladesh with the strengthening global mood of *Perestroika*, the easing of Cold War tensions and the movement towards South Asian regional cooperation did not eventuate. India's increasing domestic instability and continually tense relations with Pakistan ensured that defensiveness and distrust remained characteristic of Indo–Bangladesh relations. The United States was more inclined to leave the region in India's hands, rather than give disproportionate military assistance to Pakistan, but tensions did not ease automatically. Declining superpower interest also meant that the smaller states, such as Bangladesh, faced a much more difficult task in arousing international attention and support for their grievances, knowing that outside assistance or intervention was unlikely to be forthcoming. India had considerable leeway during this later period to act as it saw fit in the region, representing, according to M.A. Carranza, 'a golden opportunity for India to mend fences with its smaller neighbours'.[2] India's need for military predominance in South Asia was no longer driven by Cold War imperatives, but the opportunity to improve relations with its South Asian neighbours was not acted upon. India's increasing domestic insecurity and instability, and its tense relations with Sri Lanka as well as Pakistan, meant that there was little chance or incentive to improve relations with Bangladesh.

Indo–Pakistani rivalry, reinforced by the ongoing territorial dispute over Kashmir, has been a feature endemic to the South Asian region since Partition, pervading all South Asian interstate relationships. India's treatment of Bangladesh has been coloured by this rivalry, but not to the same extent that it has influenced Bangladesh's relations with Pakistan, instilling relations between the latter parties with comparative warmth and stability. Indo–Pakistani rivalry has therefore been considered as the most influential category of pressures to affect Bangladesh–Pakistan relations. While comparatively cordial, Bangladesh's relations with Pakistan were based on shared insecurities, rather than on more positive aspects, with the result that those relations did not mature noticeably.

The domestic preoccupations of the Pakistan and Bangladesh governments have also been of considerable influence on relations, but domestic irritants have not been sufficient to sour relations irreparably. Pakistan's domestic problems have been somewhat more influential in impeding relations than have those of Bangladesh. The lack of progress in relations in the late 1980s represented a prime example of how Pakistan's domestic difficulties could impinge on the relationship. Benazir Bhutto's fledgling regime, beset by the tasks of quelling ethnic violence and holding on to power, had little hesitation in sacrificing improved relations with Bangladesh in the interests of domestic political necessity. The Bangladesh government's embryonic, somewhat naive, efforts to pursue a mediatory role in South Asia and to take a generally more independent stance were looked upon by Pakistan with suspicion rather than respect. The Bangladesh leadership also failed to explore fresh diplomatic avenues, tending instead to harp almost reflexively on time-worn disputes between the two states.

Personalities, rather than compatible regimes, also played an integral role in the course of Bangladesh–Pakistan relations. Forceful individuals such as Zulfikar Ali Bhutto and Ziaur Rahman held considerable personal sway over foreign policy. The effects of Bhutto's response to Mujib's assassination represented a typical example. At the same time, the abrupt removal of such influential individuals from positions of power did not negate the stabilising and unifying effects of a mutual fear of Indian regional dominance.

Because of its pre-eminent position in the region, a large portion of the responsibility for improving South Asian interstate relations rests on India's shoulders. Each of the three states under study has faced considerable, and increasing, political, economic, civil and communal strife, but India has always been in the strongest position of the three to deal with domestic difficulties. India's successive governments have been plagued by problems such as political mismanagement, corruption, the dominance of personalities, overcentralisation and communal and ethnic violence, but so have those of Pakistan and Bangladesh, often to a much greater degree. India's political institutions and democratic structure have also shown extreme resilience, whereas for Bangladesh and Pakistan the struggle to establish and maintain viable, democratic forms of government has been much greater.[3] Bangladesh and Pakistan are both more vulnerable to external political manipulation than India. If there is to be an improvement in Bangladesh's relations with India, and in South Asian international relations generally, then India is most able to initiate necessary changes. Unfortunately, according to Judith Brown, the Indian government has been typified by a 'limited capacity to engineer change', and is becoming more subject to the pressure of powerful, self-serving political groups.[4] Brown does believe, nonetheless, that the process of political decay in India is 'neither inevitable nor irreversible', subject to the actions of politicians with vision and integrity.[5] The argument that India is simply interested in preserving regional peace and finds difficulty in doing so because of its politically unstable, militarily-dominated and over-sensitive neighbours has been shown in this study to be inadequate. India has played on the instability of its neighbours in furthering its political aims. So, too, have the smaller states played on India's regional dominance to attract international and domestic support, although in a less subtle manner, making it easier for India to lay blame on the other states for the lack of regional cooperation.

Less obvious obstructions, such as India's resistance to multilateral negotiation and its preoccupation with preserving the regional status quo, are more difficult to pinpoint. Each of the South Asian states, including India, has overplayed regional and domestic tensions. A 'no-war, no-peace' position in South Asia has allowed the smaller states to internationalise issues, obtain military assistance and justify martial law.[6] It has also been used by India to deny concessions and to take a tough stance with the other states. India's recalcitrance in offering concessions has been exemplified by its reluctance to accept Pakistan's proposals for nuclear non-proliferation in South Asia, while at the same time supporting the elimination of nuclear weapons at the global level.[7] Improved relations with China in the 1990s and the ending of the Cold War have not been sufficient incentives for India to initiate military restraint and regional arms control and, to date, India continues to acquire sophisticated weaponry aimed at keeping Pakistan and China in check.[8] A compromise on the nuclear front would enhance India's international prestige and ease regional tensions, without necessarily arousing a domestic outcry, as would occur with attempts to back down on the major bone of contention in the region: the dispute over Kashmir. Unless India begins to show a greater willingness to compromise and accommodate the concerns of the smaller states, it is unlikely that significant improvements in South Asian cooperation will occur.

While India is in a better political and economic position to initiate improvements in South Asian interstate relations, Bangladesh does have considerable potential to develop a mediatory role in South Asia. Bangladesh has already demonstrated its maturity in the international arena, as exemplified by its election in 1978 to a two-year term on the United Nations Security Council; its initiative in proposing and helping to establish the South Asian Association for Regional Cooperation (SAARC); its hosting of the Islamic Foreign Ministers' Conference in 1983, and the Bangladesh foreign minister's election as President of the 41st Session of the United Nation's General Assembly in 1986. Bangladesh is also in a position to distance itself somewhat from the rivalry and antagonism which pervade the Indo–Pakistan relationship and which have been so influential in the course of South Asian interstate relations as a whole.

Because the regional realm is considered to have had the greatest impact on Bangladesh's foreign relations, it seems logical that any improvements in those relations, particularly with India, will take place within the regional context. Neither bilateral nor extra-regional negotiations and fora have proved effective in solving South Asian problems. Improving economic links within South Asia has often been put forward as an informal, indirect means by which a confidence-building process might begin to take shape in South Asia. The launching of SAARC represented the first step in using a regional approach to ease South Asian disharmony. The continued existence of the forum is a feat not to be underestimated, whether or not significant achievements have as yet been forthcoming. It is unlikely that improved economic relations, one of the main aims of SAARC, will generate political cooperation and change in the region. Economic reform is more predicated by political will than vice versa, as expressed by Kishore Dash:

> [I]f regional economic cooperation is left to market forces alone, it would take decades. Therefore, conscious efforts at the political level and demonstration of political will by the South Asian leaders are absolutely

necessary for the growth of regional economic cooperation in South Asia.[9]

It may be that SAARC's specifically regional focus is a vital ingredient necessary before long-term improvements in relations between each of the South Asian states can occur. The evolution of SAARC offers considerable scope for on-going study. Despite its timorous beginnings, the Association may, in time, become a much more effective body. Perhaps a predominantly environmental, rather than economic, focus might be more effective, especially as the natural incentives for improved regional trade are minimal. If SAARC was able to implement effective measures in tackling the region's escalating environmental difficulties, such as those caused by overpopulation, natural hazards, scarcity of resources and environmental degradation, it would have marked beneficial consequences for interstate relations, in particular, between Bangladesh and India, many of their disputes having an environmental as well as political dimension.

Since the establishment of SAARC, Bangladesh has begun to take a more active role in South Asian interstate negotiations and mediation. While Bangladesh's mediatory efforts have been regarded somewhat askance by India and Pakistan, the prospects for Bangladesh to become more effective, at least within the realm of negotiation, appear to be positive. With its strong political and cultural links with both India and Pakistan, Bangladesh is in an ideal position to contribute meaningfully to discussions aimed at easing the main source of tension in the region: the rivalry between India and Pakistan. Bangladesh's effectiveness in the regional sphere will improve particularly if its relationship with India stabilises and strengthens. There are some signs that Indo–Bangladesh relations are finding a firmer footing, particularly with the signing of a 30-year treaty on the sharing of the Ganges water in December 1996.[10] The continued survival of Bangladesh's parliamentary democracy, despite the political upheavals of 1996, also bodes well for Bangladesh's future stability. If Bangladesh can set the laudable regional example of maintaining a stable political structure and cordial relations with both India and Pakistan, then its potential to devise well aimed initiatives for regional reconciliation which are, in turn, taken seriously, will be greatly enhanced.

Notes and References

1 General Influences on Bangladesh's Foreign Policy

1. The South Asian region is usually defined as consisting of seven states: Bangladesh, India, Pakistan, Sri Lanka, Nepal, Bhutan and the Maldives.
2. For an analysis of east-wing subordination see W.H. Morris-Jones, 'Pakistan Post Mortem and the Roots of Bangladesh', in M.M. Khan and H.M. Zafarullah, *Politics and Bureaucracy in a New Nation: Bangladesh*, Dacca, 1980, pp. 26–34.
3. B. Sen Gupta, *Regional Cooperation and Development in South Asia, Vol. 1*, New Delhi, 1986, p.19.
4. Ainslee Embree points out that this partial borrowing also can be coloured with admiration for the values and attitudes of the former rulers. A.T. Embree, *Imagining India*, Delhi, 1989, p. 188.
5. In pre-British times, Bengal enjoyed relative autonomy. Although Bengal became part of the Mughal empire in 1576, it was ruled independently of the central government virtually until the death of Aurangzeb (1707), the last significant Mughal ruler. See D.A. Wright, *Bangladesh: Origins and Indian Ocean Relations (1971–1975)*, New Delhi, 1988, p. 17.
6. P. Ghosh applies to the South Asian states the notion that differing stages of political development lead to conflicting strategic and diplomatic positions. P.S. Ghosh, *Cooperation and Conflict in South Asia*, New Delhi, 1989, pp. 3, 14 and 229.
7. C. Clapham, and W. Wallace (eds), *Foreign Policy Making in Developing States*, Westmead, 1977, p. 174.
8. B. Buzan, 'Peace, Power and Security: Contending Concepts in the Study of International Relations', *Journal of Peace Research*, vol. 21, no. 2, 1984, p. 121.
9. H.A. Kissinger, 'Domestic Structure and Foreign Policy', in J.N. Rosenau, *International Politics and Foreign Policy: A Reader in Research and Theory*, New York, 1969, pp. 261–2.
10. T. Maniruzzaman, *The Security of Small States in the Third World*, Canberra, ANU, 1982, p. 15.
11. The problems associated with diplomatic recognition of Bangladesh were most pronounced in relation to the Islamic states. For a detailed discussion see: Wright, *Bangladesh: Origins and Indian Ocean Relations*, pp. 221–42.
12. *The Bangladesh Observer*, 2 May 1976.
13. *Ibid.*, 25 March 1982.
14. C. Thomas, *In Search of Security: The Third World in International Relations*, Boulder, 1987, p. 7. Thomas particularly points to the United States for its lack of understanding in dealing with 'third world' states.
15. For a succinct discussion of the basis for this factionalism, see M. Rashiduzzaman, 'Changing Political Patterns in Bangladesh: Internal Constraints and External Fears', in Khan, Zafarullah, *Politics*, pp. 176–95.
16. For example, in 1995, the strength of the Bangladesh army, navy and air force personnel was, 156 000, 8000 and 6500, respectively, whereas the Indian equivalent was vastly greater: 1.14 million, 55 000, and 110 000, respectively. Furthermore, compared with India's arsenal in 1995 of 2600 tanks, Bangladesh had 140.

See *The Statesman's Year-Book: A Statistical, Political and Economic Account of the States of the World for the Year 1996–1997*, London, 1996, pp. 182–3, 641–2.

17. For examples of proponents of this view, see: H. Wiberg, 'The Security of Small Nations: Challenges and Defences', *Journal of Peace Research*, vol. 24, no. 4, 1987, p. 340. However, Wiberg does stress that the military dimension is not the only one. [See p. 354.] See also R.G.C. Thomas (ed.), *The Great Power Triangle and Asian Security*, 1983, p. 71, and B. Buzan (*et al.*), *South Asian Insecurity and the Great Powers*, New York, 1986, pp. 8–30.

18. See M. Rahman Shelley, *Emergence of a New Nation in a Multi-Polar World: Bangladesh*, Washington, D.C., 1978, p. 19, and K. Subrahmanyam, 'India and Its Neighbours: A Conceptual Framework of Peaceful Co-existence', in U.S. Bajpai (ed.), *India and Its Neighbourhood*, New Delhi, 1986, p. 109.

19. The 'primordialist/instrumentalist' debate became prominent particularly due to the writings of two South Asia specialists, Paul Brass and Francis Robinson. See P.R. Brass, *Language, Religion and Politics in North India*, London, 1974, and F. Robinson, *Separatism among Indian Muslims: The Politics of the United Provinces' Muslims, 1860–1923*, London, 1974.

20. For a discussion specifically related to the pre-Pakistan period, see A. Roy, 'The Bengal Muslim "Cultural Mediators" and the Bengal Muslim Identity in the Nineteenth and Early Twentieth Centuries', *South Asia: Journal of South Asian Studies*, vol. 10, no. 1, 1987, pp. 11–34.

21. See D.A. Wright, 'Islam and Bangladeshi Polity', *South Asia: Journal of South Asian Studies*, vol. 10, no. 1, 1987, p. 15.

22. P.R. Brass, *Ethnicity and Nationalism: Theory and Comparison*, New Delhi, 1991, p. 74.

23. Financial loans and a vastly unequal trading relationship have made Bangladesh a major debtor to India. See C. Baxter, 'Bangladesh at Ten: An Appraisal of a Decade of Political Development', *The World Today*, vol. 38, no. 2, February 1982, p. 78.

24. M. Franda, *Bangladesh: The First Decade*, New Delhi, 1982, p. 281.

25. T.A. Keenleyside, 'Nationalist Indian Attitudes Towards Asia: A Troublesome Legacy For Post-Independence Indian Foreign Policy', *Pacific Affairs*, vol. 55, no. 2, 1982, p. 210–1.

26. *Ibid.*, p. 211.

27. R. Tagore, *Towards Universal Man*, London, 1961, p. 57.

28. *Ibid.*, p. 91.

29. *Ibid.*, p. 249.

30. *Ibid.*, p. 66.

31. Keenleyside, 'Nationalist Indian Attitudes', p. 214–15. For some of Nehru's comments on Asian unity and India's role, presented at the Inter-Asian Conference, New Delhi in March 1947, see: S. Gopal (ed.), *Selected Works of Jawaharlal Nehru*, Second Series, vol. 2, New Delhi, pp. 501–9.

32. L. Ziring (ed.), *The Subcontinent in World Politics: India, Its Neighbors, and the Great Powers*, New York, 1978, p. 85.

33. M.A. Bhatty, 'Strategic Balance In South Asia Including the Adjacent Ocean', *World Review*, vol. 31, no. 1, 1992, p. 26.

34. R. Kumar, 'India's Political Identity: Nation-State or Civilisation-State', *Indian Ocean Review*, vol. 4, no. 4, 1991, pp. 23, 26. Ravinder Kumar is the Director of the Nehru Memorial Museum, New Delhi.

35. A.T. Embree, 'Indian Civilization and Regional Cultures: The Two Realities', in P. Wallace (ed.), *Region and Nation in India*, New Delhi, 1985, pp. 19–39.

36. *Ibid.*, p. 21. Ravinder Kumar makes the point that the unity and character of Indian society is determined not so much by the Brahmanical 'high culture' as it is later by the 'middle' traditions of devotional theism, as embodied in the bhakti movement which became prominent after the first millennium C.E.R. Kumar, 'The Past and the Present: An Indian Dialogue', *Nehru Memorial Museum and Library, Occasional Papers on Perspectives on Indian Development*, no. I, New Delhi, March 1989, p. 23 (unpublished).

37. Embree, 'Indian Civilization and Regional Cultures', p. 24.

38. *Ibid.*, pp. 25–6.

39. *Ibid.*, p. 24.

40. *Ibid.*, p. 34.

41. *Ibid.*, p. 35.

42. Ghosh, *Cooperation and Conflict*, p. 37.

43. Bangladeshi concerns about Indian interference were manifested within months of achieving independence as exemplified by their insistence that Indian troops be withdrawn from Bangladesh. This was despite their much-needed assistance in the wake of the war. For details, see Wright, *Bangladesh: Origins and Indian Ocean Relations (1971–1975)*, pp. 125–31.

44. C. Bateman points to Indian activities in Sri Lanka, Sikkim, Bhutan and Nepal as immediate examples of such meddling. See C. Bateman, 'National Security and Nationalism in Bangladesh', *Asian Survey*, vol. 19, no. 8, August 1979, p. 784. Even India's assistance to Bangladesh in 1971 was, certainly from Pakistan's point of view, a form of meddling. Much is said of India's humble wish simply to preserve the status quo in South Asia, but such semantics do not negate, for example, the many repercussions of Indian assistance in Bangladesh's war of independence.

45. S. Mansingh, *India's Search For Power: Indira Gandhi's Foreign Policy 1966–1982*, New Delhi, 1984, p. 263. See also n. 44.

46. Stephen Cohen interprets the militarisation of India as a corrosion of its 'political soul', as personified by Mahatma Gandhi and Jawaharlal Nehru. S.P. Cohen, 'Dimensions of Militarism in South Asia', *Defence Journal* (Karachi), no. 7, July 1984, p. 9, cited in, Ghosh, *Cooperation and Conflict*, p. 221.

47. Ghosh, *Cooperation and Conflict*, p. 221.

48. *Times of India* (Bombay), 8 November 1975.

49. P.K. Mishra, *South Asia in International Politics*, Delhi, 1984, p.148. See also K. Subrahmanyam, 'India and Its Neighbours: A Conceptual Framework of Peaceful Co-existence', in Bajpai (ed.), *India and its Neighborhood*, pp. 123–4, where Subrahmanyam states: 'A number of people in this country readily accept the apparently plausible thesis advanced in our neighbouring countries that a large and militarily powerful India constitutes a threat to them and is hegemonistic. Historically this thesis is untenable in terms of India's pattern of behaviour in the last four decades.' See also pp. 125–6.

50. Mansingh, *India's Search*, p. 262.

51. Buzan, 'Peace, Power and Security', p. 123.

52. Ghosh, *Cooperation and Conflict*, p. 57.

53. Buzan, 'Peace, Power and Security', pp. 110–11.

54. See Chapters 7 and 8.

55. East-wing feelings of insecurity were exacerbated particularly during the 1965 war between India and Pakistan, where East Pakistan was left defenceless against a possible Indian attack. For details, see D.A. Wright, *India–Pakistan Relations: 1962–1969*, New Delhi, 1989, pp. 99–100.

56. B. Prasad, *India's Foreign Policy: Studies in Continuity and Change*, New Delhi, 1979, pp. 107–8.
57. Mansingh, *India's Search*, p. 269.
58. W.H. Morris-Jones, 'India – More Questions Than Answers', *Asian Survey*, vol. 24, no. 8, 1984, p. 809.
59. P.V.N. Rao, *Reflections on Non-Alignment*, New Delhi [1992], p. 8.
60. N. Jetly, 'India and the Domestic Turmoil in South Asia', in U. Phadnis (ed.), *Domestic Conflicts in South Asia, Vol. 1: Political Dimensions*, New Delhi, 1986, p. 80.
61. *The Bangladesh Observer*, 13 August 1976.
62. *Ibid.*, 14 August 1976.
63. Mansingh, *India's Search*, p. 262.
64. 'As Mrs Gandhi Sees It', interview with Indira Gandhi by Fatma Zakaria, *Times of India* (New Delhi), 14 August 1983.
65. T. George *et al.*, *Security in Southern Asia 2: India and the Great Powers*, Aldershot, 1984, p. 204.
66. Bangladesh is one of the poorest countries in the world. *The Europa World Year Book 1996, Volume 1*, London, 1996, p. 502. See also Table 1.1.
67. The Grameen Bank currently works in 36 000 villages in Bangladesh (almost half the total number of villages) and annually gives out 4 million loans to the rural poor, operating through 62 000 lending centres with staff of over 12 000. 94 per cent of these loans are given to female heads of households. M. Yunus, *Towards a Poverty-Free World*, paper delivered at the 'Bangladesh: Democracy and Development' Conference organised by the National Centre for South Asian Studies, Melbourne, held at the Royal Melbourne Institute of Technology (22–23 March 1997).
68. 'Persistence of Poverty in Bangladesh', *Grameen Poverty Research*, vol. 2, no. 1, January 1996, p. 2. According to another report, produced by the 'independent Pakistan-based Human Development Centre, headed by a former Pakistan finance minister, Mr Mahbub ul Haq', South Asia was 'going backwards in all main social development indicators, despite higher rates of economic growth', the benefits of which had not 'trickled down' to the poor. The report also concluded that South Asian poverty eclipsed even that of sub-Saharan Africa. Admittedly, the report was produced partly in response to the Australian government's decision in 1996 to cut aid to South Asia, while maintaining funding for Africa. *The Sydney Morning Herald*, 19 April 1997.
69. *Ibid.*
70. See Table 1.1.
71. According to the World Bank, Bangladesh's population growth rate between 1990–1995 was 1.6 per cent. *Bangladesh Country Overview* (updated 22 January 1977, cited 7 February 1997) World Bank Group: <http://www.worldbank.org/html/extdr/offrep/sas/b.htm>.
72. Population Reference Bureau: *1995 World Population Data Sheet – Bangladesh* (updated 5 February, cited 7 February 1997): <http://dbdev.ciesin.org:8989/cgi-bin/wdb/wdbprb/fdf/PRBWDS/>.
73. For a history of the pro-aid/anti-aid debate, see Anisul Islam, 'Foreign Aid and Economic Development', in H. Zafarullah *et al.* (eds), *Policy Issues in Bangladesh*, New Delhi, 1994, pp. 107–8.
74. S. Rahman, 'Bangladesh in 1989: Internationalization of Political and Economic Issues', *Asian Survey*, vol. 30, no. 2, 1990, p. 155. The obvious response which could be made to this criticism is that the donors have not allowed for the real conditions in Bangladesh.

75. Islam, 'Foreign Aid', pp. 97–135.
76. T. Maniruzzaman, 'The Fall of the Military Dictator: 1991 Elections and the Prospect of Civilian Rule in Bangladesh', *Pacific Affairs*, vol. 65, no. 2, 1992, p. 217.
77. Islam, 'Foreign Aid', p. 97. By contrast, the ratio of aid to GDP for India was only 2 per cent in 1990. *Ibid.*, p. 101.
78. *Ibid.*, pp. 100–1.
79. *Ibid.*, p. 98.
80. Commodity aid grants declined from 84 per cent in 1972 to 30 per cent in 1990 and project aid grants dropped from 53 per cent to 38 per cent in 1990. *Ibid.*, p. 100.
81. *Ibid.*, p. 105, and *The Europa World Year Book 1996*, p. 502.
82. Islam, 'Foreign Aid', pp. 105–6.
83. R. Sobhan, 'Bangladesh and the World Economic System: the Crisis of External Dependence', in S.R. Chakravarty, and V. Narain (eds), *Bangladesh, Vol. 3: Global Politics*, New Delhi, 1988, p. 30.
84. *Ibid.*
85. *Ibid.*
86. *Ibid.*
87. *Ibid.*, p. 31.
88. *Ibid.*
89. *Ibid.*, p. 43.
90. Maniruzzaman, 'The Fall of the Military Dictator', p. 218.
91. *Ibid.*
92. *Ibid.*
93. Unpaid loans from Development Financing Institutions (DFIs) amounted to 11 000 million Taka in 1991 (approximately US$290 million). *Ibid.*, p. 219.
94. Sobhan, 'Bangladesh', p. 43.
95. *Ibid.*, pp. 43–4.
96. Islam, 'Foreign Aid', p. 104.
97. B.N. Ghosh, *Political Economy of Neocolonialism in Third World Countries*, New Delhi, 1985, p. 21.
98. *Ibid.*, p. 36.
99. *Ibid.*, p. 32.
100. Sobhan, 'Bangladesh', pp. 30–50.
101. At the end of 1993, India's total external debt was US$91 781 million. The cost of debt servicing for India is also high, being 28.4 per cent of export earnings in 1993. *The Europa World Year Book 1996, Volume 1*, p. 1539.
102. For example, severe flooding and loss of life occurred in Bangladesh in 1985, 1987, 1988 and 1991.
103. Islam, 'Foreign Aid', p. 103.
104. *Ibid.*
105. *Ibid.* For a similar viewpoint see M.M. Khan and S.A. Husain (eds), *Bangladesh Studies: Politics, Administration, Rural Development and Foreign Policy*, Dhaka, 1986, pp. 250–54.
106. E. Ahamed (ed.), *Foreign Policy of Bangladesh: A Small State's Imperative*, Dhaka, 1984, p. 89.
107. *The Europa World Year Book 1996, Volume 1*, London, 1996, p. 502.
108. C. Baxter, 'Bangladesh in 1990: Another New Beginning?', *Asian Survey*, vol. 31, no. 2, 1991, p. 151, and *The Europa World Year Book 1993, Volume 1*, London, 1993, p. 453.

109. R. Sobhan, *The Crisis of External Dependence: The Political Economy of Foreign Aid to Bangladesh*, London, 1982, pp. 142, 240. The United States supplied US$577 million in aid during the same period. See also Islam, 'Foreign Aid', p. 104.
110. Islam, 'Foreign Aid', p. 102.
111. Canada has more than doubled its aid to Bangladesh, increasing its share of total aid from 2.7 per cent in 1972 to 5.7 per cent in 1990. *Ibid.*
112. Franda, *Bangladesh*, p. 282 and Z.R. Khan, *Leadership in the Least Developed Nation: Bangladesh*, Syracuse, 1983, pp. 165–6. For details of one of Zia's trips to obtain Islamic support and aid, see *The Bangladesh Observer*, 22 May 1976.
113. Franda, *Bangladesh*, p. 280.
114. *The Bangladesh Observer*, 27 August 1980, 31 August 1980.
115. See for example Zia's address to the United Nations General Assembly in August 1980, when he presented his 10-point plan for the 'restructuring of the global economic order' in order to 'remove the ever widening disparity between the developed and the developing nations'. *Ibid.*, 27 August 1980.
116. *Ibid.*, 8 March 1977, 5 July 1979, 8 November 1979.
117. *Ibid.*, 16 May 1980.
118. *Ibid.*, 8 December 1985.
119. *Ibid.*, 30 October 1983.
120. *New York Times* (New York), 11 April 1982.
121. For example, Chinese links with Bangladesh were continually publicised with great fanfare in the Bangladesh press. See *The Bangladesh Observer*, 4 November 1983, 16 June 1987, 11 December 1988.
122. Jetly, 'India', p. 73.
123. M. Franda and A. Rahman, 'India, Bangladesh and the Superpowers', in P. Wallace (ed.), *Region and Nation in India*, New Delhi, 1985, p. 263.
124. See Chapter 6.

2 1975–81: Indo–Pakistani Rivalry and Indian Party Politics

1. S.S. Bindra, *Indo–Bangladesh Relations*, New Delhi, 1982, p. 62.
2. C.J. Gulati, *Bangladesh: Liberation to Fundamentalism (A Study of Volatile Indo–Bangladesh Relations)*, New Delhi, 1988, p. 221.
3. U.S. Bajpai (ed.), *India and Its Neighbourhood*, New Delhi, 1986, p. 294.
4. There is a tendency for pro-Indian analysts to consider the 'external influences' upon Bangladesh's foreign policy to include Pakistan but not India.
5. P. Ghosh, *Cooperation and Conflict in South Asia*, New Delhi, 1989, p. 1.
6. L. Lifschultz, *Bangladesh: The Unfinished Revolution*, London, 1979, p. 102.
7. Within days of the 7 November coup, China extended its 'warm support to the new Government of Bangladesh', already having extended diplomatic recognition in October, shortly after Mujib's assassination. See *The Bangladesh Observer*, 12 November 1975.
8. *New York Times*, February 2, 1976.
9. *Times of India* (New Delhi), 8 November 1975.
10. *Ibid.*
11. *The Bangladesh Observer*, 24 November 1975.
12. *Ibid.*
13. *New York Times*, February 2, 1976. The tension between India and Pakistan was eased by the signing of the Simla Agreement in 1972 and diplomatic relations

between India and Pakistan were restored in July 1976. Nevertheless, relations have tended to remain cool and wary to the present day.

14. These included: the drawn-out negotiations over the return of POWs to Pakistan and the debate over the holding of war crimes trials which provided useful leverage for the Indian government against Pakistan. See D.A. Wright, *Bangladesh: Origins and Indian Ocean Relations (1971–1975)*, New Delhi, 1988, pp. 169–89.

15. *New York Times*, December 31, 1975.

16. *Times of India* (New Delhi), 31 January 1976. For the Bangladesh government's response to India's denial of assistance to the 'miscreants' and to the accusation of anti-Indianism, see *The Bangladesh Observer*, 1 February 1976.

17. For an in-depth history of the dispute, see A. Lamb, *Kashmir: A Disputed Legacy, 1846–1990*, Hertingfordbury, 1991.

18. Lamb, *Kashmir*, p. 231.

19. According to Richard Sisson and Leo Rose, India had 'compromised its non-alignment principles and involved the Soviet Union – and, for a few years in the 1950s, China – in South Asia as a counter force to the United States. [This was particularly in response to Pakistan's military alliances involving the United States via SEATO and CENTO]. Kashmir was by no means the only critical issue in these developments, but it assumed a major symbolic role for both the Indian and Pakistani governments'. R. Sisson and L.E. Rose, *War and Secession: Pakistan, India and the Creation of Bangladesh*, New Delhi, 1990, p. 40.

20. Lamb, *Kashmir*, p. 241.

21. See L. Ziring, 'Pakistan and India: Politics, Personalities, and Foreign Policy', *Asian Survey*, vol. 18, no. 7, 1978, pp. 714–15.

22. The demise of the Janata Party's unity was caused partly by ideological factionalism. For an analysis, see L.I. Rudolph and S.H. Rudolph, 'Rethinking Secularism: Genesis and Implications of the Textbook Controversy, 1977–79', *Pacific Affairs*, vol. 56, no. 1, 1983, pp. 15–37.

23. According to the Janata government's minister for external affairs, A.B. Vajpayee, the government's emphasis on non-alignment represented the restoration of 'idealism and principled behaviour in the conduct of India's foreign policy'. A.B. Vajpayee, 'India's Foreign Policy Today', in B. Prasad, *India's Foreign Policy: Studies in Continuity and Change*, New Delhi, 1979, p. 9.

24. J. Das Gupta, 'The Janata Phase: Reorganization and Redirection in Indian Politics', *Asian Survey*, vol. 19, no. 4, 1979, p. 396.

25. Once in power, the Desai government made a series of gestures of friendship to the Carter administration in the USA and these were quickly reciprocated. See *New York Times*, July 5, 1977, where Desai explained that since being installed as prime minister, he and President Carter had exchanged private letters regularly, expressing similar values with regard to a wide variety of subjects.

26. Relations between India and China had already started to improve under Mrs Gandhi with India and China agreeing to exchange ambassadors on 15 April 1976. *New York Times*, April 16, 1976. In further improving ties with China, Desai's government aimed to off-set excessive Soviet influence and hence pursue a more independent foreign policy. See W.K. Andersen, 'India in Asia: Walking on a Tightrope', *Asian Survey*, vol. 19, no. 12, 1979, p. 1249.

27. See Ziring, 'Pakistan and India', p. 728.

28. *The Bangladesh Observer*, 8 April 1977.

29. *Ibid.* For a comment in the western press on Desai's attempts to reassure India's neighbours, see *The Times* (London), 31 March 1977.

30. *The Bangladesh Observer*, 8 April 1977.
31. *The Bangladesh Observer*, 11 June 1977.
32. See *ibid.* and *The Times* (London), 30 August 1977.
33. *The Bangladesh Observer*, 30 November 1977.
34. For a thorough analysis of the rationale behind the Indian government's decision to construct the barrage, see B. Crow (*et al.*), *Sharing the Ganges: The Politics and Technology of River Development*, New Delhi, 1995, pp. 55–74.
35. Wright, *Bangladesh*, p. 154.
36. For a detailed study of the effects (which range from disrupted fishing, navigation and irrigation to salination of farming soil), and the Indian government's generally unsympathetic responses, see see Crow (*et al.*), *Sharing the Ganges*, pp. 124–8, and K. Begum, *Tension over the Farakka Barrage: A Techno-Political Tangle in South Asia*, Stuttgart, 1988, pp. 128–51. See also *The Bangladesh Observer*, 12 February 1976, in which many of the perceived ill-effects of the barrage were described. India's tendency to disregard Bangladeshi fears with regard to the barrage is exemplified by the following, somewhat glib, statement made by India's minister for external affairs, Yeshwantrao Chavan: 'According to the best information and expert assessment available with the Government of India, any withdrawal of the waters of the Ganga in Bangladesh or in India ought not to have any adverse consequences for either country because of the abundance of water throughout the year, except for the lean season of mid-March to mid-May. In fact, no adverse effects in Bangladesh during the lean season last year were observed by the Indian members of the joint teams of experts that had been set up under the Agreement of 18th April, 1975.' *Lok Sabha Debates*, 9 March 1976. Whatever observations were made by the Bangladesh experts are conspicuous by their absence in the minister's statement.
37. The following comment appeared in *The Bangladesh Observer*, 6 February 1976: 'A fresh agreement has to be reached if India wants to withdraw water through her Farakka Barrage during the ensuing dry season. Therefore, the Statesman [Calcutta] report on the withdrawal of 40,000 cusecs long before the beginning of the lean months without prior agreement with her lower riparian counterpart is not only surprising but also shocking'. See also *The Bangladesh Observer*, 14 September 1976 and *The Times* (London), 23 March 1976.
38. The Farakka Barrage issue became the focus of considerable attention in Bangladesh from February 1976, not long after Zia came to power, when the dry season operation of the barrage had begun to take effect. See *The Bangladesh Observer*, 12, 15, 19, 24, 29 February 1976, 6, 14, 18, 24, 26 March 1976.
39. *Ibid.*, 23 June 1976.
40. *Ibid.*, 26 August 1976.
41. *Ibid.*
42. *Ibid.*, 14 September 1976.
43. *The Statesman* (Delhi), 11 September 1976.
44. This statement was made by the United Nations following a debate held in November 1976, which had been prompted by Bangladesh's appeal in September to the UN for an impartial hearing on the Farakka issue. See *The Statesman* (Delhi), 26 November 1976. See also *The Bangladesh Observer*, 30 September 1976 and 16 November 1976.
45. For details of the talks, held between December 1976 and January 1977, see *The Bangladesh Observer*, 7 December 1976, and 16, 24 January 1977. See also *The Statesman* (Delhi), 9 December 1976 and 24 January 1977.
46. *The Statesman* (Delhi), 25 January 1976.

47. Three rounds of inconclusive talks had already been held between November 1976 and January 1977.

48. *Amrita Bazar Patrika* (Calcutta), 19 April 1977. See also *The Bangladesh Observer*, 19 April 1977, for a more cautious appraisal of the announcement.

49. *Amrita Bazar Patrika* (Calcutta), 22 April 1977. See also *The Times* (London), 8 September 1977. Criticism of the accord was not restricted to West Bengal, coming also from those in the opposition parties (including Mrs Gandhi) and even some members of the ruling Janata Party. See K. Singh, *India and Bangladesh*, Delhi, 1987, pp. 118–19, 124.

50. *Amrita Bazar Patrika* (Calcutta), 22 April 1977.

51. For details of the accord and an account of the history of the Farakka dispute, see *The Bangladesh Observer*, 6 November 1977. A full copy of the agreement is also available in Singh, *India and Bangladesh*, pp. 162–6.

52. Khushida Begum dismisses the five-year accord as failing 'to ease the situation'. Begum, *Tension*, 1988, p. 187.

53. *The Bangladesh Observer*, 12 October 1977. For the West Bengal press reply, see *Amrita Bazar Patrika* (Calcutta), 15 October 1977.

54. *The Bangladesh Observer*, 20 December 1977.

55. For details of the various proposals for augmentation of the Ganges – which range from the construction of dams on Ganges tributaries to the building of a link canal from the Brahmaputra to the Ganges, see M.R. Islam, 'The Ganges Water Dispute: An Appraisal of a Third Party Settlement', *Asian Survey*, vol. 27, no. 8, 1987, pp. 922–6. See also map 7 (p. 00).

56. *The Bangladesh Observer*, 19 April 1979. For an equally optimistic comment from the Indian press, see *Times of India* (New Delhi), 18 April 1979.

57. *New York Times*, April 19, 1979.

58. *Amrita Bazar Patrika* (Calcutta), 21 January 1980.

59. *Ibid.*

60. For example, see *Amrita Bazar Patrika* (Calcutta), 4 March 1980, *The Bangladesh Observer*, 4 March 1980, 9 April 1980 and 9 January 1981.

61. For example, see *The Bangladesh Observer*, 23 January 1980 and 15 February 1980.

62. Moreover, other matters were receiving greater attention and providing more useful political mileage for Zia and Mrs Gandhi, such as the crackdown on illegal immigration of Bangladeshis into Assam and the ownership dispute over New Moore Island in the Bay of Bengal.

63. *The Bangladesh Observer*, 24 March 1980, 12 July 1980, 9 January 1981 and 10 January 1981.

64. Begum, *Tension*, p. 191.

65. For details of the October 1982 accord, see *Asian Recorder*, November 5–11, 1982, p. 16871. For details of the slight advantage to India, see Singh, *India and Bangladesh*, p. 137.

66. The name 'Neumoor' (which later became 'New Moore') was first given to the island by the British Admiralty in 1971. When the dispute over the island's ownership flared between India and Bangladesh in 1980, India renamed the island 'Purbasha', while Bangladesh called it South Talpatty. The name 'New Moore' has been used because it carries a less biased connotation than the others.

67. According to a communiqué appearing in the *Asian Recorder*, the two leaders 'discussed the delay in the implementation of the land boundary agreement of 1974 and agreed that all necessary measures be taken to overcome the difficulties in order that the agreement could be implemented as speedily as possible . . . The

two sides noted that their 'fruitful and constructive' discussions had contributed greatly towards increasing mutual trust and friendship between the two countries'. *The Asian Recorder,* May 28–June 3, 1979, p. 14903. See also *Times of India* (New Delhi), 18 April 1979.

68. For a detailed account, see Gulati, *Bangladesh,* pp. 174–83.
69. *Lok Sabha Debates,* vol. 21, no. 22, 20 December 1978, pp. 244–5.
70. Between early July and mid-August 1981, 8000 Bangladeshis on the two enclaves were encircled and besieged by armed Indians alleged to be receiving assistance from the Border Security Forces. *The Bangladesh Observer,* 11 August 1981. According to the same report, several Bangladeshis had died of starvation in the siege.
71. *Lok Sabha Debates,* vol. 21, no. 22, 20 December 1978, p. 22.
72. The West Bengal government also played upon the issue, using legal action to delay the Indian government from handing over the corridor until 1990. See A.K.M. Abdus Sabur, 'Bangladesh–India Relations: An Overview', in B. Bastiampillai (ed.), *India and Her South Asian Neighbours,* Colombo, 1992, p. 167.
73. A 'char' is a term for a silted islet formed in a river. The Muhuri Char is situated on the Indo–Bangladesh border, between Noakhali and Tripura districts, near the Indian town of Belonia. (see map 5, p. 46.) For a history of the dispute, see Bindra, *Indo–Bangladesh Relations,* pp. 48–53.
74. *The Bangladesh Observer,* 7 November 1979.
75. *Ibid.*
76. *Ibid.*
77. *Ibid.,* 5 December 1979.
78. *Amrita Bazar Patrika* (Calcutta), 13 November 1979.
79. For example, Bindra, *Indo–Bangladesh Relations,* p. 49, where the date given for the required demolition of the spurs should have been 20 October 1979, instead of 2 October. See *The Bangladesh Observer,* 7 November and 5 December 1979.
80. It is commonplace and predictable that the Bangladeshi and Indian press should present accounts which favoured their respective governments, clouding whatever may have been the reality. The contrasting viewpoints can be compared between those given in *The Bangladesh Observer,* and those in the *Amrita Bazar Patrika* (Calcutta). See *The Bangladesh Observer,* 7 November and 6 December 1979, and *Amrita Bazar Patrika* (Calcutta), 6–10, 13, 18–19, 21 November 1976.
81. I. Hossain, 'Bangladesh–India Relations: Issues and Problems', *Asian Survey,* vol. 21, no. 11, 1981, p. 1124.
82. *Lok Sabha Debates,* 30 January 1980.
83. Should be 45 acres.
84. *Amrita Bazar Patrika* (Calcutta), 13 November 1979.
85. *New York Times,* December 29, 1979.
86. *Amrita Bazar Patrika* (Calcutta), 9 November 1979.
87. *New York Times,* December 3, 1979.
88. *Ibid.*
89. *The Bangladesh Observer,* 7 November 1979.
90. The size of the island has been given a wide range of interpretations, varying from 2 square kilometres: Gulati, *Bangladesh,* p. 162, to 288 square kilometres: Hossain, 'Bangladesh–India Relations', p. 1124. According to a report in *The Bangladesh Observer,* 26 May 1981, the figure of 228 square kilometres was an estimate of how large the island would become by 1991. Also complicating matters was the controversy over whether or not New Moore island was in fact comprised of two separate islands. See *The Bangladesh Observer,* 2 July 1980.

91. See M.H. Rahman, 'Delimitation of Maritime Boundaries: A Survey of Problems in the Bangladesh Case', *Asian Survey*, vol. 24, no.12, 1984, pp. 1302–17.

92. This provided an additional reason for Bangladesh's claim to the island, since it could have been created largely from Bangladeshi soil. See Rahman, 'Delimitation', p. 1308.

93. The amount of sea bed which it was claimed India stood to gain varied from approximately 25 000 square kilometres to 65 000 square kilometres. See Gulati, *Bangladesh*, p. 170.

94. M. Franda, *Bangladesh: The First Decade*, New Delhi, 1982, p. 294.

95. *The Bangladesh Observer*, 2 July 1980.

96. India's 'evidence' appeared in *The Bangladesh Observer*, 26 May 1981: '"All the documents show that the island belongs to us and there is no question of a dispute or Bangladesh having a claim on it", a Foreign Office spokesman said . . . Data derived from satellite have established that the New Moore island lies 5.2 kms from the nearest point on the mainland coast of India while the distance from Bangladesh coast is 7.5 kms.'

97. *Asian Recorder*, 2–8 July 1981, p. 16101.

98. During Desai's visit to Dhaka, he emphasised the need to 'resolve the questions of maritime boundary on a mutually satisfactory basis'. *The Bangladesh Observer*, 19 April 1979.

99. For examples see *Far Eastern Economic Review*, 'Unilateral annexation: 164 square kilometres', 2 May 1980, p. 38, and *The Bangladesh Observer*, 8 April 1981.

100. *Far Eastern Economic Review*, 2 May 1980, p. 38. The Indian flag was hoisted on 12 March 1980.

101. Gulati, *Bangladesh*, p. 164.

102. *The Bangladesh Observer*, 19 August 1980.

103. *Ibid.*

104. *Ibid.*, 18 August 1980.

105. *The Statesman* (Delhi) 18 August 1980, *The Bangladesh Observer*, 18 August 1980.

106. *The Bangladesh Observer*, 6 December 1980.

107. *Ibid.*

108. *Ibid.*, 8 April 1981.

109. *Ibid.*

110. *Amrita Bazar Patrika* (Calcutta), 17 May 1981.

111. *The Bangladesh Observer*, 18 May 1981.

112. *Ibid.*

113. *Amrita Bazar Patrika* (Calcutta), 20 May 1981.

114. *The Indian Express*, quoted in *The Bangladesh Observer*, 20 May 1981. For a summary of another example of an Indian opinion opposed to the Indian government's handling of New Moore, see *The Bangladesh Observer*, 19 July 1981.

115. The issue gave Sheikh Hasina, daughter of Mujibur Rahman and leader of the Awami League (H) opposition party, the opportunity both to criticise her rival, Ziaur Rahman, and to counter her pro-Indian reputation in Bangladesh. Returning from six years of asylum in India, Hasina launched her political activities in Bangladesh during the New Moore island dispute, declaring India's actions to be a 'gross violation of all international laws and the principle of coexistence'. *The Bangladesh Observer*, 21 May 1981.

116. For the complete text of the White Paper, see *ibid.*, 27 May 1981.

117. *Ibid.* Parliament also put on record its strong protest against the actions of the Indian government, considering them to be 'in clear violation of the agreements

and understanding reached with the Government of Bangladesh and of internationally accepted norms and practices'. *Ibid.*

118. *Ibid.*, 28 May 1981.

119. Zia was assassinated on 30 May 1981, barely three days after Parliament's resolution on New Moore Island had been passed. In the opinion of some scholars, Zia's political position was particularly shaky at the time, causing him to take a strong anti-Indian stance over the New Moore Island issue in order to create a diversionary focus and thereby consolidate his support. For examples, see Bindra, *Indo–Bangladesh Relations*, pp. 61–2, and N. Jetly, 'India and the Domestic Turmoil in South Asia', in U. Phadnis (ed.), *Domestic Conflicts in South Asia, vol. 1: Political Dimensions*, New Delhi, 1986, p. 73.

120. For example, in June 1981, at the Islamic Foreign Minister's Conference in Baghdad, the Bangladesh government formally aired its grievances against India with regard to New Moore Island, but with little obvious impact. See *The Bangladesh Observer*, 12 and 15 June 1981.

121. In the months following Zia's assassination, a few standard calls were made for a joint survey of the island. For examples, see *ibid.*, 24 and 29 July 1981.

122. Territorial and water-sharing issues are still notable sources of friction between the two states in the 1990s.

123. F.A. Vali, *Politics of the Indian Ocean Region: The Balances of Power*, New York, 1976, p. 237.

124. Bindra, *Indo–Bangladesh Relations*, p. 62.

125. See Chapter 5.

3   1982–4: A New Beginning or the Darkest Hour?

1. S. Mansingh, *India's Search For Power: Indira Gandhi's Foreign Policy 1966–1982*, New Delhi, 1984, p. 262.

2. S. Tharoor, *Reasons of State: Political Development and India's Foreign Policy Under Indira Gandhi, 1966–1977*, New Delhi, 1982, pp. 361–2.

3. *Ibid.*, pp. 54–5.

4. J. Manor (ed.), *Nehru to the Nineties: The Changing Office of Prime Minister in India*, London, 1994, p. 8.

5. N. Chakravartty, 'Bangladesh', in U.S. Bajpai (ed.), *India and Its Neighbourhood*, New Delhi, 1986, p. 294.

6. For example, see N. Chakravartty, 'Bangladesh', p. 294, and C.J. Gulati, *Bangladesh: Liberation to Fundamentalism (A Study of Volatile Indo–Bangladesh Relations)*, New Delhi, 1988, p. 78.

7. See P.S. Ghosh, *Cooperation and Conflict in South Asia*, New Delhi, 1989, p. 96 and Gulati, *Bangladesh*, p. 85. According to analyst William Richter, Ershad was less antagonistic to India than Zia was, but 'considerably less pro-India than Mujib'. W.L. Richter, 'Mrs. Gandhi's Neighborhood: Indian Foreign Policy Toward Neighboring Countries', *Journal of Asian and African Studies*, vol. XXII, nos. 3–4, 1987, p. 254.

8. P.S. Ghosh states: 'The fall of Sheikh Mujibur Rahman marked the watershed in Indo–Bangla relations and the growth of religious fanaticism and Bangladesh's change of stance in foreign policy seriously impaired [those relations].' P.S. Ghosh, *Cooperation and Conflict*, p. 88. Ghosh also describes military rule in Bangladesh as having a negative impact on Indo–Bangladesh relations. *Cooperation and Conflict*, p. 95.

9. L. Ziring, *Bangladesh: From Mujib to Ershad, An Interpretive Study*, Oxford, 1992, p. 153.

10. The shift in Bangladesh's foreign policy following Mujib's assassination has been described as a 'slap in the face of India'. See L. Lifschultz, 'New Delhi's 'views' on the Dacca Coups', *Far Eastern Economic Review*, November 28, 1975, p. 17.
11. Examined in detail in Chapter 5.
12. *Times of India* (New Delhi), 25 March 1982.
13. *Ibid.* Mrs Gandhi's reaction was in glaring contrast to her response to Ziaur Rahman's coup which prompted her to declare: '[T]hings happening in "our neighbourhood" were not entirely good and cause us grave concern."' *Times of India* (Bombay), 8 November 1975. See also Chapter 1, n. 55.
14. *Ibid.*
15. *Ibid.*
16. *Ibid.*
17. *Ibid.*
18. *Ibid.*
19. According to D.A. Wright, even Zia's critics within Bangladesh 'have admitted that oppression was not a characteristic of his government'. D.A. Wright, 'Bangladesh and Its Indian Ocean Neighbours', *Bangladesh Bulletin*, vol 6, no. 2, May 1979, p. 5.
20. See Chapter 6.
21. R.L. Hardgrave, 'India in 1984: Confrontation, Assassination, and Succession', *Asian Survey*, vol. 25, no. 2, 1985, p. 131.
22. P. Ghosh, *Cooperation and Conflict*, p. 64. The 'other' political forces to which Ghosh refers include the Islamic orthodox, Marxists and the military.
23. *The Bangladesh Observer* (Dhaka), 25 March 1982.
24. S. Ganguly, 'The Prime Minister and Foreign and Defence Policies', in Manor, p. 154.
25. Tharoor, *Reasons of State*, p. 351.
26. *Ibid.*
27. *Ibid.*
28. *Ibid.*, p. 350.
29. At the conclusion of his visit, Rao expressed 'India's firm belief in "nurturing" a relationship with Bangladesh based on friendship, co-operation and mutual respect for each other's sovereignty and territorial integrity'. *Times of India* (New Delhi), 23 May 1982. For further details of Rao's visit to Dhaka and the wide range of issues discussed, see *The Bangladesh Observer* (Dhaka), 23–24 May 1982 and *Times of India* (New Delhi), 23–24 May 1982.
30. *The Bangladesh Observer* (Dhaka), 14 October 1982.
31. *Ibid.*, 15 October 1982.
32. *Times of India* (New Delhi), 16 October 1982.
33. The reason for this was that the 1977 agreement was, after all, a temporary, non-binding one and could be revoked upon its expiry – as Khurshida Begum has pointed out. K. Begum, *Tension over the Farakka Barrage: A Techno–Political Tangle in South Asia*, Stuttgart, 1988, pp. 184–5.
34. *The Bangladesh Observer* (Dhaka), 8 October 1982.
35. *Times of India* (New Delhi), 9 October 1982.
36. The lease was subsequently challenged legally by residents of West Bengal, thwarting the implementation of the lease and protracting the issue. Gulati, *Bangladesh*, p. 182. In late June 1992 India finally leased (maintaining sovereignty over) the corridor to Bangladesh for 999 years. *The Europa World Year Book 1996, Volume 1*, London, 1996, p. 501.

37. *The Bangladesh Observer* (Dhaka), 8 October 1982.
38. *Ibid.*
39. *Ibid.*
40. *Ibid.*
41. According to Kuldeep Singh, the MOU placed India in a better position than previously because the agreement stipulated that during periods of exceptionally lean flow the water would be divided via consultations between both governments, rather than by a guaranteed minimum of 80 per cent to Bangladesh, as had applied with the 1977 agreement. K. Singh, *India and Bangladesh*, Delhi, 1987, p. 137. India's argument was that the MOU allowed for greater flexibility during times of extreme drought. See Editorial, *Times of India* (New Delhi), 9 October 1982.
42. These proposals had been put forward in 1974, but more formally in 1978, in response to the need for long-term planning outlined in the 1977 Agreement. See K. Begum, *Tension*, p. 192, and B. Crow *et al.*, *Sharing the Ganges: The Politics and Technology of River Development*, New Delhi, 1995, p. 106.
43. See *Lok Sabha* debates, vol. 17, no. 16, 7 August 1978, pp. 86–7, and *The Bangladesh Observer* (Dhaka), 31 May 1979. See also B.M. Abbas, *The Ganges Waters Dispute*, New Delhi, 1982, pp. 118–24. Begum, *Tension*, pp. 197–8. The rejection of each other's option continued throughout the remainder of Zia's regime. See *Asian Recorder*, 19 February 1981, p. 15891.
44. Begum, *Tension*, p. 202.
45. *Ibid.*, pp. 202–3. For Begum's summary of the possible side-effects of the link canal, see pp. 197–8.
46. Begum, *Tension*, p. 198.
47. Pro-canal arguments were boosted by the World Bank's unperturbed approval of the scheme, describing it as 'practical and reasonable'. S.S. Bindra, *Indo–Bangladesh Relations*, New Delhi, 1982, p. 120.
48. For example, Singh, *Bangladesh*, p. 924. For a pro-canal viewpoint, see C.J. Gulati, *India and Bangladesh*, p. 120–3.
49. Begum, *Tension*, p. 204.
50. India's preference for a bilateral approach was made clear during the UN discussions on Farakka in November 1976, where Indian Foreign Secretary, Mr Jagat Mehta insisted that the UN should avoid interfering directly in the Farakka issue and instead allow India and Bangladesh to resolve their differences via bilateral negotiations. See *The Statesman* (Delhi), 18 November 1976.
51. *Times of India* (New Delhi), 25 March 1982, pp. 210–15. In reviewing Begum's study of the Barrage, Kazi Mamun criticises Begum for not emphasising that Indian qualms about including Nepal in the augmentation talks with Bangladesh were because of Nepal's advantageous, upper-riparian position on the Brahmaputra. See 'Book Reviews', *Pacific Affairs*, vol. 62, 1989, pp. 414–15.
52. By May 1984, the expiry date of the MOU, the Farakka augmentation plans had not advanced beyond the stalemate level of 1978. See *The Bangladesh Observer* (Dhaka), 7 May 1984 and *Asian Recorder*, June 17–23, 1984, p. 17798.
53. Perhaps the most worrysome outcome of the link canal for Bangladesh was the likelihood that India would have control over the canal offtake and outfall, thus placing Bangladesh in a similar position of vulnerability as had been created by the Farakka Barrage itself. See Singh, *India and Bangladesh*, p. 130.
54. Begum, *Tension*, pp. 228–9.
55. *Times of India* (New Delhi), 9 October 1982.
56. Gulati, *Bangladesh*, p. 85.

57. S.D. Muni, *Pangs of Proximity: India and Sri Lanka's Ethnic Crisis*, New Delhi, 1993, p. 21.
58. *The Bangladesh Observer* (Dhaka), 20 October 1982.
59. See *Times of India* (New Delhi), 9 October 1982 and *New York Times* (New York), 29 July 1982.
60. Such as the intensifying autonomy demands of the Sikh political group, the Akali Dal.
61. Muni, *Pangs of Proximity*, pp. 27–8.
62. See Chapter 2.
63. Mansingh, *India's Search*, p. 299.
64. Bindra, *Anglo–Bangladesh Relations*, p. 86.
65. P.J. Bertocci, 'Bangladesh in 1984: A Year of Protracted Turmoil', *Asian Survey*, vol. 25, no. 2, 1985, pp. 155–68. For details of the trade agreement renewal which went a little further to redress the trade imbalance against Bangladesh, see *Asian Recorder*, 4–10 November 1984, p. 18017.
66. W.H. Morris-Jones, 'India – More Questions Than Answers', *Asian Survey*, vol. 24, no. 8, 1984, p. 811.
67. *Ibid.*, pp. 813–4. Many other analysts have also made this point.
68. R.L. Hardgrave, 'India in 1983: New Challenges, Lost Opportunities', *Asian Survey*, vol. 24, no. 2, 1984, p. 209.
69. See R.L. Hardgrave, *India Under Pressure*, Boulder, 1984, p. 4, and W.H. Morris-Jones, 'India', pp. 813–14.
70. Hardgrave, *India Under Pressure*, p. 73.
71. Ghosh, *Cooperation and Contact*, p. 81. For a similar point of view, see S. Mansingh, *India's Search*, p. 271.
72. For sample accounts which describe India's perspective of the disturbances in Assam and Tripura, see *The Statesman* (Delhi), 11 July 1980 and *Amrita Bazar Patrika* (Calcutta), 22 October 1980. In the latter account, Mrs Gandhi also added the 'foreign hand' ingredient, accusing 'certain foreign powers' of exploiting the unrest at India's expense.
73. M. Weiner, *Sons of the Soil: Migration and Ethnic Conflict in India*, New Jersey, 1978, p. 80.
74. Population in Assam grew between 1961 and 1981 at an average of 35.52 per cent while the rest of India grew at an average 24.76 per cent. *Census of India, 1981*, Series 1, India, Paper 1 of 1981, cited in Gulati, *Bangladesh*, p. 140.
75. Weiner, *Sons of the Soil*, pp. 75–143.
76. Morris-Jones, 'India', p. 811. This view is held by other analysts, such as Weiner, *Sons of the Soil*, p.83, and C.J. Gulati who has conducted a detailed study of the Assam problem and Bangladeshi infiltration. See Gulati, *Bangladesh*, p. 130.
77. Morris-Jones, 'India', p. 811.
78. *Ibid.* Morris-Jones also points out that Assam has been impoverished by the central government's failure to compensate Assam adequately for the substantial contribution its products (oil and tea, in particular) have made to the national income.
79. Hardgrave, 'India in 1983', p. 210.
80. Morris-Jones, 'India', p. 811. See also *The Bangladesh Observer* (Dhaka), 28 February 1983, and *Times of India* (New Delhi), 28 February and 6 March 1983. According to the *New York Times*, August 28, 1983, at least 5000 were killed in the election violence.
81. Hardgrave, 'India in 1983', p. 210.
82. *Times of India* (New Delhi), 4 April 1983.

83. *Times of India* (New Delhi), 4 April 1983.
84. Hardgrave, 'India in 1983', p. 210.
85. *Ibid.* After the February violence in Assam, illegal immigrants were reported as opting to move into areas such as Bihar and West Bengal instead, hence the Indian government's decision to fence the entire Indo–Bangladesh border. See *New York Times*, August 28, 1983.
86. *The Bangladesh Observer* (Dhaka), 3 August 1983.
87. *Ibid.*
88. *Times of India* (New Delhi), 22 August 1983.
89. L.R. Baral, 'SARC, But No 'Shark': South Asian Regional Cooperation in Perspective', *Pacific Affairs*, vol. 58, no. 3, 1985, p. 412.
90. *Times of India* (New Delhi), 13 August 1983.
91. *The Bangladesh Observer* (Dhaka), 3 September 1983. For details of the fence announcement see *Times of India* (New Delhi) 13 August 1983.
92. *Times of India* (New Delhi), 22 August 1983.
93. *The Bangladesh Observer* (Dhaka), 15 August 1983. Ershad's stand lacked credibility and according to most analysts of the issue, considerable numbers of Bengali Muslims and Bangladeshis have entered Assam illegally, especially since 1970. Morris-Jones has described the post-1970 migration as a 'veritable invasion'. Morris-Jones, *India*, p. 811. According to Indian officials, more than 9,000 'infiltrators' from Bangladesh were arrested between January and June 1983. *New York Times*, August 28, 1983.
94. Hardgrave, 'India in 1983', p. 210.
95. *New York Times*, August 28, 1983.
96. Although kept on a tight rein, political parties were beginning to unify their opposition to Ershad's enforcement of martial law, with a hartal demanding a return to democratic government being held on 1 November 1983. *The Bangladesh Observer* (Dhaka), 2 November 1983.
97. *Asian Recorder*, 22–28 October 1983, p. 17421.
98. See *The Bangladesh Observer* (Dhaka), 22–26 April and 29 October 1984, *New York Times*, April 22 and 25, 1984 and *Times of India* (New Delhi), 22 and 24–26 April 1984.
99. *Times of India* (New Delhi), 27 April 1984.
100. The fence was located provocatively 9 inches within Indian territory. *The Economist*, V. 291, 28 April 1984, p. 47.
101. It was, in fact, 1981.
102. *Times of India* (New Delhi), 25 April 1984.
103. According to the *Economist*, V. 291, 28 April 1984, p. 47, the fence would 'almost certainly add a new item to the smugglers' inventory: barbed wire'.
104. *Ibid.*
105. Gulati, *Bangladesh*, p. 182.
106. *The Bangladesh Observer* (Dhaka), 27 October 1984. Part of the tension between India and Pakistan arose from India's accusations that Pakistan was giving assistance to Sikh separatists in the Punjab.
107. According to official data, communal incidents and the number of persons killed in India has risen 'alarmingly' since the mid-1980s. For example, in 1975, 205 incidents were recorded, while in 1985 there were 525. See S.D. Muni, 'Ethnic Conflicts, Federalism and Democracy in India', in S.D. Muni (ed.), *Understanding South Asia: Essays in the Memory of Late Professor (Mrs) Urmila Phadnis*, New Delhi, 1994, p. 149.

4   1985–90: The 'New Era' of Regional Amity and Cooperation

1. N.D. Palmer, *The New Regionalism in Asia and the Pacific*, Lexington, 1991, p. 2.
2. *Ibid.*, p. 17.
3. *Ibid.*, p. 11. In December 1987, US Secretary of State George Schultz commented: 'regional associations . . . are fast becoming an important and effective new milieu for political and economic interactions in the world . . . Regional, political, and religious blocs of nations . . . now provide platforms for a number of countries to exercise influence in global affairs', cited in Palmer, *The New Regionalism*, p. 16.
4. This comment was made by Peter Lyon, cited in Palmer, *The New Regionalism*, p. 75.
5. The SARC organisation was launched formally in August 1983 by the seven South Asian foreign ministers, but the December 1985 summit was attended by all the heads of government, giving greater stature to the organisation. See *The Bangladesh Observer* (Dhaka), 8 December 1985.
6. In 1980, the share of intra-SAARC trade of the SAARC member countries was on average only 3.2 per cent. By 1989, the figure had actually dropped – to 2.9 per cent. 'SAARC Regional Study on Trade, Manufactures and Services', cited in, S.D. Muni (ed.), *Understanding South Asia: Essays in the Memory of Late Professor (Mrs) Urmila Phadnis*, New Delhi, 1994, p. 231.
7. *Times of India* (New Delhi), 9 December 1985.
8. *Ibid.*, 10 December 1985.
9. The following assessment was made in a recent overview of SAARC's achievements:
    > Thus it is to be observed that, in ten years of existence, SAARC has provided itself with an institutional framework, has seen the development of numerous programmes of cooperation in the economic, cultural, scientific and technical domains, has made it possible to increase contacts at the highest political levels and has given experts, scholars and academicians the opportunity to exchange ideas at innumerable conferences and seminars on SAARC. This is a far from negligible and virtually unexpected balance, if it is seen in comparison with bilateral political relations, which have not always been on a fair course'. G. Boquerat *et al.*, *SAARC Economic and Political Atlas*, Pondy Papers in Social Sciences, No. 20, Pondicherry, 1996, p. 17.
10. Such as the control and use of rivers.
11. As an example: Rajiv Gandhi viewed SAARC as 'pointing the way to collective self-reliance in order to overcome problems of poverty, illiteracy, malnutrition and disease in the area', *Times of India* (New Delhi), 8 December 1985, and Ziaul Haq commented that SAARC would 'make a signal contributor to the consolidation of peace and stability in the area'. *The Bangladesh Observer* (Dhaka), 9 December 1985.
12. For details of the reasons for the shift in India's foreign policy, see Harish Kapur, 'India's Foreign Policy Under Rajiv Gandhi', *The Round Table*, vol. 304, 1987, pp. 469–79.
13. *Glasnost* (openness) and *Perestroika* (restructuring) were policies implemented in the late 1980s by the Soviet leader, Mikhail Gorbachev. They were aimed at making the Soviet government more open and answerable to the public and at implementing political and economic reform in the Soviet Union.
14. Kapur, 'India's Foreign Policy', p. 471.
15. The United States was prepared to offer some sensitive defence technology to India, but in the long term, the USSR was considered by India as a more

reliable source of military equipment and spare parts. Kapur, 'India's Foreign Policy', pp. 470–1.

16. A. Kapur, 'Indian Foreign Policy: Perspectives and Present Predicaments', *The Round Table*, vol. 295, 1985, p. 236.

17. Warmer relations between China and the Soviet Union culminated in May 1989, with Mikhail Gorbachev's historic visit to China.

18. Kapur, 'Indian Foreign Policy', 236.

19. Some confidence-building measures were eventually implemented on India's part to improve relations, such as Rajiv's ice-breaking trip to China in December 1988, the first such visit since Nehru's in 1954. According to *The Bangladesh Observer*, 25 December 1988, Rajiv's trip had 'broken the ice in Sino–Indian relations', but the road to friendship between the two 'Asian giants' was 'still paved with doubts'. The ever-present tension over border deliniation was further reinforced in April and May 1987, when Himalayan border clashes occurred between Indian and Chinese forces.

20. H. Kapur, *India's Foreign Policy, 1947–92: Shadows and Substance*, New Delhi, 1994, p. 206. The potential for conflict erupting between China and India has also extended to the naval sphere with each expanding its naval capability since the 1980s. China continues to put pressure on India by supplying Pakistan with weaponry, such as surface-to-surface missiles, which China has been sending regularly to Pakistan since 1991. R. Thakur, *The Politics and Economics of India's Foreign Policy*, London, 1994, p. 74.

21. S. Ganguly, 'The Prime Minister and Foreign and Defence Policies', in J. Manor (ed.), *Nehru to the Nineties: The Changing Office of Prime Minister in India*, London, 1994, p. 155.

22. *Times of India* (New Delhi), 27 February 1986. (Article by Girilal Jain, 'Rajiv Gandhi's Personality').

23. Kapur, *India's Foreign Policy*, p. 194.

24. *Far Eastern Economic Review*, vol. 131, 2 January 1986, p. 29.

25. *The Bangladesh Observer* (Dhaka), 18 October 1985.

26. *Ibid.*

27. *Ibid.*

28. *Ibid.*

29. *Ibid.*, 19 October 1985.

30. *Ibid.*, 19 October 1985.

31. B. Crow *et al.*, *Sharing the Ganges: The Politics and Technology of River Development*, New Delhi, 1995, p. 201.

32. *Ibid.*, pp. 203–4.

33. *The Bangladesh Observer* (Dhaka), 11 December 1985.

34. B.G. Verghese, *Waters of Hope: Integrated Water Resource Development and Regional Cooperation within the Himalayan–Ganga–Brahmaputra–Barak Basin*, New Delhi, 1990, p. 366.

35. The issue of tribal insurgency will be discussed in detail in Chapter 6.

36. *Times of India* (New Delhi), 10 December 1985.

37. *Far Eastern Economic Review*, vol. 131, 2 January 1986, p. 29. The announcement was made on 17 December 1985.

38. *Times of India* (New Delhi), 10 December 1985.

39. *Far Eastern Economic Review*, vol. 131, 2 January 1986, p. 29.

40. The visit was planned for April 1986, but was cancelled due to increasing Indo–Pakistani tension over alleged Pakistani assistance to Sikh extremists in the Punjab.

41. *Far Eastern Economic Review*, vol. 131, 2 January 1986, p. 29.
42. *Ibid.*
43. *Ibid.*
44. For a summary, see S. Wolpert, *A New History of India*, 4th edn, New York, 1993, pp. 426–7. According to Wolpert, Rajiv ousted the finance minister, V.P. Singh from the cabinet because of Singh's attempts to uncover embarrassing and corrupt government dealings, such as the Bofors defense contract.
45. Wolpert, *A New History*, p. 427. Of particular concern to Rajiv's party was the loss of the Haryana by-election, Haryana state being considered a long-time bastion of Congress-I support.
46. *Ibid.*
47. Ganguly, 'The Prime Minister', p. 155.
48. Kapur, *India's Foreign Policy*, pp. 196–7.
49. Ganguly, 'The Prime Minister', p. 156.
50. *Ibid.*
51. *The Bangladesh Observer* (Dhaka), 18 March 1986.
52. *Times of India* (New Delhi), 9 December 1985.
53. *Far Eastern Economic Review*, vol. 131, 2 January 1986, p. 29.
54. See *Keesing's Contemporary Archives*, vol. XXI, December 1985, p. 34052 and *ibid.*, vol. XXXII, July 1986, p. 34483.
55. *Ibid.*, December 1985, p. 34052.
56. *New York Times* (New York), 18 January 1986.
57. *The Bangladesh Observer* (Dhaka), 10 April 1986.
58. *Ibid.*
59. *Keesing's Contemporary Archives*, vol. XXXII, July 1986, p. 34483.
60. Crow *et al.*, *Sharing the Ganges*, p. 202.
61. *Ibid.*, p. 189.
62. The Bangladesh government's role will be examined in Chapter 6.
63. Crow *et al.*, *Sharing the Ganges*, p. 202.
64. *Ibid.*
65. *The Bangladesh Observer* (Dhaka), 18 November 1986.
66. Crow *et al.*, *Sharing the Ganges*, p. 206.
67. *Ibid.*
68. *Ibid.*, p. 207.
69. *Ibid.*, p. 208.
70. *Ibid.*, pp. 194–5.
71. *Ibid.*, p. 195.
72. *Ibid.*
73. Verghese, *Waters of Hope*, p. 209.
74. Joint Rivers Commission, Dhaka, 'Position Paper on the Issues of the Memorandum of Understanding of November 1985', 19.3.87, cited in Begum, *Tension over the Farakka Barrage: A Techno-Political Tangle in South Asia*, Stuttgart, 1988, p. 248.
75. Crow *et al.*, *Sharing the Ganges*, p. 191.
76. To be examined in Chapter 6.
77. Crow *et al.*, *Sharing the Ganges*, p. 249.
78. *Ibid.*, p. 216. A new JCE was eventually formed in 1992.
79. For a summary of the arguments see Verghese *Waters of Hope*, p. 371. Most of the flooding in 1988 derived from the Brahmaputra and Meghna rivers, not the Ganges.

80. This was exemplified by the following comment by Ershad: 'The main source of flood control lies across the geographical bounds of Bangladesh and as such, cooperation of regional countries, India, Nepal, Bhutan and China was vitally necessary to keep Bangladesh from recurring disaster.' *The Bangladesh Observer* (Dhaka), 17 October 1988.

81. Verghese, *Waters of Hope*, p. 373.

82. *The Far Eastern Economic Review*, 13 October 1988, p. 24.

83. *Ibid.*

84. *Ibid.*

85. Verghese, *Water of Hope*, p. 372.

86. *Ibid.* The aim of the model was to allow planners 'to posit the full range of possible flow conditions and test simulated engineering works'.

87. *Ibid.*

88. For a summary, see S.D. Muni, *Pangs of Proximity: India and Sri Lanka's Ethnic Crisis*, New Delhi, 1993, pp. 76–83.

89. Wolpert, *A New History*, p. 431.

90. For details of Indo–Pakistani relations at that time see S. Yasmeen, 'India and Pakistan: Why the Latest Exercise in Brinkmanship?', *Australian Journal of Politics and History*, vol. 34, no. 1, 1988/89, pp. 64–72.

91. R. Thakur, 'India After Nonalignment', *Foreign Affairs*, Spring, 1992, p. 171.

92. Ganguly, '*The Prime Ministers*' p. 156.

93. This was the first visit by an Indian External Affairs Minister for three years.

94. *The Far Eastern Economic Review*, 15 March 1990, p. 29.

95. *The Bangladesh Observer* (Dhaka), 18 February 1990.

96. *Ibid.*, 19 February 1990.

97. The coalition government collapsed in November 1990 largely because of opposition from within by the Hindu extremist Bharatiya Janata Party (BJP). Hindu–Muslim communal tension was exacerbated by the BJP over the Babri Masjid (at Ayodhya), a mosque allegedly built on the ruins of a Hindu temple marking what was believed to be the birthplace of the Hindu deity, Lord Ram.

98. *The Bangladesh Observer* (Dhaka), 18 July 1990.

99. Thakur, *Politics and Economics*, p. 165.

100. Kapur, *India's Foreign Policy, 1947–92: Shadows and Substance, op. cit.*, p. 135.

101. In 1988, Pakistan ranked as the fourth largest recipient of US military aid after Israel, Egypt and Turkey. S. Yasmeen, 'India and Pakistan', p. 69.

5   1975–81: Military Ascendancy in Bangladesh

1. For a summary of the reasons why Mujib's popularity plummeted, see L. Jenkins, 'The Sins of the Father', *Newsweek*, August 25, 1975, p. 11.

2. The August 1975 coup against Mujib was carried out by disgruntled elements in the military, although the Majors who killed Mujib were 'used as pawns by more sophisticated political forces', L. Lifschultz, *Bangladesh: The Unfinished Revolution*, London, 1979, p. 102. Nevertheless, it is unlikely that those forces would have participated in the coup if Mujib had continued to receive popular support. It is therefore not surprising that Zia went to considerable lengths to cultivate mass appeal.

3. The 'four pillars' espoused by Mujib and the principles upon which the 1972 Bangladesh constitution was based were: nationalism, secularism, socialism and democracy. These principles followed closely the four principles attributed to Jawaharlal Nehru of India: democracy, socialism, secularism and non-alignment. Nehru's, and

hence Mujib's understanding of a 'secular' state was essentially one in which religious minority groups would have equal rights with the majority religious group. See M. Brecher, *Nehru: A Political Biography*, London, 1959, p. 621. It did not necessarily imply that the Indian or Bangladesh governments should not be based on religious principles.

4. C.H. Bateman, 'National Security and Nationalism in Bangladesh', *Asian Survey*, vol. 19, no. 8, August 1979, p. 781. According to 'numerous reports', Pakistani military equipment worth about US$50 million was taken back to India. See M. Rashiduzzaman, 'Changing Political Patterns in Bangladesh: Internal Constraints and External Fears', in M.M. Khan and H.M Zafarullah (eds), *Politics and Bureaucracy in a New Nation: Bangladesh*, Dacca, 1980, p. 193.

5. The vague wording of Article 9 of the Friendship Treaty caused greatest concern in Bangladesh because it seemed to imply that even a domestic threat to Mujib's regime could invite Indian intervention:

> 'Each of the high contracting parties shall refrain from giving any assistance to any third party taking part in an armed conflict against the other party. In case either party is attacked or threatened with attack, the high contracting parties shall immediately enter into mutual consultations in order to take appropriate effective measures to eliminate the threat and thus ensure the peace and security of their countries.'
>
> *Asian Recorder*, 15–21 April 1972, p. 10720.

6. L. Lifschultz, 'New Delhi's 'views' on the Dacca Coups', *Far Eastern Economic Review*, 28 November 1975, p. 17.

7. In a Presidential order on 6 June 1975, Sheikh Mujib announced the creation of a national party, known as the Bangladesh Krishak Sramik Awami League (BAKSAL) which was to be the only party allowed under the Constitution. See *Asian Recorder*, 2–8 July 1975, p. 12659.

8. Zillur Khan explores the process of politicisation of the armed forces in Pakistan, and subsequently Bangladesh, being stimulated particularly by the need to aid the civil administration during crises such as floods, famines and epidemics. Z.R. Khan, 'Politicization of the Bangladesh Military: A Response to Perceived Shortcomings of Civilian Government', *Asian Survey*, vol. 21, no. 5, 1981, pp. 551–64.

9. A.G. Noorani, *India, the Superpowers and the Neighbours: Essays in Foreign Policy*, New Delhi, 1985, p. 55.

10. J. Uyangoda, 'Indo–Bangladesh Relations in the 1970s: Bangladeshi Perspectives', in S.U. Kodikara (ed.), *South Asian Strategic Issues: Sri Lankan Perspectives*, New Delhi, 1990, p. 67.

11. C.P. O'Donnell, *Bangladesh: Biography of a Muslim Nation*, Boulder, 1984, p. 212.

12. See *New York Times*, November 18, 1975. According to A. Mascarenhas, the leader of the abortive November 3 coup, Khalid Musharraf, was unfairly accused of attempting a 'sell-out to India and restoring a Mujibist government in Bangladesh', but did nothing to dispel the charge. A. Mascarenhas, *Bangladesh: A Legacy of Blood*, 1986, pp. 104–5.

13. L. Lifschultz, 'The Crisis Has Not Passed', *Far Eastern Economic Review*, December 5, 1975, p. 30.

14. Wright, *Bangladesh: Origins and Indian Ocean Relations (1971–1975)*, Sterling, 1988, p. 154.

15. The reasons for military politicisation in Bangladesh are numerous and complex and will be discussed in greater depth later in the chapter. They relate largely to the Independence War of 1971, and to Mujib's attempts to restrain the military.

16. *The Bangladesh Observer*, 15 August 1978.
17. *Ibid.*
18. The Fifth Amendment to the Bangladesh Constitution, passed on 5 April 1979, contained many checks on the sovereignty of the parliament. In particular, it validated all proclamations and martial law orders given since 15 August 1975 and retained controversial aspects of Mujib's Fourth Amendment to the constitution by which an all-powerful presidential form of government had been introduced. See A. Haque, 'Bangladesh 1979: Cry for a Sovereign Parliament', *Asian Survey*, vol. 20, no. 2, 1980, p. 221. See also *The Constitution of the People's Republic of Bangladesh: As Modified up to 28th February, 1979* [Dacca] [n.d.], p. 23. The military dominance of the elected National Assembly has been pointed out by Zillur Khan, who states that 30 per cent of the representatives were 'informers of the military regime'. Z.R. Khan, *Leadership in the Least Developed Nation: Bangladesh*, Syracuse, 1983, p. 149.
19. For a comparison between Zia and Ayub, see M.M. Khan and J.P. Thorp (eds), *Bangladesh: Society, Politics and Bureaucracy*, Dhaka, 1984, p. 107. Zillur Khan goes a step further by pointing out that Zia's efforts to militarise the government were much more subtle and sophisticated than Ayub's. Z.R. Khan, *Leadership in the Least Developed Nation*, p. 149.
20. The JSD had initiated a sepoy revolution in the military and reinstalled Zia as leader of the armed forces, expecting him to instigate their demands for social revolution.
21. S.S. Islam, 'The State in Bangladesh Under Zia (1975–81)', *Asian Survey*, vol. 24, no. 5, 1984, p. 568. For details of Taher's sentencing in a closed and dubious military tribunal, see *The Bangladesh Observer*, 18 July 1976. The sentence was carried out also under secrecy on 21 July 1976, to ensure that there would be no interference from Taher's supporters. Mascarenhas, *Bangladesh*, pp. 115–17. Also, media censorship appeared to be well in place because the execution was not reported in *The Bangladesh Observer*.
22. It was normal practice for officer cadets of the JRB to travel to Dehra Dun in India [India's Sandhurst] to undergo a year-long military course. In January 1975, the force was estimated to be 25 000 (almost half of the combined strength of the Bangladesh army, navy and airforce) and Mujib's intention was to increase the figure to 130 000. Adding to the military rivalry was the enormous amount of funding provided to the JRB, while the regular army was kept on a tight budget. The JRB was also alleged to have carried out torturing of captives and killing of Mujib's political opponents. See *Far Eastern Economic Review*, 'Power to Mujib's Private Army', 10 January, 1975.
23. Also spelled 'Mir Jafar'. Mir Jafar has remained a symbol for treachery in the Bengal region because of his opportunistic arrangement with the British under Clive during the Battle of Plassey in 1757.
24. *The Bangladesh Observer*, 24 November 1975.
25. For press reports, see *Times of India* (New Delhi), 21, 22 April 1976. See also *The Times* (London), 21 April 1976 and *New York Times*, April 22, 1976.
26. For example, in February 1976, the Indian government finally agreed to form a joint inquiry committee with Bangladesh to investigate the guerrilla border activities. While this meant that a step forward in cooperation had been achieved, the limitations of such an inquiry, and the way in which India easily held the upper hand, were obvious from the outset. The Director General of the Indian Border Security Force agreed that border instability existed and needed

investigating, but he emphatically denied, even before that investigation took place, the possibility that 'any miscreants were operating from inside Indian territory or that sanctuary was being allowed to any miscreants from Bangladesh'. *The Bangladesh Observer*, 14 February 1976. Moreover, the final report promised to be ready within thirty days, never eventuated, being shelved after ineffective border talks held in January 1977, *ibid.*, 30 January 1977.

27. *Ibid.*, 30 January 1977.

28. For details of the socialist character of the Bangladesh liberation movement, see: T. Maniruzzaman, *Radical Politics and the Emergence of Bangladesh*, Dhaka, 1975, pp. 47–55. Maniruzzaman points out that the political orientation of those who fought in the war shifted to a position which was further left than that of the regular Awami League. See p. 49.

29. Committed leftist leader and fellow commander, Abu Taher, was a close friend of Zia's during the war, although after the 7 November coup, Zia chose to crush the leftist sepoy revolutionaries and execute Taher, seeing their activities as a threat to military stability and his own plans for power consolidation.

30. This statement was part of Taher's testimony delivered between 12 and 15 July in Dhaka Central Jail to the Special Martial Law Tribunal which sentenced him to be executed on the 21 July. See L. Lifschultz, *Bangladesh: The Unfinished Revolution*, p. 87. For the first publication of Taher's last testimony, see L. Lifschultz, 'Abu Taher's Last Testament: Bangladesh: The Unfinished Revolution', *Economic and Political Weekly* (Bombay), Special Number, August 1977, pp. 1303–53.

31. For details of Zia's crackdown on the JSD and its revolutionary Twelve Demands, see Lifschultz, 'The Crisis Has Not Passed', pp. 28–34.

32. Long-time rival of Sheikh Mujib, Maulana Bhashani had become particularly outspoken against Mujib's economic mismanagement and pro-Indian policy in the last three years of Mujib's regime. For examples, see *Morning News* (Dhaka), 19 May 1973 and 15 April 1974. For Bhashani's explanation of what he meant by 'Islamic socialism', see *Morning News* (Dhaka), 8 August 1973.

33. E. Ahamed, 'Dominant Bureaucratic Elites in Bangladesh,' in M.M. Khan and H.M. Zafarullah, *Politics and Bureaucracy in a New Nation: Bangladesh*, Dacca, 1980, p. 150.

34. *Ibid.*, p. 155.

35. It has been pointed out that Zia's Islamic emphasis was not of an extreme nature because it was based on the backlash against the discredited Awami League's secular rule rather than the rise of extreme Islamic fundamentalism. See D.A. Wright, 'Islam and Bangladeshi Polity', *South Asia: Journal of South Asian Studies*, vol. 10, no. 2, December 1987, p. 21.

36. Traditionally, the Islam practised in rural Bangladesh was of a more liberal form, being Sufi and Indic-influenced. See D. Walker, 'Islam and Nationalism in Bangladesh', *Hamdard Islamicus*, vol. 14, no. 2, 1991, p. 39.

37. *The Bangladesh Observer*, 14 March 1976.

38. *Ibid.*

39. *Ibid.*, 2 May 1976.

40. S. Oren, 'After the Bangladesh Coups', *The World Today*, vol. 32, no. 1, January 1976, p. 21.

41. *Ibid.*

42. A. Roy, 'The Bengal Muslim "Cultural Mediators" and the Bengal Muslim Identity in the Nineteenth and Early Twentieth Centuries', *South Asia*, vol. 10, no. 1, 1987, p. 28.

43. Wright, 'Islam and Bangladeshi Polity', pp. 21–2.
44. 'The Proclamations (Amendment) order, 1977', in *The Constitution of the People's Republic of Bangladesh: As Modified up to 28th February, 1979*, pp. 153–4.
45. *Ibid.*, p. 152. See also *The Bangladesh Observer*, 23 April 1977.
46. 'The Proclamations (Amendment) order, 1977', p. 154.
47. *The Bangladesh Observer*, 23 January 1978.
48. For example, in May 1976, Zia attended an Islamic Foreign Minister's Conference in Istanbul and afterwards visited Saudi Arabia and Iran, returning delighted with the improved prospects for Muslim aid to Bangladesh. See *The Bangladesh Observer*, 22 May 1976. Other examples include Zia's diplomatic visit to Saudi Arabia in 1977, *ibid.*, 29 July 1977; the Iraqi Vice-President's visit to Bangladesh in 1978, *Ibid.*, 4 July 1978; Zia's talks with Indonesian President, Suharto in Jakarta in 1978, *ibid.*, 29 July 1978; and in 1980, at a seminar in Dhaka organised by the World Islamic Council, Zia reiterated that Bangladesh was 'determined to work with the Islamic countries for fostering stronger Islamic unity', *ibid.*, 25 December 1980.
49. Government of Bangladesh, Ministry of Finance, External Resources Division, 'Flow of External Resources into Bangladesh' (as of June 30, 1981), pp. 20–2 and pp. 26–76, cited in M.M. Khan and S.A. Husain (eds), *Bangladesh Studies: Politics, Administration, Rural Development and Foreign Policy*, Dhaka, 1986, p. 251. See also *The 1979 Statistical Yearbook of Bangladesh*, Dacca, p. 346. Most of the aid came from Saudi Arabia.
50. The extreme poverty of Bangladesh is best illustrated by examining the state's *per capita* GNP. In 1975, Bangladesh, along with Laos and Mali, had the lowest rate in the world, being US$90. In the same year, India had a *per capita* income of US$140, while Pakistan's was even higher, at US$160. This has partly resulted from the heavy economic dependency upon agriculture, with 91.2 per cent of Bangladesh's population living in rural areas in 1974 (as opposed to 79.4 per cent in India). In 1974–5, agriculture provided 63.1 per cent of GDP. See *The 1979 Statistical Yearbook of Bangladesh*, Dacca, pp. 517, 526–8.
51. H. Evans, 'Bangladesh: South Asia's Unknown Quantity', *Asian Affairs*, New Series, vol. 19, October 1988, p. 309.
52. The heavy dependence on foreign assistance was reflected in the Bangladesh budget for fiscal year 1979–80 (July–June), whereby it was calculated that the state's development programmes for the following fiscal year would depend for a 'relatively high' 73 per cent of their financing on foreign aid. Also according to this budget, Bangladesh had received foreign aid commitments of US$7.713 billion between December 1971 and June 1979. See S. Kamaluddin, 'Agriculture's Growing Pains', *Far Eastern Economic Review*, 22 June, 1979, p. 86. According to the *New York Times*, 6 June 1978, Bangladesh had received, since gaining independence, nearly US$6 billion in aid, including US$1 billion from the United States.
53. Wright, 'Bangladesh: Foreign Policy For the 1980s', *Bangladesh Bulletin*, vol. 14, 1987, p. 22–3.
54. Ahamed (ed.), 'Dominant Bureaucratic Elites', p. 12.
55. D.A. Wright, 'Destructive Features of Bangladeshi Political Life', *Probaho*, vol. 1, no. 3, 1991, p. 23.
56. India had been a major contributor of aid to Bangladesh between 1971 and 1974, providing, for example, US$84 million in project-aid. After 1974–5, no project-aid was committed by India, it being provided instead largely by the

West, Middle Eastern states and the USSR. See *The 1979 Statistical Yearbook of Bangladesh*, Dacca, pp. 347–8.

57. *New York Times*, August 29, 1980.
58. Particularly Saudi Arabia and OPEC. See *The 1979 Statistical Yearbook of Bangladesh*, Dacca, p. 346.
59. See L. Ziring, 'Pakistan and India: Politics, Personalities, and Foreign Policy', *Asian Survey*, vol. 18, no. 7, 1978, p. 711, and L. Ziring (ed.), *The Subcontinent in World Politics: India, Its Neighbors, and the Great Powers*, New York, p. 116.
60. *The Times* (London), 19 March 1981.
61. For details of the speedy reconciliation between Bangladesh and Pakistan once Zia had come to power, see *New York Times*, February 2, 1976.
62. Within days of the 7 November coup, China extended its 'warm support to the new Government of Bangladesh'. See *The Bangladesh Observer*, 12 November 1975. In April 1977, following Zia's successful goodwill tour of China in January (during which an economic and technical agreement was signed), Premier of the People's Republic of China, Hua Kuo-feng, expressed confidence that 'the friendly relations and cooperations between China and Bangladesh would increasingly grow in strength and develop through joint efforts of their two Governments and peoples', *The Bangladesh Observer*, 8 April 1977. See also *ibid.*, 4 January 1977.
63. Due to the smuggling of raw jute into India, Bangladesh was believed to have lost about US$50 million in foreign exchange in those years. See Rashiduzzaman, 'Changing Political Patterns' p. 193.
64. Ziring (ed.), *The Subcontinent in World Politics*, p. 10.
65. *The Bangladesh Observer*, 26 January 1977.
66. *New York Times*, October 4, 1976.
67. Gulati, *Bangladesh*, p. 209.
68. R. Sobhan, *The Crisis of External Dependence: The Political Economy of Foreign Aid to Bangladesh*, London, 1982, p. 125.
69. According to Rehman Sobhan, the OPEC states have 'invariably' given untied aid to Bangladesh, allowing Bangladesh to retain maximum flexibility in investment decisions. Sobhan, *The Crisis*, p. 153.
70. Sobhan, *The Crisis*, pp. 149–53. Sobhan has provided an astute and balanced assessment of Indo–Bangladesh economic relations in the 1970s, bringing out the complex tie between political and economic considerations in those relations.
71. Indian aid to Bangladesh between December 1971 and June 1972 totalled US$222.7 million, sufficient to avert an impending famine. Sobhan, *The Crisis*, pp. 139–40.
72. In the late 1970s, Indian jute exports were actually losing ground in the world market due to competition from supplies and synthetic substitutes from Bangladesh. See Ministry of Information and Broadcasting (comp.), *India. A Reference Annual: 1982*, New Delhi, 1982, p. 344.
73. Sobhan, *The Crisis*, pp. 140, 142.
74. For details of why this occurred, see Sobhan, *The Crisis*, pp. 130–31.
75. *The Bangladesh Observer*, 13 January 1976. See also *Times of India* (New Delhi), 13 January 1976. According to the report in the *Times of India*, trade had declined sharply over the preceding three years, Indian exports to Bangladesh falling from Rs. 58.78 crores in 1973–4 to Rs. 42.17 crores in 1974–5 and Rs. 16.50 crores between July and December 1975. The decline in trade and the trade imbalance are also revealed in the imports from Bangladesh which fell from Rs. 17.05 crores in 1973–4 to Rs. 9.18 crores in 1974–5 and Rs. 9 crores between

July and December 1975. The leader of the Bangladesh delegation at the talks, M. Nurul Islam, expressed his satisfaction with the 'definite, concrete and positive steps' which had been taken at the talks.

76. The trade agreement was especially congenial for poorer Bangladesh. India's decision to increase imports from Bangladesh was a reasonably magnanimous gesture because those goods were either already oversupplied or had had problems with price and quality control. See *Times of India* (New Delhi), 13 January 1976.

77. Morarji Desai and the Janata coalition party came to power in India in March 1977, ousting Mrs Gandhi in the national elections.

78. *Asian Recorder*, 25 June–1 July 1978, p. 14373.

79. *Ibid.*, 25 November–1 December 1980, p. 15759.

80. Such as those associated with disputes over territory and the checking of illegal Bangladeshi immigration into India. For example, see *New York Times* (New York), October 28, 1980, for a comment on India's revived 'anti-immigrant drive'.

81. Particularly by arousing entrenched fears of colonial exploitation, as had been carried out by West Pakistan before 1971. See I. Hossain, 'Bangladesh–India Relations: Issues and Problems', *Asian Survey*, vol. 21, no. 11, 1981, pp. 1116–7. According to Hossain, Mujib's trade pact with India was ostensibly aimed to promote trade between the two states, but in reality, resulted in large scale smuggling. *Ibid.*, p. 1117.

82. A large increase in aid from the United States was obtained by Zia, particularly from 1976 to 1979, where US$648.1 million was received, as opposed to US$379.5 million provided during the preceding years between 1971 and 1975. See Government of Bangladesh, Ministry of Finance, External Resources Division, 'Flow of External Resources into Bangladesh, as of June 30, 1981', pp. 20–2 and 26–76, cited in Khan and Husain (eds), *Bangladesh Studies*, pp. 251–2.

83. See *New York Times*, December 31, 1975.

84. H.A. Kissinger, 'Domestic Structure and Foreign Policy', in J.N. Rosenau, *International Politics and Foreign Policy: A Reader in Research and Theory*, New York, 1969, p. 272.

85. Ahamed (ed.), 'Dominant Bureaucratic Elites', p. 4.

86. Wright, 'Destructive Features of Bangladeshi Political Life', p. 24.

87. B. Buzan *et al.*, *South Asian Insecurity and the Great Powers*, New York, 1986, pp. 7–8.

88. According to Lawrence Ziring, approximately 26 coup attempts occurred during Zia's rule, culminating in his assassination by a disgruntled military officer in May 1981. See L. Ziring, *Bangladesh: From Mujib to Ershad – An Interpretive Study*, Oxford, 1992, pp. 140–1.

6 1982–90: Political Manoeuvres and Ethnic Violence

1. Editorial, *Times of India* (New Delhi), 25 March 1982.

2. L. Ziring, *Bangladesh: From Mujib to Ershad, An Interpretive Study*, Oxford, 1992, p. 140.

3. While there is still some controversy over the subject, the official explanation was that a disgruntled Freedom Fighter officer, Muhammad Abul Manzur, along with a small group of supporting officers, carried out the assassination. See A. Mascarenhas, *A Legacy of Blood*, London, 1986, pp. 160–83.

4. Ziring, *Bangladesh*, p. 144.

5. S. Hassan, 'Transitional Politics In Bangladesh: A Study of Sattar's Interim Presidency', *India Quarterly*, vol. 39, no. 3, 1983, p. 264.

6. This issue had intensified due to Zia's civilianising policies. See Z.R. Khan, 'Bangladesh in 1981: Change, Stability, and Leadership', *Asian Survey*, vol. 22, no. 2, 1982, p. 165.

7. According to S. Hassan, Zia's 'youth, vigour and dedication had earned him the respect of his countrymen' and his sudden death had thrown the country into 'chaos and uncertainty', leaving Sattar's interim government with little option but to 'honour Zia's international commitments and carry forward his domestic policies and objectives'. Hassan, 'Transitional Politics', p. 263.

8. The fragility of Sattar's position is revealed, for example, in the comment by Marcus Franda that Zia's death had occurred 'at a point when things had started to go sour but had not yet deteriorated'. M. Franda, *Bangladesh: The First Decade*, New Delhi, 1982, p. 324.

9. *The Bangladesh Observer* (Dhaka), 25 March 1982.

10. M.A. Rahman, 'Bangladesh in 1983: A Turning Point for the Military', *Asian Survey*, vol. 24, no. 2, 1984, p. 151.

11. M. Ataur Rahman points out that while 'political, economic and social conditions' were 'fast deteriorating' under Sattar, popular acceptance of Ershad's coup had resulted more from widespread disillusionment with Sattar's 'uninspiring' regime than anything else. M.A. Rahman, p. 151.

12. *The Bangladesh Observer* (Dhaka), 25 March 1982.

13. Rahman, 'Bangladesh in 1983', p. 150.

14. *Ibid.*, p. 151.

15. See also Chapter 3.

16. *Times of India*, 25 March 1982.

17. See Chapters 3 and 4.

18. See Chapter 8.

19. *The Bangladesh Observer* (Dhaka), 8 June 1988.

20. See S.D. Muni, *Pangs of Proximity: India and Sri Lanka's Ethnic Crisis*, New Delhi, 1993, p. 28.

21. B. Crow *et al.*, *Sharing the Ganges: The Politics and Technology of River Development*, New Delhi, 1995.

22. See Chapter 3.

23. *The Economist*, 'Bangladesh floods: drowned by politics', vol. 308, 17 September 1988, p. 38.

24. Crow *et al.*, *Sharing the Ganges*, p. 193.

25. *Ibid.*, p. 198.

26. *Ibid.*

27. *Ibid.*, p. 193.

28. *Ibid.*

29. *Ibid.*

30. *Ibid.*

31. *Ibid.*, p. 194.

32. *Ibid.*, p. 198.

33. *Ibid.*, pp. 194–5.

34. *Ibid.*, p. 210.

35. B.G. Verghese, *Waters of Hope: Integrated Water Resource Development and Regional Cooperation within the Himalayan–Ganga–Brahmaputra–Barak Basin*, New Delhi, 1990, pp. 374–5.

36. See Chapters 2 and 3.

37. For examples, see *The Bangladesh Observer* (Dhaka), 18 April 1988 (Bangladesh viewpoint); and. K.P. Khanal, 'Impact of Domestic Conflicts on Regional

Cooperation in South Asia', in B. Sen Gupta, *Regional Cooperation and Development in South Asia, Vol. 2,* New Delhi, 1986 p. 195 (Indian viewpoint).

38. Useful sources dealing with the Chittagong Hill Tract tribal insurgency include S.M. Ali, *The Fearful State: Power, People and Internal War in South Asia,* London, 1993, pp. 162–203; M. Rahman Shelley (ed.), *The Chittagong Hill Tracts of Bangladesh: The Untold Story,* Dhaka, 1992; U. Phadnis *et al.* (eds), *Domestic Conflicts in South Asia, Vol. 1: Political Dimensions,* New Delhi, 1986, pp. 55–83; W. Van Schendel, 'The Invention of the "Jummas": State Formation and Ethnicity in Southeastern Bangladesh', *Modern Asian Studies,* vol. 26, no. 1, 1992, pp. 95–128; *Far Eastern Economic Review,* 'Intractable hills: autonomy plan fails to appease the rebels', 5 April 1990, pp. 22–4; and S.S. Ahsan and B. Chakma, 'Problems of National Integration in Bangladesh: The Chittagong Hill Tracts', *Asian Survey,* vol. XXIX, no. 10, October 1989, pp. 959–70.

39. The figure ranges from 11 to 13, depending on the source. See Ali, *The Fearful State.,* p. 166.

40. The figures are based on a variety of sources: 1991 Census, Bangladesh Bureau of Statistics, cited in Rahman Shelley (ed.), *The Chittagong Hill Tracts,* p. 50; Ali, *The Fearful State,* pp. 166–7; Van Schendel, 'The Invention of the "Jummas"', p. 95; *Far Eastern Economic Review,* 'Intractable hills: autonomy plan fails to appease the rebels', 5 April 1990, p. 24.

41. Van Schendel, 'The Invention of the "Jummas"', p. 95.

42. *Ibid.,* p.102.

43. *Ibid.*

44. *Ibid.,* p. 108.

45. *ibid.,* pp. 102–4.

46. As an example, Van Schendel quotes Abdus Sattar, a prominent Bangladeshi writer on tribal affairs in the 1970s, who described the hill people thus:
   Their way of life is timeless. Their cultural configuration is still intact, the outlines still hard and sharply drawn against the contrasting background of civilization with no sign of dimming...If there is no education it will further widen the gap between the civilized and the pre-civilized. Isolated and left behind the tribes will become more inward-looking and aggressive...The tribals are usually simple, credulous and jovial folks. As long as they have enough to eat they are not much bothered by worries...They are of deep interest to any one who wants to discover man in his raw form.' Abdus Sattar, *Tribal Culture in Bangladesh,* Dacca, Muktadhara, 1975, pp. 4–7, cited in Van Schendel, 'The Invention of the "Jummas"' pp. 103–4.

47. Van Schendel, 'The Invention of the "Jummas"', pp. 104–6.

48. Ali, *The Fearful State,* p. 170.

49. *Ibid.,* p. 175.

50. *Ibid.,* p. 171.

51. For a thorough analysis of the Act of 1900 see Rahman Shelley (ed.), *The Chittagong Hill Tracts.,* pp. 73–106.

52. Van Schendel, 'The Invention of the "Jummas"', p. 111.

53. *Ibid.,* p. 115.

54. *Ibid.,* pp. 115–16.

55. Ahsan and Chakma put the figure at 98 per cent. Ahsan and Chakma, 'Problems of National Integration', pp. 965–6. S.M. Ali puts the figure at approximately 89 per cent. Ali, *The Fearful State,* p. 167.

56. Van Schendel, 'The Invention of the "Jummas"', p. 95.

57. Ali, *The Fearful State*, p. 177.
58. *Ibid.*, p. 179.
59. *Ibid.*
60. *Ibid.*, pp. 181–2.
61. *Ibid.* See also: Chris Mullin, 'The CIA Conspiracy', *Far Eastern Economic Review*, vol. 36, no. 89, 1975, pp. 149–50.
62. Ali, *The Fearful State*, p. 182.
63. *Ibid.*
64. *Ibid.*
65. The 1971 war resulted in divided loyalties within the tribal groups. Some supported the Mizo and Naga insurgents in India and hence sided with the Pakistan central government. Others joined the Bengali Liberation Army but were not trusted and became disillusioned. Many Montagnards who fled into India during the war found, on their return, that their land had been occupied by Bengali settlers. This resulted in armed conflict over land claims. For further information, see Ali, *The Fearful State*, pp. 182–3.
66. Ahsan and Chakma, 'Problems of National Integration', p. 967.
67. *Ibid.*, p. 968.
68. 'Larma's Debate in the Parliament,' *Bangladesh National Assembly Debates*, 1:6, 23 January 1974, cited in Ahsan and Chakma, 'Problems of National Integration', p. 968.
69. For example, according to an Anti-Slavery report (submitted to a UN human rights subcommission working group on indigenous peoples) about 300 unarmed tribal men, women and children were massacred by Bangladeshi troops and armed Bengali immigrants at the village of Kaokhali Bazar on 25 March 1980. Anti-Slavery Society, *The Chittagong Hill Tracts: Militarization, Oppression and the Hill Tribes*, Indigenous Peoples and Development Series, Report No. 2, London, Anti-Slavery Society, 1984, p. 55.
70. For example, on 31 May 1984, members of the *Shanti Bahini* killed 175 settlers, including 33 women. *Asian Recorder*, 29 July–4 August 1984, p. 17861. See also *Far Eastern Economic Review*, 'Intractable hills: autonomy plan fails to appease the rebels', 5 April 1990, p. 23. According to an Amnesty International report, the Bangladesh government was responsible for many human rights abuses in the CHT including deliberate and unlawful political killings. The Bangladesh government categorically rejected these accusations. Amnesty International, *Bangladesh: Unlawful Killings and Torture in the Chittagong Hill Tracts*, London, 1986, pp. 10–11.
71. *Ibid.*, p. 11.
72. *The Bangladesh Observer* (Dhaka), 23 March 1988.
73. *Asian Recorder*, 29 July–4 August 1984, p. 17862.
74. *Ibid.*
75. Ali, *The Fearful State*, p.193. The figure for surrendered guerrillas varies. According to the *New York Times*, only 2000 had surrendered by October 1986. *New York Times*, October 23, 1986.
76. See *Keesing's Contemporary Archives*, vol. XXXII, July 1986, p. 34483 and vol. XXXIII, December 1987, p. 35574.
77. By June 1986, approximately 20 000 troops and armed police were placed on alert throughout southeast Bangladesh. According to the Madras paper, *The Hindu*, the Bangladeshi soldiers operating in the CHT were also being trained in counterinsurgency methods by the British Special Air Service (SAS). *Keesing's Contemporary Archives*, vol. XXXII, July 1986, p. 34483.

78. *Keesing's Contemporary Archives*, vol. XXXIII December 1987, p. 35574. India claimed that aproximately 44 000 Chakma refugees were sheltering in five camps in Tripura, while Bangladesh put the figure at much less – about 30 000. See also *The Bangladesh Observer* (Dhaka), 18 April 1988. According to a report by Amnesty International, the refugee crisis was sparked by the Bangladesh army carrying out 'thousands of arbitrary arrests' and killing and torturing 'innocent tribespeople at will.' *New York Times*, October 23, 1986.

79. See Chapter 4.

80. *Far Eastern Economic Review*, 'Intractable hills: autonomy plan fails to appease the rebels', 5 April 1990, p. 22.

81. *Ibid.*

82. *Ibid.*, p. 24.

83. For example in May 1988, BNP leader, Begum Khaleda Zia demanded the 'ousting of the present autocratic government' for, amongst other things, its 'failure to ensure security' of the people in the Chittagong Hill Tracts. *Bangladesh Observer* (Dhaka), 5 May 1988.

84. The Bangladesh media habitually described the CHT violence in highly emotive terms, without exception placing blame on the *Shanti Bahini*. The following are a couple of examples of media descriptions: 'Their [the *Shanti Bahini's*] heinous design is manifested in the orgy of repeated violence in the Chittagong Hill Tracts. The latest brutal attack…resulting in the death of eleven persons was part of that heinous design': *The Bangladesh Observer* (Dhaka), 8 June 1987; and, 'The villagers found no words to narrate the cold blooded holocaust perpetrated by the Shanti Bahini', *The Bangladesh Observer* (Dhaka), 3 May 1988.

85. *Far Eastern Economic Review*, 'Intractable hills: autonomy plan fails to appease the rebels', 5 April 1990, p. 24.

86. This appears to be a distortion of events. The Chakma refugees had fled into India to escape the large-scale reprisal attacks by Bangladesh forces and armed Bengali settlers which occurred in response to a series of *Shanti Bahini* killings in the region. See *Far Eastern Economic Review*, 'Intractable hills: autonomy plan fails to appease the rebels', 5 April 1990, p. 22.

87. *The Bangladesh Observer* (Dhaka), 6 May 1988.

88. *Ibid.* See also *Far Eastern Economic Review*, 'Playing the India Hand', 26 May 1988.

89. *The Bangladesh Observer* (Dhaka), 6 May 1988.

90. *New York Times*, October 23, 1986.

91. In June 1989, following further *Shanti Bahini* attacks, the *New York Times* put the refugee figure at 51 000, of which 9000 were estimated to have fled to India in the preceding fortnight. *New York Times*, June 11, 1989.

92. *The Bangladesh Observer* (Dhaka), 14 June 1989

93. *Ibid.*

94. *New York Times*, June 11, 1989. According to the *New York Times* article, *Shanti Bahini* weapons were also obtained from raids on Bangladeshi military units and by picking up large caches of Chinese semi-automatic weapons during the 1971 war.

95. *Far Eastern Economic Review*, 'Intractable hills: autonomy plan fails to appease the rebels', 5 April 1990, pp. 23–4.

96. *Far Eastern Economic Review*, 'In the Tribal Tangle', 20 August 1987, p. 21.

97. *The Bangladesh Observer* (Dhaka), 9 January 1987.

98. See *Far Eastern Economic Review*, 'In the Tribal Tangle', 20 August 1987, pp. 21–2 and *Far Eastern Economic Review*, 'Talking with the Tribals', 1 September 1988, pp. 32–3.

99. *Far Eastern Economic Review*, 'In the Tribal Tangle', 20 August 1987, p. 22. See also 'Dhaka not training TNV guerillas', *The Bangladesh Observer* (Dhaka), 30 January 1988.
100. Between 1976 and 1986, 2000–3000 were estimated to have been killed, while a further 3000 were estimated to have died owing to poor health care in the Tripura refugee camps between 1986 and 1989. See *New York Times*, October 23, 1986 and *The Bangladesh Observer* (Dhaka), 22 June 1989. Violence, including massacres, have continually occurred in the CHT to the present day. For a recent outbreak and attempts at mediation, see *Dhaka Bangladesh* (Internet Edition of Daily News), 25 September 1996, 29 January 1997, and 4 February 1997 <http://www.dhaka-bangladesh.com/ index.html>.
101. *Far Eastern Economic Review*, 'An ill wind in the East', 19 December 1985, p. 26.
102. *Far Eastern Economic Review*, 'Intractable hills: autonomy plan fails to appease the rebels', 5 April 1990, p. 24.
103. *Ibid.*, p. 23.
104. The number of *Shanti Bahini* had dropped to about 500 by 1990. *Ibid.*
105. *Far Eastern Economic Review*, 'Talking with the Tribals', 1 September 1988, p. 32.
106. *The Bangladesh Observer* (Dhaka), 19 February 1990.
107. *Ibid.*
108. *Ibid.*
109. *The Asian Recorder*, 28 May–3 June 1979, p. 14903, and *New York Times*, April 19, 1979.
110. *The Asian Recorder*, 28 May–3 June 1979, p. 14903.
111. For example: Khanal, 'Impact of Domestic Conflicts', p. 173.
112. T.H. Eriksen, 'Ethnicity Versus Nationalism', *Journal of Peace Research*, vol. 28, no. 3, 1991, p. 277.
113. *Ibid.*
114. According to the 1991 Census, approximately 15 per cent of Bangladesh's population was non-Muslim. *Statesman's Year-book 1993–1994*, London, 1993, p. 190.
115. For examples, see *Times of India*, 17 July 1987; Khanal, 'Impact of Domestic Conflicts', p. 192 and Nancy Jetly, 'India and the Domestic Turmoil in South Asia', in U. Phadnis *et al.* (eds), *Domestic Conflicts*, pp. 72–3.
116. See Chapter 1.

7 1975–81: Catalysts and Covergences of Interest

1. For example, see: S.S. Islam, 'Bangladesh–Pakistan Relations: From Conflict to Cooperation', in E. Ahamed (ed.), *Foreign Policy of Bangladesh: A Small State's Imperative*, Dhaka, 1984, pp. 52–63; C. Baxter, *Bangladesh: A New Nation In An Old Setting*, Boulder, 1984, pp. 101–2; C.P. O'Donnell, *Bangladesh: Biography of a Muslim Nation*, Boulder, 1984, pp. 212, 218; S.N. Kaushik, 'Pakistan's Relations with Bangladesh: An Overview of the Perception of the Leaders of the Two Countries', in S.R. Chakravarty and V. Narain (eds), *Bangladesh, Volume Three: Global Politics*, New Delhi, 1988, pp. 155–69. The chapter by Kaushik contains the most detail, but it is written from a pro-Bangladesh standpoint.
2. S.N. Kaushik does discuss this period. See Kaushik, 'Pakistan's Relations', pp. 156–63.
3. *Ibid.*
4. Islam, 'Bangladesh–Pakistan Relations', pp. 52–3.

5. B. Buzan *et al.*, *South Asian Insecurity and the Great Powers*, New York, 1986, p. 9.
6. *Ibid.*
7. Ambassadors were exchanged between Bangladesh and Pakistan in January 1976. See *Pakistan Times* (Lahore), 3 January and 13 January 1976.
8. For a discussion of Bhutto's reasons for officially recognising Bangladesh, see L. Ziring, 'Pakistan and India: Politics, Personalities, and Foreign Policy', *Asian Survey*, vol. 18, no. 7, 1978, p. 711.
9. Concerning Pakistan's recognition of Bangladesh, Bhutto declared: 'I do not say I like this decision. I do not say I want this decision. I do not say I am very happy today'. See *The Times* (London), 23 February 1974.
10. See *Far Eastern Economic Review*, 29 August 1975, p. 13.
11. This was largely due to growing disillusionment with Mujib's policies and his pro-Indian position.
12. Bangladeshi officials declared: 'We are disappointed that a great opportunity has been missed in taking a giant step forward in reconciliation . . . We found a total lack of response to the problems that are basic'. *New York Times*, June 30, 1974.
13. *New York Times* (New York), February 2, 1976.
14. *Newsweek*, 'Death of the Bangabandhu', August 25, 1975, p. 12.
15. This comment was made by a Pakistani government official in Islamabad. See *New York Times* (New York), February 2, 1976.
16. *Ibid.*
17. *Pakistan Times* (Lahore), November 12, 1975.
18. *New York Times*, February 2, 1976.
19. For an interpretation of Zia ul-Haq's efforts to use religion in consolidating power see: O. Noman, *Pakistan: A Political and Economic History Since 1947*, 2nd edn, London, 1990, pp. 144–54.
20. Camilleri and Teichmann make the point that states 'domesticate religion and morality' in order to 'use them in the service of state values and policies'. J. Camilleri and M. Teichmann, *Security and Survival: The New Era in International Relations*, South Yarra, 1973, p. 15. In the case of Pakistan and Bangladesh, individual leaders, rather than 'the state', have used this technique to secure power.
21. Tushar K. Barua, 'Military Regime in Pakistan and Bangladesh: A Contrast in Political Processes' in M.M. Khan and J.P. Thorp (eds), *Bangladesh: Society, Politics and Bureaucracy*, Dhaka, 1984, p. 75.
22. *Ibid.*
23. Further evidence for this will be provided in the chapter (p. 000).
24. T. Maniruzzaman, *The Security of Small States in the Third World*, Canberra, ANU., 1982, p. 15. E. Ahamed also writes that the most important objective of foreign policy is the maintenance of the state's 'sovereignty, political independence and territorial integrity.' Ahamed (ed.), *Foreign Policy*, p. 4.
25. K.J. Holsti, *International Politics: A Framework for Analysis*, 2nd edn, Englewood Cliffs, New Jersey, 1972, p. 371.
26. *Ibid.*
27. C. Hill, 'Theories of Foreign Policy Making for the Developing Countries', in C. Clapham (ed.), *Foreign Policy Making in Developing States*, Westmead, 1977, p. 7. Robert Good put forward the idea that foreign policy has often served to keep an 'in-group' in power. *Ibid.*
28. *Ibid.*
29. Holsti, *International Politics*, p. 379.

30. *Ibid.*
31. *Ibid.*, p. 380.
32. Hill, 'Theories', p. 10.
33. C. Clapham, 'Conclusion: Comparative Foreign Policy and Developing States', in Clapham (ed.), *Foreign Policy Making*, p. 169.
34. *Pakistan Times* (Lahore), 1 May 1976.
35. *Ibid.* A memorandum of 'understanding banking arrangements' was signed the following day, on 1 May 1976.
36. *Ibid.*, 3 May 1976.
37. Islam, 'Bangladesh–Pakistan Relations', p. 57.
38. *Pakistan Times* (Lahore), 16 May 1976.
39. Ziring, 'Pakistan and India', p. 726.
40. In May 1976, for example, Bhutto emphasised the primacy of Islam and its supremacy over political and economic ideology, declaring that 'while our religion, detached from alien accretions and the workings of obscurantism, sanctions, absorbs and encompasses our economic ideology and political philosophy, a political system and economic methodology cannot even pretend to embrace the full range and scope of a religion like Islam. *Pakistan Times* (Lahore), 15 May 1976.
41. *Bangladesh Observer*, 31 August 1977.
42. *Ibid.*, 23 December 1977.
43. *Asian Recorder*, 8–14 January 1978, p. 14109.
44. A Joint Economic Commission between Pakistan and Bangladesh was established in July 1979. *Ibid.*, 3–9 September 1979, pp. 15065–6.
45. *Bangladesh Observer*, 12 July 1980.
46. *Pakistan Times* (Lahore), 3 August 1978.
47. Kaushik, 'Pakistan's Relations', p. 164.
48. O'Donnell, *Bangladesh*, p. 218.
49. For details of the amounts requested, totalling approximately Tk. 257 crore, see Islam, 'Bangladesh–Pakistan Relations', pp. 57–9.
50. D.A. Wright, *Bangladesh: Origins and Indian Ocean Relations (1971–1975)*, New Delhi, 1988, pp. 186–7, 193–4.
51. O'Donnell, *Bangladesh*, p. 218. Ziaur Rahman had commented that the repatriation of 'non-locals' would start 'very soon'. *Bangladesh Observer*, 24 December 1977.
52. *Bangladesh Observer*, 23 December 1978.
53. *Ibid.*, 26 October 1980.
54. *Ibid.*, 27 October 1980.
55. *Ibid.*
56. *The Bangladesh Times*, 11 August 1983, cited in Islam, 'Bangladesh–Pakistan Relatons', p. 59.
57. *Bangladesh Observer*, 27 October 1980.
58. L. Ziring *et al.* (eds), *Pakistan: The Long View*, Durham, 1977, p. 6.
59. S. Tahir-Kheli, 'The Foreign Policy of 'New' Pakistan', *Orbis*, vol. 20, no. 3, Fall 1976, p. 734.
60. *Asian Recorder*, 4–10 March 1972, p. 10645.
61. *Ibid.*, p. 10648.
62. Tahir-Kheli, 'The Foreign Policy of 'New' Pakistan', p. 735.
63. As well as consolidating Pakistan's links with China, Bhutto also reaffirmed Pakistan's ties with the Islamic states which had supported Pakistan during the

war, by offering his thanks in person in his 'journey among brothers' in 1972. See Tahir-Kheli, 'The Foreign Policy of 'New' Pakistan', p. 734.

64. According to Bhutto, this was what the Simla Agreement offered. See Tahir-Kheli, 'The Foreign Policy of 'New' Pakistan', p. 740.

65. *Pakistan Times* (Lahore), 20 December 1975.

66. Tahir-Kheli, 'The Foreign Policy of 'New' Pakistan', p. 753.

67. As referred to in Chapter 5, Article 9 of the Friendship Treaty, signed between Bangladesh and India in March 1972, implied that an anti-Indian regime in Bangladesh could be removed legitimately by the Indian government. For details of the treaty, see *Asian Recorder*, 15–21 April 1972, p. 10720.

68. *Pakistan Times* (Lahore), 25 November 1975.

69. *Ibid.*, 12 November 1975.

70. *Bangladesh Observer*, 21 July 1976.

71. Such as Pakistan's official recognition of Bangladesh and the release of POWs.

72. S.M.M. Razvi, 'Conflict and Cooperation in South Asia', *The Round Table*, no. 299, 1986, p. 269.

73. S.P. Cohen, 'India, South Asia and the Superpowers: War and Society' in P. Wallace (ed.), *Region and Nation in India*, New Delhi, 1985, p. 234.

8 1982–90: A Maturing of Relations?

1. Relations between Pakistan and Bangladesh have received little scholarly attention in the literature. For a brief, biased and descriptive account of relations during Ershad's regime, see S.N. Kaushik, 'Pakistan's Relations with Bangladesh: An Overview of the Perception of the Leaders of the Two Countries', in S.R. Chakravarty and V. Narain (eds), *Bangladesh, Volume Three: Global Politics*, New Delhi, 1988, pp. 165–8. See also S.S. Islam, 'Bangladesh–Pakistan Relations: From Conflict to Cooperation', in E. Ahamed (ed.) *Foreign Policy of Bangladesh: A Small State's Imperative*, Dhaka, 1984, pp. 52–63.

2. Mainly in India, Pakistan and Sri Lanka.

3. R.B. Rais, 'Pakistan in the Regional and Global Power Structure', *Asian Survey*, vol. 31, no. 4, 1991, p. 383.

4. T.P. Thornton, 'Between the Stools? U.S. Policy Towards Pakistan During the Carter Administration', *Asian Survey*, vol. 22, no. 10, October 1982, p. 971.

5. W.H. Wriggins, 'Pakistan's Search for a Foreign Policy After the Invasion of Afghanistan', *Pacific Affairs*, vol. 57, no. 2, 1984, p. 298.

6. *Ibid.*, p. 285.

7. For a relevant article, see Wriggins, 'Pakistan's Search', pp. 284–303.

8. The US assistance included F-16 aircraft, Cobra gunship helicopters, M48A5 tanks and Harpoon missiles. Pakistan became the fourth largest recipient of US military aid after Israel, Egypt and Turkey. S. Yasmeen, 'India and Pakistan: Why the Latest Exercise in Brinkmanship?', *Australian Journal of Politics and History*, vol. 34, no. 1, 1988/89, p. 69.

9. This emphasis was partly in response to the 1979 Iranian Islamic revolution and the ousting of the Shah of Iran.

10. *Dawn*, 25 November 1981.

11. *Ibid.*

12. The attachés were found trying, for unexplained reasons, to set fire to 600 rolls of movie film. *New York Times* (New York), April 11, 1982.

13. *Ibid.*

14. *Ibid.*

15. *Ibid.*
16. *Daily News*, 21 August 1982, cited in Kaushik, 'Pakistan's Relations', p. 165.
17. See Chapter 7.
18. *The Bangladesh Observer* (Dhaka), 5 October 1982.
19. *Ibid.*, and *New York Times* (New York), May 18, 1986.
20. *The Bangladesh Observer* (Dhaka), 25 October 1982.
21. *Ibid.*
22. *Ibid.*, 12–13 August 1983.
23. *Ibid.*, 7, 8, and 11 December 1983.
24. *Ibid.*, 12 August 1983.
25. *Ibid.*
26. *Ibid.*
27. *Ibid.*
28. *Ibid.*
29. For background detail, see Chapter 7.
30. *The Bangladesh Observer* (Dhaka), 13 August 1983.
31. *Ibid.*
32. *Ibid.*, 7 December 1983. *Ummah* means the 'community of believers'.
33. *Ibid.*, 11 December 1983.
34. The organisation, called the *Rabita El Alam Al Islami* (The World Muslim League) was based in Mecca and was reported to have received pledges from various Arab oil-producing nations to pay for the rehabilitation project. *New York Times* (New York), July 11, 1988. See also *The Bangladesh Observer* (Dhaka), 11 July 1988.
35. *The Bangladesh Observer* (Dhaka), 11 July 1988.
36. *Ibid.*, 6 June 1985. Approximately 11 000 people died in the cyclone. *Keesing's Contemporary Archives*, vol. XXXI, December 1985, p. 34051.
37. Immediate aid was offered by countries such as Saudi Arabia, Japan, the United States and the United Kingdom. *Keesing's Contemporary Archives*, vol. XXXI, December 1985, p. 34051.
38. *The Bangladesh Observer* (Dhaka), 6 June 1985.
39. See Chapter 4.
40. *Muhajireen* descendants use the same term to describe themselves. For an historical overview of this linguistic, cultural group, see I.H. Malik, 'Ethno–Nationalism in Pakistan: A Commentary on Muhajir Qaumi Mahaz (MQM) in Sindh', *South Asia, Journal of South Asian Studies*, vol. XVIII, no 2, 1995, pp. 50–2.
41. Malik, 'Ethno–Nationalism', p. 59.
42. *Ibid.*, pp. 53–4.
43. Yasmeen, 'India and Pakistan', p. 69. Communal riots occurring in Karachi from November 1986 to January 1987, primarily between the *Muhajireen* and the Pushtuns, resulted in over 200 dead and 500 wounded.
44. *Ibid.* Further violence erupted in Karachi in September 1988, with more than 400 being killed during two days of rioting. Malik, 'Ethno–Nationalism', p. 61.
45. Migrant People's Movement.
46. The Biharis and the *Muhajireen* shared a common past as both groups originated as refugees who had fled India in 1947, the former moving to East Pakistan and the latter moving to the west wing. No doubt, the MQM wished to expand its support base, but the full explanation for why the MQM decided to take up the Bihari cause after Zia ul-Haq's death is unclear. Malik, 'Ethno–Nationalism', p. 63.

47. J. Bray, 'Pakistan in 1989: Benazir's Balancing Act', *The Round Table*, no. 310, 1989, pp. 194–5.
48. S.V.R. Nasr, 'Democracy and the Crisis of Governability in Pakistan', *Asian Survey*, vol. 32, no. 6, 1992, p. 523.
49. *Ibid.*, p. 525.
50. *Ibid.*, p. 529.
51. *Ibid.*
52. *The Bangladesh Observer* (Dhaka), 4 October 1989.
53. *Ibid.*, 2 October 1989.
54. *Far Eastern Economic Review*, 'Left in limbo: Bhutto appears to backtrack on the Biharis issue', 19 October 1989, p. 23.
55. *The Times* (London), 25 and 27 October 1989.
56. *Ibid.*
57. J. Bray, 'Nawaz Sharif's New Order in Pakistan', *The Round Table*, no. 318, 1991, p. 181.
58. *The Bangladesh Observer* (Dhaka), 8 June 1988.
59. Nasr, 'Democracy', p. 529.
60. P.S. Bhogal, 'Pakistan's India Policy: Shift from Zia to Benazir', *India Quarterly*, vol. XLV, no. 1, January–March 1989, p. 43.
61. Nasr, 'Democracy', p. 529.
62. *Ibid.*, p. 529–30.
63. *Ibid.*, p. 530.
64. Bray, 'Pakistan in 1989', pp. 198–9.
65. Nasr, 'Democracy', p. 523.
66. L. Ziring, 'Pakistan and India: Politics, Personalities, and Foreign Policy', *Asian Survey*, vol. 18, no. 7, 1978, p. 719.
67. Plans for the SAARC foreign minister's meeting, scheduled to be held in Islamabad later in the month, were disrupted by a dispute between Sri Lanka and India. Sri Lanka was insisting that India withdraw the Indian Peace-Keeping Force from its soil or it would refuse to attend the meeting and, furthermore, would not host the following year's SAARC summit. Bangladesh's foreign minister, Anisul Islam Mahmud, made an impromptu visit to India and Sri Lanka in an attempt to mediate in the dispute and to persuade Sri Lanka to cease agitation and attend the meeting. As host for the foreign minister's meeting, Pakistan considered that it had the responsibility to mediate and ought to have been consulted properly by Bangladesh. For details, see *Far Eastern Economic Review*, 'Strained relations: Bangladesh initiative over SAARC upsets Pakistan', 3 August 1989, p. 23.
68. *Ibid.*
69. *Ibid.*
70. In August 1992, for example, Bangladesh's new Prime Minister, Khaleda Zia, revitalised the Bihari issue, along with other outstanding matters such as asset-sharing, to strengthen her domestic popularity. The Pakistan government, then under Nawaz Sharif, was receptive to reopening the Bihari issue because he had the support of the MQM and hoped, in turn, to antagonise and put pressure on his opponent, Benazir, and her Sindhi-based PPP. For details see *Far Eastern Economic Review*, 'The begum's gambit: Khaleda's plan to return Pakistani refugees', 6 August 1992, p. 23.
71. For an analysis of Pakistan's quest for nuclear capability, see Gowher Rizvi, 'The Rivalry Between India and Pakistan' in B. Buzan *et al.*, *South Asian Insecurity and the Great Powers*, New York, 1986, pp. 120–1.

Conclusion

1. K.P. Khanal, 'Impact of Domestic Conflicts on Regional Cooperation in South Asia', in B. Sen Gupta, (ed.), *Regional Cooperation and Development in South Asia*, vol. 2, New Delhi, 1986, p. 192 and Nancy Jetly, 'India and the Domestic Turmoil in South Asia', in U. Phadnis *et al.*, (eds), *Domestic Conflicts in South Asia, vol. 1: Political Dimensions*, New Delhi, 1986, pp. 72–3.
2. M.E. Carranza, 'Rethinking Indo–Pakistani Nuclear Relations', *Asian Survey*, vol. 36, no. 6, June 1996, pp. 562–3.
3. Despite the post-Ershad upheavals in Bangladesh, a democratic structure is becoming established in Bangladesh and has survived the challenges to date.
4. J.M. Brown, *Modern India: The Origins of an Asian Democracy*, 2nd edn, Oxford, 1994, pp. 396–7.
5. *Ibid.*, p. 397.
6. S.P. Cohen, 'India, South Asia, and the Superpowers: War and Society', in P. Wallace (ed.), *Region and Nation in India*, New Delhi, 1985, p. 241.
7. Carranza, 'Rethinking Indo–Pakistan Nuclear Relations', p. 565.
8. In March 1997 India acquired 40 long-range, multi-role Sukhoi-30MK (Su-30) jet aircraft from Russia for approximately US$1.8 billion. These aircraft were purchased to 'counter the potential threat posed by F-16 and Mirage 2000 fighters in service with Pakistan'. The Su-30s were also more sophisticated than the batch of 70 Su-27s purchased in 1996 by China, allowing India to play 'an enhanced role across South, South-East and East Asian countries, principally to counter Chinese ambitions'. *The Australian* (Canberra), 17 March 1997.
9. K.C. Dash, 'The Political Economy of Regional Cooperation in South Asia', *Pacific Affairs*, vol. 69, no. 2, 1996, p. 207.
10. The treaty is, nevertheless, controversial, with Opposition parties in both India and Bangladesh raising strong criticisms. Ishtiaq Hossain, *Bangladesh–India Ganges Water Sharing Treaty: Problems and Prospects*, paper delivered at the 'Bangladesh: Democracy and Development' Conference organised by the National Centre for South Asian Studies, Melbourne, held at the Royal Melbourne Institute of Technology (22–23 March 1997).

Bibliography

NEWSPAPERS

The Australian (Canberra)
Amrita Bazar Patrika (Calcutta)
The Bangladesh Observer (Dhaka)
The Daily Star (Dhaka, Weekly Internet Edition)
Dawn (Karachi)
Dhaka Bangladesh (Internet Edition of Daily News) –
   <http://www.dhaka-bangladesh.com/index.html>
The Guardian Weekly (London)
Morning News (Dhaka)
New York Times (New York)
Overseas Hindustan Times (New Delhi)
Pakistan Times (Lahore)
The Statesman (Delhi)
The Times (London)
Times of India (Bombay)
Times of India (New Delhi)

OFFICIAL DOCUMENTS

Government of Bangladesh

Rahman, W. (comp.)   *Bangladesh and the United Nations*, Dhaka, Ministry of Information, 1986.

The Constitution of the People's Republic of Bangladesh: As Modified up to 28th February, 1979, [Dacca], [n.d.].

Statistical Pocketbook of Bangladesh 1994, Dhaka, Bangladesh Bureau of Statistics, Statistics Division, Ministry of Planning, Government of the People's Republic of Bangladesh, [1994].

The 1991 Statistical Yearbook of Bangladesh, Dhaka, Bangladesh Bureau of Statistics, Statistics Division, Ministry of Planning, Government of the People's Republic of Bangladesh, November 1991.

The 1979 Statistical Yearbook of Bangladesh, Dacca, Bangladesh Bureau of Statistics, Statistics Division, Ministry of Planning, Government of the People's Republic of Bangladesh.

Government of India

Ministry of Information and Broadcasting (comp.) *India. A Reference Annual: 1982*, New Delhi, Publications Division, Ministry of Information and Broadcasting, 1982.

PARLIAMENTARY DEBATES

India: *Lok Sabha* debates, 1975–83.

OTHER CONTEMPORARY SOURCES

Asian Recorder, 1958–92.
Bhutto, B.   *Foreign Policy in Perspective*, Lahore, Classic, 1978.
Bhutto, Z.A.   *The Great Tragedy*, 2nd edn, Karachi, Pakistan People's Party, 1971.
Bhutto, Z.A.   *The Third World: New Directions*, London, Quartet Books, 1977.
Gangal, S.C. (ed.)   *India Foreign Policy: A Documentary Study of India's Foreign Policy Since the Installation of the Janata Government on 24 March 1977*, New Delhi, Young Asia Publications, 1980.
Jain, R.K. (ed.)   *Soviet South Asian Relations 1947–1978*, vol. 2: *Pakistan, Bangladesh, Nepal, Sri Lanka*, Atlantic Highlands, Humanities Press, 1979.
Keesing's Contemporary Archives, 1947–86.
Keesing's Record of World Events, 1987–91.
Khan, M.A.   *Friends Not Masters: A Political Autobiography*, London, Oxford University Press, 1967.
Rao, P.V.N.   *Reflections on Non-Alignment*, New Delhi, Ministry of External Affairs, Government of India, [1992].
Singh, S.K. (ed.)   *Bangladesh Documents*, 2 vols, New Delhi, Ministry of Information and Broadcasting, n.d.
United Nations   Economic and Social Commission for Asia and the Pacific, *Statistical Yearbook for Asia and the Pacific: 1982*, Bangkok, ESCAP, n.d.

BOOKS

Abbas, B.M.   *The Ganges Waters Dispute*, New Delhi, Vikas, 1982.
Ahamed, E.   *Military Rule and the Myth of Democracy*, Dhaka, University Press, 1988.
Ahamed, E. (ed.)   *Foreign Policy of Bangladesh: A Small State's Imperative*, Dhaka, University Press, 1984.
Ahmed, A.S.   *Discovering Islam: Making Sense of Muslim History and Society*, London, Routledge, 1988.
Akhtar, J.D.   *The Saga of Bangladesh*, Delhi, Oriental Publishers, 1971.
Ali, S.M.   *The Fearful State: Power, People and Internal War in South Asia*, London, Zed Books, 1993.
Ali, S.M.   *Civil–Military Relations in the Soft State: The Case of Bangladesh*, European Network of Bangladesh Studies/EC Research Paper, no. 1/6-94, Bath, ENBS, School of Social Sciences, University of Bath [1994].
Ali, T.   *Pakistan: Military Rule or People's Power*, New York, W. Morrow, 1970.
Amnesty International.   *Bangladesh: Unlawful Killings and Torture in the Chittagong Hill Tracts*, London, Amnesty International Publications, 1986.
Anderson, B.   *Imagined Communities*, 2nd edn, London, Verso, 1991.
Anti-Slavery Society.   *The Chittagong Hill Tracts: Militarization, Oppression and the Hill Tribes*, Indigenous Peoples and Development Series, Report no. 2, London, Anti-Slavery Society, 1984.
Appadorai, A. and Rajan, M.S.   *India's Foreign Policy and Relations*, New Delhi, South Asian Publishers, 1985.
Asghar Khan, M.A. (ed.)   *Islam, Politics and the State: The Pakistan Experience*, London, Zed Books, 1985.
Research Institute for Peace and Security, Tokyo (comp.)   *Asian Security 1995–96*, London, Brassey's, 1995.

Ayoob, M. (ed.) *Conflict and Intervention in the Third World*, Canberra, ANU Press, 1980.

Bajpai, U.S. (ed.) *India and Its Neighbourhood*, New Delhi, Lancer International, 1986.

Bandyopadhyay, S. *et al.* (eds) *Bengal: Communities, Development and States*, New Delhi, Manohar, 1994.

Banerjee, D.N. *East Pakistan: A Case-Study in Muslim Politics*, Delhi, Vikas, 1969.

Banerjee, S. *India's Simmering Revolution: The Naxalite Uprising*, London, Zed Press, 1982.

Barnds, W.J. *India, Pakistan and the Great Powers*, London, Pall Mall Press, 1972.

Bastiampillai, B. (ed.) *India and Her South Asian Neighbours*, Colombo, Bandaranaike Centre for International Studies, 1992.

Baxter, C. *Bangladesh: A New Nation In An Old Setting*, Boulder, Westview, 1984.

Begum, K. *Tension over the Farakka Barrage: A Techno–Political Tangle in South Asia*, Stuttgart, Steiner Verlag Wiesbaden, 1988.

Bhargava, G.S. *Pakistan in Crisis*, 2nd edn, Delhi, Vikas Publishing House, 1971.

Bhatnagar, Y. *Mujib: The Architect of Bangladesh: A Political Biography*, Delhi, Indian School Supply Depot, 1971.

Bhattacharjea, Ajit (ed.) *Dateline Bangladesh*, Bombay, Jaico Publishing House, 1971.

Bhattacharjee, G.P. *Renaissance and Freedom Movement in Bangladesh*, Calcutta, Minerva Associates, 1973.

Bindra, S.S. *Indo–Bangladesh Relations*, New Delhi, Deep and Deep, 1982.

Biswas, J. *US–Bangladesh Relations: A Study of the Political and Economic Development During 1971–81*, Calcutta, Minerva Associations, 1984.

Blinkenberg, L. *India–Pakistan: The History of Unsolved Conflicts*, Munksgaard, Dansk Udenrigspolitisk Instituts, 1972.

Boquerat, G. *et al.* *SAARC Economic and Political Atlas*, Pondy Papers in Social Sciences, no. 20, Pondicherry, French Institute, 1996.

Bowman, L.W. and Clark, I. (eds) *The Indian Ocean in Global Politics*, Boulder, Westview, 1981.

Brass, P.R. *Language, Religion and Politics in North India*, London, Cambridge University Press, 1974.

Brass, P.R. 'The Politics of India since Independence', in *The New Cambridge History of India*, vol. 4, no. 1, Cambridge, Cambridge University Press, 1990.

Brass, P.R. *Ethnicity and Nationalism: Theory and Comparison*, New Delhi, Sage, 1991.

Brecher, M. *Nehru: A Political Biography*, London, Oxford University Press, 1959.

Broomfield, J.H. *Elite Conflict in a Plural Society*, Berkeley, University of California Press, 1968.

Broomfield, J.H. *Mostly About Bengal: Essays in Modern South Asian History*, New Delhi, Manohar, 1982.

Brown, J.M. *Modern India: The Origins of an Asian Democracy*, 2nd edn, Oxford, Oxford University Press, 1994.

Burke, S.M. *Pakistan's Foreign Policy: An Historical Analysis*, London, Oxford University Press, 1973.

Burke, S.M. *Mainsprings of Indian and Pakistani Foreign Policies*, Minneapolis, University of Minnesota Press, 1974.

Burki, S.H. *Pakistan: A Nation in the Making*, Boulder, Westview, 1986.

Buzan, B. *et al.* *South Asian Insecurity and the Great Powers*, New York, St Martin's Press, 1986.

Callard, K. *Pakistan: A Political Study*, London, Allen and Unwin, 1968.

Camilleri, J. *Chinese Foreign Policy: The Maoist Era and its Aftermath*, Oxford, Martin Robertson, 1980.

Camilleri, J. and Teichmann, M. *Security and Survival: The New Era in International Relations*, South Yarra, Heineman Educational, 1973.

Cassen, R. (ed.) *Soviet Interests in the Third World*, London, Sage, 1985.

Chakrabarti, R. *The Political Economy of India's Foreign Policy*, Calcutta, K.P. Bagchi, 1982.

Chakrabarti, S.K. *The Evolution of Politics in Bangladesh, 1947–1978*, New Delhi, Associated, 1978.

Chakrabarty, D. *Rethinking Working-Class History: Bengal 1890–1940*, Princeton, Princeton University Press, 1989.

Chakravarti, P.C. *The Evolution of India's Northern Borders*, London, Asia Publishing House, 1971.

Chakravarty, S.R. *Bangladesh: The Nineteen Seventy-Nine Elections*, New Delhi, South Asian Publishers, 1988.

Chakravarty, S.R. and Narain, V. (eds) *Bangladesh*, vols. 1–3, New Delhi, South Asian Publishers, 1988.

Chatterjee, R.K. *India's Land Borders: Problems and Challenges*, New Delhi, Sterling, 1978.

Chatterji, B.C. *Renaissance and Reaction in Nineteenth Century Bengal*, Calcutta, Minerva, 1977.

Chitty, N. *Framing South Asian Transformation: An Examination of Regional Views on South Asian Cooperation*, New Delhi, South Asian Publishers, 1994.

Cheema, P.I. *Conflict and Cooperation in the Indian Ocean: Pakistan's Interests and Choices*, Canberra, Strategic and Defence Studies Centre, ANU, 1980.

Chopra, M.K. *India and the Indian Ocean: New Horizons*, New Delhi, Sterling, 1982.

Chopra, P. (ed.) *Challenge of Bangladesh: A Special Debate*, Bombay, Popular Prakashan, 1971.

Chopra, P. (ed.) *Contemporary Pakistan: New Aims and Images*, New Delhi, Vikas, 1983.

Choudhury, G.W. *Constitutional Development in Pakistan*, 2nd edn, Vancouver, University of British Columbia, 1969.

Choudhury, G.W. *The Last Days of United Pakistan*, Nedlands, University of Western Australia Press, 1974.

Choudhury, G.W. *India, Pakistan, Bangladesh and the Major Powers: Politics of a Divided Subcontinent*, New York, Free Press, 1975.

Clapham, C. (ed.) *Foreign Policy Making in Developing States*, Westmead, Saxon House, 1977.

Crow, B. *et al.* *Sharing the Ganges: The Politics and Technology of River Development*, New Delhi, Sage Publications, 1995.

Das, M. *From Nation to Nation: A Case Study of Bengali Independence*, Calcutta, Minerva Associates, 1981.

Das Gupta, J. *Language, Conflict and National Development. Group Politics and National Language Policy in India*, Los Angeles, University of California Press, 1970.

Dasgupta, A. and Lechner, G. *Development Aid Today*, New Delhi, Mosaic Books, 1995.

De, A. *Roots of Separatism in Nineteenth Century Bengal*, Calcutta, Ratna Prakashan, 1974.

Embree, A.T. *Imagining India*, Delhi, Oxford University Press, 1989.

Esposito, J.L. (ed.) *Islam in Asia: Religion, Politics and Society*, New York, Oxford University Press, 1987.

The Europa World Year Book 1993, Volume 1, London, Europa Publications, 1993.

The Europa World Year Book 1996, Volume 1, London, Europa Publications, 1996.

Faaland, J.   *Aid and Influence: The Case of Bangladesh*, New York, St Martin's Press, 1980.

Faaland, J. and Parkinson, J.R.   *Bangladesh: The Test Case For Development*, London, C. Hurst, 1976.

Feldman, H.   *From Crisis to Crisis: Pakistan 1962–69*, London, Oxford University Press, 1972.

Feldman, H.   *The End and the Beginning: Pakistan, 1969–1971*, London, Oxford University Press, 1975.

Franda, M.   *Bangladesh: The First Decade*, New Delhi, South Asian Publishers, 1982.

Frankel, J.   *International Politics: Conflict and Harmony*, London, Allen Lane, 1969.

Frankel, J.   *International Relations in a Changing World*, Oxford, Oxford University Press, 1979.

George, T. *et al.*   *Security in Southern Asia 2: India and the Great Powers*, Aldershot, Gower, 1984.

Ghosh, B.N.   *Political Economy of Neocolonialism in Third World Countries*, New Delhi, Sterling, 1985.

Ghosh, P.S.   *Cooperation and Conflict in South Asia*, New Delhi, Manohar, 1989.

Ghosh, S.   *The Role of India in the Emergence of Bangladesh*, Calcutta, Minerva Associates, 1983.

Gilmartin, D.   *Empire and Islam: Punjab and the Making of Pakistan*, Berkeley, University of California Press, 1988.

Gopal, S. (ed.)   *Selected Works of Jawaharlal Nehru*, Second Series, Volume 2, New Delhi, Jawaharlal Nehru Memorial Fund, 1984.

Gordon, L.A.   *Bengal and The Indian Nationalist Movement: A Study of Regionalism, Politics and Thought*, Cambridge, Cambridge University Press, 1969.

Gordon, S. *et al.*   *Security and Security Building in the Indian Ocean Region*, Canberra, Strategic and Defence Studies Centre, ANU, 1996.

Gulati, C.J.   *Bangladesh: Liberation to Fundamentalism (A Study of Volatile Indo–Bangladesh Relations)*, New Delhi, Commonwealth Publishers, 1988.

Hardgrave, R.L.   *India Under Pressure*, Boulder, Westview, 1984.

Hardy, P.   *The Muslims of British India*, London, Cambridge University Press, 1972.

Harrison, S.S.   *India: The Most Dangerous Decades*, Princeton, Princeton University Press, 1960.

Hasanuzzaman, A.M. (ed.)   *Bangladesh: Crisis of Political Development*, Dhaka, Jahangirnagar University, 1988.

Haynes, D.E.   *Rhetoric and Ritual in Colonial India: The Shaping of a Public Culture in Surat City, 1852–1928*, Berkeley, University of California Press, 1991.

Holbraad, C. (ed.)   *Superpowers and World Order*, Canberra, ANU Press, 1971.

Holsti, K.J.   *International Politics: A Framework for Analysis*, 2nd edn, Englewood Cliffs, New Jersey, Prentice-Hall, 1972.

Hossain, G.   *General Ziaur Rahman and the BNP: Political Transformation of a Military Regime*, Dhaka, University Press, 1988.

Huntington, S.P.   *Political Order in Changing Societies*, New Haven, Yale University Press, 1968.

Huque, A.S.   *Politics and Administration in Bangladesh: Problems of Participation*, Dhaka, University Press, 1988.

Indological Studies and Research in India: Progress and Prospects, Proceedings of a Seminar held at the Ramakrishna Mission Institute of Culture, Gol Park, Calcutta, 1991.

Islam, N.   *Development Planning in Bangladesh: A Study in Political Economy*, Dhaka University Press, 1977.

Islam, R. *A Tale of Millions: Bangladesh Liberation War – 1971*, 2nd edn, Dhaka, Chittaranjan Saha Muktadhara, 1986.

Jackson, R. *South Asian Crisis; India, Pakistan and Bangla Desh: A Political and Historical Analysis of the 1971 War*, New York, Praeger, 1975.

Jahan, R. *Bangladesh Politics: Problems and Issues*, Dhaka, University Press, 1980.

Jain, G. *Pakistan Military Elite*, Delhi, G. Jain, 1971.

Jain, R. *US–PAK Relations, 1947–1983*, New Delhi, Radiant Publishers, 1983.

Jalal, A. *The Sole Spokesman: Jinnah, The Muslim League, and the Demand for Pakistan*, Cambridge, Cambridge University Press, 1982.

Jannuzi, F.T. *India in Transition: Issues of Political Economy in a Plural Society*, Boulder, Westview, 1989.

Jervis, R. *Perception and Misperception in International Politics*, Princeton, Princeton University Press, 1976.

Johnson, B.L.C. *Bangladesh*, New York, Barnes & Noble, 1975.

Kapur, H. *India's Foreign Policy, 1947–92: Shadows and Substance*, New Delhi, Sage Publications, 1994.

Karim, A.K.N. *The Dynamics of Bangladesh Society*, Delhi, Vikas, 1980.

Kazancigil, A. (ed.) *The State in Global Perspective*, Aldershot, Gower, 1986.

Kegley C.W., Jr. *Controversies in International Relations Theory: Realism and the Neoliberal Challenge*, New York, St Martin's Press, 1995.

Khan, I. (ed.) *Fresh Perspectives on India and Pakistan*, Oxford, Bougainvillea Books, 1985.

Khan, M.A. *Generals in Politics: Pakistan 1958–1982*, New Delhi, Vikas, 1983.

Khan, M.A. *Islam, Politics and the State: The Pakistan Experience*, London, Zed Books, 1985.

Khan, M.M. and Husain, S.A. (eds) *Bangladesh Studies: Politics, Administration, Rural Development and Foreign Policy*, Dhaka, Centre for Adminstration Studies, Dhaka University, 1986.

Khan, M.M. and Thorp, J.P. (eds) *Bangladesh: Society, Politics and Bureaucracy*, Dhaka, Centre for Administrative Studies, 1984.

Khan, M.M. and Zafarullah, H.M. (eds) *Politics and Bureaucracy in a New Nation: Bangladesh*, Dacca, Centre for Administrative Studies, 1980.

Khan, Z.R. *Leadership in the Least Developed Nation: Bangladesh*, Syracuse University Press, 1983.

Khan, Z.R. *Martial Law to Martial Law: Leadership Crisis in Bangladesh*, Dhaka, University Press, 1984.

Khilnani, N.M. *Realities of Indian Foreign Policy*, New Delhi, ABC Publishers, 1984.

Kodikara, S.U. *Strategic Factors in Interstate Relations in South Asia*, Canberra, Strategic and Defence Studies Centre, ANU, 1979.

Kodikara, S.U. 'Role of Extra-Regional Powers and South Asian Security', in S.U. Kodikara (ed.), *South Asian Strategic Issues: Sri Lankan Perspectives*, New Delhi, Sage, 1990, pp. 34–54.

Kopf, D. *The Brahmo Samaj and the Shaping of the Modern Indian Mind*, Princeton, Princeton University Press, 1979.

Kukreja, V. *Civil–Military Relations in South Asia: Pakistan, Bangladesh and India*, New Delhi, Sage, 1991.

Kulkarni, V.B. *Pakistan: Its Origin and Relations With India*, New Delhi, Sterling, 1988.

Lal, S. *Bangla–Pak Polities*, New Delhi, Election Archives, 1985.

Lamb, A. *Kashmir: A Disputed Legacy, 1846–1990*, Hertingfordbury, Roxford Books, 1991.

Lifschultz, L. *Bangladesh: The Unfinished Revolution*, London, Zed Press, 1979.

Linklater, A. *Men and Citizens in the Theory of International Relations*, 2nd edn, London, Macmillan, 1990.

Low, D.A. (ed.) *The Political Inheritance of Pakistan*, London, Macmillan, 1991.

Majumdar, R.C. *History of Modern Bengal*, 2 vols. Calcutta, G. Bharadwaj, 1978–81.

Maniruzzaman, T. *Radical Politics and the Emergence of Bangladesh*, Dacca, Bangladesh Books International Ltd, 1975.

Maniruzzaman, T. *The Bangladesh Revolution and its Aftermath*, Dacca, Bangladesh Books International Ltd, 1980.

Maniruzzaman, T. *The Security of Small States in the Third World*, Canberra, Strategic and Defence Studies Centre, ANU, 1982a.

Maniruzzaman, T. *Group Interests and Political Changes: Studies of Pakistan and Bangladesh*, New Delhi, South Asian Publishers, 1982b.

Manor, J. (ed.) *Nehru to the Nineties: The Changing Office of Prime Minister in India*, London, Hurst & Co., 1994.

Mansingh, S. *India's Search For Power: Indira Gandhi's Foreign Policy 1966–1982*, New Delhi, Sage, 1984.

Mascarenhas, A. *The Rape of Bangladesh*, Delhi, Vikas, n.d.

Mascarenhas, A. *A Legacy of Blood*, London, Hodder & Stoughton, 1986.

Masselos, J. *Nationalism on the Indian Subcontinent: An Introductory History*, Melbourne, Nelson, 1972.

Masselos, J. (ed.) *India: Creating a Modern Nation*, New Delhi, Sterling, 1990.

McLellan, D.S. *The Theory and Practice of International Relations*, 4th edn, Englewood Cliffs, New Jersey, Prentice-Hall, 1974.

McMillen, D.H. (ed.) *Asian Perspectives on International Security*, London, Macmillan, 1984.

Mehrotra, S. 'The Political Economy of Indo–Soviet Relations', in R. Cassen (ed.), *Soviet Interests in the Third World*, London, Sage, 1985.

Miller, J.B.D. *The Politics of the Third World*, London, Oxford University Press, 1966.

Mishra, P.K. *South Asia in International Politics*, Delhi, UDH Publishers, 1984.

Misra, K.P. (ed.) *Janata's Foreign Policy*, New Delhi, Vikas, 1979.

Misra, K.P. (ed.) *Studies in Indian Foreign Policy*, New Delhi, Vikas, 1969.

Muni, S.D. *Pangs of Proximity: India and Sri Lanka's Ethnic Crisis*, New Delhi, Sage, 1993.

Muni, S.D. (ed.) *Understanding South Asia: Essays in the Memory of Late Professor (Mrs) Urmila Phadnis*, New Delhi, South Asian Publishers, 1994.

Muni, S.D. and Muni, A. *Regional Cooperation in South Asia*, New Delhi, National Publishing House, 1984.

Munir, M. *Pakistan From Jinnah to Zia: A Study in Ideological Convulsions*, New Delhi, Document Press [1980].

Nanda, B.R. (ed.) *Indian Foreign Policy: The Nehru Years*, New Delhi, Vikas, 1976.

Narain, V. *Foreign Policy of Bangladesh (1971–1981): The Context of National Liberation Movement*, Jaipur, Aalekh, 1987.

Nizami, T.A. *The Communist Party and India's Foreign Policy*, New Delhi, Assoc. Publishing House, 1971.

Noman, O. *Pakistan: A Political and Economic History Since 1947*, 2nd edn, London, Kegan Paul International, 1990.

Noorani, A.G. *India, the Superpowers and the Neighbours: Essays in Foreign Policy*, New Delhi, South Asian Publications, 1985.

Northedge, F.S. (ed.) *The Foreign Policies of the Powers*, rev. edn, London, Faber & Faber, 1974.

O'Donnell, C.P. *Bangladesh: Biography of a Muslim Nation*, Boulder, Westview, 1984.
Palmer, N.D. *The New Regionalism in Asia and the Pacific*, Lexington, Lexington Books, 1991.
Pantham, T. *Political Theories and Social Reconstruction: A Critical Survey of the Literature on India*, New Delhi, Sage Publications, 1995.
Parmanand, *Political Development in South Asia*, New Delhi, Sterling, 1988.
Penrose, E.F. *The Revolution in International Relations: A Study in the Changing Nature and Balance of Power*, London, Frank Cass, 1965.
Pettman, R. *International Politics: Balance of Power, Balance of Productivity, Balance of Ideologies*, Melbourne, Longman Cheshire, 1991.
Phadnis, U. *Ethnicity and Nation-Building in South Asia*, New Delhi, Sage, 1989.
Phadnis, U. (ed.) *Domestic Conflicts in South Asia, vol. 1: Political Dimensions*, New Delhi, South Asian Publishers, 1986.
Prasad, B. *India's Foreign Policy: Studies in Continuity and Change*, New Delhi, Vikas, 1979.
Puchkov, V.P. *Political Development of Bangladesh 1971–1985*, New Delhi, Patriot, 1989.
Rajan, M.S. *India's Foreign Relations During the Nehru Era*, Bombay, Asia Publishing House, 1976.
Rajan, M.S. and Ganguly, S. (eds) *Great Power Relations, World Order and the Third World*, New Delhi, Vikas, 1981.
Razia Akter Banu, U.A.B. *Islam in Bangladesh*, Leiden, Brill, 1992.
Robinson, F. *Separatism among Indian Muslims: The Politics of the United Provinces' Muslims, 1860–1923*, London, Cambridge University Press, 1974.
Rosenau, J.N. *International Politics and Foreign Policy: A Reader in Research and Theory*, New York, Free Press, 1969.
Rowland, J. *A History of Sino–Indian Relations: Hostile Co-existence*, Princeton, Princeton University Press, 1967.
Said, E.W. *Orientalism*, London, Penguin, 1978.
Sayeed, K.B. *The Political System of Pakistan*, Boston, Houghton-Mifflin, 1967.
Sayeed, K.B. *Pakistan: The Formative Phase 1857–1948*, 2nd edn, London, Oxford University Press, 1968.
Scalapino, R.A. *et al.* (eds) *Internal and External Security Issues in Asia*, Berkeley, Institute of East Asian Studies, University of California, 1986.
Schuler, E. and Schuler K. *Public Opinion and Constitution-Making in Pakistan, 1958–1962*, East Lansing, Michigan State University, 1967.
Seal, A. *The Emergence of Indian Nationalism: Competition and Collaboration in the Later Nineteenth Century*, London, Cambridge University Press, 1971.
Segal, G. 'Sino–Soviet Relations in the Third World', in R. Casson, (ed.), *Soviet Interests in the Third World*, London, Sage, 1985.
Sen, S. *Muslim Politics in Bengal, 1937–1947*, New Delhi, Impex, India [1976].
Sen, R. *A Case Study of Political Elites in Bangladesh, 1947–70*, University of Sussex [1977].
Sen Gupta, B. (ed.) *Regional Cooperation and Development in South Asia*, 2 vols, New Delhi, South Asian Publishers, 1986.
Sen Gupta, J. *History of Freedom Movement in Bangladesh, 1943–1973: Some Involvement*, Calcutta, Naya Prokash, 1974.
Shamasastry, R. (trans.) *Kautilya's Arthasastra*, 8th edn, Mysore, Mysore Printing and Publishing House, 1967.
Sharma, S.R. *Bangladesh Crisis and Indian Foreign Policy*, New Delhi, Young Asia, 1978.

Shelley, M. Rahman, *Emergence of a New Nation in a Multi-Polar World: Bangladesh,* Washington DC, University Press of America, 1978.

Shelley, M. Rahman, (ed.) *The Chittagong Hill Tracts of Bangladesh: The Untold Story,* Dhaka, Centre for Development Research, 1992.

Shulman, M.D. (ed.) *East–West Tensions in the Third World,* New York, W.W. Norton, 1986.

Singh, K. *India and Bangladesh,* Delhi, Anmol Publications, 1987.

Singhal, D.P. *India and World Civilization,* 2 vols, London, Sidgwick & Jackson, 1972a.

Singhal, D.P. *Pakistan,* Englewood Cliffs, New Jersey, Prentice-Hall, 1972b.

Singhal, D.P. *A History of the Indian People,* London, Methuen, 1983.

Sisson, R. and Rose, L.E. *War and Secession: Pakistan, India and the Creation of Bangladesh,* New Delhi, Vistaar Publications, 1990.

Sobhan, R. *The Crisis of External Dependence: The Political Economy of Foreign Aid To Bangladesh,* London, Zed Press, 1982.

The Statesman's Year-Book: A Statistical, Political and Economic Account of the States of the World for the Year 1996–1997, London, Macmillan, 1996.

Stephens, I. *Ten Years of Pakistan, 1947–1957,* Karachi, Pakistan Publications, 1957.

Tagore, R. *Towards Universal Man,* London, Asia Publishing House, 1961.

Talbot, I. *Provincial Politics and the Pakistan Movement: The Growth of the Muslim League in North-West and North-East India 1937–47,* Karachi, Oxford University Press, 1988.

Tayeeb, A. *Pakistan: A Political Geography,* London, Oxford University Press, 1966.

Taylor, D. and Yapp, M. (eds) *Political Identity in South Asia,* London, Curzon Press, 1979.

Thakur, R. *The Politics and Economics of India's Foreign Policy,* London, Hurst & Co., 1994.

Tharoor, S. *Reasons of State: Political Development and India's Foreign Policy Under Indira Gandhi, 1966–1977,* New Delhi, Vikas, 1982.

Thomas, C. *In Search of Security: The Third World in International Relations,* Boulder, Rienner, 1987.

Thomas, R.G.C. (ed.) *The Great Power Triangle and Asian Security,* Lexington Books, 1983.

Uyangoda, J. 'Indo–Bangladesh Relations in the 1970s: Bangladeshi Perspectives', in S.U. Kodikara (ed.), *South Asian Strategic Issues: Sri Lankan Perspectives,* New Delhi, Sage, 1990, pp. 67–81.

Vajpayee, A.B. *Continuity and Change in India's Foreign Policy,* New Delhi, Ministry of External Affairs, 1978.

Vajpayee, A.B. *New Dimensions of India's Foreign Policy,* New Delhi, Vision Books, 1979.

Vali, F.A. *Politics of the Indian Ocean Region: The Balances of Power,* New York, Free Press, 1976.

Varma, S.P. and Misra, K.P. (eds) *Foreign Policies in South Asia,* Bombay, Orient Longmans, 1969.

Varma, S.P. and Narain, V. (eds) *Pakistan Political System in Crisis: Emergence of Bangladesh,* Jaipur, South Asian Studies Centre, University of Rajasthan, 1972.

Verghese, B.G. *Waters of Hope: Integrated Water Resource Development and Regional Cooperation within the Himalayan–Ganga–Brahmaputra–Barak Basin,* New Delhi, Oxford and IBH Publishing, 1990.

Wallace, P. (ed.) *Region and Nation in India,* New Delhi, Oxford and IBH, 1985.

Weiner, M. *Sons of the Soil: Migration and Ethnic Conflict in India*, New Jersey, Princeton University Press, 1978.

Werake, M. 'China and South Asia: Some Historical Perspectives', in S.U. Kodikara (ed.), *South Asian Strategic Issues: Sri Lankan Perspectives*, New Delhi, Sage, 1990, pp. 55–66.

Westergaard, K. *State and Rural Society in Bangladesh: A Study in Relationship*, London, Curzon, 1985.

Wight, M. *Power Politics*, (eds) H. Bull and C. Holbraad, Leicester, Leicester University Press, 1978.

Wink, A. (ed.) *Islam, Politics and Society in South Asia*, New Delhi, Manohar, 1991.

Wolpert, S. *A New History of India*, 4th edn, New York, Oxford University Press, 1993.

Wriggins, W.H. *et al.* *Dynamics of Regional Politics: Four Systems on the Indian Ocean Rim*, New York, Columbia University Press, 1992.

Wright, D.A. *Bangladesh: Origins and Indian Ocean Relations (1971–1975)*, New Delhi, Sterling Publishers Private, 1988.

Wright, D.A. *India–Pakistan Relations: 1962–1969*, New Delhi, Sterling Publishers Private, 1989.

Zafarullah, H. (ed.) *The Zia Episode in Bangladesh Politics*, New Delhi, South Asian Publishers, 1996.

Zafarullah, H. *et al.* (eds) *Policy Issues in Bangladesh*, New Delhi, South Asian Publishers, 1994.

Ziring, L. *Bangladesh: From Mujib to Ershad, An Interpretive Study*, Oxford, Oxford University Press, 1992.

Ziring, L. (ed.) *The Subcontinent in World Politics: India, its Neighbors, and the Great Powers*, New York, Praeger, 1978.

Ziring, L. *et al.* (eds) *Pakistan: The Long View*, Durham, Duke University Press, 1977.

ARTICLES

Afroz, S. 'The Cold War and the United States Military Aid to Pakistan 1947–1960: A Reassessment', *South Asia*, vol. XVII, no. 1, 1994, pp. 57–72.

Ahamed, E. 'Development Strategy in Bangladesh: Probable Political Consequences', *Asian Survey*, vol. 18, no. 11, 1978, pp. 1168–80.

Ahamed, E. and Nazneen, D.R.J.A. 'Islam in Bangladesh: Revivalism or Power Politics?', *Asian Survey*, vol. 30, no. 8, 1990, pp.795–808.

Ahmad, A. 'Pakistan Faces Democracy: A Provisional Nationality', *The Round Table*, April 1971, pp. 227–37.

Ahmed, A.S. 'Postmodernist Perceptions of Islam: Observing the Observer', *Asian Survey*, vol. 31, no. 3, March 1991, pp. 213–31.

Ahmed, E. 'Development Strategy: Class and Regional Interests of the Ruling Elites in Pakistan', *Indian Economic and Social History Review*, vol. 15, no. 4, October–December 1978, pp. 421–49.

Ahsan, S.S. and Chakma, B. 'Problems of National Integration in Bangladesh: The Chittagong Hill Tracts', *Asian Survey*, vol. XXIX, no. 10, October 1989, pp. 959–70.

Ajami, F. 'The Summoning: "But They Said, We Will Not Hearken"', *Foreign Affairs*, vol. 72, no. 4, September–October 1993, pp. 2–9.

Akhyar, M.A. 'Pakistan: The Way Ahead From Martial Law', *South Asian Review*, vol. 3, no. 1, October 1969, pp. 23–30.

Alam, A.M.Q. 'Privatisation Policy and the Problem of Industrial Development in Bangladesh', *South Asia*, New Series, vol. 12, no. 2, 1989, pp. 49–68.

Alam, S.M.S. 'The Military and the Crisis of Political Hegemony in Bangladesh', *South Asia Bulletin*, vol. 10, no. 2, 1990, pp. 32–41.

Amin, N. 'The Pro-Chinese Communist Movement in Bangladesh', *Journal of Contemporary Asia*, vol. 15, no. 3, 1985, pp. 349–60.

Andersen, W.K. 'India in Asia: Walking on a Tightrope', *Asian Survey*, vol. 19, no. 12, 1979, pp. 1241–53.

Andersen, W.K. 'India in 1981: Stronger Political Authority and Social Tension', *Asian Survey*, vol. 22, no. 2, 1982, pp. 119–35.

Andersen, W.K. 'India in 1982: Domestic Challenges and Foreign Policy Successes', *Asian Survey*, vol. 23, no. 2, 1983, pp. 111–22.

Ayoob, M. 'Pakistan's Political Development, 1947 to 1970: Bird's Eye View', *Economic and Political Weekly*, January 1971, pp. 199–204.

Ayoob, M. 'Two Faces of Political Islam: Iran and Pakistan Compared', *Asian Survey*, vol. 19, no. 6, 1979, pp. 535–46.

Baral, L.R. 'SARC, But No "Shark": South Asian Regional Cooperation in Perspective', *Pacific Affairs*, vol. 58, no. 3, 1985, pp. 411–26.

Bartley, R.L. 'The Case for Optimism: The West Should Believe in Itself', *Foreign Affairs*, vol. 72, no. 4, September–October 1993, pp. 15–18.

Bateman, C.H. 'National Security and Nationalism in Bangladesh', *Asian Survey*, vol. 19, no. 8, August 1979, pp. 780–8.

Baxter, C. 'Bangladesh at Ten: An Appraisal of a Decade of Political Development', *The World Today*, vol. 38, no. 2, February 1982, pp. 73–80.

Baxter, C. 'Democracy and Authoritarianism in South Asia', *Journal of International Affairs*, vol. 38, Winter 1985, pp. 307–19.

Baxter, C. 'Continuing Problems in Bangladesh', *Current History*, March 1986, pp. 121–4.

Baxter, C. 'The Struggle For Development in Bangladesh', *Current History*, December, 1989, pp 437–40.

Baxter, C. 'Bangladesh in 1990: Another New Beginning?', *Asian Survey*, vol. 31, no. 2, 1991, pp. 146–52.

Baxter, C. 'Bangladesh: A Parliamentary Democracy, if They Can Keep It', *Current History*, vol. 91, no. 563, March 1992, pp. 132–6.

Baxter, C. and Rashiduzzaman, M. 'Bangladesh Votes: 1978 and 1979', *Asian Survey*, vol. 21, no. 4, 1981, pp. 485–500.

Beg, M.A. 'Intra-SAARC Trade: A Dwindling Feature', *India Quarterly*, vol. XLVI, no. 1, January–March 1990, pp. 47–89.

Bertocci, P.J. 'Bangladesh in the Early 1980s: Praetorian Politics in an Intermediate Regime', *Asian Survey*, vol. 22, no. 10, 1982, pp. 988–1008.

Bertocci, P.J. 'Bangladesh in 1984: A Year of Protracted Turmoil', *Asian Survey*, vol. 25, no. 2, 1985, pp. 155–68.

Bertocci, P.J. 'Bangladesh in 1985: Resolute Against the Storms', *Asian Survey*, vol. 26, no. 2, 1986, pp. 224–34.

Bhandari, R. *et al.* 'NAM in the Present Global Scenario: Discussion', *India Calling*, October 1992, pp. 2–5.

Bhargava, R. 'How Not to Defend Secularism', *South Asia Bulletin*, vol. XIV, no. 1, 1994, pp. 33–41.

Bhattacharya, V. 'India and Bangladesh', *India Quarterly*, vol. XLI, no. 1, January–March 1985, pp. 44–51.

Bhatty, M.A. 'Strategic Balance In South Asia Including the Adjacent Ocean', *World Review*, vol. 31, no. 1, 1992, pp. 24–31.

Bhogal, P.S. 'Pakistan's India Policy: Shift from Zia to Benazir', *India Quarterly*, vol. XLV, no. 1, January–March 1989, pp. 35–45.

Binyan, L. 'Civilization Grafting: No Culture is an Island', *Foreign Affairs*, September–October 1993, vol. 72, no. 4, pp. 19–21.

Bray, J. 'Pakistan in 1989: Benazir's Balancing Act', *The Round Table*, no. 310, 1989, pp. 192–200.

Bray, J. 'Nawaz Sharif's New Order in Pakistan', *The Round Table*, no. 318, 1991, pp. 179–90.

Budhraj, V.S. 'Moscow and the Birth of Bangladesh', *Asian Survey*, vol. 13, no. 5, May 1973, pp. 482–95.

Buzan, B. 'Peace, Power and Security: Contending Concepts in the Study of International Relations', *Journal of Peace Research*, vol. 21, no. 2, 1984, pp. 109–25.

Carranza, M.E. 'Rethinking Indo–Pakistani Nuclear Relations', *Asian Survey*, vol. 36, no. 6, June 1996, pp. 561–73.

Chakrabarty, B. 'The 1947 United Bengal Movement: A Thesis Without a Synthesis', *Indian Economic and Social History Review*, vol. 30, no. 4, 1993, pp. 467–88.

Chakrabarty, D. 'Modernity and Ethnicity in India', *South Asia*, New Series, Special Issue, 1994, pp. 143–55.

Chicherov, A.I. 'South Asia and the Indian Ocean in the 1980s: Some Trends Towards Changes In International Relations', *Asian Survey*, vol. 24, no. 11, November 1984, pp. 1117–30.

Choudhury, G.W. 'The East Pakistan Political Scene, 1955–1957', *Pacific Affairs*, vol. 30, no. 4, 1957, pp. 312–20.

Choudhury, G.W. 'Bangladesh: Why It Happened', *International Affairs*, vol. 48, no. 2, April 1972, pp. 242–9.

Chowdhury, M.H. 'Religious Parties in Bangladesh', reprinted from *Chittagong University Studies*, Part 1, vols 3 and 4, 1979 and 1980, pp. 1–16.

Crow, B. 'Why are the Ganges and Brahmaputra Undeveloped? Politics and Stagnation in the Rivers of South Asia', *Bulletin of Concerned Asian Scholars*, vol. 13, no. 4, October–December 1981, pp. 35–48.

Dally, P. 'India and the 'Non-Aligned' Nations', *Asian Outlook*, May 1986, pp. 4–8.

Das Gupta, J. 'The Janata Phase: Reorganization and Redirection in Indian Politics', *Asian Survey*, vol. 19, no. 4, 1979, pp. 390–403.

Dash, K.C. 'The Political Economy of Regional Cooperation in South Asia', *Pacific Affairs*, vol. 69, no. 2, 1996, pp. 185–209.

Deo, A.R. 'India's Foreign Policy: South Asian Neighbours', *World Focus: Monthly Discussion Journal*, vol. 12, nos 11–12, November–December 1991, pp. 27–32.

The Economist 'Sweeping dissent under a red carpet', vol. 289, 3 December 1983a, p.40.

The Economist 'Ershad entitled', vol. 289, 17 December 1983b, p. 36.

The Economist 'A fence that makes bad neighbours', vol. 291, 28 April 1984a.

The Economist 'One thwarts, the other courts', vol. 293, 8 December 1984b, pp. 32–4.

The Economist 'Progress in Bangladesh means not going backwards', vol. 296, 20 July 1985, pp. 33–4.

The Economist 'Bangladesh floods: drowned by politics', vol. 308, 17 September 1988, pp. 38–40.

Eriksen, T.H. 'Ethnicity Versus Nationalism', *Journal of Peace Research*, vol. 28, no. 3, 1991, pp. 263–78.

Evans, H.   'Bangladesh: South Asia's Unknown Quantity', *Asian Affairs*, New Series, vol. 19, October 1988, pp. 309–17.

Far Eastern Economic Review   'Power to Mujib's private army', 10 January 1975a, pp. 27–8.

Far Eastern Economic Review   'The CIA Conspiracy', vol. 36, no. 89, 1975b, pp. 149–50.

Far Eastern Economic Review   'Sheikh Mujib pays the ultimate price', 29 August 1975c, pp. 10–14.

Far Eastern Economic Review   'The Sheikh's legacy of confusion', 5 September 1975d, pp. 15–19.

Far Eastern Economic Review   'A smile from the Chinese', 19 September 1975e, pp. 26–8.

Far Eastern Economic Review   'Unilateral annexation: 164 square kilometres', 2 May 1980, p. 38.

Far Eastern Economic Review   'Human ebb and flow', 15 December 1983, pp. 42–4.

Far Eastern Economic Review   'Food and politics', 30 August 1984, p. 32.

Far Eastern Economic Review   'Hey there, neighbour', 25 April 1985a, p. 48.

Far Eastern Economic Review   'An ill wind in the east: The explosive mix of tribal and border tension', 19 December 1985b, pp. 26–8.

Far Eastern Economic Review   'Greedy for Ganga's goodies', 19 December 1985c, pp. 26–7.

Far Eastern Economic Review   'Smiles and salaams: Gandhi and Zia step up efforts to improve ties', 2 January 1986a, p. 29.

Far Eastern Economic Review   'The right to rule', 30 January 1986b, p. 16.

Far Eastern Economic Review   'The general's gambit', 31 July 1986c, pp. 22–4.

Far Eastern Economic Review   'Slow but sure start: Saarc leaders agree on some cooperative ventures', 4 December 1986d, pp. 26–7.

Far Eastern Economic Review   'Lacking in leadership', 12 February 1987a, p. 22.

Far Eastern Economic Review   'In the tribal tangle', 20 August 1987b, pp. 21–2.

Far Eastern Economic Review   'A carrot-and-stick game', 10 December 1987c, pp. 28–9.

Far Eastern Economic Review   'Calling on Uncle Sam', 7 April 1988a, pp. 35–6.

Far Eastern Economic Review   'The Security scenario', 5 May 1988b, pp. 40–1.

Far Eastern Economic Review   'A religious wrangle', 26 May 1988c, pp. 40–1.

Far Eastern Economic Review   'Playing the India hand', 26 May 1988d, pp. 40–1.

Far Eastern Economic Review   'A law unto himself: master manipulator who dominated politics and the military', 1 September 1988e, pp. 19–21.

Far Eastern Economic Review   'Talking with tribals', 1 September 1988f, pp. 32–4.

Far Eastern Economic Review   'Stemming the flood', 13 October 1988g, pp. 24–5.

Far Eastern Economic Review   'Politics of legitimacy', 20 July 1989a, p. 28.

Far Eastern Economic Review   'Strained relations: Bangladesh initiative over Saarc upsets Pakistan', 3 August 1989b, p. 23.

Far Eastern Economic Review   'Left in limbo: Bhutto appears to backtrack on the Biharis issue', 19 October 1989c, p. 23.

Far Eastern Economic Review   'A calming influence', 15 March 1990a, p. 29.

Far Eastern Economic Review   'Intractable hills: autonomy plan fails to appease the rebels', 5 April 1990b, pp. 22–4.

Far Eastern Economic Review   'Politics of disarray', 25 October 1990c, p. 21.

Far Eastern Economic Review   'Full circle: cycle of repression returns with emergency rule', 6 December 1990d, p. 13.

Far Eastern Economic Review   'Exit Ershad', 13 December 1990e, pp. 10–11.

Far Eastern Economic Review   'Too close for comfort: geopolitics worries the subcontinent', 24 January 1991a.

Far Eastern Economic Review 'Trade without tariff: the country has become a smuggler's paradise', 8 August 1991b, pp. 16–17.

Far Eastern Economic Review 'The Arakan exodus: Rangoon precipitates new problem for Dhaka', 26 March 1992a, pp. 22, 26.

Far Eastern Economic Review 'Anxious neighbours: Asean members break silence on refugee issue', 26 March 1992b, pp. 26–8.

Far Eastern Economic Review 'Country of choice: Bihari refugees to return to Pakistan', 25 June 1992c, p. 23.

Far Eastern Economic Review 'The begum's gambit: Khaleda's plan to return Pakistani refugees', 6 August 1992d, p. 23.

Feldman, H. 'The Toppling of Ayub Khan: Pent Up Passions and Grievances', *The Round Table*, July 1969, pp. 255–63.

Franda, M.F. 'Communism and Regional Politics in East Pakistan', *Asian Survey*, July 1970, pp. 588–606.

Gardezi, H.N. 'Politics of Religion in Pakistan's Elections: An Assessment, *South Asia Bulletin*, vol. XIV, no. 1, 1994, pp. 110–13.

Ghosh, P. 'Bangladesh at the Crossroads: Religion and Politics', *Asian Survey*, vol. 33, no. 7, July 1993, pp. 697–710.

Ghosh, S. 'Constitutional Changes in Bangladesh: Process of Political Development', *India Quarterly*, vol. 42, no. 4, 1986, pp. 391–404.

Grameen Poverty Research, 'Persistence of Poverty in Bangladesh', vol. 2, no. 1, January 1996, pp. 1–2.

Grant, J. *et al.* 'Huntington's "The Clash of Civilizations?"', *Asian Studies Review*, vol. 18, no. 1, July 1994, pp. 1–30.

Haass, R.N. 'South Asia: Too Late to Remove the Bomb?', *Orbis*, Winter, 1988, pp. 107–18.

Halim, M.A. 'Bargaining Power of the Third World Countries', *Politics, Administration and Change*, vol. 5, no. 1, January–June 1980, pp. 68–73.

Haque, A. 'Pak–China Friendship, 1960–70 – Collusion?', *Jahangirnagar Review* (reprint), vol. 2, 1978.

Haque, A. 'Pakistan's China Policy and Chinese Diplomacy in the Sixties – An Appraisal', *Jahangirnagar Review* (reprint), vol. 3, 1979.

Haque, A. 'Bangladesh 1979: Cry for a Sovereign Parliament', *Asian Survey*, vol. 20, no. 2, 1980, pp. 217–30.

Haque, A. 'Bangladesh in 1980: Strains and Stresses – Opposition in the Doldrums, *Asian Survey*, vol. 21, no. 2, 1981, pp. 188–202.

Haque, A. 'Political Forces, Values and External Politics: Their Interaction: The Case of Pakistan – 1947–70', *Journal of the Asiatic Society of Bangladesh* (reprint), vol. 23, no. 3, December 1978.

Hardgrave, R.L. 'India in 1983: New Challenges, Lost Opportunities', *Asian Survey*, vol. 24, no. 2, 1984, pp. 209–18.

Hardgrave, R.L. 'India in 1984: Confrontation, Assassination, and Succession', *Asian Survey*, vol. 25, no. 2, 1985, pp. 131–44.

Hart, G. 'Agrarian Structures and the State in Java and Bangladesh', *The Journal of Asian Studies*, vol. 47, no. 2, May 1988, pp. 249–67.

Hashmi, T.-I. 'The Communalisation of Class Struggle: East Bengal Peasantry, 1923–29', *Indian Economic and Social History Review*, vol. 25, no. 2, 1988, pp. 171–204.

Hassan, S. 'Transitional Politics In Bangladesh: A Study of Sattar's Interim Presidency', *India Quarterly*, vol. 39, no. 3, 1983, pp. 263–80.

Horn, R.C.   'The Soviet Union and Sino–Indian Relations', *Orbis*, Winter 1983, pp. 889–906.

Hossain, I.   'Bangladesh–India Relations: Issues and Problems', *Asian Survey*, vol. 21, no. 11, 1981, pp. 1115–28.

Humayun, S.   'East Pakistan and West Pakistan Alienation: A Background', *Journal of the Pakistan Historical Society*, vol. 39, Part 3, July 1991, pp. 279–97.

Huntington, S.P.   'The Clash of Civilizations?', *Foreign Affairs*, Summer 1993a, vol. 72, no. 3, pp. 22–49.

Huntington, S.P.   'If Not Civilizations, What? Paradigms of the Post-Cold War World', *Foreign Affairs*, November–December 1993b, vol. 72, no. 5, pp. 187–94.

Huque, A.S. and Akhter, M.Y.   'The Ubiquity of Islam: Religion and Society in Bangladesh', *Pacific Affairs*, vol. 60, no. 2, 1987, pp. 200–21.

Husain, Z.   'Maulana Sayyid Abul A'la Maududi: An Appraisal of his Thought and Political Influence', *South Asia*, New Series, vol. 9, no. 1, 1986, pp. 61–81.

Iftekharuzzaman,   'Bangladesh in the Changing World: Challenges and Options at Home', *Bangladesh Institute of International and Strategic Studies Journal*, vol. 13, no. 2, April 1992, pp. 187–222.

Irshad, A.   'Indian Military Power and Policy', *Bangladesh Institute of International and Strategic Studies Journal*, vol. 10, no. 4, 1989, pp. 388–410.

Islam, M.R.   'The Ganges Water Dispute: An Appraisal of a Third Party Settlement, *Asian Survey*, vol. 27, no. 8, 1987, pp. 918–34.

Islam, N.   'Islam and National Identity: The Case of Pakistan and Bangladesh', *International Journal of Middle East Studies*, vol. 13, 1981, pp. 55–72.

Islam, S.S.   'The State in Bangladesh Under Zia (1975–81)', *Asian Survey*, vol. 24, no. 5, 1984, pp. 556–73.

Islam, S.S.   'Relative State Autonomy and Development Strategy in Bangladesh', 1975–1981', *Pacific Affairs*, vol. 59, no. 4, Winter 1986–7, pp. 563–76.

Islam, S.S.   'Bangladesh in 1986: Entering a New Phase', *Asian Survey*, vol. 27, no. 2, 1987, pp. 163–72.

Islam, S.S.   'Bangladesh in 1987: A Spectrum of Uncertainties', *Asian Survey*, vol. 28, no. 2, 1988, pp. 163–71.

Jenkins, L.   'The Sins of the Father', *Newsweek*, August 25, 1975, p. 11.

Jetly, N.   'Sino–Indian Relations: A Quest for Normalization', *India Quarterly*, vol. XLII, no. 1, January–March 1986, pp. 53–68.

Kabir, F.   'Bureaucracy in Bangladesh: The Political Involvement and Influence', *Bangladesh Institute of International and Strategic Studies Journal*, vol. 12, no. 2, April 1991.

Kabir, M.G.   'Religion, Language and Nationalism in Bangladesh', *Journal of Contemporary Asia*, vol. 17, no. 4, 1987.

Kamaluddin, S.   'Agriculture's Growing Pains', *Far Eastern Economic Review*, 22 June, 1979, pp. 86–8.

Kapur, A.   'Indian Foreign Policy: Perspectives and Present Predicaments', *The Round Table*, no. 295, 1985, pp. 230–9.

Kapur, A.   'The Indian Subcontinent: The Contemporary Structure of Power and the Development of Power Relations', *Asian Survey*, vol. 28, no. 7, July 1988, pp. 693–710.

Kapur, H.   'India's Foreign Policy Under Rajiv Gandhi', *The Round Table*, no. 304, 1987, pp. 469–80.

Keenleyside, T.A.   'The Inception of Indian Foreign Policy: The Non-Nehru Contribution', *South Asia*, New Series, vol. 4, no. 2, 1981, pp. 63–78.

Keenleyside, T.A. 'Nationalist Indian Attitudes Towards Asia: A Troublesome Legacy For Post-Independence Indian Foreign Policy', *Pacific Affairs*, vol. 55, no. 2, 1982, pp. 210–30.

[Khan, K.W.] 'Pakistan From Within – A Three-way Split', *The Round Table*, January 1972, pp. 15–27.

Khan, Z.R. 'Politicization of the Bangladesh Military: A Response to Perceived Short-comings of Civilian Government', *Asian Survey*, vol. 21, no. 5, 1981, pp. 551–64.

Khan, Z.R. 'Bangladesh in 1981: Change, Stability, and Leadership', *Asian Survey*, vol. 22, no. 2, 1982, pp. 163–70.

Khan, Z.R. 'Islam and Bengali Nationalism', *Asian Survey*, vol. 25, no. 8, 1985, pp. 834–51.

Khilnani, N.M. 'India's Political and Economic Policies Towards Her Neighbours', *The Round Table*, no. 301, 1987, pp. 53–8.

Khilnani, N.M. 'The Follies, Fumblings, and Frustrations of India's Recent Foreign Policy', *The Round Table*, no. 321, 1992, pp. 57–9.

Kirkpatrick, J.J. *et al.* 'The Modernizing Imperative: Tradition and Change', *Foreign Affairs*, September–October 1993, vol. 72, no. 4, pp. 22–6.

Kochanek, S.A. 'The Rise of Interest Politics in Bangladesh', *Asian Survey*, vol. 36, no. 7, July 1996, pp. 704–22.

Kohli, M. 'The Non-Aligned Movement and the Super Powers in Historical Perspective', *Quarterly Review of Historical Studies*, vol. 25, no. 3, 1985, pp. 8–22.

Kohli, M. 'Indian Foreign Policy: A Geo-Political Perspective', *India Quarterly*, vol. XLVI, no. 4, October–December 1990, pp. 33–40.

Kothari, R. 'State Building in the Third World: Alternative Strategies', *Politics, Administration and Change*, vol. 5, no. 1, January–June 1980, pp. 91–108.

Kumar, R. 'India's Political Identity: Nation-State or Civilisation-State', *Indian Ocean Review*, vol. 4, no. 4, 1991, pp. 23, 26.

Lambert, R.D. 'Factors in Bengali Regionalism in Pakistan', *Far Eastern Survey*, April 1959, pp. 49–58.

Lenneberg, C. 'Women and Political Leadership in India: Able Politicians or Token Presences?', *Asian Studies Review*, vol. 17, no. 3, April 1994, pp. 6–14.

Lifschultz, L. 'New Delhi's "views" on the Dacca Coups', *Far Eastern Economic Review*, 28 November 1975a, pp. 16–17.

Lifschultz, L. 'The Crisis Has Not Passed', *Far Eastern Economic Review*, 5 December 1975b, pp. 28–34.

Lifschultz, L. 'Abu Taher's Last Testament: Bangladesh: The Unfinished Revolution', *Economic and Political Weekly* (Bombay), Special Number, August 1977, pp. 1303–53.

Ling, T. 'Creating a New State: The Bengalis of Bangladesh', *South Asian Review*, vol. 5, no. 3, April 1974, pp. 221–9.

Ludden, D. 'History Outside Civilisation and the Mobility of South Asia', *South Asia: Journal of South Asian Studies*, New Series, vol. 17, no. 1, June 1994, pp. 1–23.

Lyon, P. 'Bangladesh Since Mujib', *World Survey*, May–June, nos 89–90, 1976, pp. 1–15.

Madan, T.N. 'Secularism in Its Place', *Journal of Asian Studies*, vol. 46, no. 4, 1987, pp. 747–58, pp. 747–59.

Mahbubani, K. 'The Dangers of Decadence: What the Rest can Teach the West', *Foreign Affairs*, vol. 72, no. 4, September–October 1993, pp. 10–14.

Majeed, A. 'Indian Security Perspectives in the 1990s', *Asian Survey*, vol. 30, no. 11, 1990, pp. 1084–98.

Makeig, D.C. 'War, No-War, and the India–Pakistan Negotiating Process', *Pacific Affairs*, vol. 60, no. 2, 1987, pp. 271–94.

Malik, I.H.   'Ethno–Nationalism in Pakistan: A Commentary on Muhajir Qaumi Mahaz (MQM) in Sindh', *South Asia*, vol. XVIII, no 2, 1995, pp. 49–72.

Malik, I.H.   'The State and Civil Society in Pakistan', *Asian Survey*, vol. 36, no. 7, July 1996, pp. 673–90.

Maniruzzaman, T.   'Bangladesh in 1976: Struggle for Survival as an Independent State', *Asian Survey*, vol. 17, no. 2, 1977, pp. 191–200.

Maniruzzaman, T.   'The Fall of the Military Dictator: 1991 Elections and the Prospect of Civilian Rule in Bangladesh', *Pacific Affairs*, vol. 65, no. 2, 1992, pp. 203–24.

Maniruzzaman, T.   'Group Interests in Pakistan Politics, 1947–1958', *Pacific Affairs*, vol. 39, nos 1 and 2, 1966, pp. 83–98.

Mashreque, M.S.   'Kinship and Power Structure in a Bangladesh Village: Findings of Research and Some Policy Recommendations for Rural Development', *Politics, Administration and Change*, vol. 12, no. 2, 1987, pp. 42–53.

Mayer, P.   'Tombs and Dark Houses: Ideology, Intellectuals, and Proletarians in the Study of Contemporary Indian Islam', *Journal of Asian Studies*, vol. 40, no. 3, 1981, pp. 481–97.

Milner, D.   'Pakistan: A Hope for Democracy', *Asian Review*, vol. 2, no. 4, July 1969, pp. 277–86.

Misra, K.P.   'The Farakka Accord', *The World Today*, vol. 34, no. 2, 1978, pp. 41–4.

Morris-Jones, W.H.   'India – More Questions Than Answers', *Asian Survey*, vol. 24, no. 8, 1984, pp. 809–16.

Muni, S.D.   'India and the Post-Cold War World: Opportunities and Challenges', *Asian Survey*, vol. 31, no. 9, 1991, pp. 862–74.

Narain, I.   'India in 1985: Triumph of Democracy', *Asian Survey*, vol. 26, no. 2, 1986, pp. 253–69.

Narain, I. and Dutta, N.   'India in 1986: The Continuing Struggle', *Asian Survey*, vol. 27, no. 2, 1987, pp. 181–93.

Nasr, S.V.R.   'Democracy and the Crisis of Governability in Pakistan', *Asian Survey*, vol. 32, no. 6, 1992, pp. 521–37.

Newsweek, 'Death of the Bangabandhu', August 25, 1975, pp. 10–12.

Oldenburg, P.   'A Place Insufficiently Imagined: Language, Belief, and the Pakistan Crisis of 1971', *Journal of Asian Studies*, vol. 44, no. 4, 1985, pp. 711–31.

Oren, S.   'After the Bangladesh Coups', *The World Today*, vol. 32, no. 1, January 1976, pp. 18–24.

Osmany, S.H   'Cardinal Elements of Nationalism in Bangladesh', *Bangladesh Institute of International and Strategic Studies Journal*, vol. 12, no. 2, April 1991.

Qureshi, S.A.   'An Analysis of Contemporary Pakistani Politics: Bhutto Versus the Military', *Asian Survey*, vol. 19, no. 9, 1979, pp. 910–21.

Prabhakara, M.S.   'BJP and the North-East, *South Asia Bulletin*, vol. XIV, no. 1, 1994, pp. 66–71.

Pradhan, P.   'Nuclear Pakistan: India's Response', *India Quarterly*, vol. XLIII, no. 1, January–March 1987, pp. 1–14.

Rahman, M.A.   'East Pakistan – The Roots of Estrangement', *South Asian Review*, vol. 3, no. 3, April 1970, pp. 235–9.

Rahman, M.A.   'Bangladesh in 1982: Beginnings of the Second Decade', *Asian Survey*, vol. 23, no. 2, 1983, pp. 149–57.

Rahman, M.A.   'Bangladesh in 1983: A Turning Point for the Military', *Asian Survey*, vol. 24, no. 2, 1984, pp. 240–9.

Rahman, M.H.   'Delimitation of Maritime Boundaries: A Survey of Problems in the Bangladesh Case', *Asian Survey*, vol. 24, no.12, 1984, pp.1302–17.

Rahman, S. 'Issues and Agenda for South Asia Regional Cooperation: A Bangladeshi Perspective', *Asian Survey*, vol. 25, no. 4, 1985, pp. 405–25.

Rahman, S. 'Bangladesh in 1988: Precarious Institution Building amid Crisis Management', *Asian Survey*, vol. 29, no. 2, 1989, pp. 216–22.

Rahman, S. 'Bangladesh in 1989: Internationalization of Political and Economic Issues', *Asian Survey*, vol. 30, no. 2, 1990, pp. 150–7.

Rais, R.B. 'Pakistan in the Regional and Global Power Structure', *Asian Survey*, vol. 31, no. 4, 1991, pp. 378–92.

Rajan. M.S. 'Non-Alignment: The Dichotomy Between Theory and Practice in Perspective', *India Quarterly*, vol. 36, no. 1, 1980, pp. 43–66.

Rao, R.V.R.C. 'Regional Cooperation in South Asia', *The Round Table*, no. 293, 1985, pp. 53–65.

Rashiduzzaman, M. 'The National Assembly of Pakistan under the 1962 Constitution', *Pacific Affairs*, vol. 42, no. 4, Winter 1969–70.

Rashiduzzaman, M. 'The National Awami Party of Pakistan: Leftist Politics in Crisis', *Pacific Affairs*, vol. 43, no. 1, Spring 1970a, pp. 394–409.

Rashiduzzaman, M. 'The Awami League in the Political Development of Pakistan', *Asian Survey*, July, 1970b, pp. 574–87.

Rashiduzzaman, M. 'Bangladesh in 1977: Dilemmas of the Military Rulers', *Asian Survey*, vol. 18, no. 2, 1978, pp. 126–34.

Rashiduzzaman, M. 'Bangladesh 1978: Search for a Political Party', *Asian Survey*, vol. 19, no. 2, 1979, pp. 191–7.

Razvi, S.M.M. 'Conflict and Cooperation in South Asia', *The Round Table*, no. 299, 1986, pp. 269–79.

Reeves, P. 'The Congress and the Abolition of Zamindari in Uttar Pradesh', *South Asia*, New Series, vol. 8, nos 1 and 2, 1985, pp. 154–67.

Richter, W.L. 'Persistent Praetorianism: Pakistan's Third Military Regime', *Pacific Affairs*, vol. 51, no. 3, 1978, pp. 406–26.

Richter, W.L. 'The Political Dynamics of Islamic Resurgence in Pakistan', *Asian Survey*, vol. 19, no. 6, 1979, pp. 547–57.

Richter, W.L. 'Mrs Gandhi's Neighborhood: Indian Foreign Policy Toward Neighboring Countries', *Journal of Asian and African Studies* vol. XXII, nos 3–4, 1987, pp. 250–65.

Rose, L.E. 'The Superpowers in South Asia: A Geostrategic Analysis', *Orbis*, Summer 1978, pp. 395–413.

Roy, A. 'The Bengal Muslim "Cultural Mediators" and the Bengal Muslim Identity in the Nineteenth and Early Twentieth Centuries', *South Asia*, vol. 10, no. 1, 1987, pp. 11–34.

Roy, A.K. 'National and Communist Forces at Cross-roads in Bangladesh', *United Asia*, vol. 23, no. 3, 1971, pp. 164–71.

Rubinoff, A.C. 'The Multilateral Imperative in India's Foreign Policy', *The Round Table*, no. 319, 1991, pp. 313–34.

Rudolph, L.I. and Rudolph, S.H. 'Rethinking Secularism: Genesis and Implications of the Textbook Controversy, 1977–79', *Pacific Affairs*, vol. 56, no. 1, 1983, pp. 15–37.

Sanger, C. 'The Struggles of Bangladesh', *International Perspectives*, September–October 1984, pp. 16–18.

Satyamurthy, T.V. 'Indo–Bangladesh Relations: A Structural Perspective', *Asia Quarterly*, no. 1, 1977, pp. 52–75.

Sayeed, K.B. 'The Political Role of Pakistan's Civil Service', *Pacific Affairs*, vol. 31, no. 2, June 1958, pp. 131–46.

Seth, S.P. 'China as a Factor in Indo–Pakistani Politics', *The World Today*, vol. 25, no. 1, January 1969.

Shafqat, S. 'Pakistan Under Benazir Bhutto', *Asian Survey*, vol. 36, no. 7, July 1996, pp. 655–72.

Shamsul Alam, S.M. 'The Military and the Crisis of Political Hegemony in Bangladesh', *South Asia Bulletin*, vol. 10, no. 2, 1990, pp. 32–41.

Sharma, R. 'Nehru's World-View: An Alternative to the Superpowers' Model of International Relations', *India Quarterly*, vol. XLV, no. 4, October–December 1989, pp. 324–32.

Shelley, M.R. 'Bangladesh – Origins and Prospects', *Contemporary Review*, July 1973.

Singh, D. 'Role of Bilateralism in Solving Mutual Conflicts with Special Reference to Tin Bigha Issue', *India Quarterly*, vol. XLIX, no. 4, October–December 1993, pp. 59–66.

Sisson, R. 'India in 1989: A Year of Elections in a Culture of Change', *Asian Survey*, vol. 30, no. 2, 1990, pp. 111–25.

Sisson, R. and Majmundar, M. 'India in 1990: Political Polarization', *Asian Survey*, vol. 31, no. 2, 1991, pp. 103–12.

Sobhan, R. 'Social Forces in the Basic Democracies', *Asian Review*, vol. 1, no. 3, April 1968.

Suhrawardy, H.S. 'Political Stability and Democracy in Pakistan', *Foreign Affairs*, vol. 35, no. 3, April 1957, pp. 422–31.

Tahir-Kheli, S. 'The Foreign Policy of "New" Pakistan', *Orbis*, vol. 20, no. 3, Fall 1976, pp. 733–57.

Tasker, R. and Kamaluddin, S. 'Martial Law, Democracy and the Future', *Far Eastern Economic Review*, 12 October 1979, pp. 30–1.

Thakur, R. 'India After Nonalignment', *Foreign Affairs*, Spring, 1992, pp. 165–82.

Thakur, R. 'India and the United States', *Asian Survey*, vol. 36, no. 6, June 1996, pp. 574–91.

Thomas, J.W. 'Work for the Poor of East Pakistan', *Asian Review*, vol. 2, no. 1, October 1968.

Thomas, R.G.C. 'Security Relationships in Southern Asia: Differences in the Indian and American Perspectives', *Asian Survey*, vol. 21, no. 7, 1981, pp. 689–709.

Thornton, T.P. 'Between the Stools? US Policy Towards Pakistan During the Carter Administration', *Asian Survey*, vol. 22, no. 10, October 1982, pp. 959–77.

Thornton, T.P. 'The New Phase in US–Pakistan Relations', *Foreign Affairs*, vol. 68, no. 3, Summer 1989.

Thorp, J.P. 'Bangladesh, Bangladesh! – A Review Article', *Journal of Asian Studies*, vol. 45. no. 4, 1986, pp. 789–97.

Tilman, R.O. 'Burma in 1986: The Process of Involution Continues', *Asian Survey*, vol. 27, no. 2, February 1987, pp. 254–63.

Van Schendel, W. 'The Invention of the "Jummas": State Formation and Ethnicity in Southeastern Bangladesh', *Modern Asian Studies*, vol. 26, no. 1, 1992, pp. 95–128.

Vivekanandan, B. 'The Indian Ocean as a Zone of Peace: Problems and Prospects', *Asian Survey*, vol. 21, no. 12, 1981, pp. 1237–48.

Walker, D. 'Islam and Nationalism in Bangladesh', *Hamdard Islamicus*, vol. 14, no. 2, 1991, pp. 35–63.

Wallensteen, P. 'Universalism Vs. Particularism: On the Limits of Major Power Order', *Journal of Peace Research*, vol. 21, no. 3, 1984, pp. 243–56.

Wariavwalla, B. 'India in 1987: Democracy on Trial', *Asian Survey*, vol. 28, no. 2, 1988, pp. 119–25.

Weinbaum, M.G. 'Civic Culture and Democracy in Pakistan', *Asian Survey*, vol. 36, no. 7, 1996, pp. 639–54.

Wiberg, H. 'The Security of Small Nations: Challenges and Defences', *Journal of Peace Research*, vol. 24, no. 4, 1987, pp. 339–63.

Wilcox, W. 'Political Change in Pakistan: Structures, Functions, Constraints and Goals', *Pacific Affairs*, vol. 41, no. 3, 1968, pp. 341–54.

Wilcox, W. 'Pakistan: A Decade of Ayub', *Asian Survey*, vol. 9, no. 2, February 1969, pp. 87–93.

Wilcox, W. 'Pakistan in 1969: Once Again at the Starting Point', *Asian Survey*, vol. 10, no. 2, February 1970.

Wilson, A. Jeyaratnam 'The Foreign Policies of India's Immediate Neighbours: A Reflective Interpretation', *Journal of Asian and African Studies*, vol. XXV, nos 1–2, 1990, pp. 42–59.

Wink, A. 'Sovereignty and Universal Dominion in South Asia', *Indian Economic and Social History Review*, vol. 21, no. 3, 1984, pp. 265–92.

Wriggins, W.H. 'Pakistan's Search for a Foreign Policy After the Invasion of Afghanistan', *Pacific Affairs*, vol. 57, no. 2, 1984, pp. 284–303.

Wright, D.A. 'An Australian Perception of Bangladesh: 1971–78', *Bangladesh Bulletin*, vol. 6, no. 1, Febuary 1979a, pp. 5–12.

Wright, D.A. 'Bangladesh and Its Indian Ocean Neighbours', *Bangladesh Bulletin*, vol. 6, no. 2, May 1979b, pp. 3–10.

Wright, D.A. 'Diplomatic Relations Between the States of the Indian Subcontinent', *World Review*, vol. 22, no. 4, 1983, pp. 70–9.

Wright, D.A. 'Bangladesh: Foreign Policy For the 1980s', *Bangladesh Bulletin*, vol. 14, 1987a, pp. 21–9.

Wright, D.A. 'Bangladeshi Identity and Nationalism', *Bangladesh Bulletin*, vol. 14, 1987b, pp. 2–10.

Wright, D.A. 'Islam and Bangladeshi Polity', *South Asia: Journal of South Asian Studies*, vol. 10, no. 2, December 1987c, pp. 15–27.

Wright, D.A. 'Destructive Features of Bangladeshi Political Life', *Probaho*, vol. 1, no. 3, 1991, pp. 22–5.

Wright, R. 'Islam, Democracy and the West', *Foreign Affairs*, Summer 1992.

Yasmeen, S. 'India and Pakistan: Why the Latest Exercise in Brinkmanship?', *Australian Journal of Politics and History*, vol. 34, no. 1, 1988/89, pp. 64–72.

Ziring, L. 'Pakistan and India: Politics, Personalities, and Foreign Policy', *Asian Survey*, vol. 18, no. 7, 1978, pp. 706–30.

Ziring, L. 'From Islamic Republic To Islamic State In Pakistan', *Asian Survey*, vol. 24, no. 9, 1984, pp. 931–46.

UNPUBLISHED

Abrar, C.R. *State, Regime and Authoritarianism: The Bangladesh Case*, paper delivered at the International Seminar on South Asia's Security in the 1990s: Primacy of its Internal Dimension, organised by the Bangladesh Institute of International and Strategic Studies (BIISS), Dhaka (5–7 January 1992).

Choudhury, D. *Bangladesh and South Asia*, paper delivered at the Sixth National Conference of the Bangladesh Political Science Association held at Jahangirnagar University (16–17 February 1991).

Hassan, S.   *Bangladesh Foreign Policy: Issues and Challenges,* paper delivered at the First Annual Conference of the Bangladesh Society of International Studies, Bangladesh Institute of International and Strategic Studies (BIISS), Dhaka (31 January 1989).

Husain, A.   *Ethnicity and Security of Bangladesh,* paper delivered at the Regional Seminar on South Asia's Security in the 1990s: Primacy of its Internal Dimension, organised by the Bangladesh Institute of International and Strategic Studies (BIISS) Dhaka, (5–7 January 1992).

Hossain, Ishtiaq   *Bangladesh–India Ganges Water Sharing Treaty: Problems and Prospects,* paper delivered at the 'Bangladesh: Democracy and Development' Conference organised by the National Centre for South Asian Studies, Melbourne, held at the Royal Melbourne Institute of Technology (22–23 March 1997).

Islam, M.N.   *The Farakka Barrage: A Man–Made Disaster for Bangladesh,* paper delivered at the Seventh National Conference (1993) of the Bangladesh Political Science Association held at the University of Chittagong.

Kumar, R.   'The Past as a Mirror of the Future', *Nehru Memorial Museum and Library, Occasional Papers on History and Society,* no. IX, New Delhi, 1983.

Kumar, R.   'The Roots of Democracy in India', *Nehru Memorial Museum and Library, Occasional Papers on History and Society,* no. XXXVII, New Delhi, March 1987.

Kumar, R.   'The Past and the Present: An Indian Dialogue', *Nehru Memorial Museum and Library, Occasional Papers on Perspectives on Indian Development,* no. I, New Delhi, March 1989a.

Kumar, R.   'The Structure of Politics in India on the Eve of Independence', *Nehru Memorial Museum and Library, Occasional Papers on History and Society,* Second Series, no. XVI, New Delhi, January 1989b.

Momen, N.   *Strengths and Weaknesses of Bangladesh's Diplomacy,* paper delivered at a seminar on 'Bangladesh Foreign Policy: Issues and Challenges', organised by the Bangladesh Society of International Studies, 31 January 1989 at the Bangladesh Institute of International and Strategic Studies (BIISS), Dhaka.

Nuruzzaman, M.   *Confidence–Building in South Asia: A Bangladeshi Perspective,* paper delivered at the Regional Seminar on South Asia's Security in the 1990s: Primacy of its Internal Dimension, organised by the Bangladesh Institute of International and Strategic Studies (BIISS), Dhaka (5–7 January 1992).

Rehman, A.A.   *Secularism and Secularisation: The Bangladesh Experience, 1971–86,* paper delivered at Asian Studies Association of Australia Conference, Sydney (11–16 May 1986).

Roy, A.   'Salience of Islam in South Asian Politics: Pakistan and Bangladesh', in K. McPherson and Vicziany, M. (eds), *Australia and South Asia: A Blueprint For 2001, Draft Report, June 1993,* Perth/Melbourne, Indian Ocean Centre For Peace Studies, University of Western Australia and Monash Asia Institute, Monash University, 1988.

Wright, D.A.   *Ziaur Rahman and His Presidency of Bangladesh,* paper delivered at Australia–Bangladesh Society Zia Parishad, Sydney, 9 November 1991.

Wright, D.A.   *Towards the New Millennium: Bangladeshi Democracy in the 1990s,* paper delivered at the 'Bangladesh: Democracy and Development' Conference organised by the National Centre for South Asian Studies, Melbourne, held at the Royal Melbourne Institute of Technology (22–23 March 1997).

Yunus, M.   *Towards a Poverty-Free World,* paper delivered at the 'Bangladesh: Democracy and Development' Conference organised by the National Centre for South Asian Studies, Melbourne, held at the Royal Melbourne Institute of Technology (22–23 March 1997).

Index